BOOKS BY

E. D. H. JOHNSON

The Alien Vision of Victorian Poetry   *1952*
Sources of the Poetic Imagination in Tennyson, Browning, and Arnold

EDITOR

The World of the Victorians   *1964*
The Poetry of Earth   *1966*

CARLISLE

Maryport

Workington

ISLE OF MAN

Whitehaven

SKIDDAW
△
SADDLEBACK
△
Loweswater
Keswick   Penruddock
CASTLE RIGG
St.Bees
Emmerdale Br.   △ DERWENT WATER   Penrith
CASTLE
CRAG △   ○ Grange
Egremont
EAGLE CRAG △
Borrowdale   ULZWATER
Gosforth   WAST WATER   HELVELLYN
△
SCA FELL   Appleby
Rydal   ○○ Ambleside
Grasmere   ○ Kentmere

I R I S...

Broughton   ○ Windermere
WINDERMERE WATER

○ Kendal

Ulverston

0   8 MI.

Holyhead

ANG.

CAER...

CAMBRIAN M...

MER...

Aberystwyth

CARD.

PEMB. W   A
Milford Haven   CARM.
Carmarthen
Pembroke   BR...

SWANSEA
RHONDD...
GLAM.
BRISTOL CHANNEL CARDIFF

MILES

0   25

Bideford

Bridgw...

E   DEVON   Tiverton
N
CORNWALL   SO...
DARTMOOR   • Exeter
Penzance   PLYMOUTH
Torquay

Portla...

E N G L I S H   C H...

Indian ink drawing for The Bright Cloud, *by Samuel Palmer, c. 1831–32*

THE POETRY
OF EARTH

A COLLECTION OF
ENGLISH NATURE WRITINGS

*SELECTED, WITH AN INTRODUCTION
AND CRITICAL PREFACES
BY*

E. D. H. JOHNSON

ATHENEUM *NEW YORK*

1974

ACKNOWLEDGMENTS

Grateful acknowledgment is due to the following:

Clarendon Press, Oxford: for permission to print extracts from *Correspondence of Thomas Gray*, edited by Paget Toynbee and Leonard Whibley (1935), 3 vols.; and from *Collected Letters of Samuel Taylor Coleridge, 1785–1806*, edited by E. L. Griggs (1956), 2 vols.

Macmillan and Co. Ltd., London, and St. Martin's Press, Inc., New York: for permission to print extracts from *Journals of Dorothy Wordsworth*, edited by E. de Selincourt (1941), 2 vols.

Routledge and Kegan Paul Ltd., London, and to the editors: for permission to print extracts from *The Prose of John Clare*, edited by J. W. and Anne Tibble (1951).

Oxford University Press, London, and to the editors: for permission to print extracts from *The Journals and Papers of Gerard Manley Hopkins*, edited by Humphry House and Graham Storey (1959).

Jonathan Cape Ltd., London, and to the Executors of the Estate of Mrs. Essex Hope: for permission to print extracts from *Kilvert's Diary*, edited by William Plomer (1960), 3 vols.

FOR LAURIE

The poetry of earth is never dead . . . Keats

Introduction

The ever-expanding ranks of those who turn to nature for respite from the wearisome demands of existence in the twentieth century have a spiritual kinship with the company of writers here brought together. If, as a result of the spread of knowledge, today's nature lover finds himself more often a gleaner than a trail-breaker in the fields of scientific exploration, he nonetheless is animated by the same impulses to which earlier generations of inquirers responded. Not for him anymore than for them is there meaning in C. P. Snow's distinction between the two cultures. Like his predecessors, he simultaneously inhabits the twin worlds of fact and poetry. Indeed, he has inherited their perception that the poetry is in the fact. It is not, then, that the attitudes reflected in the following pages will seem remote to a contemporary audience, although the scenes that called forth these attitudes may well instill nostalgia for the vanishing away of so much wild, fresh beauty. In its depths human nature has happily suffered no changes commensurate with the violence which modern man has inflicted on the face of the earth. Hence the need to escape into those fairer landscapes which survive through the lovingly accurate observations left by country dwellers in times past.

The treatment of natural history as a branch of literature is a long-standing tradition among the English. The golden age of this genre of writing, however, lasted for little more than a century between, roughly, 1770 and 1880. Prior to the earlier date the amateur naturalist commanded too little information to be able to pursue his researches with any confidence in their value; in more recent times he is likely to be dismayed at the outset by the very extent of specialized knowledge. When the Renaissance reawakened men to the significance of the tangible world, the natural sciences had not progressed very far beyond the teachings of Aristotle and Pliny; and the great investigators of the sixteenth and seventeenth centuries were further hampered by the fabulous and legendary accretions which had grown up about their subjects during the Middle Ages. It was from this legacy of superstition that Francis Bacon and his followers, the founders of The Royal Society, sought to emancipate the thought of the age. The new appeal to empirical evidence is embodied in the title of one of Sir Thomas Browne's most popular works: *Pseudodoxia Epidemica, or Enquiries into very many received tenets and commonly-presumed truths, which examined prove but Vulgar and Common Errors* (1646).

Browne has some claim to be regarded as the progenitor of the great line of English field-naturalists on the basis of his *Notes and Letters on the Natural History of Norfolk*, dating from the 1660's, although not published until 1835. By the end of the Victorian period the conditions fostering such genially informal records of regional flora and fauna had largely ceased to exist, not only as a result of the retreat of wild-life before the encroachments of an urbanized society, but also because the mass of data available for codification and analysis had given priority to the laboratory scientist. As early as 1882, in an article entitled "A Few Words about the Nineteenth Century," the positivist Frederic Harrison commented on the disappearance of nature lovers of the breed of Gilbert White as one of the more deplorable signs of the times:

A hundred years ago, a naturalist was a man who, having mastered, say, some millions of observations, had, if he possessed a mind of vigour, some idea of what Nature is. Now, there are millions of billions of possible observations, all in many different sciences, and as no human brain can deal with them, men mark off a small plot, stick up a notice to warn off intruders, and grub for observations there. And so a naturalist now often knows nothing about Nature, but devotes himself to one hundredth or thousandth part of Nature—say the section of *Annelida*—and of these, often to one particular worm, or he takes the *Gasteropods*, and then he confines himself to a particular kind of snail; and then after twenty years he publishes a gigantic book about the co-ordination of the maculae of the wings of the extinct *Lepidoptera*, or it may be the genesis of the tails of the various parasites that inhabited the palaeozoic flea. I don't say but what this microscopic, infinitely vast, infinitesimally small, work has got to be done. But it has its dangers, and saps all grip and elasticity of mind, when it is done in a crude, mechanical way, by the medal-hunting crowd.

The appeal of natural history sprang from certain interdependent assumptions about the phenomenal world which were common property in the late eighteenth and nineteenth centuries. These may be categorized under three headings: that the study of nature is intellectually rewarding; that it is spiritually edifying; and that it is aesthetically gratifying. With the dawn of the Renaissance natural scientists throughout Europe began to probe the mysteries of the animal and vegetable creation; but before the layman could benefit from their discoveries, some measure of system had to be introduced into the collecting, describing, and comparing of specimens. The initial impetus to a widespread interest in nature studies was provided by the work on the classification of species accomplished by John Ray in the late seventeenth century. In the following period Ray's pioneering contributions were greatly refined by the Swedish taxonomist, Carl Linnaeus, who said: "The first step of science is to know one thing from another. This knowledge consists in their specific distinctions; but in order that it may be fixed and permanent distinct names must be given to different things, and those names must be recorded and remembered." Equipped with Linnaeus' *Systema Naturae*, the would-be naturalist had for the first time a reliable guide to help him pick his way through the maze of wonders revealed to the observing eye.

In pre-Darwinian days science and religion were not antagonistic; indeed Protestant theology encouraged the wave of curiosity about the workings of nature released by the Renaissance. So long as the fixity of species was not called in question, the identification of living forms and the examination of their structure and behavior were construed as promoting the glory of God, whose providential will was manifest in his handiwork. Nevertheless, the accumulating evidence that the natural world was under the reign of invariable law, in accordance with uniformi-

ix

tarian rather than catastrophic theories of biological progress, subtlely undermined the authority of the Christian revelation and promoted the more rationalistic approach to religious faith which goes by the name of deism. The deistic argument from design is most clearly stated in William Paley's *Natural Theology: or, Evidences of the Existence and Attributes of the Deity, collected from the Appearances of Nature* (1802). The title of this enormously influential work indicates how extensively eighteenth-century religious thought had been influenced by the findings of science. Yet, these early inquirers, it must be remembered, remained firm Christians, confident of the devout tendency of their researches. "Thus," Sir Thomas Browne could write, in his *Religio Medici* (1642), "there are two Books from whence I collect my Divinity; besides that written one of God, another of His servant Nature, that universal and publick Manuscript, that lies expans'd unto the Eyes of all: those that never saw Him in the one, have discover'd Him in the other." With greater eloquence John Ray set forth the credo of succeeding generations of naturalists in *The Wisdom of God manifested in the Works of Creation* (1691):

Let it not suffice to be book-learned, to read what others have written and to take upon trust more falsehood than truth, but let us ourselves examine things as we have opportunity, and converse with Nature as well as with books. . . . The treasures of Nature are inexhaustible. . . . I know that a new study at first seems very vast, intricate and difficult: but after a little resolution and progress, after a man becomes a little acquainted, as I may so say, with it, his understanding is wonderfully cleared up and enlarged, the difficulties vanish, and the thing grows easy and familiar. . . . Some reproach methinks it is to learned men that there should be so many animals still in the world whose outward shape is not yet taken notice of or described, much less their way of generation, food, manners, uses, observed. If man ought to reflect upon his Creator the glory of all his works, then ought he to take notice of them all and not to think anything unworthy of his cognizance.

The reverential spirit inspired by perception of divinely appointed order in the animate world was inseparable from the pleasure which the sensitive observer derived from its beauty and harmony, interpreted as additional proof of the creator's beneficence. The *Religio Medici* again crystallizes an attitude which seized the imagination of Browne's followers: "I hold there is a general beauty in the works of God, and therefore no deformity in any kind or species of creature whatsoever. . . . Now Nature is not at variance with Art, nor Art with Nature, they being both servants of His Providence. Art is the perfection of Nature." With the emergence of the romantic sensibility after the middle of the eighteenth century came a greatly heightened appreciation of natural beauty. The religious impulse took less orthodox forms of expression, as men turned increasingly to nature for the release of hitherto repressed feelings. Over the resultant burst of nature poetry from Cowper through Wordsworth to Tennyson there is no need to linger; four of the writers in this collection, Gray, Coleridge, Clare, and Hopkins, are, after all, primarily remembered as poets. It is worth remarking, however, that the literature of romanticism had its graphic counterpart in another indigenous development, the school of English landscape painters. Gainsborough and Richard Wilson were contemporaries of Gilbert White; and the artistic style originated by them is coextensive with the period under consideration. In one of his lectures John Constable had this to say about the principles which informed his artistic practice: "Painting is a science, and should be pursued as an inquiry into the laws of nature. Why, then, may not landscape painting be considered as a branch of natural philosophy, of which pictures are but the experiments?" To invoke the names of Constable's contemporaries—Girtin and Turner, Crome and Cotman, De Wint and Cox—is to conjure up their luminous delineations of those bucolic scenes amidst which the naturalists (many of whom were accomplished draftsmen as well) wandered with equal delight.

Loren Eiseley distinguishes between two traditions which have governed the study of natural history in England: "One stems directly from the purely scientific and experimental approach of Bacon . . . The other more gracious, humane tradition descends through John Ray and Gilbert White, two parson-

xi

naturalists, to the literary observers of later centuries, men such as Thoreau and Hudson." The examples here gathered are all the work of *out-of-door* as opposed to *in-door* naturalists, in the phraseology of Leonard Jenyns' *Observations in Natural History* (1846). Viewed as a group, their careers conform to certain patterns which help to explain their communal interest in the natural world, as well as the circumstances which favored its cultivation. White, Coleridge, Kingsley, Hopkins, and Kilvert were all clerics who found happiness in rural benefices. Knapp, Waterton, and St. John, as members of the squirearchy, lived on country estates, while yeoman blood flowed in the veins of Cobbett, Clare, and Jefferies. From such dwellers on the land familiarity with the lore of nature can be taken for granted. Their homogeneity is further emphasized by certain uniform traits of temperament which promoted intimacy with the natural world. Without being recluses, these writers were by and large unworldly and sufficiently at odds with the temper of their times to dislike and resolutely avoid city life. White, Gray, and Dorothy Wordsworth never married; and many of the others felt ill-at-ease under domestic or social constraint. Love of solitude bred among them a strong sense of individuality, nurtured, indeed, eccentricities and oddities of behavior, frequently engaging but too often aggravated by an inherent tendency to melancholy, which in the cases of Dorothy Wordsworth and Clare verged over into actual madness.

With the possible exception of Gosse, the contributions of these naturalists have been passed over by the historians of science. Yet, who is to say how much the great theoretical achievements of the biological sciences owe to the work of gifted amateurs? Darwin's important investigation of earthworms, for example, grew out of facts to which White had drawn his attention in *The Natural History of Selborne*. In the Preface to *The Aquarium* Gosse perceptively described the *modus operandi* of field-naturalists of the old school:

The habits of animals will never be thoroughly known till they are observed in detail. Nor is it sufficient to mark them with attention now and then; they must be closely watched, their various actions carefully noted, their behav-

xii

iour under different circumstances, and especially those movements which seem to us mere vagaries, undirected by any suggestible motive or cause, well examined. A rich fruit of result, often new and curious and unexpected, will, I am sure, reward any one who studies living animals in this way. The most interesting parts, by far, of published Natural History are those minute, but graphic particulars, which have been gathered by an attentive watching of individual animals.

From the foregoing passage emerge two implications about the methods and purposes of the early natural historians which go far to explain their enduring appeal. In the first place, they confined themselves as scrupulously as possible to first-hand impressions White's term for this procedure was *autopsia*, denoting the observer's open-minded reliance on the evidence of his own eyes. Shorn of abstract speculation and hearsay, their descriptions have the authenticity of direct experience. Secondly, their concern was with *animate* nature, unlike the closet scientist who anatomizes his specimens in the laboratory. This means that in their writings they were constantly endeavoring to capture and portray the living drama of the natural world in all its vibrant inter-relatedness.

For the true field-naturalist physical setting is an all-important component of his investigations, since the habits of animals are so much subject to environmental factors. The zeal which the English nature lovers brought to the study of creatures in their native habitats was intensified by the strength of their emotional attachment to districts hallowed by other associations. Each of the following selections testifies to its author's deep and affectionate familiarity with the region which he is describing: whether it be the Cumberland lakes of Dorothy Wordsworth, the Northamptonshire fens of Clare, the Scottish highlands of St. John, or the Devonshire shores of Gosse. No novel or poem can match in particularity and fullness of detail the evocations of the English countryside, while it was still unspoiled, which irradiate the following pages. The fact that the writers were so unselfconsciously attuned to ways of life that retained their perennial vitality imparts to their scenes an atmosphere of serenity and quiet felicity now only discoverable in the remote wilds. Even so perceptive a work as W. H. Hudson's *Nature in Downland*, published in 1900, shows in its deliberate striving for local color a quality of artifice wholly alien to the author's predecessors, who wrote untroubled by forebodings of the doom in store for the open spaces they loved.

The joyful wonder at the spectacle of nature so pervasively reflected in this collection is also in part traceable to pre-Darwinian habits of mind. Evolutionary speculations had been current for at least a century prior to the publication of *The Origin of Species* in 1859; and Darwin's contemporaries were less disturbed by his hypothesis that living species have descended by modification from more primitive forms than they were by the great biologist's explanation of how evolution takes place: namely, through a ruthless struggle for survival in which the selection of favorable variations is determined by chance. The bleak implications of this theory permanently destroyed the spiritual consolation which men had hitherto derived from the exploration of natural phenomena, by discrediting its basic premises. The Darwinian version of a world perpetually torn by chaotic conflict, of "Nature, red in tooth and claw" in Tennyson's grim phrase, was wholly incompatible with the older belief that natural order and harmony prevail throughout creation. Likewise, the proposition that evolution occurs in a largely fortuitous way challenged the concept of divine providence, depriving life of all meaning and placing it at the mercy of Hardy's "Crass Casualty." The nature lovers who came before Darwin were undisturbed by the pessimistic surmises which haunted Hardy's generation; and indeed, on the part of scientists at least, the early opposition to the Darwinian hypothesis was to a great extent generated by the realization that, deprived of its traditional religious sanctions, the study of natural history could never again address man's moral and aesthetic faculties in the ways so feelingly expressed by John Leonard Knapp in the following passage from *The Journal of a Naturalist:*

> And perhaps none of the amusements of human life are more satisfactory and dignified, than the investigation and survey of the workings and ways of Providence in this

created world of wonders, filled with his never-absent power; it occupies and elevates the mind, is inexhaustible in supply, and, while it furnishes meditation for the closet of the studious, gives to the reflections of the moralizing rambler admiration and delight, and is an engaging companion, that will communicate an interest to every rural walk.

Certainly, the pleasure to be derived from these pages is due to the authors' genius for communicating the all-sufficing delight with which they pursued their daily adventures, whether they were bent on collecting specimens or were content simply to observe and ruminate on the beauties and surprises that lay in wait. This vein of writing appears at its best in guises which invite the reader's intimacy; and with this in mind, the selections have been culled from letters, notebooks, journals and diaries, as well as the essay. Much of the material has the informal ease only to be found where there was no original intention to publish; and nearly all of it observes the fine line that divides scientific or purely expository from consciously literary prose. The writer's individuality comes across, but as if by accident. He unfailingly writes with his eye on the object; yet its meaning to him is what ultimately matters. In their responses the present company perfectly exemplifies what Keats meant by "negative capability," that is, the capacity to live in and for the immediate experience. Cowper, another poet who was also a passionate countryman, penned the naturalist's apologia in one of his letters: "My descriptions are all from nature: not one of them second-handed. My delineations of the heart are from my own experience: not one of them borrowed, or in the least conjectural."

This collection does not pretend to offer more than a sampling from among the literary riches that come under the heading of natural history. For every figure for whom room has been found, it has been necessary to exclude one equally attractive, while the informed reader will doubtless look in vain for favorite passages from the authors chosen. It is to be hoped, however, that there is enough here to suggest the variety and excellence of a too often neglected region of English writing.

Princeton, New Jersey

CONTENTS

CONTENTS

ILLUSTRATIONS

ILLUSTRATIONS

Gilbert White

The Goatsucker, or Fern Owl;
from Thomas Pennant's The British Zoology, 1766

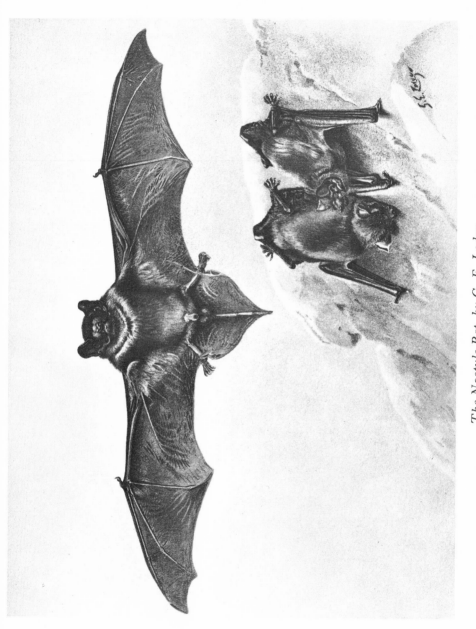

The Noctule Bat, by G. E. Lodge

Gilbert White
[1720–1793]

Few books have the power to make converts to a way of life. In this select company belongs Gilbert White's *The Natural History and Antiquities of Selborne*, which from its publication in 1789 has lured generations of amateur naturalists out-of-doors to join the ranks of Selbornians. White's enchanting blend of science, antiquarianism, and folk-lore has passed through nearly 100 editions, and has given direction to the activities of figures as unlike as Coleridge, to whom it was "this sweet delightful book," and Darwin, who on reading it in youth, wondered "why every gentleman did not become an ornithologist." Its elusive, but enduring charm is, as much as anything, attributable to the happy concurrence of the right man with the right time and the right place.

Selborne is a rural village in eastern Hampshire, so secluded that even Cobbett, that inveterate frequenter of byways, had to cast about to find it in 1823. The locality, however, is graced by an extraordinary diversity of terrain within small compass, its topographical features including in pleasant proximity open moor, downs, farmland, woods, ponds, and streams, with all the resulting varieties of soil and vegetation. Here White for more than sixty years led his quiet bachelor's existence in "The Wakes," a house built by his grandfather. After taking his degree at Oriel College, Oxford, and entering orders, he served during most of his career as curate, either in Selborne or adjoining parishes, refusing all opportunities for preferment since they would have meant leaving his beloved region. Throughout a life devoid of external incident he fulfilled his ministerial office with undeviating rectitude, and with the kindliness, simplicity, courtesy, and humor which illuminate his writings. "The mind that produced the 'Selborne,'" wrote the great landscape painter, John Constable, "is such a one as I have always envied.

. . . Surely the serene and blameless life of Mr. White, so exempt from the folly and quackery of the world, must have fitted him for the clear and intimate view he took of nature."

From boyhood White had been unusually attentive to the spectacle of the natural world, and in 1751 he began to keep a *Garden Kalendar.* Through his brother Benjamin, a London publisher and bookseller, he came to know the leading English zoologist of the day, Thomas Pennant, who invited him to write letters communicating his discoveries. He was also soon in correspondence with the Hon. Daines Barrington, a Welsh barrister with scientific interests and the deviser of the *Naturalist's Journal* in which from 1767 White kept his records. To Barrington goes the credit for suggesting that the letters, originally intended solely for Pennant and himself, should be amplified to make up a book. No small part of the unique savor of *Selborne* derives from the writer's wise decision to retain the epistolary form so congenial to his easy-going and candid temperament.

Although he was familiar with the standard authorities, Ray, Willughby, Linnaeus, White described himself as "an outdoor naturalist, one who takes his observations from the subject himself, and not from the writings of others." He added the harvest mouse and the great noctule bat to the list of British fauna. For all his ardent curiosity, he professed "never to lose sight of utility," so that later and more systematic naturalists found that they could almost invariably rely on the accuracy of his field notes. At the same time he exhibited a most engaging openness of mind, proclaiming that "candour forbids me to say absolutely that any fact is false, because I have never been witness to such a fact"; and this pliancy on occasion led him astray, as when, persuaded by Barrington's theory that swallows and martins were not migratory, he devoted much fruitless effort to trying to locate their places of hibernation. White's book was twenty years in the making; and his leisurely way of accumulating data allowed time not only to assimilate his findings, but also to speculate on their theoretical significance. He was among the first to call attention to the phenomenon of protective coloration as an example of adaptive function; and his observations led him very early to conclude that: "The two great motives which regulate

4

the proceedings of the brute creation are love and hunger. . . ."

White conceived of natural history as, in his own words, "an inquiry . . . into the life and conversation of animals." In their freshness and immediacy his notations give the impression of having been jotted down *in situ*, with a full awareness not only of how behavior is related to environment, but also of the interdependence of all forms of animate being. *Selborne* evokes a quite matchless feeling for the rhythm and harmony of the natural world, its wholeness and unity, that universal concord which for White was evidence of a divine economy never more wonderful than in its humble manifestations. Thus, the author's pioneer invesigations of the habits of the *Lumbricidae* lead, typically enough, to the reflection that: "Earth-worms, though in appearance a small and despicable link in the chain of Nature, yet, if lost, would make a lamentable chasm."

Year Selborne. Place. Soil.	Therm.	Barom.	Wynd	Inches of Rain or Sn. Size of Hail-st.	Weather.	Trees first in leaf—Plants—Fungi first appear.	Plants first ap. flower: Moss & vegetate.	first in Birds and Insects appear, or fish, and other animals.	Observations with regard to	Miscellaneous Observations, and Memorandums.
June 18. Sunday. 8 12 4 8	71.	29 6/10	S.W. N.		cloudy hot dark with air. sweet even.					Wheat looks well. Phallus impudicus stinks
19. Monday. 8 12 4 8	62½	29 7/10	N.E. N. N.E.		dark deep & blue, sweet even.					Great honey-dew. Began cutting my meadow grass. Grass very short.
20. Tuesday. 8 12 4 8	71¾	29 6/10	N. S.W.		great dew. bright. cloudy: about sultry: sweet even.		Agrimonia Eupatoria.			Barley shoots into ear. Meadow-grass very short indeed.
21. Wednes. 8 12 4 8	71.	29 70½	N. S.W. N.		fine thro' sun. freshair. bright cool gale.		Hay makes at a vast rate.			Barley begins to ripen. Vast crops of plums, currants, & goose-berries.
22. Thurs. 8 12 4 8	73.	29 7/10	S. W.		grey dull sky with fresh wind. cloudy about.		House martins which bred in our old nest, got the second brood off: they build themselves.			Wheat begins to ripen at Hartley. There has been the great breed of bees this summer.
23. Friday. 8 12 4 8	65.	29 40½	S.W. S.W. S.W.		sun. hot. dark & windy. dark & spitting.		new ones by 10 days. or a fortnight.			about half a crop: it is very short & fine.
24. Saturday. 8 12 4 8	64½	29 5/10	W. S.W.		bright delightful. soft rain for hours. grey mild & mild.					Indeed which lay it rain on the plants & loss of horses appears in the forest: it seems to abound more in moist...

From *The Natural History and Antiquities of Selborne.*

Letters to Thomas Pennant, Esquire

LETTER XXI

Selborne, Nov. 28, 1768

DEAR SIR,

WITH regard to the *oedicnemus*, or stone-curlew, I intend to write very soon to my friend near *Chichester*, in whose neighbourhood these birds seem most to abound; and shall urge him to take particular notice when they begin to congregate, and afterwards to watch them most narrowly whether they do not withdraw themselves during the dead of the winter. When I have obtained information with respect to this circumstance, I shall have finished my history of the *stone-curlew;* which I hope will prove to your satisfaction, as it will be, I trust, very near the truth. This gentleman, as he occupies a large farm of his own, and is abroad early and late, will be a very proper spy upon the motions of these birds: and besides, as I have prevailed on him to buy the Naturalist's Journal (with which he is much delighted), I shall expect that he will be very exact in his dates. It is very extraordinary, as you observe, that a bird so common with us should never straggle to you.

And here will be the properest place to mention, while I

think of it, an anecdote which the above-mentioned gentleman told me when I was last at his house; which was that, in a warren joining to his outlet, many daws (*corvi monedulæ*) build every year in the rabbit-burrows under ground. The way he and his brothers used to take their nests, while they were boys, was by listening at the mouths of the holes; and, if they heard the young ones cry, they twisted the nest out with a forked stick. Some water-fowls (*viz.* the puffins) breed, I know, in that manner; but I should never have suspected the daws of building in holes on the flat ground.

Another very unlikely spot is made use of by daws as a place to breed in, and that is *Stonehenge*. These birds deposit their nests in the interstices between the upright and the impost stones of that amazing work of antiquity: which circumstance alone speaks the prodigious height of the upright stones, that they should be tall enough to secure those nests from the annoyance of shepherd-boys, who are always idling round that place.

One of my neighbours last *Saturday*, *November* the 26th, saw a martin in a sheltered bottom: the sun shone warm, and the bird was hawking briskly after flies. I am now perfectly satisfied that they do not all leave this island in the winter.

You judge very right, I think, in speaking with reserve and caution concerning the cures done by toads: for, let people advance what they will on such subjects, yet there is such a propensity in mankind towards deceiving and being deceived, that one cannot safely relate any thing from common report, especially in print, without expressing some degree of doubt and suspicion.

Your approbation, with regard to my new discovery of the migration of the ring-ousel, gives me satisfaction; and I find you concur with me in suspecting that they are foreign birds which visit us. You will be sure, I hope, not to omit to make inquiry whether your ring-ousels leave your rocks in the autumn. What puzzles me most, is the very short stay they make with us; for in about three weeks they are all gone. I shall be very curious to remark whether they will call on us at their return in the spring, as they did last year.

I want to be better informed with regard to ichthyology. If fortune had settled me near the sea-side, or near some great river, my natural propensity would soon have urged me to have made myself acquainted with their productions: but as I have lived mostly in inland parts, and in an upland district, my knowledge of fishes extends little farther than to those common sorts which our brooks and lakes produce.

LETTER XXII

Selborne, Jan. 2, 1769

Dear Sir,

As to the peculiarity of jackdaws building with us under the ground in rabbit-burrows, you have, in part, hit upon the reason; for, in reality, there are hardly any towers or steeples in all this country. And perhaps, *Norfolk* excepted, *Hampshire* and *Sussex* are as meanly furnished with churches as almost any counties in the kingdom. We have many livings of two or three hundred pounds a year, whose houses of worship make little better appearance than dovecots. When I first saw *Northamptonshire*, *Cambridgeshire* and *Huntingdonshire*, and the fens of *Lincolnshire*, I was amazed at the number of spires which presented themselves in every point of view. As an admirer of prospects, I have reason to lament this want in my own country; for such objects are very necessary ingredients in an elegant landscape.

What you mention with respect to reclaimed toads raises my curiosity. An ancient author, though no naturalist, has well remarked that "*Every kind of beasts, and of birds, and of serpents, and things in the sea, is tamed, and hath been tamed, of mankind*".

It is a satisfaction to me to find that a green lizard has

9

actually been procured for you in *Devonshire;* because it corroborates my discovery, which I made many years ago, of the same sort, on a sunny sandbank near *Farnham* in *Surrey.* I am well acquainted with the south hams of *Devonshire;* and can suppose that district, from its southerly situation, to be a proper habitation for such animals in their best colours.

Since the ring-ousels of your vast mountains do certainly not forsake them against winter, our suspicions that those which visit this neighbourhood about *Michaelmas* are not *English* birds, but driven from the more northern parts of *Europe* by the frosts, are still more reasonable; and it will be worth your pains to endeavour to trace from whence they come, and to inquire why they make so very short a stay.

In your account of your error with regard to the two species of herons, you incidentally gave me great entertainment in your description of the heronry at *Cressi-hall;* which is a curiosity I never could manage to see. Fourscore nests of such a bird on one tree is a rarity which I would ride half as many miles to have a sight of. Pray be sure to tell me in your next whose seat *Cressi-hall* is, and near what town it lies. I have often thought that those vast extents of fens have never been sufficiently explored. If half a dozen gentlemen, furnished with a good strength of water-spaniels, were to beat them over for a week, they would certainly find more species.

There is no bird, I believe, whose manners I have studied more than that of the *caprimulgus* (the goat-sucker), as it is a wonderful and curious creature: but I have always found that though sometimes it may chatter as it flies, as I know it does, yet in general it utters it's jarring note sitting on a bough; and I have for many an half hour watched it as it sat with it's under mandible quivering, and particularly this summer. It perches usually on a bare twig, with it's head lower than it's tail, in an attitude well expressed by your draughtsman in the folio *British Zoology.* This bird is most punctual in beginning it's song exactly at the close of day; so exactly that I have known it strike up more than once or twice just at the report of the *Portsmouth* evening gun, which we can hear when the weather is still. It appears to me past all doubt that it's notes are formed by organic impulse, by the powers of the parts of it's windpipe, formed for sound, just as cats pur. You will credit me, I hope, when I assure you that, as my neighbours were assembled in an hermitage on the side of a steep hill where we drink tea, one of these churn-owls came and settled on the cross of that little straw edifice and began to chatter, and continued his note for many minutes: and we were all struck with wonder to find that the organs of that little animal, when put in motion, gave a sensible vibration to the whole building! This bird also sometimes makes a small squeak, repeated four or five times; and I have observed that to happen when the cock has been pursuing the hen in a toying way through the boughs of a tree.

It would not be at all strange if your bat, which you have procured, should prove a new one, since five species have been found in a neighbouring kingdom. The great sort that I mentioned is certainly a non-descript: I saw but one this summer, and that I had no opportunity of taking.

Your account of the *Indian-grass* was entertaining. I am no angler myself; but inquiring of those that are, what they supposed that part of their tackle to be made of? they replied "of the intestines of a silkworm".

Though I must not pretend to great skill in entomology, yet I cannot say that I am ignorant of that kind of knowledge: I may now and then perhaps be able to furnish you with a little information.

The vast rains ceased with us much about the same time as with you, and since we have had delicate weather. Mr. *Barker*, who has measured the rain for more than thirty years, says, in a late letter, that more has fallen this year than in any he ever attended to; though, from *July* 1763 to *January* 1764, more fell than in any seven months of this year.

11

LETTER XXIII

Selborne, February 28, 1769

DEAR SIR,

IT is not improbable that the *Guernsey* lizard and our green lizards may be specifically the same; all that I know is, that, when some years ago many *Guernsey* lizards were turned loose in *Pembroke* college garden, in the university of *Oxford*, they lived a great while, and seemed to enjoy themselves very well, but never bred. Whether this circumstance will prove any thing either way I shall not pretend to say.

I return you thanks for your account of *Cressi-hall;* but recollect, not without regret, that in *June* 1746 I was visiting for a week together at *Spalding*, without ever being told that such a curiosity was just at hand. Pray send me word in your next what sort of tree it is that contains such a quantity of herons' nests; and whether the heronry consists of a whole grove or wood, or only of a few trees.

It gave me satisfaction to find that we accorded so well about the *caprimulgus:* all I contended for was to prove that it often chatters sitting as well as flying; and therefore the noise was voluntary, and from organic impulse, and not from the resistance of the air against the hollow of its mouth and throat.

If ever I saw any thing like actual migration, it was last *Michaelmas-day*. I was travelling, and out early in the morning: at first there was a vast fog; but, by the time that I was got seven or eight miles from home towards the coast, the sun broke out into a delicate warm day. We were then on a large heath or common, and I could discern, as the mist began to break away, great numbers of swallows (*hirundines rusticæ*) clustering on the stunted shrubs and bushes, as if they had roosted there all night. As soon as the air became clear and

12

pleasant they all were on the wing at once; and, by a placid and easy flight, proceeded on southward towards the sea: after this I did not see any more flocks, only now and then a straggler.

I cannot agree with those persons that assert that the swallow kind disappear some and some gradually, as they come, for the bulk of them seem to withdraw at once: only some stragglers stay behind a long while, and do never, there is the greatest reason to believe, leave this island. Swallows seem to lay themselves up, and to come forth in a warm day, as bats do continually of a warm evening, after they have disappeared for weeks. For a very respectable gentleman assured me that, as he was walking with some friends under *Merton-wall* on a remarkably hot noon, either in the last week in *December* or the first week in *January*, he espied three or four swallows huddled together on the moulding of one of the windows of that college. I have frequently re-marked that swallows are seen later at *Oxford* than else-where: is it owing to the vast massy buildings of that place, to the many waters round it, or to what else?

When I used to rise in a morning last autumn, and see the swallows and martins clustering on the chimnies and thatch of the neighbouring cottages, I could not help being touched with a secret delight, mixed with some degree of mortifica-tion: with delight, to observe with how much ardour and punctuality those poor little birds obeyed the strong impulse towards migration, or hiding, imprinted on their minds by their great Creator; and with some degree of mortification, when I reflected that, after all our pains and inquiries, we are yet not quite certain to what regions they do migrate; and are still farther embarrassed to find that some do not actually migrate at all.

These reflections made so strong an impression on my imagination, that they became productive of a composition that may perhaps amuse you for a quarter of an hour when next I have the honour of writing to you.

13

LETTER XL

Selborne, Sept. 2, 1774

DEAR SIR,

BEFORE your letter arrived, and of my own accord, I had been remarking and comparing the tails of the male and female swallow, and this ere any young broods appeared; so that there was no danger of confounding the dams with their *pulli:* and besides, as they were then always in pairs, and busied in the employ of nidification, there could be no room for mistaking the sexes, nor the individuals of different chimnies the one for the other. From all my observations, it constantly appeared that each sex has the long feathers in it's tail that give it that forked shape; with this difference, that they are longer in the tail of the male than in that of the female.

Nightingales, when their young first come abroad, and are helpless, make a plaintive and a jarring noise; and also a snapping or cracking, pursuing people along the hedges as they walk: these last sounds seem intended for menace and defiance.

The grasshopper-lark chirps all night in the height of summer.

Swans turn white the second year, and breed the third.

Weasels prey on moles, as appears by their being sometimes caught in mole-traps.

Sparrow-hawks sometimes breed in old crows' nests, and the kestril in churches and ruins.

There are supposed to be two sorts of eels in the island of *Ely.* The threads sometimes discovered in eels are perhaps their young: the generation of eels is very dark and mysterious.

Hen-harriers breed on the ground, and seem never to settle on trees.

14

When redstarts shake their tails they move them horizontally, as dogs do when they fawn: the tail of a wagtail, when in motion, bobs up and down like that of a jaded horse.

Hedge-sparrows have a remarkable flirt with their wings in breeding-time; as soon as frosty mornings come they make a very piping plaintive noise.

Many birds which become silent about *Midsummer* reassume their notes again in *September;* as the thrush, blackbird, woodlark, willow-wren, &c.; hence *August* is by much the most mute month, the spring, summer and autumn through. Are birds induced to sing again because the temperament of autumn resembles that of spring?

Linnæus ranges plants geographically; palms inhabit the tropics, grasses the temperate zones, and mosses and lichens the polar circles; no doubt animals may be classed in the same manner with propriety.

House-sparrows build under eaves in the spring; as the weather becomes hotter they get out for coolness, and nest in plum-trees and apple-trees. These birds have been known sometimes to build in rooks' nests, and sometimes in the forks of boughs under rooks' nests.

As my neighbour was housing a rick he observed that his dogs devoured all the little red mice that they could catch, but rejected the common mice; and that his cats ate the common mice, refusing the red.

Red-breasts sing all through the spring, summer, and autumn. The reason that they are called autumn songsters is, because in the two first seasons their voices are drowned and lost in the general chorus; in the latter their song becomes distinguishable. Many songsters of the autumn seem to be the young cock red-breasts of that year: notwithstanding the prejudices in their favour, they do much mischief in gardens to the summer-fruits.

The titmouse, which early in *February* begins to make two quaint notes, like the whetting of a saw, is the marsh titmouse: the great titmouse sings with three cheerful joyous notes, and begins about the same time.

Wrens sing all the winter through, frost excepted.

House-martins came remarkably late this year both in *Hampshire* and *Devonshire:* is this circumstance for or against either hiding or migration?

Most birds drink sipping at intervals; but pigeons take a long continued draught, like quadrupeds.

Notwithstanding what I have said in a former letter, no grey crows were ever known to breed on *Dartmoor;* it was my mistake.

The appearance and flying of the *scarabæus solstitialis*, or fern-chafer, commence with the month of *July*, and cease about the end of it. These scarabs are the constant food of *caprimulgi*, or fern-owls, through that period. They abound on the chalky downs and in some sandy districts, but not in the clays.

In the garden of the *Black-bear* inn in the town of *Reading* is a stream or canal running under the stables and out into the fields on the other side of the road: in this water are many carps, which lie rolling about in sight, being fed by travellers, who amuse themselves by tossing them bread: but as soon as the weather grows at all severe these fishes are no longer seen, because they retire under the stables, where they remain till the return of spring. Do they lie in a torpid state? if they do not, how are they supported?

The note of the white-throat, which is continually repeated, and often attended with odd gesticulations on the wing, is harsh and displeasing. These birds seem of a pugnacious disposition; for they sing with an erected crest and attitudes of rivalry and defiance; are shy and wild in breeding-time, avoiding neighbourhoods, and haunting lonely lanes and commons; nay even the very tops of the *Sussex-downs*, where there are bushes and covert; but in *July* and *August* they bring their broods into gardens and orchards, and make great havock among the summer-fruits.

The black-cap has in common a full, sweet, deep, loud, and wild pipe; yet that strain is of short continuance, and his motions are desultory; but when that bird sits calmly and engages in song in earnest, he pours forth very sweet, but inward melody, and expresses great variety of soft and gentle modulations, superior perhaps to those of any of our warblers, the nightingale excepted.

Black-caps mostly haunt orchards and gardens; while they warble their throats are wonderfully distended.

The song of the redstart is superior, though somewhat like that of the white-throat: some birds have a few more notes than others. Sitting very placidly on the top of a tall tree in a village, the cock sings from morning to night: he affects neighbourhoods, and avoids solitude, and loves to build in orchards and about houses; with us he perches on the vane of a tall maypole.

The fly-catcher is of all our summer birds the most mute and the most familiar; it also appears the last of any. It builds in a vine, or a sweetbriar, against the wall of an house, or in the hole of a wall, or on the end of a beam or plate, and often close to the post of a door where people are going in and out all day long. This bird does not make the least pretension to song, but uses a little inward wailing note when it thinks it's young in danger from cats or other annoyances: it breeds but once, and retires early.

Selborne parish alone can and has exhibited at times more than half the birds that are ever seen in all *Sweden;* the former has produced more than one hundred and twenty species, the latter only two hundred and twenty-one. Let me add also that it has shown near half the species that were ever known in *Great-Britain.*

On a retrospect, I observe that my long letter carries with it a quaint and magisterial air, and is very sententious; but, when I recollect that you requested stricture and anecdote, I hope you will pardon the didactic manner for the sake of the information it may happen to contain.

17

GILBERT WHITE

Letters to the Honourable Daines Barrington

LETTER XIII

April 12, 1772

DEAR SIR,

WHILE I was in *Sussex* last autumn my residence was at the village near *Lewes*, from whence I had formerly the pleasure of writing to you. On the first of *November* I remarked that the old tortoise, formerly mentioned, began first to dig the ground in order to the forming it's hybernaculum, which it had fixed on just beside a great tuft of hepaticas. It scrapes out the ground with it's fore-feet, and throws it up over it's back with it's hind; but the motion of it's legs is ridiculously slow, little exceeding the hour-hand of a clock; and suitable to the composure of an animal said to be a whole month in performing one feat of copulation. Nothing can be more assiduous than this creature night and day in scooping the earth, and forcing it's great body into the cavity; but, as the noons of that season proved unusually warm and sunny, it was continually interrupted, and called forth by the heat in the middle of the day; and though I continued there till the thirteenth of *November*, yet the work remained unfinished. Harsher weather, and frosty mornings, would have quickened it's operations. No part of it's behaviour ever struck me more than the extreme timidity it always expresses with regard to rain; for though it has a shell that would secure it against the wheel of a loaded cart, yet does it discover as much solicitude about rain as a lady dressed in all her best attire, shuffling away on the first sprinklings, and running it's head up in a corner. If attended to, it becomes an excellent

18

weather-glass; for as sure as it walks elate, and as it were on tiptoe, feeding with great earnestness in a morning, so sure will it rain before night. It is totally a diurnal animal, and never pretends to stir after it becomes dark. The tortoise, like other reptiles, has an arbitrary stomach as well as lungs; and can refrain from eating as well as breathing for a great part of the year. When first awakened it eats nothing; nor again in the autumn before it retires: through the height of the summer it feeds voraciously, devouring all the food that comes in it's way. I was much taken with it's sagacity in discerning those that do it kind offices: for, as soon as the good old lady comes in sight who has waited on it for more than thirty years, it hobbles towards it's benefactress with aukward alacrity; but remains inattentive to strangers. Thus not only "*the ox knoweth his owner, and the ass his master's crib,*" but the most abject reptile and torpid of beings distinguishes the hand that feeds it, and is touched with the feelings of gratitude!

P.S. In about three days after I left *Sussex* the tortoise retired into the ground under the hepatica.

LETTER XV

Selborne, July 8, 1773

DEAR SIR,

SOME young men went down lately to a pond on the verge of *Wolmer-forest* to hunt flappers, or young wild-ducks, many of which they caught, and, among the rest, some very minute yet well-fledged wild-fowls alive, which upon examination I found to be teals. I did not know till then that teals ever bred in the south of *England*, and was much pleased with the discovery: this I look upon as a great stroke in natural history.

19

We have had, ever since I can remember, a pair of white owls that constantly breed under the eaves of this church. As I have paid good attention to the manner of life of these birds during their season of breeding, which lasts the summer through, the following remarks may not perhaps be unacceptable:—About an hour before sunset (for then the mice begin to run) they sally forth in quest of prey, and hunt all round the hedges of meadows and small enclosures for them, which seem to be their only food. In this irregular country we can stand on an eminence and see them beat the fields over like a setting-dog, and often drop down in the grass or corn. I have minuted these birds with my watch for an hour together, and have found that they return to their nests, the one or the other of them, about once in five minutes; reflecting at the same time on the adroitness that every animal is possessed of as far as regards the well being of itself and offspring. But a piece of address, which they shew when they return loaded, should not, I think, be passed over in silence.—As they take their prey with their claws, so they carry it in their claws to their nest: but, as the feet are necessary in their ascent under the tiles, they constantly perch first on the roof of the chancel, and shift the mouse from their claws to their bill, that the feet may be at liberty to take hold of the plate on the wall as they are rising under the eaves.

White owls seem not (but in this I am not positive) to hoot at all: all that clamorous hooting appears to me to come from the wood kinds. The white owl does indeed snore and hiss in a tremendous manner; and these menaces well answer the intention of intimidating: for I have known a whole village up in arms on such an occasion, imaging the church-yard to be full of goblins and spectres. White owls also often scream horribly as they fly along; from this screaming probably arose the common people's imaginery species of *screech-owl*, which they superstitiously think attends the windows of dying persons. The plumage of the remiges of the wings of every species of owl that I have yet examined is remarkably soft and pliant. Perhaps it may be necessary that the wings of these birds should not make much resistance or rushing, that they may be enabled to steal through the air unheard upon a nimble and watchful quarry.

While I am talking of owls, it may not be improper to mention what I was told by a gentleman of the county of *Wilts*. As they were grubbing a vast hollow pollard-ash that had been the mansion of owls for centuries, he discovered at the bottom a mass of matter that at first he could not account for. After some examination, he found it was a congeries of the bones of mice (and perhaps of birds and bats) that had been heaping together for ages, being cast up in pellets out of the crops of many generations of inhabitants. For owls cast up the bones, fur, and feathers, of what they devour, after the manner of hawks. He believes, he told me, that there were bushels of this kind of substance.

When brown owls hoot their throats swell as big as an hen's egg. I have known an owl of this species live a full year without any water. Perhaps the case may be the same with all birds of prey. When owls fly they stretch out their legs behind them as a balance to their large heavy heads: for as most nocturnal birds have large eyes and ears they must have large heads to contain them. Large eyes I presume are necessary to collect every ray of light, and large concave ears to command the smallest degree of sound or noise.

LETTER XVIII

Selborne, Jan. 29, 1774

DEAR SIR,

THE house-swallow, or chimney-swallow, is undoubtedly the first comer of all the *British hirundines;* and appears in general on or about the thirteenth of *April*, as I have re-

21

marked from many years observation. Not but now and then a straggler is seen much earlier: and, in particular, when I was a boy I observed a swallow for a whole day together on a sunny warm *Shrove Tuesday;* which day could not fall out later than the middle of *March*, and often happened early in *February*.

It is worth remarking that these birds are seen first about lakes and mill-ponds; and it is also very particular, that if these early visitors happen to find frost and snow, as was the case of the two dreadful springs of 1770 and 1771, they immediately withdraw for a time. A circumstance this much more in favour of hiding than migration; since it is much more probable that a bird should retire to it's hybernaculum just at hand, than return for a week or two only to warmer latitudes.

The swallow, though called the chimney-swallow, by no means builds together in chimnies, but often within barns and out-houses against the rafters; and so she did in *Virgil's* time:

> "————*Antè*
> "*Garrula quàm tignis nidos suspendat hirundo.*"

In *Sweden* she builds in barns, and is called *ladu swala*, the barn-swallow. Besides, in the warmer parts of *Europe* there are no chimnies to houses, except they are *English-built:* in these countries she constructs her nest in porches, and gate-ways, and galleries, and open halls.

Here and there a bird may affect some odd, peculiar place; as we have known a swallow build down the shaft of an old well, through which chalk had been formerly drawn up for the purpose of manure: but in general with us this *hirundo* breeds in chimnies; and loves to haunt those stacks where there is a constant fire, no doubt for the sake of warmth. Not that it can subsist in the immediate shaft where there is a fire; but prefers one adjoining to that of the kitchen, and disregards the perpetual smoke of that funnel, as I have often observed with some degree of wonder.

Five or six or more feet down the chimney does this little bird begin to form her nest about the middle of *May*, which consists, like that of the house-martin, of a crust or shell composed of dirt or mud, mixed with short pieces of straw to render it tough and permanent; with this difference, that whereas the shell of the martin is nearly hemispheric, that of the swallow is open at the top, and like half a deep dish: this nest is lined with fine grasses, and feathers which are often collected as they float in the air.

Wonderful is the address which this adroit bird shews all day long in ascending and descending with security through so narrow a pass. When hovering over the mouth of the funnel, the vibrations of her wings acting on the confined air occasion a rumbling like thunder. It is not improbable that the dam submits to this inconvenient situation so low in the shaft, in order to secure her broods from rapacious birds, and particularly from owls, which frequently fall down chimnies, perhaps in attempting to get at these nestlings.

The swallow lays from four to six white eggs, dotted with red specks; and brings out her first brood about the last week in *June*, or the first week in *July*. The progressive method by which the young are introduced into life is very amusing: first, they emerge from the shaft with difficulty enough, and often fall down into the rooms below: for a day or so they are fed on the chimney-top, and then are conducted to the dead leafless bough of some tree, where, sitting in a row, they are attended with great assiduity, and may then be called *perchers*. In a day or two more they become *flyers*, but are still unable to take their own food; therefore they play about near the place where the dams are hawking for flies; and, when a mouthful is collected, at a certain signal given, the dam and the nestling advance, rising towards each other, and meeting at an angle; the young one all the while uttering such a little quick note of gratitude and complacency, that a person must have paid very little regard to the wonders of Nature that has

23

not often remarked this feat.

The dam betakes herself immediately to the business of a second brood as soon as she is disengaged from her first; which at once associates with the first broods of *house-martins;* and with them congregates, clustering on sunny roofs, towers, and trees. This hirundo brings out her second brood towards the middle and end of *August.*

All the summer long is the swallow a most instructive pattern of unwearied industry and affection; for, from morning to night, while there is a family to be supported, she spends the whole day in skimming close to the ground, and exerting the most sudden turns and quick evolutions. Avenues, and long walks under hedges, and pasture-fields, and mown meadows where cattle graze, are her delight, especially if there are trees interspersed; because in such spots insects most abound. When a fly is taken a smart snap from her bill is heard, resembling the noise at the shutting of a watch-case; but the motion of the mandibles are too quick for the eye.

The swallow, probably the male bird, is the *excubitor* to house-martins, and other little birds, announcing the approach of birds of prey. For as soon as an hawk appears, with a shrill alarming note he calls all the swallows and martins about him; who pursue in a body, and buffet and strike their enemy till they have driven him from the village, darting down from above on his back, and rising in a perpendicular line in perfect security. This bird also will sound the alarm, and strike at cats when they climb on the roofs of houses, or otherwise approach the nests. Each species of hirundo drinks as it flies along, sipping the surface of the water; but the swallow alone, in general, *washes* on the wing, by dropping into a pool for many times together: in very hot weather house-martins and bank-martins dip and wash a little.

The swallow is a delicate songster, and in soft sunny weather sings both perching and flying; on trees in a kind of concert, and on chimney tops: is also a bold flyer, ranging to distant downs and commons even in windy weather, which the other species seem much to dislike; nay, even frequenting exposed sea-port towns, and making little excursions over the salt water. Horsemen on wide downs are often closely attended by a little party of swallows for miles together, which plays before and behind them, sweeping around, and collecting all the sculking insects that are roused by the trampling of the horses' feet: when the wind blows hard, without this expedient, they are often forced to settle to pick up their lurking prey.

This species feeds much on little *coleoptera*, as well as on gnats and flies; and often settles on dug ground, or paths, for gravels to grind and digest it's food. Before they depart, for some weeks, to a bird, they forsake houses and chimnies, and roost in trees; and usually withdraw about the beginning of *October;* though some few stragglers may appear on at times till the first week in *November.*

Some few pairs haunt the new and open streets of *London* next the fields, but do not enter, like the house-martin, the close and crowded parts of the city.

Both male and female are distinguished from their congeners by the length and forkedness of their tails. They are undoubtedly the most nimble of all the species: and when the male pursues the female in amorous chase, they then go beyond their usual speed, and exert a rapidity almost too quick for the eye to follow.

After this circumstantial detail of the life and discerning στοργη of the swallow, I shall add, for your farther amusement, an anecdote or two not much in favour of her sagacity:—

A certain swallow built for two years together on the handles of a pair of garden-shears, that were stuck up against the boards in an out-house, and therefore must have her nest spoiled whenever that implement was wanted: and, what is stranger still, another bird of the same species built it's nest on the wings and body of an owl that happened by accident to hang dead and dry from the rafter of a barn. This owl, with the nest on it's wings, and with eggs in the nest, was brought

25

as a curiosity worthy the most elegant private museum in *Great-Britain*. The owner, struck with the oddity of the sight, furnished the bringer with a large shell, or conch, desiring him to fix it just where the owl hung: the person did as he was ordered, and the following year a pair, probably the same pair, built their nest in the conch, and laid their eggs.

The owl and the conch make a strange grotesque appearance, and are not the least curious specimens in that wonderful collection of art and nature.

Thus is instinct in animals, taken the least out of it's way, an undistinguishing, limited faculty; and blind to every circumstance that does not immediately respect self-preservation, or lead at once to the propagation or support of their species.

LETTER XXVIII

Selborne, Jan. 8, 1776

DEAR SIR,

IT is the hardest thing in the world to shake off superstitious prejudices: they are sucked in as it were with our mother's milk; and, growing up with us at a time when they take the fastest hold and make the most lasting impressions, become so interwoven into our very constitutions, that the strongest good sense is required to disengage ourselves from them. No wonder therefore that the lower people retain them their whole lives through, since their minds are not invigorated by a liberal education, and therefore not enabled to make any efforts adequate to the occasion.

Such a preamble seems to be necessary before we enter on the superstitions of this district, lest we should be suspected of exaggeration in a recital of practices too gross for this enlightened age.

But the people of *Tring*, in *Hertfordshire*, would do well to remember, that no longer ago than the year 1751, and within twenty miles of the capital, they seized on two superannuated wretches, crazed with age, and overwhelmed with infirmities, on a suspicion of witchcraft; and, by trying experiments, drowned them in a horse-pond.

In a farm-yard near the middle of this village stands, at this day, a row of pollard-ashes, which, by the seams and long cicatrices down their sides, manifestly show that, in former times, they have been cleft asunder. These trees, when young and flexible, were severed and held open by wedges, while ruptured children, stripped naked, were pushed through the apertures, under a persuasion that, by such a process, the poor babes would be cured of their infirmity. As soon as the operation was over, the tree, in the suffering part, was plastered with loam, and carefully swathed up. If the parts coalesced and soldered together, as usually fell out, where the feat was performed with any adroitness at all, the party was cured; but, where the cleft continued to gape, the operation, it was supposed, would prove ineffectual. Having occasion to enlarge my garden not long since, I cut down two or three such trees, one of which did not grow together.

We have several persons now living in the village, who, in their childhood, were supposed to be healed by this superstitious ceremony, derived down perhaps from our *Saxon* ancestors, who practised it before their conversion to Christianity.

At the south corner of the *Plestor*, or area, near the church, there stood, about twenty years ago, a very old grotesque hollow pollard-ash, which for ages had been looked on with no small veneration as a *shrew-ash*. Now a shrew-ash is an ash whose twigs or branches, when gently applied to the limbs of cattle, will immediately relieve the pains which a beast suffers from the running of a *shrew-mouse* over the part affected: for it is supposed that a shrew-mouse is of so baneful and deleterious a nature, that wherever it creeps over

27

a beast, be it horse, cow, or sheep, the suffering animal is afflicted with cruel anguish, and threatened with the loss of the use of the limb. Against this accident, to which they were continually liable, our provident fore-fathers always kept a shrew-ash at hand, which, when once medicated, would maintain it's virtue for ever. A shrew-ash was made thus: —Into the body of the tree a deep hole was bored with an auger, and a poor devoted shrew-mouse was thrust in alive, and plugged in, no doubt, with several quaint incantations long since forgotten. As the ceremonies necessary for such a consecration are no longer understood, all succession is at an end, and no such tree is known to subsist in the manor, or hundred.

As to that on the *Plestor*,

"The late vicar stubb'd and burnt it,"

when he was way-warden, regardless of the remonstrances of the by-standers, who interceded in vain for it's preservation, urging it's power and efficacy, and alledging that it had been

"Religione patrum multos servata per annos".

LETTER XLII

"Omnibus animalibus reliquis certus et uniusmodi, et in suo cuique genere incessus est: aves solæ vario meatu feruntur, et in terrâ, et in äere."

PLIN., Hist. Nat., lib. x., cap. 38.

Selborne, Aug. 7, 1778

DEAR SIR,

A GOOD ornithologist should be able to distinguish birds by their air as well as by their colours and shape; on the ground as well as on the wing, and in the bush as well as in the hand. For, though it must not be said that every *species* of birds has a manner peculiar to itself, yet there is somewhat in most

28

genera at least, that at first sight discriminates them, and enables a judicious observer to pronounce upon them with some certainty. Put a bird in motion

"——*Et vera incessu patuit————*."

Thus *kites* and *buzzards* sail round in circles with wings expanded and motionless; and it is from their gliding manner that the former are still called in the north of *England gleads*, from the *Saxon* verb *glidan*, to glide. The *kestrel*, or *wind-hover*, has a peculiar mode of hanging in the air in one place, his wings all the while being briskly agitated. *Hen-harriers* fly low over heaths or fields of corn, and beat the ground regularly like a pointer or setting-dog. *Owls* move in a buoyant manner, as if lighter than the air; they seem to want ballast. There is a peculiarity belonging to *ravens* that must draw the attention even of the most incurious—they spend all their leisure time in striking and cuffing each other on the wing in a kind of playful skirmish; and, when they move from one place to another, frequently turn on their backs with a loud croak, and seem to be falling to the ground. When this odd gesture betides them, they are scratching themselves with one foot, and thus lose the center of gravity. *Rooks* sometimes dive and tumble in a frolicsome manner; *crows* and *daws* swagger in their walk; *wood-peckers* fly *volatu undoso*, opening and closing their wings at every stroke, and so are always rising or falling in curves. All of this genus use their tails, which incline downward, as a support while they run up trees. *Parrots*, like all other hooked-clawed birds, walk aukwardly, and make use of their bill as a third foot, climbing and ascending with ridiculous caution. All the *gallinæ* parade and walk gracefully, and run nimbly; but fly with difficulty, with an impetuous whirring, and in a straight line. *Magpies* and *jays* flutter with power-less wings, and make no dispatch; *herons* seem incumbered with too much sail for their light bodies; but these vast hollow wings are necessary in carrying burdens, such as large fishes, and the like; *pigeons*, and particularly the sort called *smiters*, have a way of clashing their wings the one against the other over their backs with a loud snap; another variety called *tumblers* turn themselves over in the air. Some birds have movements peculiar to the season of love: thus *ring-doves*, though strong and rapid at other times, yet in the spring hang about on the wing in a toying and playful manner; thus the *cock-snipe*, while breeding, forgetting his former flight, fans the air like the wind-hover; and the *green-finch* in particular exhibits such languishing and faultering gestures as to appear like a wounded and dying bird; the *king-fisher* darts along like an arrow; *fern-owls*, or *goat-suckers*, glance in the dusk over the tops of trees like a meteor; *starlings* as it were swim along, while *missel-thrushes* use a wild and desultory flight; *swallows* sweep over the surface of the ground and water, and distinguish them-selves by rapid turns and quick evolutions; *swifts* dash round in circles; and the *bank-martin* moves with frequent vacilla-tions like a butterfly. Most of the small birds fly by jerks, rising and falling as they advance. Most small birds hop; but *wagtails* and *larks* walk, moving their legs alternately. *Sky-larks* rise and fall perpendicularly as they sing; *woodlarks* hang poised in the air; and *titlarks* rise and fall in large curves, singing in their descent. The *white-throat* uses odd jerks and gesticulations over the tops of hedges and bushes. All the *duck-kind* waddle; *divers* and *auks* walk as if fettered, and stand erect on their tails: these are the *compedes* of *Linnæus*. *Geese* and *cranes*, and most wild-fowls, move in figured flights, often changing their position. The secondary *remiges* of *Tringæ*, *wild-ducks*, and some others, are very long, and give their wings, when in motion, an hooked ap-pearance. *Dabchicks*, *moor-hens*, and *coots*, fly erect, with their legs hanging down, and hardly make any dispatch; the reason is plain, their wings are placed too forward out of the true centre of gravity; as the legs of *auks* and *divers* are situated too backward.

LETTER XLIII

Selborne, Sept. 9, 1778

DEAR SIR,

FROM the motion of birds, the transition is natural enough to their notes and language, of which I shall say something. Not that I would pretend to understand their language like the *vizier;* who, by the recital of a conversation which passed between two owls, reclaimed a sultan, before delighting in conquest and devastation; but I would be thought only to mean that many of the winged tribes have various sounds and voices adapted to express their various passions, wants, and feelings; such as anger, fear, love, hatred, hunger, and the like. All species are not equally eloquent; some are copious and fluent as it were in their utterance, while others are confined to a few important sounds: no bird, like the fish kind, is quite mute, though some are rather silent. The language of birds is very ancient, and, like other ancient modes of speech, very elliptical; little is said, but much is meant and understood.

The notes of the eagle-kind are shrill and piercing; and about the season of nidification much diversified, as I have been often assured by a curious observer of Nature, who long resided at *Gibraltar*, where eagles abound. The notes of our *hawks* much resemble those of the king of birds. *Owls* have very expressive notes; they hoot in a fine vocal sound, much resembling the *vox humana*, and reducible by a pitch-pipe to a musical key. This note seems to express complacency and rivalry among the males: they use also a quick call and an horrible scream; and can snore and hiss when they mean to menace. *Ravens*, besides their loud croak, can exert a deep and solemn note that makes the woods to echo; the amorous sound of a *crow* is strange and ridiculous; *rooks*, in the

31

breeding season, attempt sometimes in the gaiety of their hearts to sing, but with no great success; the *parrot*-kind have many modulations of voice, as appears by their aptitude to learn human sounds; *doves* coo in an amorous and mournful manner, and are emblems of despairing lovers; the *woodpecker* sets up a sort of loud and hearty laugh; the *fern-owl*, or *goat-sucker*, from the dusk till day-break, serenades his mate with the clattering of castanets. All the tuneful *passeres* express their complacency by sweet modulations, and a variety of melody. The *swallow*, as has been observed in a former letter, by a shrill alarm bespeaks the attention of the other *hirundines*, and bids them be aware that the hawk is at hand. Aquatic and gregarious birds, especially the nocturnal, that shift their quarters in the dark, are very noisy and loquacious; as cranes, wild-geese, wild-ducks, and the like: their perpetual clamour prevents them from dispersing and losing their companions.

In so extensive a subject, sketches and outlines are as much as can be expected; for it would be endless to instance in all the infinite variety of the feathered nation. We shall therefore confine the remainder of this letter to the few domestic fowls of our yards, which are most known, and therefore best understood. At first the *peacock*, with his gorgeous train, demands our attention; but, like most of the gaudy birds, his notes are grating and shocking to the ear: the yelling of cats, and the braying of an ass, are not more disgustful. The voice of the *goose* is trumpet-like, and clanking; and once saved the Capitol at *Rome*, as grave historians assert: the hiss also of the *gander* is formidable and full of menace, and "protective of his young." Among *ducks* the sexual distinction of voice is remarkable; for, while the *quack* of the female is loud and sonorous, the voice of the *drake* is inward and harsh, and feeble, and scarce discernible. The cock *turkey* struts and gobbles to his mistress in a most uncouth manner; he hath also a pert and petulant note when he attacks his adversary. When a hen *turkey* leads forth her young brood she keeps a watchful eye; and if a bird of prey appear, though ever so high in the air, the careful mother announces the enemy with a little inward moan, and watches him with a steady and attentive look; but, if he approach, her note becomes earnest and alarming, and her outcries are redoubled.

No inhabitants of a yard seem possessed of such a variety of expression and so copious a language as common poultry. Take a chicken of four or five days old, and hold it up to a window where there are flies, and it will immediately seize it's prey, with little twitterings of complacency; but if you tender it a wasp or a bee, at once it's note becomes harsh, and expressive of disapprobation and a sense of danger. When a pullet is ready to lay she intimates the event by a joyous and easy soft note. Of all the occurrences of their life that of *laying* seems to be the most important; for no sooner has a hen disburdened herself, than she rushes forth with a clamorous kind of joy, which the cock and the rest of his mistresses immediately adopt. The tumult is not confined to the family concerned, but catches from yard to yard, and spreads to every homestead within hearing, till at last the whole village is in an uproar. As soon as a hen becomes a mother her new relation demands a new language; she then runs clocking and screaming about, and seems agitated as if possessed. The father of the flock has also a considerable vocabulary; if he finds food, he calls a favourite concubine to partake; and if a bird of prey passes over, with a warning voice he bids his family beware. The gallant *chanticleer* has, at command, his amorous phrases, and his terms of defiance. But the sound by which he is best known is his *crowing:* by this he has been distinguished in all ages as the countryman's clock or larum, as the watchman that proclaims the divisions of the night. Thus the poet elegantly stiles him:

> "———*the crested cock, whose clarion sounds*
> "*The silent hours.*"

33

A neighbouring gentleman one summer had lost most of his chickens by a sparrow-hawk, that came gliding down between a faggot pile and the end of his house to the place where the coops stood. The owner, inwardly vexed to see his flock thus diminishing, hung a setting net adroitly between the pile and the house, into which the caitiff dashed, and was entangled. Resentment suggested the law of retaliation; he therefore clipped the hawk's wings, cut off his talons, and, fixing a cork on his bill, threw him down among the brood-hens. Imagination cannot paint the scene that ensued; the expressions that fear, rage, and revenge, inspired, were new, or at least such as had been unnoticed before: the exasperated matrons upbraided, they execrated, they insulted, they triumphed. In a word, they never desisted from buffeting their adversary till they had torn him in an hundred pieces.

LETTER L

Selborne, April 21, 1780

Dear Sir,

The old *Sussex* tortoise, that I have mentioned to you so often, is become my property. I dug it out of it's winter dormitory in *March* last, when it was enough wakened to express it's resentments by hissing; and, packing it in a box with earth, carried it eighty miles in post-chaises. The rattle and hurry of the journey so perfectly roused it that, when I turned it out on a border, it walked twice down to the bottom of my garden; however, in the evening, the weather being cold, it buried itself in the loose mould, and continues still concealed.

As it will be under my eye, I shall now have an opportunity of enlarging my observations on it's mode of life, and propensities; and perceive already that, towards the time of coming forth, it opens a breathing place in the ground near it's head,

34

The Testudo Marginata; Gilbert White kept a female of this species as a pet

requiring, I conclude, a freer respiration, as it becomes more alive. This creature not only goes under the earth from the middle of *November* to the middle of *April*, but sleeps great part of the summer; for it goes to bed in the longest days at four in the afternoon, and often does not stir in the morning till late. Besides, it retires to rest for every shower; and does not move at all in wet days.

When one reflects on the state of this strange being, it is a matter of wonder to find that Providence should bestow such a profusion of days, such a seeming waste of longevity, on a reptile that appears to relish it so little as to squander more than two thirds of it's existence in a joyless stupor, and be lost to all sensation for months together in the profoundest of slumbers.

While I was writing this letter, a moist and warm afternoon, with the thermometer at 50, brought forth troops of *shell-snails;* and, at the same juncture, the *tortoise* heaved up the mould, and put out it's head; and the next morning came forth, as it were raised from the dead; and walked about till four in the afternoon. This was a curious coincidence! a very amusing occurrence! to see such a similarity of feelings between the two φερεοικοι! for so the *Greeks* call both the *snail* and the *tortoise*.

Summer birds are, this cold and backward spring, unusually late: I have seen but one swallow yet. This conformity with the weather convinces me more and more that they sleep in the winter.

More PARTICULARS *respecting the* OLD FAMILY TORTOISE, *omitted in the* Natural History.*

Because we call this creature an abject reptile, we are too apt to undervalue his abilities, and depreciate his powers of instinct. Yet he is, as Mr. *Pope* says of his lord,

* In the original edition this passage was printed at the end of the Antiquities.

"———Much too wise to walk into a well:"

and has so much discernment as not to fall down an haha; but to stop and withdraw from the brink with the readiest precaution.

Though he loves warm weather he avoids the hot sun; because his thick shell, when once heated, would, as the poet says of solid armour—"scald with safety." He therefore spends the more sultry hours under the umbrella of a large cabbage-leaf, or amidst the waving forests of an asparagus-bed.

But as he avoids heat in the summer, so, in the decline of the year, he improves the faint autumnal beams, by getting within the reflection of a fruit-wall: and, though he never has read that planes inclining to the horizon receive a greater share of warmth, he inclines his shell, by tilting it against the wall, to collect and admit every feeble ray.

Pitiable seems the condition of this poor embarrassed reptile: to be cased in a suit of ponderous armour, which he cannot lay aside; to be imprisoned, as it were, within his own shell, must preclude, we should suppose, all activity and disposition for enterprize. Yet there is a season of the year (usually the beginning of June) when his exertions are remarkable. He then walks on tiptoe, and is stirring by five in the morning; and, traversing the garden, examines every wicket and interstice in the fences, through which he will escape if possible: and often has eluded the care of the gardener, and wandered to some distant field. The motives that impel him to undertake these rambles seem to be of the amorous kind: his fancy then becomes intent on sexual attachments, which transport him beyond his usual gravity, and induce him to forget for a time his ordinary solemn deportment.

37

Thomas Gray

The White-tailed Eagle, wood engraving by Thomas Bewick (1753–1828)

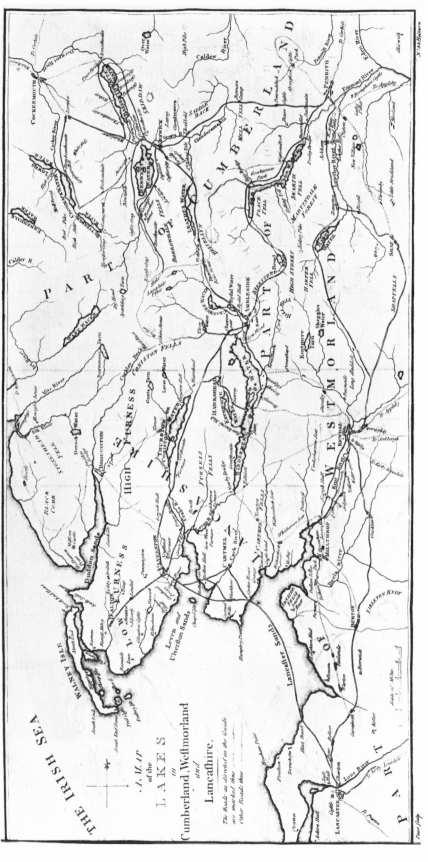

A map of the English Lake District from Thomas West's A Guide to the Lakes, 1784 edition

Thomas Gray
⌈1716–1771⌉

G ray passed the greater part of an uneventful life within the precincts of Cambridge University, first at Peterhouse and then at Pembroke College. Academic seclusion was interrupted by summer excursions about the English countryside, at once beneficial to his health and productive of data for scientific speculations. A delicate constitution had its counterpart in a caste of mind so habitually low-spirited that Gray might have been composing his own epitaph in the famous line: "And Melancholy mark'd him for her own." Already in youth a connoisseur of spiritual malaise, he was to write to his friend Richard West in 1742:

> Mine, you are to know, is a white Melancholy, or rather Leucocholy for the most part; which though it seldom laughs or dances, nor ever amounts to what one calls Joy or Pleasure, yet is a good easy sort of a state, and ça ne laisse que de s'amuser. The only fault of it is insipidity; which is apt now and then to give a sort of Ennui, which makes one form certain little wishes that signify nothing. But there is another sort, black indeed, which I have now and then felt, that has somewhat in it like Tertullian's rule of faith, Credo quia impossibile est; for it believes, nay, is sure of every thing that is unlikely, so it be but frightful; and, on the other hand, excludes and shuts its eyes to the most possible hopes, and every thing that is pleasurable; from this the Lord deliver us! for none but he and sunshiny weather can do it.

Gray's artistic fame rests securely on a handful of deeply felt and exquisitely finished poems, the product of fitful spurts of creativity which soon dried up. His culminating work, of course, is the "Elegy written in a Country Churchyard," its perennial appeal traceable in Tennyson's words to those "divine truisms that make us weep." Gray is hardly less remembered for his correspondence, which in a century of great letter-writers places him beside Walpole and Cowper. The letters declare the man: his talent for friendship, his erudition and ranging curiosity, his fastidious taste and finely discriminating critical intelligence, his sprightliness of wit ever lurking to cancel out the moods of dejection.

"Perhaps he [Gray] was the most learned man in Europe": so wrote Boswell's friend, William Johnson Temple. In devoting himself to scholarly pursuits, Gray was motivated by the twofold desire to overcome his besetting vice of indolence and to escape the boredom which followed in its train. For, as he liked to say, "To be employed is to be happy." Among the fields of knowledge which he exhaustively surveyed were classical civilization, eastern and mediaeval history, the literature of travel, English poetry with its Celtic and Scandinavian antecedents, ecclesiastical architecture. In each his mastery was acknowledged, although the accompanying plans for publication came to nothing.

Always keenly alive to the interest of the passing seasons, Gray immersed himself in the study of natural history during the last decade of his life. Like Gilbert White, he kept annual calendars in which he meticulously recorded temperature readings and weather conditions, and made detailed notations on such matters as the budding of foliage and the springing of crops, the first arrival of blossoms and fruits, the migration of birds with their songs and nesting habits. His observations and experiments were supplemented by extensive reading, especially of the great Linnaeus, whose *Systema Naturae*, first appearing in 1735, introduced system into the classification of zoological and botanical species. Gray acquired the tenth edition of this work in 1759, and filled its margins and interleaved pages with his own comments, entered in Latin as a general rule, though also in English, French, and Italian. Many of the notes are illustrated by sensitive pen-and-ink drawings of birds and insects. So absorbing was his devotion to his researches that Horace Walpole could wryly remark: "Mr. Gray often vexed me by finding him heaping notes on an interleaved *Linnaeus*, instead of pranking on his lyre."

Yet, Gray's scientific attainments were by no means those of a dilettante; there is little doubt that he would have become recognized as one of the leading entomologists in Europe had he chosen to make his findings known.

For the autumn of 1769 Gray planned a tour through the English Lakes with the physician Thomas Wharton, at whose estate, Old-Park, near Durham, he was a frequent visitor. At the last moment an attack of asthma compelled Wharton to drop out; and Gray, going on alone, kept a journal of the expedition later to be transcribed in letters to his friend, from which the following passages are taken. Gray's early visit to the Lake Country is something of a landmark in its time; and the parliamentarian Sir James Mackintosh must have had it partly in mind when he said of the poet that "he was the first discoverer of the beauties of nature in England, and has marked out the course of every picturesque journey that can be made in it." Certainly, in its fusion of accurate description with poetic sensibility this account exhibits a strain of nature writing new in English literature. Because of the love of rugged mountain scenery, expressed as early as 1739 when he passed through the Alps on the Grand Tour with Walpole, Gray has often been associated with the Romantic poets. A comparison of this journal with the ensuing selections from Dorothy Wordsworth and Coleridge, however, will show that its author responded to natural beauty not as a transcendental philosopher so much as an eighteenth-century gentleman whose eye was trained to distinguish the Picturesque or Sublime properties of the surrounding landscape. Indeed, Gray was wedded to his "glass," a kind of camera obscura for taking views which were by this agency composed into pictures.

Facsimile of a page from Thomas Gray's annotated copy of Linnaeus'
Systema Naturae, *showing Gray's drawings of moths*

From *Correspondence*

Journal of a Tour through the English Lakes

30 Sept. 1769

WIND at N.W. Clouds & sunshine. A mile & ½ from Brough on a hill lay a great army encamp'd. To the left open'd a fine valley with green meadows & hedge-rows, a Gentleman's house peeping forth from a grove of old trees. On a nearer approach appear'd myriads of horses & cattle in the road itself & in all the fields round me, a brisk stream hurrying cross the way, thousands of clean healthy People in their best party-color'd apparel, Farmers & their families, Esquires & their daughters, hastening up from the dales & down the fells on every side, glittering in the sun & pressing forward to join the throng: while the dark hills, on many of whose tops the mists were yet hanging, served as a contrast to this gay & moving scene, which continued for near two miles more along the road, and the crowd (coming towards it) reach'd on as far as Appleby.

On the ascent of the hill above Appleby the thick hanging wood & the long reaches of the Eden (rapid, clear, & full as ever) winding below with views of the Castle & Town gave much employment to the mirror: but the sun was wanting & the sky overcast. Oats & barley cut every where, but not carried in. Passed Kirby-thore, Sir W. Walston's house at Acorn-bank, Whinfield-park, Harthorn-oaks, Countess-pillar, Brougham-Castle, Mr. Brown (one of ye six Clerks) his large new house, cross'd the Eden & the Eimot (pronounce *Eeman*) with its green vale, & at 3 o'clock dined with Mrs. Buchanan, at *Penrith* on trout & partridge. In the afternoon walk'd up the *Beacon-hill* a mile to the top, saw Whinfield and Lowther-parks, & thro' an opening in the bosom of that cluster of mountains, which the Doctor well remembers, the Lake of Ulz-water, with the craggy tops of a hundred nameless hills. These to W. & S., to the N. a great extent of black & dreary plains, to E. *Cross-fell* just visible thro' mists & vapours hovering round it.

Oct. 1. Wind at S. W. a grey autumnal day, air perfectly calm & gentle. Went to see *Ulz-water* 5 miles distant. Soon left the Keswick-road & turn'd to the left thro' shady lanes along the Vale of *Eeman*, which runs rapidly on near the way, ripling over the stones. To the right is *Delmaine*, a large fabrick of pale red stone with 9 windows in front & 7 on the side built by Mr. Hassel, behind it a fine lawn surrounded by woods & a long rocky eminence rising over them. A clear & brisk rivulet runs by the house to join the Eeman, whose course is in sight & at a small distance.

Farther on appears *Hatton St. John*, a castle-like old mansion of Mr. Huddleston. Approach'd *Dunmallert*, a fine pointed hill, cover'd with wood planted by old Mr. Hassle beforemention'd, who lives always at home & delights in planting. Walk'd over a spungy meadow or two & began to mount this hill thro' a broad & strait green alley among the trees, & with some toil gain'd the summit. From hence saw the Lake opening directly at my feet majestic in its calmness, clear & smooth as a blew mirror with winding shores & low points of land cover'd with green inclosures, white farm-houses looking out among the trees, & cattle feeding. The water is almost every where border'd with cultivated lands gently sloping upwards till they reach the feet of the mountains, which rise very rude & aweful with their broken tops on either hand. Directly in front at better than 3 mile's distance, *Place-Fell*, one of the bravest among them, pushes its bold broad breast into the midst of the Lake & forces it to alter it's course, forming first a large bay to the left & then bending to the right.

I descended *Dunmallert* again by a side avenue, that was only not perpendicular, & came to *Barton*-bridge over the *Eeman*, then walking thro' a path in the wood round the bottom of the hill came forth, where the *Eeman* issues out of the lake, & continued my way along it's western shore close to the water, & generally on a level with it. Saw a cormorant flying over it & fishing. . . .

1 Oct. 1769

The figure of *Ulz-water* nothing resembles that laid down in our maps: it is 9 miles long, & (at widest) under a mile in breadth. After extending itself 3 m. & ½ in a line to S. W. it turns at the foot of *Place-Fell*, almost due West, and is here not twice the breadth of the Thames at London. It is soon again interrupted by the roots of *Helvellyn*, a lofty & very rugged mountain, & spreading again turns off to S. E., & is lost among the deep recesses of the hills. To this second turning I pursued my way about four miles along its borders beyond a village scatter'd among trees & call'd *Water-malloch*, in a pleasant grave day, perfectly calm & warm, but without a gleam of sunshine: then the sky seeming to thicken, the valley to grow more desolate, & evening drawing on, I return'd by the way I came to *Penrith*.

Oct. 2. Wind at S. E., sky clearing, *Cross-fell* misty, but the outline of the other hills very distinct. Set out at 10 for *Keswick*, by the road we went in 1767. Saw *Greystock*-town & castle to the right, which lie only 3 miles (over the Fells) from *Ulz-water*. pass'd through *Penradock* & *Threlcot* at the feet of *Saddleback*, whose furrow'd sides were gilt by the noon-day Sun, while its brow appear'd of a sad purple from the shadow of the clouds, as they sail'd slowly by it. The broad & green valley of *Gardies* and *Low-side*, with a swift stream glittering among the cottages & meadows lay to the left; & the much finer (but narrower) valley of St. *John's*

opening into it: *Hill-top* the large, tho' low, mansion of the
Gaskarths, now a Farm-house, seated on an eminence among
woods under a steep fell, was what appear'd the most con-
spicuous, & beside it a great rock like some antient tower
nodding to its fall. Pass'd by the side of *Skiddaw* & its cub
call'd *Latter-rig*, & saw from an eminence at two miles dis-
tance the Vale of Elysium in all its verdure, the sun then
playing on the bosom of the lake, & lighting up all the
mountains with its lustre.

Dined by two o'clock at the Queen's Head, & then
straggled out alone to the *Parsonage*, fell down on my back
across a dirty lane with my glass open in one hand, but broke
only my knuckles: stay'd nevertheless, & saw the sun set in
all its glory.

Oct. 3. Wind at S. E., a heavenly day. Rose at seven, &
walk'd out under the conduct of my Landlord to *Borrodale*.
The grass was cover'd with a hoar-frost, which soon melted,
& exhaled in a thin blewish smoke. Cross'd the meadows
obliquely, catching a diversity of views among the hills over
the lake & islands, & changing prospect at every ten paces,
left *Cockshut* & Castle-hill (which we formerly mounted)
behind me, & drew near the foot of *Walla-crag*, whose bare &
rocky brow, cut perpendicularly down above 400 feet, as I
guess, awefully overlooks the way: our path here tends to the
left, & the ground gently rising, & cover'd with a glade of
scattering trees & bushes on the very margin of the water,
opens both ways the most delicious view, that my eyes ever
beheld. Behind you are the magnificent heights of *Walla*-
crag; opposite lie the thick hanging woods of Lord Egre-
mont, & *Newland*-valley with green & smiling fields embos-
om'd in the dark cliffs; to the left the jaws of *Borodale*, with
that turbulent Chaos of mountain behind mountain roll'd in
confusion; beneath you, & stretching far away to the right,
the shining purity of the *Lake*, just ruffled by the breeze
enough to shew it is alive, reflecting rocks, woods, fields, &
inverted tops of mountains, with the white buildings of *Kes-*

48

wick, *Crosthwait*-church, & *Skiddaw* for a back-ground at
distance. Oh Doctor! I never wish'd more for you; & pray
think, how the glass played its part in such a spot, which is
called *Carf-close-reeds:* I chuse to set down these barbarous
names, that any body may enquire on the place, & easily find
the particular station, that I mean. This scene continues to
Barrow-gate, & a little farther, passing a brook called
Barrow-beck, we enter'd *Borodale*. The crags, named
Lodoor-banks now begin to impend terribly over your way; &
more terribly, when you hear, that three years since an im-
mense mass of rock tumbled at once from the brow, & bar'd
all access to the dale (for this is the only road) till they could
work their way thro' it. Luckily no one was passing at the
time of this fall; but down the side of the mountain & far into
the lake lie dispersed the huge fragments of this ruin in all
shapes & in all directions. Something farther we turn'd aside
into a coppice, ascending a little in front of *Lodoor* water-fall.
The height appears to be about 200 feet, the quantity of
water not great, tho' (these three days excepted) it had
rain'd daily in the hills for near two months before: but then
the stream was nobly broken, leaping from rock to rock, &
foaming with fury. on one side a towering crag, that spired
up to equal, if not overtop, the neighbouring cliffs (this lay
all in shade & darkness) on the other hand a rounder broader
projecting hill shag'd with wood & illumined by the sun,
which glanced sideways on the upper part of the cataract.
The force of the water wearing a deep channel in the ground
hurries away to join the lake. We descended again, & passed
the stream over a rude bridge. Soon after we came under
Gowder-crag, a hill more formidale to the eye & to the appre-
hension than that of *Lodoor;* the rocks atop, deep-cloven
perpendicularly by the rains, hanging loose & nodding for-
wards, seem just starting from their base in shivers: the
whole way down & the road on both sides is strew'd with piles
of the fragments strangely thrown across each other & of a
dreadful bulk. The place reminds one of those passes in the

49

Alps, where the Guides tell you to move on with speed, & say nothing, lest the agitation of the air should loosen the snows above, & bring down a mass that would overwhelm a caravan. I took their counsel here and hasten'd on in silence.

Non ragioniam di lor; ma guarda, e passa!

Oct. 3. The hills here are cloth'd all up their steep sides with oak, ash, birch, holly, &c. some of it has been cut 40 years ago, some within these 8 years, yet all is sprung again green, flourishing, & tall for its age, in a place where no soil appears but the staring rock, & where a man could scarce stand upright.

Met a civil young Farmer overseeing his reapers (for it is oat-harvest here) who conducted us to a neat white house in the village of Grange, which is built on a rising ground in the midst of a valley. Round it the mountains form an aweful amphitheatre, & thro' it obliquely runs the Derwent clear as glass, & shewing under it's bridge every trout, that passes. Beside the village rises a round eminence of rock cover'd entirely with old trees, & over that more proudly towers *Castle-crag*, invested also with wood on its sides, & bearing on its naked top some traces of a fort said to be Roman. By the side of this hill, which almost blocks up the way, the valley turns to the left & contracts its dimensions, till there is hardly any road but the rocky bed of the river. The wood of the mountains increases & their summits grow loftier to the eye, & of more fantastic forms: among them appear *Eagle's-cliff*, *Dove's-nest*, *Whitedale-pike*, &c: celebrated names in the annals of Keswick. The dale opens about four miles higher till you came to *Sea-Whaite* (where lies the way mounting the hills to the right, that leads to the *Wadd-mines*) all farther access is here barr'd to prying Mortals, only there is a little path winding over the Fells, & for some weeks in the year passable to the Dale's-men; but the Mountains know well, that these innocent people will not reveal the mysteries of their ancient kingdom, the reign of Chaos & old

50

Night. Only I learn'd, that this dreadful road dividing again leads one branch to *Ravenglas*, & the other to *Hawkshead*.

For me I went no farther than the Farmer's (better than 4 m. from Keswick) at *Grange:* his Mother & he brought us butter, that Siserah would have jump'd at, tho' not in a lordly dish, bowls of milk, thin oaten-cakes, & ale; & we had carried a cold tongue thither with us. Our Farmer was himself the Man, that last year plunder'd the Eagle's eirie: all the dale are up in arms on such an occasion, for they lose abundance of lambs yearly, not to mention hares, partridge, grous, &c. He was let down from the cliff in ropes to the shelf of rock, on which the nest was built, the people above shouting & hollowing to fright the old birds, which flew screaming round, but did not dare to attack him. He brought off the eaglet (for there is rarely more than one) & an addle egg. The nest was roundish & more than a yard over, made of twigs twisted together. Seldom a year passes but they take the brood or eggs, & sometimes they shoot one, sometimes the other Parent, but the surviver has always found a mate (probably in Ireland) & they breed near the old place. By his description I learn, that this species is the *Erne* (the Vultur *Albicilla* of Linnæus in his last edition, but in yours *Falco Albicilla*) so consult him & Pennant about it.

Walk'd leisurely home the way we came, but saw a new landscape: the features indeed were the same in part, but many new ones were disclosed by the mid-day Sun, & the tints were entirely changed. Take notice this was the best or perhaps the only day for going up Skiddaw, but I thought it better employ'd: it was perfectly serene, & hot as midsummer.

In the evening walk'd alone down to the Lake by the side of *Crow-Park* after sunset & saw the solemn colouring of night draw on, the last gleam of sunshine fading away on the hill-tops, the deep serene of the waters, & the long shadows of the mountains thrown across them, till they nearly touch'd the hithermost shore. At distance heard the murmur of many

51

waterfalls not audible in the day-time. Wish'd for the Moon, but she was *dark to me & silent, hid in her vacant interlunar cave.*

Oct. 4. Wind E., clouds & sunshine, & in the course of the day a few drops of rain. Walk'd to *Crow-park*, now a rough pasture, once a glade of ancient oaks, whose large roots still remain on the ground, but nothing has sprung from them. If one single tree had remain'd, this would have been an unparallel'd spot, & Smith judged right, when he took his print of the Lake from hence, for it is a gentle eminence, not too high, on the very margin of the water & commanding it from end to end, looking full into the *gorge* of *Borodale.* I prefer it even to *Cockshut*-hill, which lies beside it, & to which I walk'd in the afternoon: it is cover'd with young trees both sown & planted, oak, spruce, scotch-fir, &c. all which thrive wonderfully. There is an easy ascent to the top, & the view far preferable to that on Castle-hill (which you remember) because this is lower & nearer to the Lake: for I find all points, that are much elevated, spoil the beauty of the valley, & make its parts (which are not large) look poor & diminutive. While I was here, a little shower fell, red clouds came marching up the hills from the east, & part of a bright rainbow seem'd to rise along the side of Castle-hill.

From hence I got to the *Parsonage* a little before Sunset, & saw in my glass a picture, that if I could transmitt to you, & fix it in all the softness of its living colours, would fairly sell for a thousand pounds. This is the sweetest scene I can yet discover in point of pastoral beauty. The rest are in a sublimer style. . . .

Oct. 5. Wind N. E. Clouds & sunshine. Walk'd thro' the meadows & corn-fields to the Derwent & crossing it went up *How-hill.* It looks along Bassinthwaite-water & sees at the same time the course of the river & a part of the Upper-Lake with a full view of Skiddaw. Then I took my way through Portingskall village to the *Park*, a hill so call'd cover'd entirely with wood: it is all a mass of crumbling slate. Pass'd round its foot between the trees & the edge of the water, & came to a Peninsula that juts out into the lake & looks along it both ways. In front rises Walla-crag, & Castle-hill, the Town, the road to Penrith, Skiddaw & Saddleback. Returning met a brisk and cold N. Eastern blast, that ruffled all the surface of ye lake and made it rise in little waves that broke at the foot of the wood. After dinner walked up the Penrith-road 2 miles or more & turning into a corn-field to the right, call'd Castle-Rigg, saw a Druid-Circle of large stones 108 feet in diameter, the biggest not 8 feet high, but most of them still erect: they are 50 in number. The valley of St. John's appear'd in sight, & the summits of *Catchidecam* (called by Camden, *Casticand*) & *Helvellyn*, said to be as high as *Skiddaw*, & to rise from a much higher base. A shower came on, & I return'd.

Oct. 6. Wind E. Clouds & sun. Went in a chaise 8 miles along the east-side of Bassingth: Water to *Ouse-Bridge* (pronounce *Ews-bridge*) the road in some part made & very good, the rest slippery & dangerous cart-road, or narrow rugged lanes but no precipices: it runs directly along the foot of Skiddaw. Opposite to *Widhope-Brows* (cloth'd to the top with wood) a very beautiful view opens down the Lake, which is narrower & longer than that of Keswick, less broken into bays & without islands. At the foot of it a few paces from the brink gently sloping upward stands *Armathwate* in a thick grove of Scotch firs, commanding a noble view directly up the lake. At a small distance behind the house is a large extent of wood, & still behind this a ridge of cultivated hills, on which (according to the Keswick-proverb) *the Sun always shines*. The inhabitants here on the contrary call the vale of Derwent-water *the Devil's Chamber-pot*, & pronounce the name of *Skiddaw-fell* (which terminates here) with a sort of terror & aversion. *Armathwate-House* is a modern fabrick, not large, & built of dark-red stone, belonging to Mr. *Spedding*, whose Gr.father was Steward to old Sir *Ja. Lowther*, &

bought this estate of the *Himers*. So you must look for Mr. Michell in some other country. The sky was overcast & the wind cool, so after dining at a publick house, which stands here near the bridge (that crosses the Derwent just where it issues from the lake) & sauntering a little by the water-side I came home again. The turnpike is finish'd from Cocker-mouth hither (5 miles) & is carrying on to Penrith. Several little showers to-day. A man came in, who said there was snow on *Cross-fell* this morning.

Oct. 7. Market-day here. Wind N. E. Clouds & Sunshine. Little showers at intervals all day. Yet walk'd in the morning to Crow-park, & in the evening up Penrith-road. The clouds came rolling up the mountains all round very [unpromising]; yet the moon shone at intervals. It was too damp to go towards the lake. Tomorrow mean to bid farewell to Keswick.

Botany might be studied here to great advantage at another season because of the great variety of soils & elevations all lieing within a small compass. I observed nothing but several curious Lichens, plenty of gale or Dutch myrtle perfuming the borders of ye lake. This year the Wadd mine had been open'd (which is done once in 5 years) it is taken out in lumps sometimes as big as a man's fist, & will undergo no preparation by fire, not being fusible. When it is pure soft, black, & close-grain'd, it is worth sometimes 30 shillings a pound. There are no Charr ever taken in these lakes, but plenty in Butter-mere-water, which lies a little way N. of Borrodale, about Martlemas, which are potted here. They sow chiefly oats & bigg here, which are now cutting, & still on the ground. The rains have done much hurt; yet observe, the soil is so thin & light, that no day has pass'd, in which I could not walk out with ease, & you know, I am no lover of dirt. Fell-mutton is now in season for about six weeks; it grows fat on ye mountains, & nearly resembles venison: excellent Pike & Perch (here called *Bass*) trout is out of season. Partridge in great plenty.

54

Receipt to dress Perch (for Mrs. Wharton)

Wash, but neither scale, nor gut them. Broil till enough; then pull out the fins, & open them along ye back, take out the bone & all the inwards without breaking them. Put in a large lump of butter & salt, clap the sides together, till it melts, & serve very hot. It is excellent. The skin must not be eaten.

Oct. 8. Left Keswick & took the Ambleside-road in a gloomy morning. Wind E. & N. E. About 2 m. from the Town mounted an eminence call'd *Castle-rigg*, & the sun breaking out discover'd the most enchanting view I have yet seen of the whole valley behind me, the two lakes, the river, the mountains all in their glory! had almost a mind to have gone back again. The road in some few parts is not compleated, but good country-road thro' sound, but narrow & stony lanes, very safe in broad day-light. This is the case about *Causeway-foot* & among Naddle-Fells to *Lanewaite*. The vale you go in has little breadth, the mountains are vast & rocky, the fields little & poor, & the inhabitants are now making hay, & see not the sun by two hours in a day so long as at Keswick. Came to the foot of Helvellyn along which runs an excellent road, looking down from a little height on *Lee's-water* (call'd also Thirl-meer, or Wiborn-water) & soon descending on its margin. The lake from its depth looks black (tho' really clear as glass) & from the gloom of the vast crags, that scowl over it: it is narrow & about 3 miles long, resembling a river in its course. Little shining torrents hurry down the rocks to join it, with not a bush to overshadow them, or cover their march. All is rock & loose stones up to the very brow, which lies so near your way, that not half the height of Helvellyn can be seen . . .

Past by the little Chappel of Wiborn, out of which the Sunday-congregation were then issuing.

Past a beck near *Dunmail-raise*, & enter'd *Westmoreland* a second time. Now begin to see *Helm-Crag* distinguish'd from its rugged neighbours not so much by its height, as by the strange broken outline of its top, like some gigantic building demolish'd, & the stones that composed it, flung cross each other in wild confusion. Just beyond it opens one of the sweetest landscapes, that art ever attempted to imitate. (the bosom of ye mountains spreading here into a broad bason) discovers in the midst Grasmere-water. Its margin is hollow'd into small bays with bold eminences some of rock, some of soft turf, that half conceal, and vary the figure of the little lake they command, from the shore a low promontory pushes itself far into the water, & on it stands a white village with the parish-church rising in the midst of it, hanging enclosures, corn-fields, & meadows green as an emerald with their trees & hedges & cattle fill up the whole space from the edge of the water & just opposite to you is a large farm-house at the bottom of a steep smooth lawn embosom'd in old woods¸ which climb half way up the mountain's side, & discover above them a broken line of crags, that crown the scene. Not a single red tile, no flaring Gentleman's house, or garden-walls, break in upon the repose of this unsuspected paradise, but all is peace, rusticity, & happy poverty in its neatest most becoming attire.

The road winds here over *Grasmere*-hill, whose rocks soon conceal the water from your sight, yet it is continued along behind them, & contracting itself to a river communicates with Ridale-water, another small lake, but of inferior size & beauty. It seems shallow too, for large patches of reeds appear pretty far within it. Into this vale the road descends. On the opposite banks large & ancient woods mount up the hills, & just to the left of our way stands *Rydale*-hall, the family-seat of Sir Mic. Fleming, but now a farm-house, a large old-fashion'd fabrick surrounded with wood & not much too good for its present destination. Sir Michael is now on his travels, & all this timber far & wide belongs to him. I tremble for it, when he returns. Near the house rises a huge crag call'd *Rydale-head*, which is said to command a full view of Wyn-

ander-mere, & I doubt it not, for within a mile that great
Lake is visible even from the road. As to going up the crag
one might as well go up Skiddaw.

Came to Ambleside, 18 m. from Keswick meaning to lie
there, but on looking into the best bed-chamber dark & damp
as a cellar grew delicate, gave up Winandermere in despair &
resolved I would go on to *Kendal* directly, 14 m. farther. The
road in general fine turnpike, but some parts (about 3 m. in
all) not made, yet without danger.

Unexpectedly was well-rewarded for my determination.
The afternoon was fine, & the road for full 5 m. runs along
the side of Winder-mere with delicious views across it &
almost from one end to the other. It is ten miles in length, &
at most a mile over, resembling the course of some vast &
magnificent river, but no flat marshy grounds, no osier-beds,
or patches of scrubby plantation on its banks. At the head
two vallies open among the mountains, one that by which we
came down, the other *Langsledale*, in which *Wreenose* &
Hard-Knot, two great mountains, rise above the rest. From
thence the fells visibly sink & soften along its sides, some-
times they run into it (but with a gentle declivity) in their
own dark & natural complexion, oftener they are green &
cultivated with farms interspersed & round eminences on
the border cover'd with trees: towards the South it seem'd to
break into larger bays with several islands & a wider extent
of cultivation. The way rises continually till at a place call'd
Orrest-head it turns to S.E. losing sight of the water.

Pass'd by *Ings-Chappel*, & *Staveley*, but I can say no
farther, for the dusk of evening coming on I enter'd *Kendal*
almost in the dark & could distinguish only a shadow of the
Castle on a hill, & tenter-grounds spread far & wide round the
Town, which I mistook for houses. My inn promised sadly
having two wooden galleries (like Scotland) in front of it. It
was indeed an old ill-contrived house, but kept by civil sen-
sible people, so I stay'd two nights with them & fared & slept
very comfortably. . . .

Oct. 13 to visit *Gordale-Scar*. Wind N.E. Day gloomy &
cold. It lay but 6 m. from Settle, but that way was directly
over a Fell, & it might rain, so I went round in a chaise the
only way one could get near it in a carriage, which made it
full 13 m. & half of it such a road! but I got safe over it, so
there's an end, & came to *Malham* (pronounce *Maum*) a
village in the bosom of the mountains seated in a wild &
dreary valley. From thence I was to walk a mile over a very
rough ground, a torrent rattling along on the left hand. On
the cliffs above hung a few goats: one of them danced &
scratched an ear with its hind-foot in a place where I would
not have stood stock-still

for all beneath the moon.

As I advanced the crags seem'd to close in, but discover'd a
narrow entrance turning to the left between them. I followed
my guide a few paces, & lo, the hills open'd again into no
large space, & then all farther way is bar'd by a stream, that
at the height of about 50 feet gushes from a hole in the rock,
& spreading in large sheets over its broken front dashes from
steep to steep, & then rattles away in a torrent down the
valley. The rock on the left rises perpendicular with stubbed
yew-trees & shrubs, staring from its side to the height of at
least 300 feet. But these are not the thing! it is that to the
right, under which you stand to see the fall, that forms the
principal horror of the place. From its very base it begins to
slope forwards over you in one black & solid mass without
any crevice in its surface, & overshadows half the area below
with its dreadful canopy. When I stood at (I believe) full 4
yards distance from its foot, the drops which perpetually
distill from its brow, fell on my head, & in one part of the top
more exposed to the weather there are loose stones that hang
in air, & threaten visibly some idle Spectator with instant
destruction. It is safer to shelter yourself close to its bottom,
& trust the mercy of that enormous mass, which nothing but

58

Study in oil on brown paper by James Ward for his painting of Gordale Scar, 1806

an earthquake can stir. The gloomy uncomfortable day well suited the savage aspect of the place, & made it still more formidable. I stay'd there (not without shuddering) a quarter of an hour, & thought my trouble richly paid, for the impression will last for life. . . .

Dorothy Wordsworth

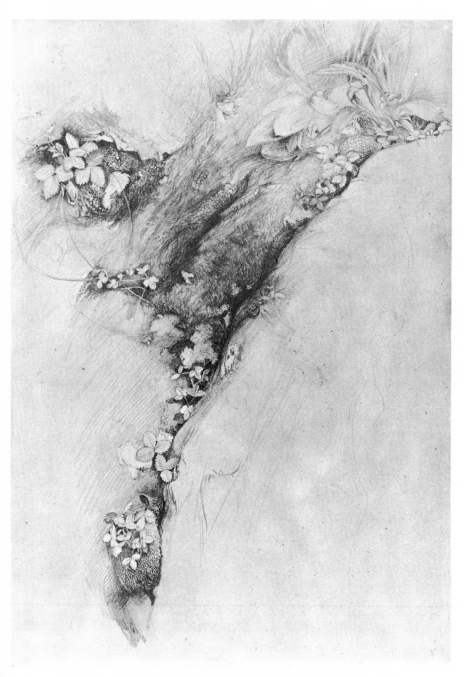

Moss and Wild Strawberry, pencil drawing by John Ruskin,
probably drawn in August 1875

Windermere, water-color by Edward Dayes (1763–1804)

Dorothy Wordsworth
[1771–1855]

Dorothy Wordsworth's outward life lies in the shade of her famous brother. Whether as his constant companion on excursions, or as his housekeeper and family mentor, or as the inspiration of some of his most imperishable poetry, she selflessly devoted herself to William's welfare. Yet, all who were fortunate enough to be admitted to the Wordsworth circle were irradiated by the aura which this remarkable woman so unobtrusively shed about her. Something of her quality emerges from De Quincey's fine tribute "that she was the very wildest (in the sense of the most natural) person I have ever known; and also the truest, most inevitable, and at the same time the quickest and readiest in her sympathy with either joy or sorrow, with laughter or with tears, with the realities of life, or the larger realities of the poets." Still more revealing is Coleridge's impression, written in June 1797 soon after their first meeting:

> Wordsworth and his exquisite sister are with me. She is a woman indeed! in mind I mean, and heart; for her person is such that if you expected to see a pretty woman, you would think her ordinary; if you expected to see an ordinary woman, you would think her pretty! but her manners are simple, ardent, impressive. In every motion her most innocent soul beams out so brightly, that who saw her would say
> "Guilt was a thing impossible in her."
> Her information various. Her eye watchful in minutest observation of nature; and her taste a perfect electrometer. It bends, protrudes, and draws in, at subtlest beauties and most recondite faults.

Dorothy's kinship with nature is celebrated in the *Journals*, which she kept as much for William's sake as for her own delight in their shared experiences. This is especially true of the Alfoxden and Grasmere Journals. The former covers the months from January to May in that wonderful year (1798) when brother and sister were living on the Quantock Hills in the southwest of England during the earliest and best days of their friendship with Coleridge, to whom they seemed "three persons and one soul." From this daily association came *Lyrical Ballads*. After their return from Germany, William and Dorothy settled at Dove Cottage in the heart of their native Lake country; and the Grasmere Journal, extending from May 1800 to January 1803, shortly after the poet's marriage to Mary Hutchinson, records Dorothy's impassioned participation in the most productive period of her brother's career.

Without William's moral fervor or Coleridge's reach of intellect, Dorothy responded to natural beauty more immediately and rapturously than either. In "Tintern Abbey" the poet refers to "the shooting lights / Of thy wild eyes," and again to her "wild ecstasies." She seems like her own description of the columbine, "a graceful slender creature, a female seeking retirement, and growing freest and most graceful where it is most alone." This quivering sensibility, so soon made glad but as easily wounded, was to have its terrible aftermath in the mental derangement which left the last twenty years of her life largely a blank, as though the emotional vitality at the core of her being had finally burnt its way through all rational restraint.

The lover of the nature poetry of Wordsworth and Coleridge will not miss in Dorothy's *Journals* the evidences of how extensively her perceptions and moods influenced their art. Indeed, William said that his sister gave him eyes; and he repaid the debt in lines which immortalize her spiritual affinities:

> *"She shall be sportive as the fawn*
> *That wild with glee across the lawn*
> *Or up the mountain springs;*
> *And hers shall be the breathing balm,*
> *And hers the silence and the calm*
> *Of mute insensate things.*

64

"*The floating clouds their state shall lend*
To her; for her the willow bend;
Nor shall she fail to see
Even in the motions of the Storm
Grace that shall mould the Maiden's form
By silent sympathy.

"*The stars of midnight shall be dear*
To her; and she shall lean her ear
In many a secret place
Where rivulets dance their wayward round,
And beauty born of murmuring sound
Shall pass into her face."

From *Journals*

Dorothy Wordsworth's Journal,
written at Alfoxden in 1798

ALFOXDEN, *January 20th*, 1798. The green paths down the hill-sides are channels for streams. The young wheat is streaked by silver lines of water running between the ridges, the sheep are gathered together on the slopes. After the wet dark days, the country seems more populous. It peoples itself in the sunbeams. The garden, mimic of spring, is gay with flowers. The purple-starred hepatica spreads itself in the sun, and the clustering snow-drops put forth their white heads, at first upright, ribbed with green, and like a rosebud when completely opened, hanging their heads downwards, but slowly lengthening their slender stems. The slanting woods of an unvarying brown, showing the light through the thin net-work of their upper boughs. Upon the highest ridge of that round hill covered with planted oaks, the shafts of the trees show in the light like the columns of a ruin.

January 21st. Walked on the hill-tops—a warm day. Sate under the firs in the park. The tops of the beeches of a brown-red, or crimson. Those oaks, fanned by the sea breeze, thick with feathery sea-green moss, as a grove not stripped of its leaves. Moss cups more proper than acorns for fairy goblets.

January 22nd. Walked through the wood to Holford. The ivy twisiting round the oaks like bristled serpents. The day

The Snowdrop, by Abraham Pether, made for Thornton's
The Temple of Flora, or Garden of Nature, *1812*

cold—a warm shelter in the hollies, capriciously bearing berries. Query: Are the male and female flowers on separate trees?

January 23rd. Bright sunshine, went out at 3 o'clock. The sea perfectly calm blue, streaked with deeper colour by the clouds, and tongues or points of sand; on our return of a gloomy red. The sun gone down. The crescent moon, Jupiter, and Venus. The sound of the sea distinctly heard on the tops of the hills, which we could never hear in summer. We attribute this partly to the bareness of the trees, but chiefly to the absence of the singing of birds, the hum of insects, that noiseless noise which lives in the summer air. The villages marked out by beautiful beds of smoke. The turf fading into the mountain road. The scarlet flowers of the moss.

January 24th. Walked between half-past three and half-past five. The evening cold and clear. The sea of a sober grey, streaked by the deeper grey clouds. The half dead sound of the near sheep-bell, in the hollow of the sloping coombe, exquisitely soothing.

January 25th. Went to Poole's after tea. The sky spread over with one continuous cloud, whitened by the light of the moon, which, though her dim shape was seen, did not throw forth so strong a light as to chequer the earth with shadows. At once the clouds seemed to cleave asunder, and left her in the centre of a black-blue vault. She sailed along, followed by multitudes of stars, small, and bright, and sharp. Their brightness seemed concentrated (half-moon).

January 26th. Walked upon the hill-tops; followed the sheep tracks till we overlooked the larger coombe. Sat in the sunshine. The distant sheep-bells, the sound of the stream; the woodman winding along the half-marked road with his laden pony; locks of wool still spangled with the dewdrops; the blue-grey sea, shaded with immense masses of cloud, not streaked; the sheep glittering in the sunshine. Returned through the wood. The trees skirting the wood, being exposed more directly to the action of the sea breeze, stripped of the net-work of their upper boughs, which are stiff and erect, like black skeletons; the ground strewed with the red berries of the holly. Set forward before two o'clock. Returned a little after four.

January 27th. Walked from seven o'clock till half-past eight. Upon the whole an uninteresting evening. Only once while we were in the wood the moon burst through the invisible veil which enveloped her, the shadows of the oaks blackened, and their lines became more strongly marked. The withered leaves were coloured with a deeper yellow, a brighter gloss spotted the hollies; again her form became dimmer; the sky flat, unmarked by distances, a white thin cloud. The manufacturer's dog makes a strange, uncouth howl, which it continues many minutes after there is no noise near it but that of the brook. It howls at the murmur of the village stream.

January 31st. Set forward to Stowey at half-past five. A violent storm in the wood; sheltered under the hollies. When we left home the moon immensely large, the sky scattered over with clouds. These soon closed in, contracting the dimensions of the moon without concealing her. The sound of the pattering shower, and the gusts of wind, very grand. Left the wood when nothing remained of the storm but the driving wind, and a few scattering drops of rain. Presently all clear, Venus first showing herself between the struggling clouds; afterwards Jupiter appeared. The hawthorn hedges, black and pointed, glittering with millions of diamond drops; the hollies shining with broader patches of light. The road to the village of Holford glittered like another stream. On our return, the wind high—a violent storm of hail and rain at the Castle of Comfort. All the Heavens seemed in one perpetual motion when the rain ceased; the moon appearing, now half veiled, and now retired behind heavy clouds, the stars still moving, the roads very dirty.

February 1st. About two hours before dinner, set forward towards Mr. Bartholemew's. The wind blew so keen in our faces that we felt ourselves inclined to seek the covert of the wood. There we had a warm shelter, gathered a burthen of large rotten boughs blown down by the wind of the preceding night. The sun shone clear, but all at once a heavy blackness hung over the sea. The trees almost *roared*, and the ground seemed in motion with the multitudes of dancing leaves, which made a rustling sound, distinct from that of the trees. Still the asses pastured in quietness under the hollies, undisturbed by these forerunners of the storm. The wind beat furiously against us as we returned. Full moon. She rose in uncommon majesty over the sea, slowly ascending through the clouds. Sat with the window open an hour in the moonlight.

February 2nd. Walked through the wood, and on to the Downs before dinner; a warm pleasant air. The sun shone, but was often obscured by straggling clouds. The redbreasts made a ceaseless song in the woods. The wind rose very high in the evening. The room smoked so that we were obliged to quit it. Young lambs in a green pasture in the Coombe, thick legs, large heads, black staring eyes.

February 3rd. A mild morning, the windows open at breakfast, the redbreasts singing in the garden. Walked with Coleridge over the hills. The sea at first obscured by vapour; that vapour afterwards slid in one mighty mass along the seashore; the islands and one point of land clear beyond it. The distant country (which was purple in the clear dull air), overhung by straggling clouds that sailed over it, appeared like the darker clouds, which are often seen at a great distance apparently motionless, while the nearer ones pass quickly over them, driven by the lower winds. I never saw such a union of earth, sky, and sea. The clouds beneath our feet spread themselves to the water, and the clouds of the sky almost joined them. Gathered sticks in the wood; a perfect stillness. The redbreasts sang upon the leafless boughs. Of a great number of sheep in the field, only one standing. Returned to dinner at five o'clock. The moonlight still and warm as a summer's night at nine o'clock.

February 4th. Walked a great part of the way to Stowey with Coleridge. The morning warm and sunny. The young lasses seen on the hill-tops, in the villages and roads, in their summer holiday clothes—pink petticoats and blue. Mothers with their children in arms, and the little ones that could just walk, tottering by their side. Midges or small flies spinning in the sunshine; the songs of the lark and redbreast; daisies upon the turf; the hazels in blossom; honeysuckles budding. I saw one solitary strawberry flower under a hedge. The furze gay with blossom. The moss rubbed from the pailings by the sheep, that leave locks of wool, and the red marks with which they are spotted, upon the wood.

February 5th. Walked to Stowey with Coleridge, returned by Woodlands; a very warm day. In the continued singing of birds distinguished the notes of a blackbird or thrush. The sea overshadowed by a thick dark mist, the land in sunshine. The sheltered oaks and beeches still retaining their brown leaves. Observed some trees putting out red shoots. Query: What trees are they?

February 17th. A deep snow upon the ground. Wm. and Coleridge walked to Mr. Bartholemew's, and to Stowey. Wm. returned, and we walked through the wood into the Coombe to fetch some eggs. The sun shone bright and clear. A deep stillness in the thickest part of the wood, undisturbed except by the occasional dropping of the snow from the holly boughs; no other sound but that of the water, and the slender notes of a redbreast, which sang at intervals on the outskirts of the southern side of the wood. There the bright green moss was bare at the roots of the trees, and the little birds were upon it. The whole appearance of the wood was enchanting;

and each tree, taken singly, was beautiful. The branches of the hollies pendent with their white burden, but still showing their bright red berries, and their glossy green leaves. The bare branches of the oaks thickened by the snow.

February 24th. Went to the hill-top. Sat a considerable time overlooking the country towards the sea. The air blew pleasantly round us. The landscape mildly interesting. The Welsh hills capped by a huge range of tumultuous white clouds. The sea, spotted with white, of a bluish grey in general, and streaked with darker lines. The near shores clear; scattered farm houses, half-concealed by green mossy orchards, fresh straw lying at the doors; hay-stacks in the fields. Brown fallows, the springing wheat, like a shade of green over the brown earth, and the choice meadow plots, full of sheep and lambs, of a soft and vivid green; a few wreaths of blue smoke, spreading along the ground; the oaks and beeches in the hedges retaining their yellow leaves; the distant prospect on the land side, islanded with sunshine; the sea, like a basin full to the margin; the dark fresh-ploughed fields; the turnips of a lively rough green. Returned through the wood.

February 26th. Coleridge came in the morning, and Mr. and Mrs. Cruikshank; walked with Coleridge nearly to Stowey after dinner. A very clear afternoon. We lay sidelong upon the turf, and gazed on the landscape till it melted into more than natural loveliness. The sea very uniform, of a pale greyish blue, only one distant bay, bright and blue as a sky; had there been a vessel sailing up it, a perfect image of delight. Walked to the top of a high hill to see a fortification. Again sat down to feed upon the prospect; a magnificent scene, *curiously* spread out for even minute inspection, though so extensive that the mind is afraid to calculate its bounds. A winter prospect shows every cottage, every farm, and the forms of distant trees, such as in summer have no distinguishing mark. On our return, Jupiter and Venus before us. While the twilight still overpowered the light of the moon, we were reminded that she was shining bright above our heads, by our faint shadows going before us. We had seen her on the tops of the hills, melting into the blue sky. . . .

March 1st. We rose early. A thick fog obscured the distant prospect entirely, but the shapes of the nearer trees and the dome of the wood dimly seen and dilated. It cleared away between ten and eleven. The shapes of the mist, slowly moving along, exquisitely beautiful; passing over the sheep they almost seemed to have more of life than those quiet creatures. The unseen birds singing in the mist.

March 7th. William and I drank tea at Coleridge's. A cloudy sky. Observed nothing particularly interesting—the distant prospect obscured. One only leaf upon the top of a tree—the sole remaining leaf—danced round and round like a rag blown by the wind.

April 15th. Set forward after breakfast to Crookham, and returned to dinner at three o'clock. A fine cloudy morning. Walked about the squire's grounds. Quaint waterfalls about, about which Nature was very successfully striving to make beautiful what art had deformed—ruins, hermitages, etc. etc. In spite of all these things, the dell romantic and beautiful, though everywhere planted with unnaturalised trees. Happily we cannot shape the huge hills, or carve out the valleys according to our fancy.

The Grasmere Journal, 1800–1803

May 14th, 1800 [*Wednesday*]. Wm. and John set off into Yorkshire after dinner at ½ past 2 o'clock, cold pork in their pockets. I left them at the turning of the Lowwood bay under the trees. My heart was so full that I could hardly speak to W. when I gave him a farewell kiss. I sate a long time upon a stone at the margin of the lake, and after a flood of tears my heart was easier. The lake looked to me, I knew not why, dull and melancholy, and the weltering on the shores seemed a heavy sound. I walked as long as I could amongst the stones of the shore. The wood rich in flowers; a beautiful yellow, palish yellow, flower, that looked thick, round, and double, and smelt very sweet—I supposed it was a ranunculus. Crowfoot, the grassy-leaved rabbit-toothed white flower, strawberries, geranium, scentless violets, anemones two kinds, orchises, primroses. The heckberry very beautiful, the crab coming out as a low shrub. Met a blind man, driving a very large beautiful Bull, and a cow—he walked with two sticks. Came home by Clappers-gate. The valley very green; many sweet views up to Rydale head, when I could juggle away the fine houses; but they disturbed me, even more than when I have been happier; one beautiful view of the Bridge, without Sir Michael's. Sate down very often, though it was cold. I resolved to write a journal of the time till W. and J. return, and I set about keeping my resolve, because I will not quarrel with myself, and because I shall give Wm. pleasure by it when he comes home again. . . .

[*May 16th*,] *Friday morning*. Warm and mild, after a fine night of rain. Transplanted radishes after breakfast, walked to Mr. Gell's with the books, gathered mosses and plants.

74

The woods extremely beautiful with all autumnal variety and softness. I carried a basket for mosses, and gathered some wild plants. Oh! that we had a book of botany. All flowers now are gay and deliciously sweet. The primrose still pre-eminent among the later flowers of the spring. Foxgloves very tall, with their heads budding. I went forward round the lake at the foot of Loughrigg Fell. I was much amused with the business of a pair of stone-chats; their restless voices as they skimmed along the water following each other, their shadows under them, and their returning back to the stones on the shore, chirping with the same unwearied voice. Could not cross the water, so I went round by the stepping-stones. The morning clear but cloudy, that is the hills were not overhung by mists. After dinner Aggy weeded onions and carrots. I helped for a little—wrote to Mary Hutchinson—washed my head—worked. After tea went to Ambleside—a pleasant cool but not cold evening. Rydale was very beauti-ful, with spear-shaped streaks of polished steel. No letters! —only one newspaper. I returned by Clappersgate. Grasmere was very solemn in the last glimpse of twilight; it calls home the heart to quietness. I had been very melancholy in my walk back. I had many of my saddest thoughts, and I could not keep the tears within me. But when I came to Grasmere I felt that it did me good. . . .

[*July*] 27*th, Sunday.* Very warm. Molly ill. John bathed in the lake. I wrote out *Ruth* in the afternoon. In the morning, I read Mr. Knight's *Landscape.* After tea we rowed down to Loughrigg Fell, visited the white foxglove, gathered wild strawberries, and walked up to view Rydale. We lay a long time looking at the lake; the shores all embrowned with the scorching sun. The ferns were turning yellow, that is, here and there one was quite turned. We walked round by Ben-son's wood home. The lake was now most still, and reflected the beautiful yellow and blue and purple and grey colours of the sky. We heard a strange sound in the Bainriggs wood, as we were floating on the water; it *seemed* in the wood, but it must have been above it, for presently we saw a raven very high above us. It called out, and the dome of the sky seemed to echo the sound. It called again and again as it flew onwards, and the mountains gave back the sound, seeming as if from their center; a musical bell-like answering to the bird's hoarse voice. We heard both the call of the bird, and the echo, after we could see him no longer. We walked up to the top of the hill again in view of Rydale—met Mr. and Miss Simpson on horseback. The crescent moon which had shone upon the water was now gone down. Returned to supper at 10 o'clock.

[*October*] *11th, Saturday.* A fine October morning. Sat in the house working all the morning. William composing. Sally Ashburner learning to mark. After dinner we walked up Greenhead Gill in search of a sheepfold. We went by Mr. Olliff's, and through his woods. It was a delightful day, and the views looked excessively chearful and beautiful, chiefly that from Mr. Olliff's field, where our house is to be built. The colours of the mountains soft and rich, with orange fern; the cattle pasturing upon the hill-tops; kites sailing in the sky above our heads; sheep bleating and in lines and chains and patterns scattered over the mountains. They come down and feed on the little green islands in the beds of the torrents, and so may be swept away. The sheepfold is falling away. It is built nearly in the form of a heart unequally divided. Look down the brook, and see the drops rise upwards and sparkle in the air at the little falls, the higher sparkles the tallest. We walked along the turf of the mountain till we came to a cattle track, made by the cattle which come upon the hills. We drank tea at Mr. Simpson's, returned at about nine—a fine mild night.

[*November*] *24th*, [1801] *Tuesday*. A rainy morning. We all were well except that my head ached a little, and I took my breakfast in bed. I read a little of Chaucer, prepared the goose for dinner, and then we all walked out. I was obliged to return for my fur tippet and spencer, it was so cold. We had intended going to Easedale, but we shaped our course to Mr. Gell's cottage. It was very windy, and we heard the wind everywhere about us as we went along the lane, but the walls sheltered us. John Green's house looked pretty under Silver How. As we were going along we were stopped at once, at the distance perhaps of 50 yards from our favourite birch tree. It was yielding to the gusty wind with all its tender twigs, the sun shone upon it, and it glanced in the wind like a flying sunshiny shower. It was a tree in shape, with stem and branches, but it was like a Spirit of water. The sun went in, and it resumed its purplish appearance, the twigs still yielding to the wind, but not so visibly to us. The other birch trees that were near it looked bright and chearful, but it was a creature by its own self among them. We could not get into Mr. Gell's grounds—the old tree fallen from its undue exaltation above the gate. A shower came on when we were at Benson's. We went through the wood—it became fair. There was a rainbow which spanned the lake from the island-house to the foot of Bainriggs. The village looked populous and beautiful. Catkins are coming out; palm trees budding; the alder, with its plumb-coloured buds. We came home over the stepping-stones. The lake was foamy with white waves. I saw a solitary butter-flower in the wood. I found it not easy to get over the stepping stones. Reached home at dinner time. Sent Peggy Ashburner some goose. She sent me some honey, with a thousand thanks. "Alas! the gratitude of men has," etc. I went in to set her right about this, and sate a while with her. She talked about Thomas's having sold his land. "Ay," says she, "I said many a time he's not come fra London to buy our land, however." Then she told me with what pains and industry they had made up their taxes, interest, etc. etc., how

77

they all got up at 5 o'clock in the morning to spin and Thomas carded, and that they had paid off a hundred pounds of the interest. She said she used to take such pleasure in the cattle and sheep. "O how pleased I used to be when they fetched them down, and when I had been a bit poorly I would gang out upon a hill and look ower 't fields and see them, and it used to do me so much good you cannot think." Molly said to me when I came in, "Poor body! she's very ill, but one does not know how long she may last. Many a fair face may gang before her." We sate by the fire without work for some time, then Mary read a poem of Daniel upon Learning. After tea Wm. read Spenser, now and then a little aloud to us. We were making his waistcoat. We had a note from Mrs. C., with bad news from poor C.—very ill. William went to John's Grove. I went to meet him. Moonlight, but it rained. I met him before I had got as far as John Baty's—he had been sur- prized and terrified by a sudden rushing of winds, which seemed to bring earth sky and lake together, as if the whole were going to enclose him in; he was glad he was in a high road.

In speaking of our walk on Sunday evening, the 22nd November, I forgot to notice one most impressive sight. It was the moon and the moonlight seen through hurrying driving clouds immediately behind the Stone-Man upon the top of the hill on the Forest Side. Every tooth and every edge of rock was visible, and the Man stood like a Giant watching from the roof of a lofty castle. The hill seemed perpendicular from the darkness below it. It was a sight that I could call to mind at any time, it was so distinct.

[*December*] *12th, Saturday.* A fine frosty morning—Snow upon the ground. I made bread and pies. We walked with Mrs. Luff to Rydale and came home the other side of the Lake, met Townley with his dogs. All looked chearful and bright. Helm Crag rose very bold and craggy, a Being by itself, and behind it was the large ridge of mountain, smooth as marble and snow white. All the mountains looked like solid stone, on our left, going from Grasmere, *i.e.* White Moss and Nab Scar. The snow hid all the grass, and all signs of vegetation, and the rocks showed themselves boldly every-where, and seemed more stony than rock or stone. The birches on the crags beautiful, red brown and glittering. The ashes glittering spears with their upright stems. The hips very beautiful, and so good!! and, dear Coleridge! I ate twenty for thee, when I was by myself. I came home first—they walked too slow for me. Wm. went to look at Langdale Pikes. We had a sweet invigorating walk. Mr. Clarkson came in before tea. We played at cards—sate up late. The moon shone upon the water below Silver-How, and above it hung, combining with Silver-How on one side, a bowl-shaped moon, the curve downwards; the white fields, glittering roof of Thomas Ashburner's house, the dark yew tree, the white fields gay and beautiful. Wm. lay with his curtains open that he might see it.

January 30th, [1802] *Saturday*. A cold dark morning. Wil-liam chopped wood—I brought it in a basket. A cold wind. Wm. slept better, but he thinks he looks ill—he is shaving now. He asks me to set down the story of Barbara Wilkin-son's turtle dove. Barbara is an old maid. She had two turtle doves. One of them died, the first year I think. The other bird continued to live alone in its cage for 9 years, but for one whole year it had a companion and daily visitor—a little mouse, that used to come and feed with it; and the dove would caress it, and cower over it with its wings, and make a loving noise to it. The mouse, though it did not testify equal delight in the dove's company, yet it was at perfect ease. The poor mouse disappeared, and the dove was left solitary till its death. It died of a short sickness, and was buried under a tree with funeral ceremony by Barbara and her maidens, and one or two others. . . .

79

[*January*] *31st, Sunday.* Wm. had slept very ill—he was tired and had a bad headache. We walked round the two lakes. Grasmere was very soft, and Rydale was extremely beautiful from the western side. Nab Scar was just topped by a cloud which, cutting it off as high as it could be cut off, made the mountain look uncommonly lofty. We sate down a long time in different places. I always love to walk that way, because it is the way I first came to Rydale and Grasmere, and because our dear Coleridge did also. When I came with Wm., 6½ years ago, it was just at sunset. There was a rich yellow light on the waters, and the Islands were reflected there. To-day it was grave and soft, but not perfectly calm. William says it was much such a day as when Coleridge came with him. The sun shone out before we reached Grasmere. We sate by the roadside at the foot of the Lake, close to Mary's dear name, which she had cut herself upon the stone. Wm. cut at it with his knife to make it plainer. We amused ourselves for a long time in watching the breezes, some as if they came from the bottom of the lake, spread in a circle, brushing along the surface of the water, and growing more delicate, as it were thinner, and of a *paler* colour till they died away. Others spread out like a peacock's tail, and some went right forward this way and that in all directions. The lake was still where these breezes were not, but they made it all alive. I found a strawberry blossom in a rock. The little slender flower had more courage than the green leaves, for *they* were but half expanded and half grown, but the blossom was spread full out. I uprooted it rashly, and I felt as if I had been committing an outrage, so I planted it again. It will have but a stormy life of it, but let it live if it can. . . .

[*February*] *23rd, Tuesday.* A misty rainy morning—the lake calm. I baked bread and pies. Before dinner worked a little at Wm.'s waistcoat—after dinner read German Grammar. Before tea we walked into Easedale. We turned aside in the Parson's field, a pretty field with 3 pretty prospects. Then we went to the first large field, but such a cold wind met us that we turn'd again. The wind seemed warm when we came out of our own door. That dear thrush was singing upon the topmost of the smooth branches of the ash tree at the top of the orchard. How long it had been perched on that same tree I cannot tell, but we had heard its dear voice in the orchard the day through, along with a chearful undersong made by our winter friends, the robins. We came home by Goan's. I picked up a few mosses by the roadside, which I left at home. We then went to John's Grove, there we sate a little while looking at the fading landscape. The lake, though the objects on the shore were fading, seemed brighter than when it is perfect day, and the Island pushed itself upwards, distinct and large. All the shores marked. There was a sweet, sea-like sound in the trees above our heads. We walked backwards and forwards some time for dear John's sake, then walked to look at Rydale. Darkish when we reached home, and we got tea immediately with candles. William now reading in Bishop Hall—I going to read German. We have a nice singing fire, with one piece of wood. Fletcher's carts are arrived but no papers from Mrs. Coleridge.

[*March 14th,*] *Sunday Morning*. William had slept badly—he got up at nine o'clock, but before he rose he had finished *The Beggar Boys*, and while we were at breakfast that is (for I had breakfasted) he, with his basin of broth before him untouched, and a little plate of bread and butter he wrote the Poem to a Butterfly! He ate not a morsel, nor put on his stockings, but sate with his shirt neck unbuttoned, and his waistcoat open while he did it. The thought first came upon him as we were talking about the pleasure we both always feel at the sight of a butterfly. I told him that I used to chase them a little, but that I was afraid of brushing the dust

81

off their wings, and did not catch them. He told me how they used to kill all the white ones when he went to school because they were Frenchmen. . . .

[*March 18th,*] *Thursday.* A very fine morning. The sun shone, but it was far colder than yesterday. I felt myself weak and William charged me not to go to Mrs. Lloyd's. I seemed indeed to myself unfit for it, but when he was gone I thought I would get the visit over if I could, so I ate a beefsteak thinking it would strengthen me; so it did, and I went off. I had a very pleasant walk—Rydale vale was full of life and motion. The wind blew briskly, and the lake was covered all over with bright silver waves, that were there each the twinkling of an eye, then others rose up and took their place as fast as they went away. The rocks glittered in the sunshine, the crows and the ravens were busy, and the thrushes and little birds sang. I went through the fields, and sate ½ an hour afraid to pass a cow. The cow looked at me, and I looked at the cow, and whenever I stirred the cow gave over eating. I was not very much tired when I reached Lloyd's—I walked in the garden—Charles is all for agriculture—Mrs. L. in her kindest way. A parcel came in from Birmingham, with Lamb's play for us, and for C. They came with me as far as Rydale. As we came along Ambleside vale in the twilight it was a grave evening. There was something in the air that compelled me to serious thought—the hills were large, closed in by the sky. It was nearly dark when I parted from the Lloyds, that is night was come on, and the moon was overcast. But, as I climbed Moss, the moon came out from behind a mountain mass of black clouds. O, the unutterable darkness of the sky, and the earth below the moon! and the glorious brightness of the moon itself! There was a vivid sparkling streak of light at this end of Rydale water, but the rest was very dark, and Loughrigg Fell and Silver How were white and bright, as if they were covered with hoar frost. The moon retired again, and appeared and disappeared several times before I reached home. Once there was no moonlight to be seen but upon the island-house and the promontory of the island where it stands. "That needs must be a holy place," etc. etc. I had many very exquisite feelings, and when I saw this lowly Building in the waters, among the dark and lofty hills, with that bright, soft light upon it, it made me more than half a poet. I was tired when I reached home, and could not sit down to reading, and tried to write verses, but alas! I gave up expecting William, and went soon to bed. Fletcher's carts came home late.

[*April*] *15th, Thursday.* It was a threatening, misty morning, but mild. We set off after dinner from Eusemere. Mrs. Clarkson went a short way with us, but turned back. The wind was furious, and we thought we must have returned. We first rested in the large boat-house, then under a furze bush opposite Mr. Clarkson's. Saw the plough going in the field. The wind seized our breath. The Lake was rough. There was a boat by itself floating in the middle of the bay below Water Millock. We rested again in the Water Millock Lane. The hawthorns are black and green, the birches here and there greenish, but there is yet more of purple to be seen on the twigs. We got over into a field to avoid some cows—people working. A few primroses by the roadside —woodsorrel flower, the anemone, scentless violets, strawberries, and that starry, yellow flower which Mrs. C. calls pile wort. When we were in the woods beyond Gowbarrow Park we saw a few daffodils close to the water-side. We fancied that the lake had floated the seeds ashore, and that the little colony had so sprung up. But as we went along there were more and yet more; and at last, under the boughs of the trees, we saw that there was a long belt of them along the shore, about the breadth of a country turnpike road. I never saw daffodils so beautiful. They grew among the mossy

stones about and about them; some rested their heads upon
these stones as on a pillow for weariness; and the rest tossed
and reeled and danced, and seemed as if they verily laughed
with the wind, that blew upon them over the lake; they
looked so gay, ever glancing, ever changing. This wind blew
directly over the lake to them. There was here and there a
little knot, and a few stragglers a few yards higher up; but
they were so few as not to disturb the simplicity, unity, and
life of that one busy highway. We rested again and again.
The bays were stormy, and we heard the waves at different
distances, and in the middle of the water, like the sea. Rain
came on—we were wet when we reached Luff's, but we
called in. Luckily all was chearless and gloomy, so we faced
the storm—we *must* have been wet if we had waited—put on
dry clothes at Dobson's. I was very kindly treated by a young
woman, the landlady looked sour, but it is her way. She gave
us a goodish supper, excellent ham and potatoes. We paid 7/-
when we came away. William was sitting by a bright fire
when I came downstairs. He soon made his way to the li-
brary, piled up in a corner of the window. He brought out a
volume of Enfield's *Speaker*, another miscellany, and an odd
volume of Congreve's plays. We had a glass of warm rum
and water. We enjoyed ourselves, and wished for Mary. It
rained and blew, when we went to bed. N.B. Deer in Gow-
barrow Park like skeletons.

April 16th, Friday (*Good Friday*). When I undrew my
curtains in the morning, I was much affected by the beauty of
the prospect, and the change. The sun shone, the wind had
passed away, the hills looked chearful, the river was very
bright as it flowed into the lake. The church rises up behind a
little knot of rocks, the steeple not so high as an ordinary
three-story house. Trees in a row in the garden under the
wall. After Wm. had shaved we set forward; the valley is at
first broken by little rocky woody knolls that make retiring
places, fairy valleys in the vale; the river winds along under
these hills, travelling, not in a bustle but not slowly, to the

lake. We saw a fisherman in the flat meadow on the other side of the water. He came towards us, and threw his line over the two-arched bridge. It is a bridge of a heavy construction, almost bending inwards in the middle, but it is grey, and there is a look of ancientry in the architecture of it that pleased me. As we go on the vale opens out more into one vale, with somewhat of a cradle bed. Cottages, with groups of trees, on the side of the hills. We passed a pair of twin Children, 2 years old. Sate on the next bridge which we crossed—a single arch. We rested again upon the turf, and looked at the same bridge. We observed arches in the water, occasioned by the large stones sending it down in two streams. A sheep came plunging through the river, stumbled up the bank, and passed close to us, it had been frightened by an insignificant little dog on the other side. Its fleece dropped a glittering shower under its belly. Primroses by the road-side, pile wort that shone like stars of gold in the sun, violets, strawberries, retired and half-buried among the grass. When we came to the foot of Brothers Water, I left William sitting on the bridge, and went along the path on the right side of the Lake through the wood. I was delighted with what I saw. The water under the boughs of the bare old trees, the simplicity of the mountains, and the exquisite beauty of the path. There was one grey cottage. I repeated *The Glow-worm*, as I walked along. I hung over the gate, and thought I could have stayed forever. When I returned, I found William writing a poem descriptive of the sights and sounds we saw and heard. There was the gentle flowing of the stream, the glittering, lively lake, green fields without a living creature to be seen on them, behind us, a flat pasture with 42 cattle feeding; to our left, the road leading to the hamlet. No smoke there, the sun shone on the bare roofs. The people were at work ploughing, harrowing, and sowing; lasses spreading dung, a dog's barking now and then, cocks crowing, birds twittering, the snow in patches at the top of the highest hills, yellow palms, purple and green twigs on the birches, ashes with their glittering spikes quite bare. The hawthorn a bright green, with black stems under the oak. The moss of the oak glossy. We then went on, passed two sisters at work (*they first passed us*), one with two pitchforks in her hand, the other had a spade. We had some talk with them. They laughed aloud after we were gone, perhaps half in wantonness, half boldness. William finished his poem before we got to the foot of Kirkstone. There we ate our dinner. There were hundreds of cattle in the vale. The walk up Kirkstone was very interesting. The becks among the rocks were all alive. Wm. showed me the little mossy streamlet which he had before loved when he saw its bright green track in the snow. The view above Ambleside very beautiful. There we sate and looked down on the green vale. We watched the crows at a little distance from us become white as silver as they flew in the sunshine, and when they went still further, they looked like shapes of water passing over the green fields. The whitening of Ambleside church is a great deduction from the beauty of it, seen from this point. We called at the Luffs, the Boddingtons there. Did not go in, and went round by the fields. I pulled off my stockings, intending to wade the beck, but I was obliged to put them on, and we climbed over the wall at the bridge. The post passed us. No letters! Rydale Lake was in its own evening brightness: the Islands and Points distinct. Jane Ashburner came up to us when we were sitting upon the wall. We rode in her cart to Tom Dawson's. All well. The garden looked pretty in the half-moonlight, half-daylight. As we went up the vale of Brother's Water more and more cattle feeding, 100 of them.

April 23rd, 1802, *Friday*. It being a beautiful morning we set off at 11 o'clock, intending to stay out of doors all the morning. We went towards Rydale, and before we got to Tom Dawson's we determined to go under Nab Scar. Thither we went. The sun shone and we were lazy. Coleridge

pitched upon several places to sit down upon, but we could
not be all of one mind respecting sun and shade, so we pushed
on to the foot of the Scar. It was very grand when we looked
up, very stony, here and there a budding tree. William ob-
served that the umbrella yew tree, that breasts the wind, had
lost its character as a tree, and had become something like to
solid wood. Coleridge and I pushed on before. We left Wil-
liam sitting on the stones, feasting with silence; and C. and I
sat down upon a rocky seat—a couch it might be under the
bower of William's eglantine, Andrew's Broom. He was be-
low us, and we could see him. He came to us, and repeated his
poems while we sate beside him upon the ground. He had
made himself a seat in the crumbling ground. After we had
lingered long, looking into the vales,—Ambleside vale, with
the copses, the village under the hill, and the green
fields—Rydale, with a lake all alive and glittering, yet but
little stirred by breezes, and our own dear Grasmere, first
making a little round lake of nature's own, with never a
house, never a green field, but the copses and the bare hills
enclosing it, and the river flowing out of it. Above rose the
Coniston Fells, in their own shape and colour—not man's
hills, but all for themselves, the sky and the clouds, and a few
wild creatures. C. went to search for something new. We saw
him climbing up towards a rock. He called us, and we found
him in a bower—the sweetest that was ever seen. The rock
on one side is very high, and all covered with ivy, which hung
loosely about, and bore bunches of brown berries. On the
other side it was higher than my head. We looked down upon
the Ambleside vale, that seemed to wind away from us, the
village *lying* under the hill. The fir-tree island was reflected
beautifully. We now first saw that the trees are planted in
rows. About this bower there is mountain-ash, common-ash,
yew-tree, ivy, holly, hawthorn, mosses, and flowers, and a
carpet of moss. Above, at the top of the rock, there is another
spot—it is scarce a bower, a little parlour on[ly], not *enclosed*
by walls, but shaped out for a resting-place by the rocks, and

the ground rising about it. It had a sweet moss carpet. We resolved to go and plant flowers in both these places to-morrow. We wished for Mary and Sara. Dined late. After dinner Wm. and I worked in the garden. C. read letter from Sara.

[*April*] *29th, Thursday.* A beautiful morning—the sun shone and all was pleasant. We sent off our parcel to Coleridge by the waggon. Mr. Simpson heard the Cuckow to-day. Before we went out, after I had written down *The Tinker*, which William finished this morning, Luff called—he was very lame, limped into the kitchen. He came on a little pony. We then went to John's Grove, sate a while at first. Afterwards William lay, and I lay, in the trench under the fence—he with his eyes shut, and listening to the waterfalls and the birds. There was no one waterfall above another—it was a sound of waters in the air—the voice of the air. William heard me breathing and rustling now and then, but we both lay still, and unseen by one another; he thought that it would be as sweet thus to lie so in the grave, to hear the *peaceful* sounds of the earth, and just to know that our dear friends were near. The lake was still; there was a boat out. Silver How reflected with delicate purple and yellowish hues, as I have seen spar; lambs on the island, and running races together by the half-dozen, in the round field near us. The copses greenish, hawthorns green. Came home to dinner, then went to Mr. Simpson—we rested a long time under a wall, sheep and lambs were in the field—cottages smoking. As I lay down on the grass, I observed the glittering silver line on the ridge of the backs of the sheep, owing to their situation respecting the sun, which made them look beautiful, but with something of strangeness, like animals of another kind, as if belonging to a more splendid world. Met old Mrs. S. at the door—Mrs. S. poorly. I got mullins and pansies. I was sick and ill and obliged to come home soon. We

88

went to bed immediately—I slept upstairs. The air coldish, where it was felt—somewhat frosty.

April 30th, Friday. We came into the orchard directly after breakfast, and sate there. The lake was calm, the day cloudy. We saw two fishermen by the lake side. William began to write the poem of *The Celandine.* I wrote to Mary H. sitting on the fur-gown. Walked backwards and forwards with William—he repeated his poem to me, then he got to work again and could not give over. He had not finished his dinner till 5 o'clock. After dinner we took up the fur gown into the Hollins above. We found a sweet seat, and thither we will often go. We spread the gown, put on each a cloak, and there we lay. William fell asleep—he had a bad headache owing to his having been disturbed the night before, with reading C.'s letter which Fletcher had brought to the door. I did not sleep, but I lay with half-shut eyes looking at the prospect as in a vision almost, I was so resigned to it. Lough-rigg Fell was the most distant hill; then came the lake, slipping in between the copses, and above the copse the round swelling field; nearer to me, a wild intermixture of rocks, trees, and slacks of grassy ground. When we turned the corner of our little shelter, we saw the church and the whole vale. It is a blessed place. The birds were about us on all sides—skobbies, robins, bull-finches. Crows now and then flew over our heads, as we were warned by the sound of the beating of the air above. We stayed till the light of day was going, and the little birds had begun to settle their singing. But there was a thrush not far off, that seemed to sing louder and clearer than the thrushes had sung when it was quite day. We came in at 8 o'clock, got tea, wrote to Coleridge, and I wrote to Mrs. Clarkson part of a letter. We went to bed at 20 minutes past 11, with prayers that William might sleep well.

May 1st, Saturday. Rose not till half-past 8, a heavenly morning. As soon as breakfast was over, we went into the garden, and sowed the scarlet beans about the house. It was a clear sky, a heavenly morning.

I sowed the flowers, William helped me. We then went and sate in the orchard till dinner time. It was very hot. William wrote *The Celandine*. We planned a shed, for the sun was too much for us. After dinner we went again to our old resting-place in the Hollins under the rock. We first lay under a holly, where we saw nothing but the holly tree, and a budding elm [?], and the sky above our heads. But that holly tree had a beauty about it more than its own, knowing as we did where we were. When the sun had got low enough, we went to the rock shade. Oh, the overwhelming beauty of the vale below, greener than green! Two ravens flew high, high in the sky, and the sun shone upon their bellies and their wings, long after there was none of his light to be seen but a little space on the top of Loughrigg Fell. We went down to tea at 8 o'clock, had lost the poem, and returned after tea. The landscape was fading: sheep and lambs quiet among the rocks. We walked towards King's, and backwards and forwards. The sky was perfectly cloudless. N.B. Is it often so? Three solitary stars in the middle of the blue vault, one or two on the points of the high hills. Wm. wrote *The Celandine*, 2nd part, to-night. Heard the cuckow to-day, this first of May.

May 6th, Thursday. A sweet morning. We have put the finishing stroke to our bower, and here we are sitting in the orchard. It is one o'clock. We are sitting upon a seat under the wall, which I found my brother building up, when I came to him with his apple. He had intended that it should have been done before I came. It is a nice, cool, shady spot. The small birds are singing, lambs bleating, cuckow calling, the thrush sings by fits, Thomas Ashburner's axe is going quietly (without passion) in the orchard, hens are cackling, flies humming, the women talking together at their doors, plumb and pear trees are in blossom—apple trees greenish—the opposite woods green, the crows are cawing. We have heard ravens. The ash trees are in blossom, birds flying all about us. The stitchwort is coming out, there is one budding lychnis, the primroses are passing their prime, celandine, violets, and wood sorrel for ever more, little geraniums and pansies on the wall. We walked in the evening to Tail End, to enquire about hurdles for the orchard shed and about Mr. Luff's flower. The flower dead! no hurdles. I went on to look at the falling wood; Wm. also, when he had been at Benson's, went with me. They have left a good many small oak trees but we dare not hope that they are all to remain. The ladies are come to Mr. Gell's cottage. We saw them as we went, and their light when we returned. When we came in we found a Magazine, and Review, and a letter from Coleridge with verses to Hartley, and Sara H. We read the review, etc. The moon was a perfect boat, a silver boat, when we were out in the evening. The birch tree is all over green in *small* leaf, more light and elegant than when it is full out. It bent to the breezes, as if for the love of its own delightful motions. Sloe-thorns and hawthorns in the hedges.

May 12th, Wednesday. A sunshiny, but coldish morning. We walked into Easedale and returned by George Rawn-son's and the lane. We brought home heckberry blossom, crab blossom, the anemone nemorosa, marsh marigold, speedwell,—that beautiful blue one, the colour of the blue-stone or glass used in jewellery—with its beautiful pearl-like chives. Anemones are in abundance, and still the dear dear primroses, violets in beds, pansies in abundance, and the little celandine. I pulled a bunch of the taller celandine. Butterflies of all colours. I often see some small ones of a pale purple lilac, or emperor's eye colour, something of the colour of that large geranium which grows by the lake side. Wm.

observed the beauty of Geordy Green's house. We see it from our Orchard. Wm. pulled ivy with beautiful berries—I put it over the chimney piece. . . .

May 14th, Friday. A very cold morning—hail and snow showers all day. We went to Brother's wood, intending to get plants, and to go along the shore of the lake to the foot. We did go a part of the way, but there was no pleasure in stepping along that difficult sauntering road in this ungenial weather. We turned again, and walked backwards and forwards in Brother's wood. William teased himself with seeking an epithet for the cuckow. I sate a while upon my last summer seat, the mossy stone. William's, unemployed, beside me, and the space between, where Coleridge has so often lain. The oak trees are just putting forth yellow knots of leaves. The ashes with their flowers passing away, and leaves coming out. The blue hyacinth is not quite full blown; gowans are coming out, marsh marigolds in full glory; the little star plant, a star without a flower. We took home a great load of gowans, and planted them in the cold about the orchard. After dinner, I worked bread, then came and mended stockings beside William; he fell asleep. After tea I walked to Rydale for letters. It was a strange night. The hills were covered over with a slight covering of hail or snow, just so as to give them a hoary winter look with the black rocks. The woods looked miserable, the coppices green as grass, which looked quite unnatural, and they seemed half shrivelled up, as if they shrank from the air. O, thought I! what a beautiful thing God has made winter to be, by stripping the trees, and letting us see their shapes and forms. What a freedom does it seem to give to the storms! . . .

Samuel Taylor Coleridge

Gate Crag, Borrowdale, pencil and water-color by John Constable, 1806

Two drawings by Alexander Cozens (d. 1786): above,
Study of a Sky; below, The Cloud

Samuel Taylor Coleridge
[1772–1834]

John Stuart Mill ascribed to Coleridge one of the "great seminal minds" of his age. The claim can be supported out of the published writings, fragmentary although they too often are; but to the poet's contemporaries it seemed that he put the best of himself into talk. Of the many accounts of his inexhaustible eloquence, none is more striking than Keats's report of their encounter near Highgate in April 1819:

> I walked with him a[t] his alderman-after-dinner pace for near two miles I suppose. In those two Miles he broached a thousand things—let me see if I can give you a list— Nightingales, Poetry—on Poetical Sensation—Metaphysics —Different genera and species of Dreams—Nightmare— a dream accompanied by a sense of touch—single and double touch—A dream related—First and second consciousness—the difference explained between will and Volition —so m[an]y metaphysicians from a want of smoking the second consciousness—Monsters—the Kraken—Mermaids —Southey believes in them—Southey's belief too much diluted—A Ghost story—Good morning—I heard his voice as he came towards me—I heard it as he moved away—I heard it all the interval—if it may be called so.

That tireless voice still reaches us in Coleridge's Conversation poems, and in his *Letters* and voluminous *Notebooks*.*

Coleridge's best years fell between 1796 and 1804, when his brilliant promise was as yet unblighted by ill health and dissipation, by irresolution and self-pity. This period spanned his so-

---

* Coleridge has been well served by his editors. The editions of the *Letters* by E. L. Griggs and of the *Notebooks* by Kathleen Coburn constitute two of the towering monuments of literary scholarship in the twentieth century.

journs at Nether Stowey and at Greta Hall in Keswick; and the constant companionship of William and Dorothy Wordsworth in these lovely regions helped to keep his senses sharp and his will vigorous. At the beginning of August 1802 he undertook the solitary mountaineering excursion through wilds deemed inaccessible by Gray a generation earlier, the record of which survives in the *Notebooks* and in Sarah Hutchinson's transcript given here. Of this exploit Gordon Wordsworth wrote: "As far as I know this is by many years the earliest record of the pleasures of rock-scrambling, or of any ascent of the Scafell group for the mere love of the fells." In its description of the terrain Coleridge's journal-letter exhibits that fusion of factual accuracy with lyricism which characterizes the Conversation poems. There had been nothing hitherto in English poetry to match the kind of sensory appeal embodied in such passages as that which concludes "Frost at Midnight":

> *Therefore all seasons shall be sweet to thee,*
> *Whether the summer clothe the general earth*
> *With greenness, or the redbreast sit and sing*
> *Betwixt the tufts of snow on the bare branch*
> *Of mossy apple-tree, while the nigh thatch*
> *Smokes in the sun-thaw; whether the eave-drops fall*
> *Heard only in the trances of the blast,*
> *Or if the secret ministry of frost*
> *Shall hang them up in silent icicles,*
> *Quietly shining to the quiet Moon.*

The full subtlety and imaginative penetration of Coleridge's response to natural phenomena is best revealed in the *Notebooks*, from which his grandson, Ernest Hartley Coleridge, edited an initial selection in 1895 under the title of *Anima Poetae*. In one of these astonishing compilations the author left the caution: "Mem. If I should die without having destroyed this and my other Memorandum Books, I trust, that these Hints and first Thoughts, often too cogitabilia rather than actual cogitata a me, may not be understood as my fixed opinions—but merely as the Suggestions of the disquisition; & acts of obedience to the apostolic command of Try all things: hold fast that which is good."

The dominant impression created by the nature notes is of an animate universe every minutest particle of which is instinct with mysterious energy: not *natura naturata*, but *natura naturans*. In this cosmic harmony man participates, discovering in each sight and sound an intimation of his organic oneness with the well-springs of being. Not long after his ascent of Scafell Coleridge wrote to a friend in September 1802:

> . . . never to see or describe any interesting appearance in nature, without connecting it by dim analogies with the moral world, proves faintness of Impression. Nature has her proper interest; & he will know what it is, who believes & feels, that every Thing has a Life of it's own, & that we are all *one Life*. A Poet's *Heart* & *Intellect* should be *combined*, *intimately combined* & *unified*, with the great appearances in Nature—& not merely held in solution & loose mixture with them, in the shape of formal Similes.

From *Collected Letters*

The Ascent of Scafell

[1–5 August 1802]

ON Sunday Augt. 1st—½ after 12 I had a Shirt, cravat, 2 pair of Stockings, a little paper & half a dozen Pens, a German Book (Voss's Poems) & a little Tea & Sugar, with my Night Cap, packed up in my natty green oil-skin, neatly squared, and put into my *net* Knapsack / and the Knap-sack on my back & the Besom stick in my hand, which for want of a better, and in spite of Mrs C. & Mary, who both raised their voices against it, especially as I left the Besom scattered on the Kitchen Floor, off I sallied—over the Bridge, thro' the Hop-Field, thro' the Prospect Bridge at Portinscale, so on by the tall birch that grows out of the center of the huge Oak, along into Newlands——Newlands is indeed a lovely Place—the houses, each in it's little Shelter of Ashes & Sycamores, just under the Road, so that in some places you might leap down on the Roof, seemingly at least—the exceeding greenness & pastoral beauty of the Vale itself, with the savage wildness of the Mountains, their Coves, and long arm-shaped & elbow-shaped Ridges—yet this wildness softened down into a congruity with the Vale by the semicircular Lines of the Crags, & of the bason-like Concavities. The Cataract between Newlands & Kescadale had but little water in it / of course, was of no particular Interest— / I passed on thro' the green steep smooth bare Kescadal/a sort of unfurnished Passage or antechamber between Newlands & Butter-

98

mere, came out on Buttermere & drank Tea at the little Inn, & read the greater part of the Revelations—the only part of the new Testament, which the Scotch Cobler read—because why? *Because it was the only part that he understood.* O 'twas a wise Cobler! . . . Conceive an enormous round Bason mountain-high of solid Stone / cracked in half & one half gone / exactly in the remaining half of this enormous Bason, does Buttermere lie, in this beautiful & stern Embracement of Rock / I left it, passed by Scale Force, the white downfal[l] of which glimmered thro' the Trees, that hang before it like bushy Hair over a madman's Eyes, and climbed 'till I gained the first Level / here it was 'every man his own pathmaker,' & I went directly cross it—upon soft mossy Ground, with many a hop, skip, & jump, & many an occasion for observing the Truth of the old Saying: where Rushes grow, A Man may go. Red Pike, a dolphin-shaped Peak of a deep red, looked in upon me from over the Fell on my Left, on my right I had, first Melbreak (the Mountain on the right of Crummock, as you ascend the Lake) then a Vale running down with a pretty Stream in it, to Loweswater / then Heck [Hen] Comb, a Fell of the same height & running in the same direction with Melbreak, a Vale on the other side too,—and at the bottom of both these Vales the Loweswater Fells running abreast. Again I reached an ascent, climbed up, & came to a ruined Sheepfold—a wild green view all around me, bleating of Sheep & noise of waters—I sate there near 20 minutes, the Sun setting on the Hill behind with a soft watery gleam; & in front of me the upper Halves of huge deep-furrowed Grasmire [Grassmoor] (the mountain on the other side of Crummock) & the huge Newland & Buttermere Mountains, & peeping in from behind the Top of Saddleback. Two Fields were visible, the highest cultivated Ground on the Newland side of Buttermere, and the Trees in those Fields were the only Trees visible in the whole Prospect.—I left the Sheepfold with regret—for of all things a ruined Sheepfold in a desolate place is the dearest to me, and fills me most with Dreams & Visions & tender thoughts of those I love best—Well! I passed a bulging roundish-headed green Hill to my Left, (and to the left of it was a frightful Crag) with a very high round-head right before me; this latter is called Ennerdale-Dodd, and bisects the ridge between Ennerdale & Buttermere & Crummock—I took it on my right hand, & came to the top of the bulging green Hill, on which I found a small Tarn, called Flatern [Floutern] Tarn, about 100 yds. in length, & not more than 7 or 8 in breadth, but O! what a grand Precipice it lay at the foot of! The half of this Precipice (called Herd house) nearest to Ennerdale was black, with green moss-cushions on the Ledges; the half nearest to Buttermere a pale pink, & divided from the black part by a great streamy Torrent of crimson Shiver, & Screes, or Shilly (as they call it). I never saw a more heart-raising Scene. I turned & looked on the Scene which I had left behind, a marvellous group of mountains, wonderfully & admirably arranged —not a single minute object to interrupt the oneness of the view, excepting those two green Fields in Buttermere —but before me the glorious Sea with the high Coast & Mountains of the Isle of Mann, perfectly distinct—& three Ships in view. A little further on, the Lake of Ennerdale (the lower part of it) came in view, shaped like a clumsy battle-dore—but it is, in reality, exactly *fiddle-shaped*. The further Bank & the higher part, steep, lofty, bare bulging Crags; the nether Bank green & pastoral, with Houses in the shelter of their own dear Trees.—On the opposite Shore in the middle & narrow part of the Lake there bulges out a huge Crag, called angling Stone / being a famous Station for anglers—and the reflection of this Crag in the Water is admirable—pillars or rather it looks like the pipes of some enormous Organ in a rich golden Color.—I travelled on to Long Moor, two miles below the foot of the Lake, & met a very hearty welcome from John Ponsonby, a Friend of Mr. Jackson's—here I stayed the night, [1 August] & the greater part of Monday—the old man went to the head of the Lake

100

with me / the mountains at the head of this Lake & Wast-dale are the Monsters of the Country, bare bleak Heads, evermore doing deeds of Darkness, weather-plots, & storm-conspiracies in the Clouds—their names are Herd house, Bowness, Wha Head, Great Gavel, the Steeple, the Pillar, & Seat Allian [Seatallan].—I left Long Moor after Tea, & proceeded to Egremont, 5 miles—thro' a very pleasant Country, part of the way by the River Enna [Ehen], with well wooded Banks, & nice green Fields, & pretty houses with Trees, and two huge Sail-cloth Manufactories—went to Girtskill, a mercer, for whom I had a Letter, but he was at Workington, so I walked on to St. Bees, 3 miles from Egremont—when I came there could not get a Bed—at last got an apology for one, at a miserable Pot-house; slept [2 August] or rather dozed, in my Clothes—breakfasted there—and went to the School & Church ruins—had read in the history of Cumbd. that there was an 'excellent Library presented to the School by Sr. James Lowther,' which proved to be some 30 odd Volumes of commentaries on the Scripture utterly worthless—& which with all my passion for ragged old Folios I should certainly make serviceable . . . for fire-lighting. Men who write Tours and County histories I have by woeful experience found out to be *damned Liars*, harsh words, but true!—It was a wet woeful oppressive morning—I was sore with my bad night—walked down to the Beach, which is a very nice hard Sand for more than a mile / but the St. Bees Head which I had read much of as a noble Cliff, might be made a song of on the Flats of the Dutch Coast—but in England 'twill scarcely bear a looking-at.—Returned to Egremont, [3 August] a miserable walk—dined there, visited the Castle, the Views from which are uncommonly interesting—I looked thro' an old wild Arch—slovenly black Houses, & gardens, as wild as a Dream, over the hills beyond them, which slip down in one place making a noticeable Gap—had a good Bed, slept well—& left Egremont this morning [4 August] after Breakfast, had a pleasant walk to

101

Calder Abbey—an elegant but not very interesting Ruin, joining to a very han[d]some Gentleman's House built of red freestone, which has the comfortable warm look of Brick without it's meanness & multitude of puny squares. This place lies just within the Line of circumference of *a Circle* of woody Hills—the area, a pretty Plain half a mile perhaps in diameter—and completely cloathed & hid with wood, except one red hollow in these low steep hills, & except behind the Abbey, where the Hills are far higher, & consist of green Fields almost (but not quite) to the Top. Just opposite to Calder Abbey, & on the Line of the Circumference, rises Ponsonby Hill, the Village of Calder Bridge, & it's interesting Mill, all in Wood, some hidden, some roofs just on a line with the Trees, some higher, but Ponsonby Hall far higher than the rest.—I regained the Road, and came to Bonewood, a single Alehouse on the top of the hill above the Village Gosforth—drank a pint of Beer (I forgot to tell you that the whole of my expences at St. Bees, a glass of Gin & Water, my Bed, & Breakfast amounted to 11d.)—from this Bonewood is a noble view of the Isle of Man on the one side, & on the other side all the bold dread tops of the Ennerdale & Wastdale Mountains / . Indeed the whole way from Egremont I had beautiful Sea Views, the low hills to my right dipping down into inverted Arches, or Angles, & the Sea, often with a Ship seen thro'—while on my left the Steeple, & Sca' Fell facing each other, far above the other Fells, formed in their interspace a great Gap in the Heaven.—So I went on, turned eastward, up the Irt, the Sea behind & Wastdale Mountains before—& here I am—

Wed. Afternoon ½ past 3, Augt. 4th. 1802—

Wastdale, a mile & half below the Foot of the Lake, at an Alehouse without a Sign, 20 strides from the Door, under the Shade of a huge Sycamore Tree, without my coat—but that I will now put on, in prudence—yes here I am / and have been

102

for something more than an hour, & have *enjoyed* a good
Dish of Tea (I carried my Tea & sugar with me) under this
delightful Tree. In the House there are only an old feeble
Woman, and a *'Tallyeur'* Lad upon the Table—all the rest of
the Wastdale World is a haymaking, rejoicing and thanking
God for this first downright summer Day that we have had
since the beginning of May.—And now I must go & see the
Lake / for immediately at the Foot of the Lake runs a low
Ridge so that you can see nothing of the Water till you are at
it's very Edge.

Between the Lake and the Mountains on the left, a low
ridge of hill runs parallel with the Lake, for more than half
it's length; & just at the foot of the Lake there is a Bank even
& smooth & low like a grassy Bank in a Gentleman's Park.
Along the hilly Ridge I walked thro' a Lane of green Hazels,
with hay-fields & Hay-makers on my Right, beyond the River
Irt, & on the other side of the River, Irton Fell with a deep
perpendicular Ravine, & a curious fretted Pillar of Clay
crosier-shaped, standing up in it—next to Ireton Fells & in
the same line are the Screes, & you can look at nothing but
the Screes tho' there were 20 quaint Pillars close by you. The
Lake is wholly hidden 'till your very Feet touch it, as one may
say / and to a Stranger the Burst would be almost overwhelm
ing. The Lake itself seen from it's Foot appears indeed of too
regular shape; exactly like the sheet of Paper on which I am
writing, except it is still narrower in respect of it's length.
(In reality however the Lake widens as it ascends, and at the
head is very considerably broader than at the foot.) But yet,
in spite of this it is a marvellous sight / a sheet of water
between 3 & 4 miles in length, the whole (or very nearly the
whole) of it's right Bank formed by the Screes, or facing of
bare Rock of enormous Height, two thirds of it's height
downwards absolutely perpendicular; & then slanting off in
Screes, or Shiver, consisting of fine red Streaks running in
broad Stripes thro' a stone colour—slanting off from the
Perpendicular, as steep as the meal newly ground from the

Miller's spout.—So it is at the foot of the Lake; but higher up this streaky Shiver occupies two thirds of the whole height, like a pointed Decanter in shape, or an outspread Fan, or a long-waisted old maid with a fine prim Apron, or—no, other things that would only fill up the Paper.—When I first came the Lake was a perfect Mirror; & what must have been the Glory of the reflections in it! This huge facing of Rock *said* to be half a mile in perpendicular height, with deep Ravin[e]s the whole *winded* [wrinkled?] & torrent-worn, except where the pink-striped Screes come in, as smooth as silk / all this reflected, turned into Pillars, dells, and a whole new-world of Images in the water! The head of the Lake is crowned by three huge pyramidal mountains, Yewbarrow, Sca' Fell, & the great Gavel; Yewbarrow & Sca' Fell nearly opposite to each other, yet so that the *Ness* (or Ridge-line, like the line of a fine Nose,) of Sca' Fell runs in behind that of Yewbarrow, while the Ness of great Gavel is still farther back, between the two others, & of course, instead of running athwart the Vale it directly faces you. The Lake & Vale run nearly from East to west. . . .

Melfell [Middle Fell] (lying South [north] of the Lake) consists of great mountain steps decreasing in size as they approach the Lake.

My Road led along under Melfell & by Yewbarrow—& now I came in sight of it's other side called Keppel Crag & then a huge enormous bason-like Cove called Green Crag [Red Pike?] / as I suppose, from there being no single Patch of Green to be seen on any one of it's perpendicular sides—so on to Kirk Fell, at the foot of which is Thomas Tyson's House where W[ordsworth] & I slept Novr. will be 3 years—& there I was welcomed kindly, had a good Bed, and left it after Breakfast.

Thursday Morning, Augt. 5th—went down the Vale almost to the water head, & ascended the low Reach between Sca' Fell and the Screes, and soon after I had gained it's height came in sight Burnmoor Water, a large Tairn . . . , it's Tail towards Sca' Fell, at its head a gap forming an inverted arch with Black Coomb & a peep of the Sea seen thro' it.—It lies directly at the Back of the Screes, & the stream that flows from it down thro' the gap, is called the Mite—and runs thro' a Vale of it's own called Miterdale, parallel with the lower part of Wastdale, and divided from it by the high Ridge called Ireton Fells. I ascended Sca' Fell by the side of a torrent, and climbed & rested, rested & climbed, 'till I gained the very summit of Sca' Fell—believed by the Shepherds here to be higher than either Helvellyn or Skiddaw—Even to Black Coomb—before me all the Mountains die away, running down westward to the Sea, apparently in eleven Ridges three parallel Vales with their three Rivers, seen from their very Sources to their falling into the Sea, where they form (excepting their Screw-like flexures) the *Trident* of the Irish Channel at Ravenglass——O my God! what enormous Mountains these are close by me, & yet below the Hill I stand on / Great Gavel, Kirk Fell, Green Crag, & behind the Pillar, then the Steeple, then the Hay Cock—on the other side & behind me, Great End, Esk Carse [Hause], Bow-fell & close to my back two huge Pyramids, nearly as high as Sca' Fell itself, & indeed parts & parts of Sca' Fell known far & near by these names, the hither one of Broad Crag, and the next to it but divided from it by a low Ridge Doe Crag, which is indeed of itself a great Mountain of stones from a pound to 20 Ton weight embedded in wooly Moss. And here I am *lounded*—so fully lounded—that tho' the wind is strong, & the Clouds are hast'ning hither from the Sea—and the whole air seaward has a lurid Look—and we shall certainly have Thunder—yet here (but that I am hunger'd & provisionless) *here* I could lie warm, and wait methinks for tomorrow's Sun / and on a nice Stone Table am I now at this moment writing to you—between 2 and 3 o'Clock as I guess / surely the first Letter ever written from the Top of Sca' Fell! But O! what a look down just under my Feet! The frightfullest Cove that might ever be seen / huge perpendicular Precipices, and one Sheep upon it's only Ledge, that surely must be crag! Tyson told me of this place, & called it Hollow Stones. Just by it & joining together, rise two huge Pillars of bare lead-colored stone— / I am no measurer / but their height & depth is terrible. I know how unfair it is to judge of these Things by a comparison of past Impressions with present—but I have no shadow of hesitation in saying that the Coves & Precipices of Helvellin are nothing to these! But [from] this sweet lounding Place I see directly thro' Borrowdale, the Castle Crag, the whole of Derwent Water, & but for the haziness of the Air I could see my own House—I see clear enough where it stands——

Here I will fold up this Letter—I have Wafers in my Inkhorn / & you shall call this Letter when it passes before you the Sca' Fell Letter / —I must now drop down, how I may into Eskdale—that lies under to my right—the upper part of it the wildest & savagest surely of all the Vales that were ever seen from the Top of an English Mountain / and the lower part the loveliest.——

Eskdale, Friday, Augt. 6th. [1802] at an Estate House called Toes

There is one sort of Gambling, to which I am much addicted; and that not of the least criminal kind for a man who has children & a Concern.—It is this. When I find it convenient to descend from a mountain, I am too confident & too indolent to look round about & wind about 'till I find a track or other symptom of safety; but I wander on, & where it is first *possible* to descend, there I go—relying upon fortune for how far down this possibility will continue. So it was yesterday afternoon. I passed down from Broadcrag, skirted the Precipices, and found myself cut off from a most sublime Crag-summit, that seemed to rival Sca' Fell Man in height, & to outdo it in fierceness. A Ridge of Hill lay low down, & divided this Crag (called Doe-crag) & Broad-crag—even as

106

the Hyphen divides the words broad & crag. I determined to go thither; the first place I came to, that was not direct Rock, I slipped down, & went on for a while with tolerable ease—but now I came (it was midway down) to a smooth perpendicular Rock about 7 feet high—this was nothing—I put my hands on the Ledge, & dropped down / in a few yards came just such another / I *dropped* that too / and yet another, seemed not higher—I would not stand for a trifle / so I dropped that too / but the stretching of the muscle[s] of my hands & arms, & the jolt of the Fall on my Feet, put my whole Limbs in a *Tremble*, and I paused, & looking down, saw that I had little else to encounter but a succession of these little Precipices—it was in truth a Path that in a very hard Rain is, no doubt, the channel of a most splendid Waterfall.—So I began to suspect that I ought not to go on / but then unfortunately tho' I could with ease drop down a smooth Rock 7 feet high, I could not *climb* it / so go on I must / and on I went / the next 3 drops were not half a Foot, at least not a foot more than my own height / but every Drop increased the Palsy of my Limbs—I shook all over, Heaven knows without the least influence of Fear / and now I had only two more to drop down / to return was impossible—but of these two the first was tremendous / it was twice my own height, & the Ledge at the bottom was [so] exceedingly narrow, that if I dropt down upon it I must of necessity have fallen backwards & of course killed myself. My Limbs were all in a tremble—I lay upon my Back to rest myself, & was beginning according to my Custom to laugh at myself for a Madman, when the sight of the Crags above me on each side, & the impetuous Clouds just over them, posting so luridly & so rapidly northward, overawed me / I lay in a state of almost prophetic Trance & Delight—& blessed God aloud, for the powers of Reason & the Will, which remaining no Danger can overpower us! O God, I exclaimed aloud—how calm, how blessed am I now / I know not how to proceed, how to return / but I am calm & fearless & confident / if this Reality were a Dream, if I were

107

asleep, what agonies had I suffered! what screams!—When the Reason & the Will are away, what remain to us but Darkness & Dimness & a bewildering Shame, and Pain that is utterly Lord over us, or fantastic Pleasure, that draws the Soul along swimming through the air in many shapes, even as a Flight of Starlings in a Wind.—I arose, & looking down saw at the bottom a heap of Stones—which had fallen abroad—and rendered the narrow Ledge on which they had been piled, doubly dangerous / at the bottom of the third Rock that I dropt from, I met a dead Sheep quite rotten—This heap of Stones, I guessed, & have since found that I guessed aright, had been piled up by the Shepherd to enable him to climb up & free the poor creature whom he had observed to be crag-fast—but seeing nothing but rock over rock, he had desisted & gone for help—& in the mean time the poor creature had fallen down & killed itself.—As I was looking at these I glanced my eye to my left, & observed that the Rock was rent from top to bottom—I measured the breadth of the Rent, and found that there was no danger of my being *wedged* in / so I put my Knap-sack round to my side, & slipped down as between two walls, without any danger or difficulty——the next Drop brought me down on the Ridge called the How / I hunted out my Besom Stick, which I had flung before me when I first came to the Rocks—and wisely gave over all thoughts of ascending Doe-Crag—for now the Clouds were again coming in most tumultuously—so I began to descend / when I felt an odd sensation across my whole Breast—not pain nor itching—& putting my hand on it I found it all bumpy—and on looking saw the whole of my Breast from my Neck [to my Navel]—& exactly all that my Kamell-hair Breast-shield covers, filled with great red heat-bumps, so thick that no hair could lie between them. They still remain / but are evidently less—& I have no doubt will wholly disappear in a few Days. It was however a startling proof to me of the violent exertions which I had made.—I descended this low Hill which was all hollow beneath me—and was like the rough green Quilt of a Bed of waters—at length two streams burst out & took their way down, one on [one] side a high Ground upon this Ridge, the other on the other—I took that to my right (having on my left this high Ground, & the other Stream, & beyond that Doe-crag, on the other side of which is Esk Halse, where the head-spring of the Esk rises, & running down the Hill & in upon the Vale looks and actually deceived me, as a great Turnpike Road—in which, as in many other respects the Head of Eskdale much resembles Langdale) & soon the channel sank all at once, at least 40 yards, & formed a magnificent Waterfall—and close under this a succession of Waterfalls 7 in number, the third of which is nearly as high as the first. When I had almost reached the bottom of the Hill, I stood so as to command the whole 8 Waterfalls, with the great triangle-Crag looking in above them, & on the one side of them the enormous more than perpendicular Precipices & *Bull's-Brows*, of Sca' Fell! And now the Thunder-Storm was coming on, again & again!—Just at the bottom of the Hill I saw on before me in the Vale, lying just above the River on the side of a Hill, one, two, three, four Objects, I could not distinguish whether Peat-hovels, or hovel-shaped Stones—I thought in my mind, that 3 of them would turn out to be stones—but that the fourth was certainly a Hovel. I went on toward them, crossing & recrossing the Becks & the River & found that they were all huge Stones—the one nearest the Beck which I had determined to be really a Hovel, retained it's likeness when I was close beside / in size it is nearly equal to the famous Bowder stone, but in every other respect greatly superior to it—it has a complete Roof, & that perfectly *thatched* with weeds, & Heath, & Mountain-Ash Bushes—I now was obliged to ascend again, as the River ran greatly to the Left, & the Vale was nothing more than the Channel of the River, all the rest of the interspace between the mountains was a tossing up & down of Hills of all sizes—and the place at which I am now writing is

109

called—*Te-as*, & spelt, *Toes*—as the Toes of Sca' Fell—. It is not possible that any name can be more descriptive of the Head of Eskdale—I ascended close under Sca' Fell, & came to a little Village of Sheep-folds / there were 5 together / & the redding Stuff, & the Shears, & an old Pot, was in the Passage of the first of them. Here I found an imperfect Shelter from a Thunder-shower—accompanied with such Echoes! O God! what thoughts were mine! O how I wished for Health & Strength that I might wander about for a Month together, in the stormiest month of the year, among these Places, so lonely & savage & full of sounds!

After the Thunder-storm I shouted out all your names in the Sheep-fold—when Echo came upon Echo / and then Hartley & Derwent & then I laughed & shouted Joanna / It leaves all the Echoes I ever heard far far behind, in number, distinctness & *humanness* of Voice—& then not to forget an old Friend I made them all say Dr. Dodd &c.—

After the Storm I passed on & came to a great Peat-road, that wound down a hill, called Maddock How, & now came out upon the first cultivated Land which begins with a Bridge that goes over a Stream, a Waterfall of considerable height & beautifully wooded above you, & a great water-slope under you / the Gill down which it falls, is called Scale Gill—& the Fall Scale Gill Force. (The word Scale & Scales is common in this Country—& is said by . . . to be derived from the Saxon Sceala; the wattling of Sheep—but judging from the places themselves, *Scale Force* & this Scale Gill Force—I think it as probable that it is derived from Scalle—which signifies a deafening Noise.) Well, I passed thro' some sweet pretty Fields, & came to a large Farm-house where I am now writing / The place is called Toes or *Te* as—the master's name John Vicars Towers—they received me hospitably / I drank Tea here & they begged me to pass the Night—which I did & supped of some excellent Salmonlings, which Towers had brought from Ravenglass whither he had been, as holding under the Earl of Egremont, & obliged 'to

ride the Fair'—a custom introduced during the times of Inse-
curity & piratical Incursion for the Protection of Ravenglass
Fair. They were a fine Family—and a Girl who did not look
more than 12 years old, but was nearly 15, was very
beautiful—with hair like vine-tendrils—. She had been long
ill—& was a sickly child—[']Ah poor Bairn! (said the
Mother) worse luck for her / she looks like a Quality Bairn,
as you may say.' This man's Ancestors have been time out of
mind in the Vale / and here I found that the common Names,
Towers, & Tozers are the same— / *er* signifies 'upon'—as
Mite-er-dale the Dale upon the River Mite / Donnerdale—a
contraction of Duddon-er-dale the Dale upon the River
Duddon—So Towers, pronounced in the Vale *Te*-ars—&
Tozers is [are] those who live on *the Toes*—i.e. upon the
Knobby feet of the Mountain / Mr. *T*ears has mended my
pen.—This morning after breakfast I went out with him, &
passed up the Vale again due East, along a higher Road, over
a heathy upland, crossed the upper part of Scale Gill, came
out upon Maddock How, & then ascending turned directly
Northward, into the Heart of the mountains; on my left the
wild Crags under which flows the Scale Gill Beck, the most
remarkable of them called Cat Crag (a wild Cat being
killed there) & on my right hand six great Crags, which
appeared in the mist all in a file—and they were all, tho' of
different sizes, yet the same shape all triangles—. Other
Crags far above them, higher up the Vale, appeared & disap-
peared as the mists passed & came / one with a waterfall,
called Spout Crag—and another most tremendous one,
called Earn [Heron] Crag—I passed on, a little way, till I
came close under a huge Crag, called Buck Crag—& imme-
diately under this is Four-foot Stone—having on it the clear
marks of four foot-steps. The Stone is in it's whole breadth
just 36 inches, (I measured it exactly) but the part that
contains the marks is raised above the other part, & is just
20½ Inches. The length of the Stone is 32½ Inches. The first
foot-mark is an Ox's foot—nothing can be conceived more

111

exact—this is 5¾ Inches wide—the second is a Boy's shoe in the Snow, 9½ Inches in length / this too is the very Thing itself, the Heel, the bend of the Foot, &c.—the third is the Foot-step to the very Life of a Mastiff Dog—and the fourth *is Derwent's very own first little Shoe*, 4 Inches in length & O! it is the sweetest Baby shoe that ever was seen.—The wie-foot in Borrowdale is contemptible; but this really does work upon my imagination very powerfully / & I will try to construct a Tale upon it / the place too is so very, very wild. I delighted the Shepherd by my admiration / & the four foot Stone is my own Christening, & Towers undertakes it shall hereafter go by that name for hitherto it has been nameless.—And so I returned & have found a Pedlar here of an interesting Physiognomy—& here I must leave off—for Dinner is ready——

View in Borrowdale, pencil and water-color by John Constable, inscribed by the artist "Borrowdale 2 Sept. 1806 morning previous to a fine day"

From *Anima Poetae*

Of
Things
Visible
and
Invisible

[A proof of] the severity of the winter,—the kingfisher [by] its slow, short flight permitting you to observe all its colors, almost as if it had been a flower.

May
20,
1799

The nightingales in a cluster or little wood of blossomed trees, and a bat wheeling incessantly round and round! The noise of the frogs was not unpleasant, like the humming of spinning wheels in a large manufactory,—now and then a distinct sound, sometimes like a duck, and sometimes like the shrill notes of sea-fowl.

Friday
evening,
Nov.
27,
1799

The immovableness of all things through which so many men were moving,—a harsh contrast compared with the universal motion, the harmonious system of motions in the country, and everywhere in Nature. In the dim light London appeared to be a huge place of sepulchres through which hosts of spirits were gliding.

Slanting pillars of misty light moved along under the sun hid by clouds.

Leaves of trees upturned by the stirring wind in twilight,—an image of paleness, wan affright.

Septem-
ber
1,
[1800]

The beards of thistle and dandelions flying about the lonely mountains like life,—and I saw them through the trees skimming the lake like swallows.

113

Dec. 19, 1800

The thin scattered rain-clouds were scudding along the sky; above them, with a visible interspace, the crescent moon hung, and partook not of the motion; her own hazy light filled up the concave, as if it had been painted and the colors had run.

March 17, 1801, Tuesday

Hartley, looking out of my study window, fixed his eyes steadily and for some time on the opposite prospect and said, "Will yon mountains *always* be?" I showed him the whole magnificent prospect in a looking-glass, and held it up, so that the whole was like a canopy or ceiling over his head, and he struggled to express himself concerning the difference between the thing and the image almost with convulsive effort. I never before saw such an abstract of *thinking* as a pure act and energy,—of thinking as distinguished from thought.

Observations and Reflections

The spring with the little tiny cone of loose sand ever rising and sinking at the bottom, but its surface without a wrinkle.

September 15, 1801

Observed the great half moon setting behind the mountain ridge, and watched the shapes its various segments presented as it slowly sunk—first the foot of a boot, all but the heel—then a little pyramid △—then a star of the first magnitude, indeed, it was not distinguishable from the evening star at its largest—then rapidly a smaller, a small, a very small star—and, as it diminished in size, so it grew paler in tint. And now where is it? Unseen—but a little fleecy cloud hangs above the mountain ridge, and is rich in amber light.

October 19, 1801

On the Greta, over the bridge by Mr. Edmundson's father-in-law, the ashes—their leaves of that light yellow which autumn gives them—cast a reflection on the river like a painter's sunshine.

The first sight of green fields with the numberless nodding gold cups, and the winding river with alders on its banks, affected me, coming out of a city confinement, with the sweetness and power of a sudden strain of music.

In natural objects we feel ourselves, or think of ourselves, only by *likenesses;* among men, too often by *differences.* Hence the soothing, love-kindling effect of rural nature—the bad passions of human societies. And why is difference linked with hatred?

Sunday, December ber 19

Remember the pear-trees in the lovely vale of Teme. Every season Nature converts me from some unloving heresy, and will make a Catholic of me at last.

Repose after agitation is like the pool under a waterfall, which the waterfall has made.

Country and Town

The rocks and stones put on a vital resemblance, and life itself seemed, thereby, to forego its restlessness, to anticipate in its own nature an infinite repose, and to become, as it were, compatible with immovability.

The Poet and the Spider

On St. Herbert's Island, I saw a large spider with most beautiful legs, floating in the air on his back by a single thread which he was spinning out, and still, as he spun, heaving on the air, as if the air beneath was a pavement elastic to his strokes. From the top of a very high tree he had spun his line; at length reached the bottom, tied his thread round a piece of grass, and reascended to spin another,—a net to hang, as a fisherman's sea-net hangs, in the sun and wind to dry.

Bright October

A drizzling rain. Heavy masses of shapeless vapor upon the mountains (O the perpetual forms of Bor-

October 21, 1803, Friday morning

rowdale!), yet it is no unbroken tale of dull sadness. Slanting pillars travel across the lake at long intervals, the vaporous mass whitens in large stains of light—on the lakeward ridge of that huge armchair of Lodore fell a gleam of softest light, that brought out the rich hues of the late autumn. The woody Castle Crag between me and Lodore is a rich flower-garden of colors—the brightest yellows with the deepest crimsons and the infinite shades of brown and green, the *infinite* diversity of which blends the whole, so that the brighter colors seem to be colors upon a ground, not colored things. Little wool-packs of white bright vapor rest on different summits and declivities. The vale is narrowed by the mist and cloud, yet through the wall of mist you can see into a bower of sunny light, in Borrowdale; the birds are singing in the tender rain, as if it were the rain of April, and the decaying foliage were flowers and blossoms. The pillar of smoke from the chimney rises up in the mist, and is just distinguishable from it, and the mountain forms in the gorge of Borrowdale consubstantiates with the mist and cloud, even as the pillar'd smoke—a shade deeper and a determinate form.

In the Visions of the Night Nov. 2, 1803, Wednesday morning, 20 minutes past 2 o'clock

The voice of the Greta and the cock-crowing. The voice seems to grow like a flower on or about the water beyond the bridge, while the cock-crowing is nowhere particular,—it is at any place I imagine and and do not distinctly see. A most remarkable sky! the moon, now waned to a perfect ostrich egg, hangs over our house almost, only so much beyond it, garden-ward, that I can see it, holding my head out of the smaller study window. The sky is covered with whitish and with dingy cloudage, thin dingiest scud close under the moon, and one side of it moving, all else moveless; but there are two great breaks of blue sky, the one stretches over our house and away toward Castlerigg, and this is speckled and blotched with

116

white cloud; the other hangs over the road, in the line of the road, in the shape of an ellipse or shuttle, I do not know what to call it,—this is unspeckled, all blue, three stars in it,—more in the former break, all unmoving. The water leaden-white, even as the gray gleam of water is in latest twilight. Now while I have been writing this and gazing between whiles (it is forty minutes past two), the break over the road is swallowed up, and the stars gone; the break over the house is narrowed into a rude circle, and on the edge of its circumference one very bright star. See! already the white mass, thinning at its edge, *fights* with its brilliance. See! it has bedimmed it, and now it is gone, and the moon is gone. The cock-crowing too has ceased. The Greta sounds on forever. But I hear only the ticking of my watch in the pen-place of my writing-desk and the far lower note of the noise of the fire, perpetual, yet seeming uncertain. It is the low voice of quiet change, of destruction doing its work by little and little.

The Night Side of Nature November 9, Wednesday night, 45 min. past 6

The town, with lighted windows and noise of the *clogged* passengers in the streets,—sound of the unseen river. Mountains scarcely perceivable except by eyes long used to them, and supported by the images of memory flowing in on the impulses of immediate impression. On the sky, black clouds; two or three dim, untwinkling stars, like full stops on damp paper, and large stains and spreads of sullen white, like a tunic of white wool seen here and there through a torn and tattered cloak of black. Whence do these stains of white proceed all over the sky, so long after sunset, and, from their indifference of place in the sky, seemingly unaffected by the west?

November 10, ½ past 2

Awoke, after long struggles, from a persecuting dream. The tale of the dream began in two *images*, in two sons of a nobleman, desperately fond of shooting, brought out by the footman to resign their

117

o'clock,
morn-
ing

property, and to be made believe that they had none. They were far too cunning for that, and as they struggled and resisted their cruel wrongers, and my interest for them, I suppose, increased, I became they, —the duality vanished,—Boyer and Christ's Hospital became concerned; yet, still, the former story was kept up, and I was conjuring him, as he met me in the street, to have pity on a nobleman's orphan, when I was carried up to bed, and was struggling up against some unknown impediment,—when a noise of one of the doors awoke me. Drizzle; the sky uncouthly marbled with white vapors and large black clouds, their surface of a fine woolly grain, but in the height and keystone of the arch a round space of sky with dim watery stars, like a friar's crown; the seven stars in the central seen through white vapor that, entirely shapeless, gave a whiteness to the circle of the sky, but stained with exceedingly thin and subtle flakes of black vapor, might be happily said in language of Boccace (describing Demogorgon, in his *Genealogia De Gli Dei*) to be *vestito d' una pallidezza affumicata.*

Tues-
day
night,
¼ after
7

The sky covered with stars, the wind up,—right opposite my window, over Brandelhow, as its centre, and extending from the gorge to Whinlatter, an enormous black cloud, exactly in the shape of an egg, —this, the only cloud in all the sky, impressed me with a demoniacal grandeur. O, for change of weather!

An
Optical
Delu-
sion

A pretty optical fact occurred this morning. As I was returning from Fletcher's, up the back lane and just in sight of the river, I saw, floating high in the air, somewhere over Mr. Banks's, a noble kite. I continued gazing at it for some time, when, turning suddenly round, I saw at an equi-distance on my right, that is, over the middle of our field, a pair of kites floating about. I looked at them for some

118

seconds, when it occurred to me that I had never before seen two kites together, and instantly the vision disappeared. It was neither more nor less than two pair of leaves, each pair on a separate stalk, on a young fruit tree that grew on the other side of the wall, not two yards from my eye. The leaves being alternate, did, when I looked at them as leaves, strikingly resemble wings, and they were the only leaves on the tree. The magnitude was given by the imagined distance, that distance by the former adjustment of the eye, which *remained* in consequence of the deep impression, the length of time I had been looking at the kite, the pleasure, etc., and [the fact that] a new object [had] impressed itself on the eye.

A Moon Set Friday, Nov. 25, 1803, morning, 45 minutes past 2

After a night of storm and rain, the sky calm and white, by blue vapor thinning into formlessness instead of clouds, the mountains of height covered with snow, the secondary mountains black. The moon descending aslant the ∨A, through the midst of which the great road winds, set exactly behind Whinlatter Point, marked A. She being an egg, somewhat uncouthly shaped, perhaps, but an ostrich's egg rather than any other (she is two nights more than a half-moon), she set behind the black point, fitted herself on to it like a cap of fire, then became a crescent, then a mountain of fire in the distance, then the peak itself on fire, one steady flame; then stars of the first, second, and third magnitude, and vanishing, upboiled a swell of light, and in the next second the whole sky, which had been *sable blue* around the yellow moon, whitened and brightened for as large a space as would take the moon half an hour to descend through.

A Sunset Monday

A beautiful sunset, the sun setting behind Newlands across the foot of the lake. The sky is cloudless, save that there is a cloud on Skiddaw, one of the highest mountains in Borrowdale, some on Helvellyn, and that the sun sets in a glorious cloud. These clouds are of various shapes, various colors, and belong to their mountains and have nothing to do with the sky. N.B.—There is something metallic, silver playfully and imperfectly gilt and highly polished, or, rather, something mother-of-pearlish, in the sun-gleams on ice, thin ice.

A Doubt- ful Experi- ment

December 30th, half past one o'clock, or, rather, Saturday morning, December 31st, put rolled bits of paper, many tiny bits of wick, some tallow, and the soap together. The whole flame, equal in size to half a dozen candles, did not give the light of one, and the letters of the book looked by the un- steady flare just as through tears or in dizziness— every line of every letter dislocated into angles, or like the mica in crumbly stones.

A rosemary tree, large as a timber tree, is a sweet sign of the antiquity and antique manners of the house against which it groweth. Rosemary (says Parkinson, *Theatrum Botanicum*, London, 1640, p. 76) is an herb of as great use with us in these days as any whatsoever, not only for physical but civil purposes—the civil uses, as all know, are at weddings, funerals, etc., to bestow on friends.

Poem. Ghost of a mountain—the forms, seizing my body as I passed, became realities—I a ghost, till I had reconquered my substance.

The old stump of the tree, with briar-roses and bramble leaves wreathed round and round—a bramble arch—a foxglove in the centre.

The steadfast rainbow in the fast-moving, fast- hurrying hail-mist! What a congregation of images and feelings, of fantastic permanence amidst the rapid change of tempest—quietness the daughter of storm.

Oct. 31, The full moon glided behind a black cloud. And
1803 what then? and who cared? It was past seven o'clock
Ave in the morning. There is a small cloud in the east,
Phoebe not larger than the moon, and ten times brighter than
Impera- she! So passes night, and all her favors vanish in
tor our minds ungrateful!

The most common appearance in wintry weather
is that of the sun under a sharp, defined level line of
a stormy cloud, that stretches one third or one half
round the circle of the horizon, thrice the height of
the space that intervenes between it and the horizon,
which last is about half again as broad as the sun.
[At length] out comes the sun, a mass of brassy
light, himself lost and diffused in his [own] strong
splendor. Compare this with the beautiful summer
set of colors without cloud.

The *hirschkäfer* (stag-beetle) in its worm state
makes its bed-chamber, prior to its metamorphosis,
half as long as itself. Why? There was a stiff horn
turned under its belly, which in the fly state must
project and harden, and this required exactly that
length.

A Saw the limb of a rainbow, footing itself on the
Sun- sea at a small apparent distance from the shore, a
Dog thing of itself—no substrate cloud or even mist visible
Dec. —but the distance glimmered through it as through
15, a thin semi-transparent hoop.
1804

Nature may be personified as the πολυμήχανος ἐργάνη,
an ever industrious Penelope, forever unravelling
what she has woven, forever weaving what she has
unravelled.

See yonder rainbow strangely preserving its form
on broken clouds, with here a bit out, here a bit in,
yet still a rainbow—even as you might place bits of
colored ribbon at distances, so as to preserve the form
of a bow to the mind. Dec. 25, 1804.

121

The
Empy-
rean

What a sky! the not yet orbed moon, the spotted oval, blue at one edge from the deep utter blue of the sky—a MASS of *pearl*-white cloud below, distant, and travelling to the horizon, but all the upper part of the ascent and all the height such *profound* blue, deep as a deep river, and deep in color, and those two depths so entirely *one*, *as* to give the meaning and explanation of the two different significations of the epithet. Here, so far from *divided*, they were scarcely *distinct*, scattered over with thin pearl-white cloudlets—hands and fingers—the largest not larger than a floating veil! Unconsciously I stretched forth my arms as to embrace the sky, and in a trance I had worshipped God in the moon—the spirit, not the form. I felt in how innocent a feeling Sabeism might have begun. Oh! not only the moon, but the depths of the sky! The moon was the *idea;* but deep sky is, of all visual impressions, the nearest akin to a feeling. It is more a feeling than a sight, or, rather, it is the melting away and entire union of feeling and sight!

Orange
Blossom
April 8,
1805

I never had a more lovely twig of orange-blossoms, with four old last year's leaves with their steady green well-placed among them, than today, and with a rose-twig of three roses [it] made a very striking nosegay to an Englishman. The orange twig was so very full of blossoms that one-fourth of the number becoming fruit of the natural size would have broken the twig off. Is there, then, disproportion here? or waste? O no! no! In the first place, here is a prodigality of beauty; and what harm do they do by existing? And is not man a being capable of Beauty even as of Hunger and Thirst? And if the latter be fit objects of a final cause, why not the former? But secondly [Nature] hereby multiplies manifold the chances of a proper number becoming fruit; in this twig, for instance, for one set of accidents that would have been fatal to the year's growth if only

Metamorphosis of the Stag-beetle, from Emile Blanchard,
Metamorphoses, Moeurs et Instincts des Insectes, *1868*

as many blossoms had been on it as it was designed
to bear fruit, there may now be three sets of accidents
—and no harm done. And, thirdly and lastly, for *me*
at *least*—or, at least, at present, for in nature doubt-
less there are many additional reasons, and possibly
for *me* at some future hour of reflection, after some
new influx of information from books or observance
—and, thirdly, these blossoms are Fruit, fruit to the
winged insect, fruit to man—yea! and of more solid
value, perhaps, than the orange itself! O how the
Bees be-throng and be-murmur it! O how the honey
tells the tale of its birthplace to the sense of sight
and odor! and to how many minute and uneyeable
insects beside! So, I cannot but think, ought I to
be talking to Hartley, and sometimes to detail all
the insects that have arts or implements resembling
human—the sea-snails, with the nautilus at their
head; the wheel-insect, the galvanic eel, etc.

Thought   Thought and reality are, as it were, two distinct
and   corresponding sounds, of which no man can say
Things   positively which is the voice and which the echo.

Oh, the beautiful fountain or natural well at
Upper Stowey! The images of the weeds which hung
down from its sides appear as plants growing up,
straight and upright, among the water-weeds that
really grow from the bottom of the well, and so vivid
was the image that for some moments, and not till
after I had disturbed the water, did I perceive that
their roots were not neighbors, and they side-by-side
companions. So, ever, then I said,—so are the happy
man's thoughts and things [or in the language of the
modern philosophers] his ideas and impressions.

Sad, drooping children of a wretched parent are
those yellowing leaflets of a broken twig, broke ere
its June.

The Pine-Tree blasted at the top was applied by
Swift to himself as a prophetic emblem of his own

decay. The Chestnut is a fine shady tree, and its wood excellent, were it not that it dies away at the *heart* first. Alas! poor me!

Moon-
light
Gleams
and
Massy
Glories

In the first [entrance to the wood] the spots of moonlight of the wildest outlines, not unfrequently approaching so near to the shape of man and the domestic animals most attached to him as to be easily confused with them by fancy and mistaken by terror, moved and started as the wind stirred the branches, so that it almost seemed like a flight of recent spirits, sylphs and sylphids dancing and capering in a world of shadows. Once, when our path was over-canopied by the meeting boughs, as I halloed to those a stone-throw behind me, a sudden flash of light dashed down, as it were, upon the path close before me, with such rapid and indescribable effect that my life seemed snatched away from me, not by terror, but by the whole attention being suddenly and unexpectedly seized hold of. If one could conceive a violent blow given by an unseen hand, yet without pain or local sense of injury, of the weight falling here or there, it might assist in conceiving the feeling. This I found was occasioned by some very large bird, who, scared by my noise, had suddenly flown upward, and by the spring of his feet or body had driven down the branch on which he was aperch.

Dreams
and
Shadows

I had a confused shadow rather than an image in my recollection, like that from a thin cloud, as if the idea were descending, though still in some measureless height.

As when the taper's white cone of flame is seen double, till the eye moving brings them into one space and then they become one—so did the idea in my imagination coadunate with your present form soon after I first gazed upon you.

125

Blue sky through the glimmering interspaces of the dark elms at twilight rendered a lovely deep yellow-green—all the rest a delicate blue.

The sunflower ought to be cultivated, the leaves being excellent fodder, the flowers eminently melliferous, and the seeds a capital food for poultry, none nourishing quicker or occasioning them to lay more eggs.

The moulting peacock, with only two of his long tail-feathers remaining, and those sadly in tatters, yet, proudly as ever, spreads out his ruined fan in the sun and breeze.

Yesterday I saw seven or eight water-wagtails following a feeding horse in the pasture, fluttering about and hopping close by his hoofs, under his belly, and even so as often to tickle his nostrils with their pert tails. The horse shortens the grass and they get the insects.

πάντα ῥεῖ Our mortal existence—what is it but a stoppage in the blood of life, a brief eddy from wind or concourse of currents in the ever-flowing ocean of pure Activity, who beholds pyramids, yea, Alps and Andes, giant pyramids, the work of fire that raiseth monuments, like a generous victor o'er its own conquest, the tombstones of a world destroyed! Yet these, too, float adown the sea of Time, and melt away as mountains of floating ice.

The Captive Bird May 16, 1808 O that sweet bird! where is it? It is encaged somewhere out of sight; but from my bedroom at the *Courier* office, from the windows of which I look out on the walls of the Lyceum, I hear it at early dawn, often, alas! lulling me to late sleep—again when I awake and all day long. It is in prison, all its instincts ungratified, yet it feels the influence of spring, and calls with unceasing melody to the Loves that dwell in field and greenwood bowers, unconscious, perhaps, that it calls in vain. O are they the songs of a happy, enduring day-dream? Has the bird hope? or does it abandon itself to the joy of its frame, a living harp of Eolus? O that I could do so!

Assuredly a thrush or blackbird encaged in London is a far less shocking spectacle, its encagement a more venial defect of just feeling, than (which yet one so often sees) a bird in a gay cage in the heart of the country,—yea, as if at once to mock both the poor prisoner and its kind mother, Nature,—in a cage hung up in a tree, where the free birds after a while, when the gaudy dungeon is no longer a scare, crowd to it, perch on the wires, drink the water, and peck up the seeds. But of all birds, I most detest to see the nightingale encaged, and the swallow, and the cuckoo. Motiveless! monstrous! But the robin! O woes' woe! woe!—he, sweet cock-my-head-and-eye, pert-bashful darling, that makes our kitchen its chosen cage.

Let us not, because the foliage waves in necessary obedience to every breeze, fancy that the tree shakes also. Though the slender branch bend, one moment to the east and another to the west, its motion is circumscribed by its connection with the unyielding trunk.

We understand nature just as if, at a distance, we looked at the image of a person in a looking-glass, plainly and fervently discoursing, yet what he uttered we could decipher only by the motion of the lips or by his mien.

That
Inward
Eye,
The
Bliss of
Solitude

The love of nature is ever returned double to us, not only the delighter in our delight, but by linking our sweetest, but of themselves perishable feelings to distinct and vivid images, which we ourselves, at times, and which a thousand casual recollections, recall to our memory. She is the preserver, the treas-

127

urer of our joys. Even in sickness and nervous diseases, she has peopled our imagination with lovely forms which have sometimes overpowered the inward pain and brought with them their old sensations. And even when all men have seemed to desert us, and the friend of our heart has passed on, with one glance from his "cold, disliking eye"—yet even then the blue heaven spreads it out and bends over us, and the little tree still shelters us under its plumage as a second cope, a domestic firmament, and the low-creeping gale will sigh in the heath-plant and soothe us by sound of sympathy till the lulled grief lose itself in fixed gaze on the purple heath-blossom, till the present beauty becomes a vision of memory.

Sometimes when I earnestly look at a beautiful object or landscape, it seems as if I were on the *brink* of a fruition still denied—as if Vision were an *appetite;* even as a man would feel who, having put forth all his muscular strength in an act of prosilience, is at the very moment *held back*—he leaps and yet moves not from his place.

Science and Philosophy

The first man of science was he who looked into a thing, not to learn whether it could furnish him with food, or shelter, or weapons, or tools, or ornaments, or *playwiths*, but who sought to know it for the gratification of *knowing;* while he that first sought to *know* in order to *be* was the first philosopher. I have read of two rivers passing through the same lake, yet all the way preserving their streams visibly distinct —if I mistake not, the Rhone and the Adar, through the Lake of Geneva. In a far finer distinction, yet in a subtler union, such, for the contemplative mind, are the streams of knowing and being. The lake is formed by the two streams in man and nature as it exists in and for man; and up this lake the philosopher sails on the junction-line of the constituent streams, still pushing upward and sounding as he goes, towards the common fountain-head of both, the mysterious source whose being is knowledge, whose knowledge is being—the adorable I AM IN THAT I AM.

Drip
Drip
Drip
Drip

The ear-deceiving imitation of a steady soaking rain, while the sky is in full uncurtainment of sprinkled stars and milky stream and dark blue interspace. The rain had held up for two hours or more, but so deep was the silence of the night that the *drip* from the leaves of the garden trees *copied* a steady shower.

The *Libellulidae* fly all ways without needing to turn their bodies—onward, backward, right, and left —with more than swallow-rivalling rapidity of wing, readiness of evolution, and indefatigable continuance.

The merry little gnats (*Tipulidae minimae*) I have myself often watched in an April shower, evidently "dancing the hayes" in and out between the falling drops, unwetted, or, rather, undown-dashed by rocks of water many times larger than their whole bodies.

The
Moon's
Halo an
Emblem
of Hope

The moon, rushing onward through the coursing clouds, advances like an indignant warrior through a fleeing army; but the amber halo in which he moves —O! it is a circle of Hope. For what she leaves behind her has not lost its radiance as it is melting away into oblivion, while, still, the other semicircle catches the rich light at her approach, and heralds her ongress.

A Land
of Bliss

The humming-moth with its glimmer-mist of rapid unceasing motion before, the humble-bee within the flowering bells and cups—and the eagle *level* with the clouds, himself a cloudy speck, surveys the vale from mount to mount. From the cataract flung on the vale, the broadest fleeces of the snowy foam light on the bank flowers or the water-lilies in the stiller pool below.

129

*Vox
Hiema-
lis
Thurs-
day
Sept.
30,
1824*

Now the breeze through the stiff and brittle-becoming foliage of the trees counterfeits the sound of a rushing stream or water-flood suddenly sweeping by. The sigh, the modulated continuousness of the murmur, is exchanged for the confusion of overtaking sounds—the self-evolution of the One for the clash or stroke of ever-commencing contact of the multitudinous, without interspace, by confusion. The short gusts rustle, and the ear feels the unlithesome dryness before the eye detects the coarser, duller, though deeper green, deadened and not [yet] awakened into the hues of decay—echoes of spring from the sepulchral vault of winter. The aged year, conversant with the forms of its youth and forgetting all the intervals, feebly reproduces them, [as it were, from] memory.

*Flowers
and
Light
April
18,
1826*

Spring flowers, I have observed, look best in the day, and by sunshine; but summer and autumnal flower-pots by lamp or candle light. I have now before me a flower-pot of cherry blossoms, polyanthuses, double violets, periwinkles, wall-flowers, but how dim and dusky they look. The scarlet anemone is an exception, and three or four of them with all the rest of the flower-glass sprays of white blossoms, and one or two periwinkles for the sake of the dark green leaves, green stems, and flexible elegant form, make a lovely group both by sun and by candle light.

William Cobbett

Ancient Trees, Lullingstone Park, Kent,
a pencil drawing of 1828 by Samuel Palmer

Cottages, Farnham, Surrey, by Thomas Rowlandson, 1784

William Cobbett
[1762–1835]

Cobbett's worldly career stands in flamboyant contrast to the quiet histories of most of the figures represented in this collection. Looking back over a turbulent life which extended from the early years of soldiering in New Brunswick and Nova Scotia to his being seated at the age of seventy in the first parliament after the passage of the Reform Act, he might have proclaimed with the old hero of Matthew Arnold's "Sohrab and Rustum":

> But now in blood and battles was my youth,
> And full of blood and battles is my age,
> And I shall never end this life of blood.

As founder and sole editor of the *Weekly Political Register* from 1802 until his death, Cobbett was the leading Radical journalist of his day; and his fearlessly belligerent assaults on entrenched interests kept him constantly at odds with governmental authority and subject to a succession of court actions. In addition to having to pay ruinous fines, he was sentenced to a term in prison and twice found it expedient to seek asylum in the United States, where he resided from 1792 to 1800 and again in 1817–1819. *Rural Rides* recounts an episode suggestive of how he throve on opposition. When a group of unruly farmers at Lewes in Sussex voted to eject him from their meeting, Cobbett, then sixty years old, says: "I rose, that they might see the man that they had to put out. Fortunately *for themselves*, not one of them attempted to approach me."

Posterity has not been much more successful than his contemporaries in reconciling the contrarieties of Cobbett's nature. Ready and implacable in his public aversions, he was at home a tenderly devoted husband and father. A revolutionary agitator for the rights of the masses in a period of cruelly repressive

133

legislation, his instinctive sympathies were yet with the Tory past. His reforming principles were offset by a host of prejudices on matters as various as the increasing use of potatoes as a staple in the national diet, the teachings of the Scottish "feelosophers," or the circulation of paper money. The two constants in Cobbett's shifting loyalties are traceable to his origins as the self-educated descendant of yeoman stock in Surrey. He never lost his deep love of the English soil nor of the agricultural populace rooted in it. For this reason the *Rural Rides*, which record his farflung wanderings through the ancient southern shires, contain the truest evidence of his qualities of heart and mind.

Cobbett was before all else a countryman. At every opportunity he fled London, which he contemptuously named "the Great Wen." He perceived with angry despair how the traditional rural economy was giving way to a new spirit of commercialism, heralded by acts of Enclosure, the supersession of cottage industries, and the traffic in landed estates. Through his writings he sought to arrest and preserve a way of life that was irretrievably passing. On his horseback journeys he made a point of shunning the great thoroughfares, convinced that "those that travel on turnpike-roads know nothing of England." Possessed of boundless curiosity and a matching stamina, he prosecuted his excursions with something of the restless delight of the great adventurers. A typical entry reads:

> I have put an end to my ride of August, September, and October, 1826, during which I have travelled five hundred and sixty-eight miles, and have slept in thirty different beds, having written three monthly pamphlets, called the *Poor Man's Friend*, and have also written (including the present one) eleven *Registers*. I have been in three cities, in about twenty market towns, in perhaps five hundred villages . . .

One can imagine Cobbett's dismay at finding passages from *Rural Rides* included in an anthology of nature writings. He travelled to collect information to support his preachments; and his descriptions rarely look beyond the ends of immediate utility: the vagaries of the seasons, the composition of the soil, the rotation of crops, the fluctuating prices of produce and livestock—

all as affecting the livelihood of hard-driven husbandmen. Yet, although casually noted and allowed to slip in as if by accident, the natural beauties of the countryside play like grace notes about the author's pragmatic observations. The very forthrightness of their rendering in Cobbett's colloquial and slightly garrulous style bears witness to the strength of those primal sympathies which, despite all hardship, knit men to their native earth.

An Earthenware Shop, Farnham, Surrey, by Thomas Rowlandson, 1784

135

From *Rural Rides*

Kensington, Friday, 4 Jan. 1822

. . . I cannot quit Battle without observing, that the country is very pretty all about it. All hill, or valley. A great deal of wood-land, in which the underwood is generally very fine, though the oaks are not very fine, and a good deal covered with *moss*. This shows, that the clay ends, before the *tap*-root of the oak gets as deep as it would go; for, when the clay goes the full depth, the oaks are always fine.—The woods are too large, and too near each other, for hare-hunting; and, as to coursing, it is out of the question here. But, it is a fine country for shooting, and for harbouring, game of all sorts.—It was rainy as I came home; but the woodmen were at work. A great many *hop-poles* are cut here, which makes the coppices more valuable than in many other parts. The women work in the coppices, shaving the bark of the hop-poles, and, indeed, at various other parts of the business. These poles are shaved to prevent *maggots* from breeding in the bark, and accelerating the destruction, of the pole. It is curious that the bark of trees should generate maggots; but it has, as well as the wood, a *sugary* matter in it. The hickory wood in America sends out from the ends of the logs when these are burning, great quantities of the finest syrup that can be imagined. Accordingly, that wood breeds maggots, or worms, as they are usually called, surprisingly. Our *ash* breeds worms very much. When the tree or pole is cut, the moist matter between the outer bark and the wood, putrifies. Thence come the maggots, which soon begin to eat their way into the wood.

136

For this reason the bark is shaved off the hop-poles, as it ought to be off all our timber trees, as soon as cut, especially the ash.—Little boys and girls, shave hop-poles, and assist in other coppice work, very nicely. And, it is pleasant work, when the weather is dry, over head. The woods, bedded with leaves as they are, are clean and dry underfoot. They are warm too, even in the coldest weather. When the ground is frozen several inches deep in the open fields, it is scarcely frozen at all in a coppice, where the underwood is a good plant, and where it is nearly high enough to cut. So that the woodman's is really a pleasant life. We are apt to think that the birds, have a hard time of it in winter. But, we forget the warmth of the woods, which far exceeds anything to be found in farm yards. When Sidmouth started me from my farm, in 1817, I had just planted my farm yard, round with a pretty coppice. But, never mind, Sidmouth and I, shall, I dare say, have plenty of time and occasion to talk about that coppice, and many other things, before we die. And, can I, when I think of these things now, *pity* those to whom Sidmouth *owed his power* of starting me!—But let me forget the subject for this time at any rate.—Woodland countries are interesting on many accounts. Not so much on account of their masses of green leaves, as on account of the variety of sights, and sounds, and incidents, that they afford. Even in winter, the coppices are beautiful to the eye, while they comfort the mind, with the idea of shelter and warmth. In spring, they change their hue from day to day, during two whole months, which is about the time from the first appearance of the delicate leaves of the birch, to the full expansion of those of the ash; and, even before the leaves come at all to intercept the view, what, in the vegetable creation, is so delightful to behold, as the bed of a coppice bespangled with primroses and blue-bells? The opening of the birch leaves, is the signal for the pheasant to begin to crow, for the blackbird to whistle, and the thrush to sing; and, just when the oak-buds begin to look reddish, and not a day before, the whole tribe of finches

137

burst forth in songs from every bough, while the lark, imitating them all, carries the joyous sounds to the sky. These are amongst the means which Providence has benignantly appointed to sweeten the toils, by which food and raiment are produced; these the English Ploughman could once hear, without the sorrowful reflection that he himself was *a pauper*, and that the bounties of nature had, for him, been scattered in vain! And, shall he never see an end to this state of things! Shall he never have the due reward of his labour! Shall unsparing taxation, never cease to make him a miserable dejected being, a creature famishing in the midst of abundance, fainting, expiring with hunger's feeble moans, surrounded by a carolling creation! O! accursed paper-money! Is there a torment surpassing the wickedness of thy inventor!

Kensington, June 24, 1822

Set out at four this morning for Redbourn, and then turned off to the Westward to go to High Wycombe, through Hempstead and Chesham. The *wheat* is good all the way. The barley and oats good enough till I came to Hempstead. But the land along here is very fine: a red tenacious flinty loam upon a bed of chalk at a yard or two beneath, which, in my opinion, is the very best *corn land* that we have in England. The fields here, like those in the rich parts of Devonshire, will bear perpetual grass. Any of them will become upland meadows. The land is, in short, excellent, and it is a real corn-country. The *trees* from Redbourn to Hempstead are very fine; oaks, ashes, and beeches. Some of the finest of each sort, and the very finest ashes I ever saw in my life. They are in great numbers, and make the fields look most beautiful. No villanous things of the *fir-tribe* offend the eye here. The custom is in this part of Hertfordshire (and, I am told it

138

continues into Bedfordshire) to leave a *border* round the ploughed part of the fields to bear grass, and to make hay from, so that, the grass being now made into hay, every corn field has a closely mowed grass walk about ten feet wide all round it, between the corn and the hedge. This is most beautiful! The hedges are now full of the shepherd's rose, honeysuckles, and all sorts of wild flowers; so that you are upon a grass walk, with this most beautiful of all flower gardens and shrubberies on your one hand, and with the corn on the other. And thus you go from field to field (on foot or on horseback), the sort of corn, the sort of underwood and timber, the shape and size of the fields, the height of the hedge-rows, the height of the trees, all continually varying. Talk of *pleasure-grounds* indeed! What, that man ever invented, under the name of pleasure-grounds, can equal these fields in Hertfordshire?—This is a profitable system too; for the ground under hedges bears little corn, and it bears very good grass. Something, however, depends on the nature of the soil: for it is not all land that will bear grass, fit for hay, perpetually; and when the land will not do that, these headlands would only be a harbour for weeds and couch-grass, the seeds of which would fill the fields with their mischievous race.—Mr. Tull has observed upon the great use of headlands.—It is curious enough, that these headlands cease soon after you get into Buckinghamshire. At first you see now-and-then a field *without* a grass headland; then, it comes to now-and-then a field *with* one; and, at the end of five or six miles, they wholly cease. Hempstead is a very pretty town, with beautiful environs, and there is a canal that comes near it, and that goes on to London. It lies at the foot of a hill. It is clean, substantially built, and a very pretty place altogether. Between Hempstead and Chesham the land is not so good. I came into Buckinghamshire before I got into the latter place. Passed over two commons. But still, the land is not bad. It is drier; nearer the chalk, and not so red. The wheat continues

139

good, though not heavy; but the barley, on the land that is not very good, is light, begins to look *blue*, and the backward oats are very short. On the still thinner lands the barley and oats must be a very short crop.—People do not sow *turnips*, the ground is so dry, and I should think that the *Swede-crop* will be very short; for *Swedes* ought to be *up* at least, by this time. If I had Swedes to sow, I would sow them now, and upon ground very deeply and finely broken. I would sow directly after the plough, not being half an hour behind it, and would roll the ground as hard as possible. I am sure the plants would come up, even without rain. And the moment the rain came, they would grow famously.—Chesham is a nice little town, lying in a deep and narrow valley, with a stream of water running through it. All along the country that I have come, the labourers' dwellings are good. They are made of what they call *brick-nog* (that is to say, a frame of wood, and a single brick thick, filling up the vacancies between the timber. They are generally covered with tile. Not *pretty* by any means; but they are good; and you see here, as in Kent, Sussex, Surrey and Hampshire, and, indeed, in almost every part of England, that most interesting of all objects, that which is such an honour to England, and that which distinguishes it from all the rest of the world, namely, *those neatly kept and productive little gardens round the labourers' houses*, which are seldom unornamented with more or less of flowers. We have only to look at these to know what sort of people English labourers are: these gardens are the answer to the *Malthuses* and the *Scarletts*. Shut your mouths, you Scotch Economists; cease bawling, Mr. Brougham, and you Edinburgh Reviewers, till *you* can show us something, not *like*, but approaching towards a likeness of *this!*

The orchards all along this country are by no means bad. Not like those of Herefordshire and the north of Kent; but a great deal better than in many other parts of the kingdom.

The cherry-trees are pretty abundant and particularly good. There are not many of the *merries*, as they call them in Kent and Hampshire; that is to say, the little black cherry, the name of which is a corruption from the French, *merise*, in the singular, and *merises* in the plural. I saw the little boys, in many places, set to keep the birds off the cherries, which reminded me of the time when I followed the same occupation, and also of the toll that I used to take in payment. The children are all along here, I mean the little children, locked out of the doors, while the fathers and mothers are at work in the fields. I saw many little groups of this sort; and this is one advantage of having plenty of room on the outside of a house. I never saw the country children better clad, or look cleaner and fatter than they look here, and I have the very great pleasure to add, that I do not think I saw three acres of *potatoes* in this whole tract of fine country, from St. Albans to Redbourn, from Redbourn to Hempstead, and from Hempstead to Chesham. In all the houses where I have been, they use the roasted rye instead of coffee or tea, and I saw one gentleman who had sown a piece of rye (a grain not common in this part of the country) for the express purpose. It costs about three farthings a pound, roasted and ground into powder.—The pay of the labourers varies from eight to twelve shillings a-week. Grass mowers get two shillings a-day, two quarts of what they call strong beer, and as much small beer as they can drink. After quitting Chesham, I passed through a wood, resembling, as nearly as possible, the woods in the more cultivated parts of Long Island, with these exceptions, that there the woods consist of a great variety of trees, and of more beautiful foliage. Here there are only two sorts of trees—beech and oak: but the wood at bottom was precisely like an American wood: none of that stuff which we generally call underwood: the trees standing very thick in some places: the shade so complete as never to permit herbage below: no bushes of any sort; and nothing to impede

141

your steps but little spindling trees here and there grown up from the seed. The trees here are as lofty, too, as they generally are in the Long Island woods, and as straight, except in cases where you find clumps of the tulip-tree, which sometimes go much above a hundred feet high as straight as a line. The oaks seem here to vie with the beeches in size, as well as in loftiness and straightness. I saw several oaks which I think were more than eighty feet high, and several with a clear stem of more than forty feet, being pretty nearly as far through at that distance from the ground, as at the bottom; and I think I saw more than one, with a clear stem of fifty feet, a foot and a half through at that distance from the ground. This is by far the finest *plank oak* that I ever saw in England. The road through the wood is winding and brings you out at the corner of a field, lying sloping to the south, three sides of it bordered by wood and the field planted as an orchard. This is precisely what you see in so many thousands of places in America. I had passed through Hempstead a little while before, which certainly gave its name to the Township in which I lived in Long Island, and which, I used to write *Hampstead*, contrary to the orthography of the place, never having heard of such a place as *Hempstead* in England. Passing through Hempstead I gave my mind a toss back to Long Island, and this beautiful wood and orchard really made me almost conceit, that I was there, and gave rise to a thousand interesting and pleasant reflections. On quitting the wood I crossed the great road from London to Wendover, went across the park of Mr. Drake, and up a steep hill towards the great road leading to Wycombe. Mr. Drake's is a very beautiful place, and has a great deal of very fine timber upon it. I think I counted pretty nearly 200 oak trees, worth, on an average, five pounds a-piece, growing within twenty yards of the road that I was going along. Mr. Drake has some thousands of these, I dare say, besides his beech; and, therefore, *he* will be able to stand a tug with the fundholders for some time. . . .

Odiham, Hampshire, Friday, 27 Sept. [1822]

From Lea we set off this morning about six o'clock to get free-quarter again at a worthy old friend's at this nice little plain market-town. Our direct road was right over the heath through Tilford to Farnham; but we veered a little to the left after we came to Tilford, at which place on the Green we stopped to look at an *oak tree*, which, when I was a little boy, was but a very little tree, comparatively, and which is now, take it altogether, by far the finest tree that I ever saw in my life. The stem or shaft is short; that is to say, it is short before you come to the first limbs; but it is full *thirty feet round*, at about eight or ten feet from the ground. Out of the stem there come not less than fifteen or sixteen limbs, many of which are from five to ten feet round, and each of which would, in fact, be considered a decent stick of timber. I am not judge enough of timber to say any thing about the quantity in the whole tree, but my son stepped the ground, and as nearly as we could judge, the diameter of the extent of the branches was upwards of ninety feet, which would make a circumference of about three hundred feet. The tree is in full growth at this moment. There is a little hole in one of the limbs; but with that exception, there appears not the smallest sign of decay. The tree has made great shoots in all parts of it this last summer and spring; and there are no appearances of *white* upon the trunk, such as are regarded as the symptoms of full growth. There are many sorts of oak in England; two very distinct; one with a pale leaf, and one with a dark leaf: this is of the pale leaf. The tree stands upon Tilford-green, the soil of which is a light loam with a hard sand stone a good way beneath, and, probably, clay beneath that. The spot where the tree stands is about a hundred and twenty feet from the edge of a little river, and the ground on which it stands may be about ten feet higher than the bed of that river.

143

In quitting Tilford we came on to the land belonging to
Waverley Abbey, and then, instead of going on to the town of
Farnham, veered away to the left towards Wrecklesham, in
order to cross the Farnham and Alton turnpike-road, and to
come on by the side of Crondall to Odiham. We went a little
out of the way to go to a place called the *Bourn*, which lies in
the heath at about a mile from Farnham. It is a winding
narrow valley, down which, during the wet season of the
year, there runs a stream beginning at the *Holt Forest*, and
emptying itself into the *Wey* just below Moor-Park, which
was the seat of Sir William Temple when Swift was residing
with him. We went to this Bourn in order that I might show
my son the spot where I received the rudiments of my educa-
tion. There is a little hop-garden in which I used to work
when from eight to ten years old; from which I have scores of
times run to follow the hounds, leaving the hoe to do the best
that it could to destroy the weeds; but the most interesting
thing was a *sand-hill*, which goes from a part of the heath
down to the rivulet. As a due mixture of pleasure with toil, I,
with two brothers, used occasionally to *disport* ourselves, as
the lawyers call it, at this sand-hill. Our diversion was this:
we used to go to the top of the hill, which was steeper than
the roof of a house; one used to draw his arms out of the
sleeves of his smock-frock, and lay himself down with his
arms by his sides; and then the others, one at head, and the
other at feet, sent him rolling down the hill like a barrel or a
log of wood. By the time he got to the bottom, his hair, eyes,
ears, nose, and mouth, were all full of this loose sand; then
the others took their turn, and at every roll, there was a
monstrous spell of laughter. I had often told my sons of this
while they were very little, and I now took one of them to see
the spot. But, that was not all. This was the spot where I was
receiving my *education;* and this was the sort of education;
and I am perfectly satisfied that if I had not received such an
education, or something very much like it; that, if I had been
brought up a milksop, with a nursery-maid everlastingly at

my heels, I should have been at this day as great a fool, as inefficient a mortal, as any of those frivolous idiots that are turned out from Winchester and Westminster School, or from any of those dens of dunces called Colleges and Universities. It is impossible to say how much I owe to that sand-hill; and I went to return it my thanks for the ability which it probably gave me to be one of the greatest terrors, to one of the greatest and most powerful bodies of knaves and fools, that ever were permitted to afflict this or any other country. . . .

Farnham, Surrey,
Thursday, Oct. 27th [1825]

We came over the heath from Thursley, this morning, on our way to Winchester. Mr. Wyndham's fox-hounds are coming to Thursley on Saturday. More than three-fourths of all the interesting talk in that neighbourhood, for some days past, has been about this anxiously looked-for event. I have seen no man, or boy, who did not talk about it. There had been a false report about it; the hounds did *not come;* and the anger of the disappointed people was very great. At last, however, the *authentic* intelligence came, and I left them all as happy as if all were young and all just going to be married. An abatement of my pleasure, however, on this joyous occasion was, that I brought away with me *one*, who was as eager as the best of them. Richard, though now only 11 years and 6 months old, had, it seems, one fox-hunt, in Herefordshire, last winter; and he actually has begun to talk rather *contemptuously* of hare-hunting. To show me that he is in no *danger*, he has been leaping his horse over banks and ditches by the road side, all our way across the country from Reigate; and he joined with such glee in talking of the expected arrival of the fox-hounds, that I felt some little pain at bringing him away. My engagement at Winchester is for Satuday; but, if

145

it had not been so, the deep and hidden ruts in the heath, in a wood in the midst of which the hounds are sure to find, and the immense concourse of horsemen that is sure to be assembled, would have made me bring him away. Upon the high, hard and open countries, I should not be afraid for him; but, here the danger would have been greater than it would have been right for me to suffer him to run.

We came hither by the way of Waverley Abbey and Moore Park. On the commons I showed Richard some of my old hunting scenes, when I was of his age, or younger, reminding him that I was obliged to hunt on foot. We got leave to go and see the grounds at Waverley, where all the old monks' garden walls are totally gone, and where the spot is become a sort of lawn. I showed him the spot where the strawberry garden was, and where I, when sent to gather *hautboys*, used to eat every remarkably fine one, instead of letting it go to be eaten by Sir Robert Rich. I showed him a tree, close by the ruins of the Abbey, from a limb of which I once fell into the river, in an attempt to take the nest of a *crow*, which had artfully placed it upon a branch so far from the trunk, as not to be able to bear the weight of a boy eight years old. I showed him an old elm tree, which was hollow even then, into which I, when a very little boy, once saw a cat go, that was as big as a middle-sized spaniel dog, for relating which I got a great scolding, for standing to which I, at last got a beating; but stand to which I still did. I have since many times repeated it; and I would take my oath of it to this day. When in New Brunswick I saw the great wild grey cat, which is there called a *Lucifee;* and it seemed to me to be just such a cat as I had seen at Waverley. I found the ruins not very greatly diminished; but, it is strange how small the mansion, and ground, and everything but the trees, appeared to me. They were all great to my mind when I saw them last; and that early impression had remained, whenever I had talked or thought of the spot; so that, when I came to see them again, after seeing the sea and so many other immense things, it seemed as if they had all been made small. This was not the case with regard to the trees, which are nearly as big here as they are any where else; and, the old cat-elm, for instance, which Richard measured with his whip, is about 16 or 17 feet round.

From Waverley we went to Moore Park, once the seat of Sir William Temple, and, when I was a very little boy, the seat of a Lady, or a Mrs. Temple. Here I showed Richard Mother Ludlum's Hole; but, alas! it is not the enchanting place that I knew it, nor that which Grose describes in his Antiquities! The semicircular paling is gone; the basins, to catch the never-ceasing little stream, are gone; the iron cups, fastened by chains, for people to drink out of, are gone; the pavement all broken to pieces; the seats, for people to sit on, on both sides of the cave, torn up, and gone; the stream that ran down a clean paved channel, now making a dirty gutter; and the ground opposite, which was a grove, chiefly of laurels, intersected by closely-mowed grass-walks, now become a poor, ragged-looking alder-coppice. Near the mansion, I showed Richard the hill, upon which Dean Swift tells us, he used to run for exercise, while he was pursuing his studies here; and I would have showed him the garden-seat, under which Sir William Temple's heart was buried, agreeably to his will; but, the seat was gone, also the wall at the back of it; and the exquisitely beautiful little lawn in which the seat stood, was turned into a parcel of divers-shaped, cockney-clumps, planted according to the strictest rules of artificial and refined vulgarity.

At Waverley, Mr. Thompson, a merchant of some sort, has succeeded (after the monks) the Orby Hunters and Sir Robert Rich. At Moore Park, a Mr. Laing, a West India planter or merchant, has succeeded the Temples; and at the castle of Farnham, which you see from Moore Park, Bishop Prettyman Tomline, has, at last, after perfectly regular and due gradations, succeeded William of Wykham! In coming up from Moore Park to Farnham town, I stopped opposite the door of a little old house, where there appeared to be a great parcel of children. "There, Dick," said I, "when I was just a little creature as that, whom you see in the door-way, I lived in this very house with my grand-mother Cobbett." He pulled up his horse, and looked *very hard at it*, but said nothing, and on we came.

East Everley (Wiltshire),
Sunday, 27th August, Evening [1826]

We set off from Uphusband on Friday, about ten o'clock, the morning having been wet. My sons came round, in the chaise, by Andover and Weyhill, while I came right across the country towards Ludgershall, which lies in the road from Andover to this place. I never knew the *flies* so troublesome, in England, as I found them in this ride. I was obliged to carry a great bough, and to keep it in constant motion, in order to make the horse peaceable enough to enable me to keep on his back. It is a country of fields, lanes, and high hedges; so that no *wind* could come to relieve my horse; and, in spite of all I could do, a great part of him was covered with foam from the sweat. In the midst of this, I got, at one time, a little out of my road, in, or near, a place called Tangley. I rode up to the garden-wicket of a cottage, and asked the woman, who had two children, and who seemed to be about thirty years old, which was the way to Ludgershall, which I knew could not be more than about *four miles* off. She did *not know!* A very neat, smart, and pretty woman; but, she did not know the way to this rotten-borough, which was, I was sure, only about four miles off! "Well, my dear good woman," said I, "but you *have been* at Ludgershall?"— "No."—"Nor at Andover?" (six miles another way)—"No." —"Nor at Marlborough?" (nine miles another way)—"No." —"Pray, were you born in this house?"—"Yes."—"And, how

148

far have you ever been from this house?"—"Oh! I have been *up in the parish* and over *to Chute*." That is to say, the utmost extent of her voyages had been about two and a half miles! Let no one laugh at her, and, above all others, let not me, who am convinced, that the *facilities*, which now exist, of *moving human bodies from place to place*, are amongst the *curses* of the country, the destroyers of industry, of morals, and, of course, of happiness. It is a great error to suppose, that people are rendered stupid by remaining always in the same place. This was a very acute woman, and as well behaved as need to be. There was, in July last (last month) a Preston-man, who had never been further from home than Chorley (about eight or ten miles), and who started *off*, *on foot*, and went, *alone*, to Rouen, in France, and back again to London, in the space of about ten days; and that, too, without being able to speak, or to understand, a word of French. N.B. Those gentlemen, who, at Green-street, in Kent, were so kind to this man, *upon finding that he had voted for me*, will be pleased to accept of my best thanks. Wilding (that is the man's name) was full of expressions of gratitude towards these gentlemen. He spoke of others who were good to him on his way; and even at Calais he found friends on my account; but he was particularly loud in his praises of the gentlemen in Kent, who had been so good and so kind to him, that he seemed quite in an extacy when he talked of their conduct.

Before I got to the rotten-borough, I came out upon a Down, just on the border of the two counties, Hampshire and Wiltshire. Here I came up with my sons, and we entered the rotten-borough together. It contained some rashers of bacon and a very civil landlady; but, it is one of the most mean and beggarly places that man ever set his eyes on. The curse, attending corruption, seems to be upon it. The look of the place would make one swear, that there never was a clean shirt in it, since the first stone of it was laid. It must have been a large place once, though it now contains only 479 persons, men, women, and children. The borough is, as to all

149

practical purposes, as much private property as this pen is my private property. Aye, aye! Let the petitioners of Manchester bawl, as long as they like, against all other evils; but, until they touch this *master-evil*, they do nothing at all.

Everley is but about three miles from Ludgershall, so that we got here in the afternoon of Friday: and, in the evening a very heavy storm came and drove away all flies, and made the air delightful. This is a real *Bown*-country. Here you see miles and miles square without a tree, or hedge, or bush. It is country of green-sward. This is the most famous place in all England for *coursing*. I was here, at this very inn, with a party eighteen years ago; and the landlord, who is still the same, recognised me as soon as he saw me. There were forty brace of greyhounds taken out into the field on one of the days, and every brace had one course, and some of them two. The ground is the finest in the world; from two to three miles for the hare to run to cover, and not a stone nor a bush nor a hillock. It was here proved to me, that the hare is, by far, the swiftest of all English animals; for I saw three hares, in one day, *run away* from the dogs. To give dog and hare a fair trial, there should be but *one* dog. Then, if that dog got so close as to compel the hare *to turn*, that would be a proof that the dog ran fastest. When the dog, or dogs, never get near enough to the hare to induce her to *turn*, she is said, and very justly, to "*run away*" from them; and, as I saw three hares do this in one day, I conclude, that the hare is the swifter animal of the two.

This inn is one of the nicest, and, in summer, one of the pleasantest, in England; for, I think, that my experience in this way will justify me in speaking thus positively. The house is large, the yard and the stables good, the landlord *a farmer* also, and, therefore, no cribbing your horses in hay or straw and yourself in eggs and cream. The garden, which adjoins the south side of the house, is large, of good shape, has a terrace on one side, lies on the slope, consists of well-disposed clumps of shrubs and flowers, and of short-grass

150

Coursing, by Henry Alken, from The National Sports of Great Britain, *1825*

very neatly kept. In the lower part of the garden there are high trees, and, amongst these, the tulip-tree and the live-oak. Beyond the garden is a large clump of lofty sycamores, and, in these a most populous rookery, in which, of all things in the world, I delight. The village, which contains 301 souls, lies to the north of the inn, but adjoining its premises. All the rest, in every direction, is bare down or open arable. I am now sitting at one of the southern windows of this inn, looking across the garden towards the rookery. It is nearly sun-setting; the rooks are skimming and curving over the tops of the trees; while, under the branches, I see a flock of several hundred sheep, coming nibbling their way in from the Down, and going to their fold.

Now, what ill-natured devil could bring Old Nic Grimshaw into my head in company with these innocent sheep? Why, the truth is this: nothing is *so swift* as *thought:* it runs over a life-time in a moment; and, while I was writing the last sentence of the foregoing paragraph, *thought* took me up at the time when I used to wear a smock-frock and to carry a wooden bottle like that shepherd's boy; and, in an instant, it hurried me along through my no very short life of adventure, of toil, of peril, of pleasure, of ardent friendship and not less ardent enmity; and after filling me with wonder, that a heart and mind so wrapped up in everything belonging to the gardens, the fields and the woods, should have been condemned to waste themselves away amidst the stench, the noise and the strife of cities, it brought me *to the present moment*, and sent my mind back to what I have yet to perform about Nicholas Grimshaw and his *ditches!*

My sons set off about three o'clock to-day, on their way to Herefordshire, where I intend to join them, when I have had a pretty good ride in this country. There is no pleasure in travelling, except on horse-back, or on foot. Carriages take your body from place to place; and, if you merely want to be *conveyed*, they are very good; but they enable you to see and to know nothing at all of the country.

Highworth, Wednesday, 6th Sept. [1826]

The great object of my visit to the Northern border of Wiltshire, will be mentioned when I get to Malmsbury, whither I intend to go to-morrow, or next day, and thence, through Gloucestershire, in my way to Herefordshire. But, an additional inducement, was to have a good long political *gossip*, with some excellent friends, who detest the borough-ruffians as cordially as I do, and who, I hope, wish as anxiously to see their fall effected, and no matter by what means. There was, however, arising incidentally, a third object, which had I known of its existence, would, of itself, have brought me from the South-West to the North-East corner of this county. One of the parishes adjoining to Highworth is that of Coleshill, which is in Berkshire, and which is the property of Lord Radnor, or Lord Folkestone, and is the seat of the latter. I was at Coleshill twenty-two or three years ago, and twice at later periods. In 1824, Lord Folkestone bought some Locust trees of me; and he has several times told me, that they were growing very finely; but, I did not know, that they had been planted at Coleshill; and, indeed, I always thought that they had been planted somewhere in the South of Wiltshire. I now found, however, that they were growing at Coleshill, and yesterday I went to see them, and was, for many reasons, more delighted with the sight, than with any that I have beheld for a long while. These trees stand in clumps of 200 trees in each, and the trees being four feet apart each way. These clumps make part of a plantation of 30 or 40 acres, perhaps 50 acres. The rest of the ground; that is to say, the ground where the clumps of Locusts do not stand, was, at the same time that the Locust clumps were, planted with chestnuts, elms, ashes, oaks, beeches, and other trees. These trees were stouter and taller than the Locust trees were, when the plantation was made. Yet, if you were

153

now to place yourself at a mile's distance from the plantation, you would not think that there was any plantation at all, except the clumps. The fact is, that the other trees have, as they generally do, made, as yet, but very little progress; are not, I should think, upon an average, more than 4½ feet, or 5 feet, high; while the clumps of Locusts are from 12 to 20 feet high; and, I think, that I may safely say, that the average height is sixteen feet. They are the most beautiful clumps of trees that I ever saw in my life. They were, indeed, planted by a clever and most trusty servant, who, to say all that can be said in his praise, is, that he is worthy of such a master as he has.

The trees are, indeed, in good land, and have been taken good care of; but, the other trees are in the same land; and, while they have been taken the same care of, since they were planted, they had not, I am sure, worse treatment before planting, than these Locust trees had. At the time when I sold them to my Lord Folkestone, they were in a field at Worth, near Crawley, in Sussex. The history of their transport is this. A Wiltshire waggon came to Worth for the trees, on the 14th of March 1824. The waggon had been stopped on the way by the snow; and, though the snow was gone off before the trees were put upon the waggon, it was very cold, and there were sharp frosts and harsh winds. I had the trees taken up, and tied up in hundreds by withes, like so many fagots. They were then put in, and upon the waggon, we doing our best to keep the roots inwards in the loading, so as to prevent them from being exposed, but as little as possible, to the wind, sun and frost. We put some fern on the top, and, where we could, on the sides; and we tied on the load with ropes, just as we should have done with a load of fagots. In this way, they were several days upon the road; and I do not know how long it was before they got safe into the ground again. All this shows how hardy these trees are, and it ought to admonish gentlemen to make pretty strict enquiries, when they have gardeners, or bailiffs, or stewards, under whose hands Locust trees die, or do not thrive.

N.B. Dry as the late summer was, I never had my Locust trees so fine as they are this year. I have some, they write me, five feet high, from seed sown just before I went to Preston the first time, that is to say, on the 13th of May. I shall advertise my trees in the next Register. I never had them so fine, though the great drought has made the number comparatively small. Lord Folkestone bought of me 13,600 trees. They are, at this moment, worth the money they cost him, and, in addition the cost of planting, and in addition to that, they are worth the fee simple of the ground (very good ground) on which they stand; and this I am able to demonstrate to any man in his senses What a difference in the value of Wiltshire, if all its Elms were Locusts! As fuel, a foot of Locust-wood is worth four or five of any English wood. It will burn better green, than almost any other wood will dry. If men want woods, beautiful woods, and *in a hurry*, let them go and see the clumps at Coleshill. Think of a wood 16 feet high, and I may say 20 feet high, in twenty-nine months from the day of planting; and the plants, on an average, not more than two feet high, when planted! Think of that: and any one may see it at Coleshill. See what efforts gentlemen make *to get a wood!* How they look at the poor slow-growing things for years; when they might, if they would, have it at once: really almost at a wish; and, with due attention, in almost any soil; and the most valuable of woods into the bargain. Mr. Palmer, the bailiff, showed me, near the house at Colehill, a Locust tree, which was planted about 35 years ago, or perhaps 40. He had measured it before. It is eight feet and an inch round at a foot from the ground. It goes off afterwards into two principal limbs; which two soon become six limbs, and each of these limbs is three feet round. So that here are six everlasting gate-posts to begin with. This tree is worth 20 pounds at the least farthing.

I saw also at Coleshill, the most complete farm yard that I ever saw, and that I believe there is in all England, many and

155

complete as English farm yards are. This was the contrivance of Mr. Palmer, Lord Folkstone's bailiff and steward. The master gives all the credit of plantation, and farm, to the servant; but the servant ascribes a good deal of it to the master. Between them, at any rate, here are some most admirable objects in rural affairs. And here, too, there is no misery amongst those who do the work; those without whom there could have been no Locust-plantations, and no farmyard. Here all are comfortable; gaunt hunger here stares no man in the face. That same disposition which sent Lord Folkestone to visit John Knight in the dungeons at Reading, keeps pinching hunger away from Coleshill. It is a very pretty spot all taken together. It is chiefly grazing land; and, though the making of cheese and bacon is, I dare say, the most profitable part of the farming here, Lord Folkestone fats oxen, and has a stall for it, which ought to be shown to foreigners, instead of the spinning jennies. A fat ox is a finer thing than a cheese, however good. There is a dairy here too, and beautifully kept. When this stall is full of oxen, and they all fat, how it would make a French farmer stare! It would make even a Yankee think, that "Old England" was a respectable "mother," after all. If I had to show this village off to a Yankee, I would blindfold him all the way to, and after I got him out of, the village, lest he should see the scare-crows of paupers on the road. . . .

Stroud (Gloucestershire),
Tuesday Forenoon, 12th Sept., 1826

I set off from Malmsbury this morning at 6 o'clock, in as sweet and bright a morning, as ever came out of the heavens, and leaving behind me as pleasant a house and as kind hosts as I ever met with in the whole course of my life, either in England or America; and that is saying a great deal indeed. This circumstance was the more pleasant, as I had never

156

before either seen or heard of, these kind, unaffected, sensible, *sans-façons*, and most agreeable friends. From Malmsbury I first came, at the end of five miles, to Tutbury, which is in Gloucestershire, there being here, a sort of dell, or ravine, which, in this place, is the boundary line of the two counties, and over which you go on a bridge, one-half of which belongs to each county. And now, before I take my leave of Wiltshire, I must observe, that, in the whole course of my life (days of *courtship* excepted, of course), I never passed seventeen pleasanter days than those which I have just spent in Wiltshire. It is, especially in the Southern half, just the sort of country that I like; the weather has been pleasant; I have been in good houses and amongst good and beautiful gardens; and, in *every* case, I have not only been most kindly entertained, but my entertainers have been of just the stamp that I like.

I saw again, this morning, large flocks of *goldfinches*, feeding on the thistle-seed, on the roadside. The French call this bird by a name derived from the thistle, so notorious has it always been, that they live upon this seed. *Thistle* is, in French, *Chardon;* and the French call this beautiful little bird *Chardonaret.* I never could have supposed, that such flocks of these birds would ever be seen in England. But, it is a great year for all the feathered race, whether wild or tame: naturally so, indeed; for every one knows, that it is the *wet* and not the *cold*, that is injurious to the breeding of birds of all sorts, whether land-birds or water-birds. They say, that there are, this year, double the usual quantity of ducks and geese: and, really, they do seem to swarm in the farmyards, wherever I go. It is a great mistake to suppose, that ducks and geese *need* water, except to drink. There is, perhaps, no spot in the world, in proportion to its size and population, where so many of these birds are reared and fatted, as in Long Island; and, it is not in one case out of ten, that they have any ponds to go to, or, that they ever see any water other than water that is drawn up out of a well.

A little way before I got to Tutbury I saw a woman digging some potatoes, in a strip of ground, making part of a field nearly an oblong square, and which field appeared to be laid out in strips. She told me, that the field was part of a farm (to the homestead of which she pointed); that it was, by the farmer, *let out* in strips to labouring people; that each strip contained a rood (or quarter of a statute acre); that each married labourer rented one strip; and that the annual rent was *a pound* for the strip. Now, the taxes being all paid by the farmer; the fences being kept in repair by him; and, as appeared to me, the land being exceedingly good; all these things considered, the rent does not appear to be too high.—This fashion is certainly a *growing* one; it is a little step towards a coming back to the ancient small life and lease-holds and common-fields! This field of strips was, in fact, a sort of common-field; and the "agriculturists," as the conceited asses of landlords call themselves, at their clubs and meetings, might, and they would if their skulls could admit any thoughts except such as relate to high prices and low wages; they might, and they would, begin to suspect, that the "dark age" people were not so very foolish, when they had so many common-fields, and when almost every man that had a family had also a bit of land, either large or small. It is a very curious thing, that the enclosing of commons, that the shutting out of the labourers *from all share* in the land; that the prohibiting of them to look at a wild animal, almost at a lark or a frog; it is curious that this hard-hearted system should have gone on, until, at last, it has produced effects so injurious and so dangerous to the grinders themselves, that they have, of their own accord, and for their own safety, begun to make a step towards the ancient system, and have, in the manner I have observed, made the labourers sharers, in some degree, in the uses, at any rate, of the soil. The far greater part of these strips of land have potatoes growing in them; but, in some cases, they have borne wheat, and, in others, barley, this year; and these have now turnips; very young, most of them, but, in some places, very fine, and in every instance, nicely hoed out. The land that will bear 400 bushels of potatoes to the acre, will bear 40 bushels of wheat; and, the ten bushels of wheat, to the quarter of an acre, would be a crop far more valuable than a hundred bushels of potatoes, as I have proved many times, in the Register. . . .

Bollitree, Wednesday, 13th Sept. [1826]

This morning was most beautiful. There has been rain here now, and the grass begins (but only begins) to grow. When I got within two hundred yards of Mr. Palmer's I had the happiness to meet my son Richard, who said that he had been up an hour. As I came along I saw one of the prettiest sights in the *flower* way that I ever saw in my life. It was a little orchard; the grass in it had just taken a start, and was beautifully fresh; and, very thickly growing amongst the grass, was the purple flowered *Colchicum*, in full bloom. They say, that the leaves of this plant which come out in the spring, and die away in the summer, are poisonous to cattle if they eat much of them in the spring. The flower, if standing by itself, would be no great beauty; but, contrasted thus, with the fresh grass, which was a little shorter than itself, it was very beautiful.

Thursley, Monday Evening, 23rd October [1826]

When I left Weston, my intention was, to go from Hambledon to Up Park, thence to Arundel, thence to Brighton, thence to East-bourne, thence to Wittersham in Kent, and then by Cranbrook, Tunbridge, Godstone and Reigate to London; but, when I got to Botley, and particularly when I

159

got to Hambledon, I found my horse's back so much hurt by
the saddle, that I was afraid to take so long a stretch, and
therefore resolved to come away straight to this place, to go
hence to Reigate, and so to London. Our way, therefore, this
morning, was over Butser-hill to Petersfield, in the first
place; then to Liphook and then to this place, in all about
twenty-four miles. Butser-hill belongs to the back chain of
the South-downs; and, indeed, it terminates that chain to the
westward. It is the highest hill in the whole country. Some
think that Hindhead, which is the famous sand-hill over
which the Portsmouth road goes at sixteen miles to the north
of this great chalk-hill; some think that Hindhead is the
higher hill of the two. Be this as it may, Butser-hill, which is
the right-hand hill of the two between which you go at three
miles from Petersfield going towards Portsmouth; this
Butser-hill is, I say, quite high enough; and was more than
high enough for us, for it took us up amongst clouds, that wet
us very nearly to the skin. In going from Mr. Goldsmith's to
the hill, it is all up hill for five miles. Now and then a little
stoop; not much; but regularly, with these little exceptions,
up hill for these five miles. The hill appears, at a distance, to
be a sharp ridge on its top. It is, however, not so. It is, in some
parts, half a mile wide or more. The road lies right along the
middle of it, from west to east, and, just when you are at the
highest part of the hill, it is very narrow from north to south;
not more, I think, than about a hundred or a hundred and
thirty yards.

This is as interesting a spot, I think, as the foot of man
ever was placed upon. Here are two valleys, one to your right
and the other to your left, very little less than half a mile
down to the bottom of them, and much steeper than a tiled
roof of a house. These valleys may be, where they join the
hill, three or four hundred yards broad. They get wider as
they get farther from the hill. Of a clear day you see all the
north of Hampshire; nay, the whole county, together with a
great part of Surrey and of Sussex. You see the whole of the

South-Downs to the eastward as far as your eye can carry you; and, lastly, you see over Portsdown Hill, which lies before you to the south; and there are spread open to your view the isle of Portsea, Porchester, Wimmering, Fareham, Gosport, Portsmouth, the harbour, Spithead, the Isle of Wight, and the ocean.

But something still more interesting occurred to me here in the year 1808, when I was coming on horseback over the same hill from Botley to London. It was a very beautiful day and in summer. Before I got upon the hill (on which I had never been before), a shepherd told me to keep on in the road in which I was, till I came to the London turnpike road. When I got to within a quarter of a mile of this particular point of the hill, I saw, at this point, what I thought was a cloud of dust; and, speaking to my servant about it, I found that he thought so too; but this cloud of dust disappeared all at once. Soon after, there appeared to arise another cloud of dust at the same place, and then that disappeared, and the spot was clear again. As we were trotting along, a pretty smart pace, we soon came to this narrow place, having one valley to our right and the other valley to our left, and, there, to my great astonishment, I saw the clouds come one after another, each appearing to be about as big as two or three acres of land, skimming along in the valley on the north side, a great deal below the tops of the hills; and successively, as they arrived at our end of the valley, rising up, crossing the narrow pass, and then descending down into the other valley and going off to the south; so that we who sat there upon our horses, were alternately in clouds and in sunshine. It is an universal rule, that if there be a fog in the morning, and that fog go from the valleys to the tops of the hills, there will be rain that day; and if it disappear by sinking in the valley, there will be no rain that day. The truth is, that fogs are clouds, and clouds are fogs. They are more or less, full of water; but, they are all water; sometimes a sort of steam, and sometimes water, that falls in drops. Yesterday morning the

161

fogs had ascended to the tops of the hills; and it was raining on all the hills round about us, before it began to rain in the valleys. We, as I observed before, got pretty nearly wet to the skin upon the top of Butser-hill; but, we had the pluck to come on, and let the clothes dry upon our backs.

I must here relate something that appears very interesting to me, and something, which, though it must have been seen by every man that has lived in the country, or, at least, in any hilly country, has never been particularly mentioned by an-body as far as I can recollect. We frequently talk of clouds coming from *dews;* and we actually see the heavy fogs be-come clouds. We see them go up to the tops of hills, and, taking a swim round, actually come, and drop down upon us, and wet us through. But, I am now going to speak of clouds, coming out of the sides of hills in exactly the same manner that you see smoke come out of a tobacco pipe, and, rising up, with a wider and wider head, like the smoke from a tobacco-pipe, go to the top of the hill or over the hill, or very much above it, and then come over the valleys in rain. At about a mile's distance from Mr. Palmer's house at Bollitree, in Here-fordshire, there is a large, long beautiful wood, covering the side of a lofty hill, winding round in the form of a crescent, the bend of the crescent being towards Mr. Palmer's house. It was here, that I first observed this mode of forming clouds. The first time I noticed it, I pointed it out to Mr. Palmer. We stood and observed cloud after cloud, come out from different parts of the side of the hill, and tower up and go over the hill out of sight. He told me that that was a certain sign that it would rain that day, for that these clouds would come back again, and would fall in rain. It rained sure enough; and I found that the country people, all round about, had this mode of the forming of the clouds as a sign of rain. The hill is called Penyard, and this forming of the clouds, they call Old Penyard's *smoking his pipe;* and it is a rule that it is sure to rain during the day, if Old Penyard smokes his pipe in the morning. These appearances take place, especially in warm and sultry weather. It was very warm yesterday morning: it had thundered violently the evening before: we felt it hot even while the rain fell upon us at Butser-hill. Petersfield lies in a pretty broad and very beautiful valley. On three sides of it are very lofty hills, partly downs and partly covered with trees: and, as we proceeded on our way from the bottom of Butser-hill to Petersfield, we saw thousands upon thousands of clouds, continually coming puffing out from different parts of these hills and towering up to the top of them. I stopped George several times to make him look at them; to see them come puffing out of the chalk downs as well as out of the woodland hills; and bade him remember to tell his father of it, when he should get home, to convince him that the hills of Hampshire, could smoke their pipes, as well as those of Herefordshire. This is a really curious matter. I have never read, in any book, anything to lead me to suppose that the observation has ever found its ways into print before. Sometimes you will see only one or two clouds during a whole morning, come out of the side of a hill; but we saw thousands upon thousands, bursting out, one after another, in all parts of these immense hills. The first time that I have leisure, when I am in the high countries again, I will have a conversation with some old shepherd about this matter: if he cannot enlighten me upon the subject, I am sure that no philosopher can. . . .

Horncastle, 13th April, morning [1830]

. . . There is one deficiency, and that, with me, a great one, throughout this country of corn and grass and oxen and sheep, that I have come over, during the last three weeks; namely, the want of *singing birds*. We are now just in that season when they sing most. Here, in all this country, I have seen and heard only about four sky-larks, and not one other singing bird of any description, and, of the small birds that

163

do not sing, I have seen only one *yellow-hammer*, and it was perched on the rail of a pound between Boston and Sibsey. Oh! the thousands of linnets all singing together on one tree, in the sand-hills of Surrey! Oh! the carolling in the coppices and the dingles of Hampshire and Sussex and Kent! At this moment (5 o'clock in the morning) the groves at Barn-Elm are echoing with the warblings of thousands upon thousands of birds. The *thrush* begins a little before it is light; next the *black bird;* next the *larks* begin to rise; all the rest begin the moment the sun gives the signal; and, from the hedges, the bushes, from the middle and the topmost twigs of the trees, comes the singing of endless variety; from the long dead grass comes the sound of the sweet and soft voice of the *white-throat* or *nettle-tom*, while the loud and merry song of the *lark* (the songster himself out of sight) seems to descend from the skies. MILTON, in his description of paradise, has not omitted the "song of earliest birds." However, every thing taken together, here, in Lincolnshire, are more good things than man could have had the conscience to *ask* of God. . . .

John Clare

The Hen-harrier, by J. Wolf, from Dresser's
A History of the Birds of Europe, 1871–81

A View in the Fens, a water-color by John Linnell (1792–1882)

John Clare
[1793–1864]

C lare limned his self-portrait in two lines:

> A peasant in his daily cares,
> A poet in his joy.

The son of a barely literate cottage farmer, he was born into a class doomed to extinction by the enclosure of public lands against which Cobbett inveighed. Yet, Clare's early years, passed in the hamlet of Helpston (which he always spelled Helpstone) near Peterborough, were hardly tinged by the tragedy to come. Despite deprivation and hard labor in the fields, his boyhood was a blissful time, from memories of which he, like Wordsworth, drew unfailing consolation in after years. Such passages as the following from his uncompleted autobiography recapture that bygone felicity:

> I often pulld my hat over my eyes to watch the rising
> of the lark or to see the hawk hang in the summer sky & the
> kite take its circles round the wood I often lingered a min-
> ute on the woodland stile to hear the wood-pigeons clapping
> their wings among the dark oaks I hunted curious flowers
> in rapture & muttered thoughts in their praise I lovd the
> pasture with its rushes & thistles & sheep tracks I adored
> the wild marshy fen with its solitary hernshaw sweeing
> along in its mellancholy sky I wandered the heath in rap-
> tures among the rabbit burrows & golden blossomed furze
> I dropped down on the thymy molehill or mossy eminence
> to survey the summer landscape as full of rapture as now I
> markd the varied colors in flat spreading fields checkerd
> with closes of different tinted grain like the colors in a map
> the copper tinted colors of clover in blossom the sun-tannd
> green of the ripening hay the lighter hues of wheat & bar-
> ley intermixd with the sunny glare of the yellow carlock &

the sunset imitation of the scarlet headaches with the blue cornbottles crowding their splendid colors in large sheets over the land & troubling the cornfields with destroying beauty the different greens of the woodland trees the dark oak the paler ash the mellow lime the white poplar peeping above the rest like leafy steeples the grey willow shining chilly in the sun as if the morning mist still lingered on its cool green I felt the beauty of these with eager delight the gadflys noonday hum the fainter murmur of the beefly 'spinning in the evening ray' the dragonflys in spangled coats darting like winged arrows down the thin stream the swallow darting through its one archd brig the shepherd hiding from the thunder shower in a hollow dotterel the wild geese skudding along & making all the letters of the alphabet as they flew the motley clouds the whispering wind that muttered to the leaves & summer grasses as it flitted among them like things at play I observd all this with the same raptures as I have done since but I knew nothing of poetry it was felt & not uttered Most my sundays was spent in this manner about the fields

A copy of James Thomson's *The Seasons*, acquired when he was thirteen, released the poetic impulse in Clare. His first volume, appropriately entitled *Poems Descriptive of Rural Life and Scenery*, by John Clare, A Northamptonshire Peasant, appeared in 1820. It met with spectacular success, passing through four editions within a year; but the editor's Introduction, while well-intentioned, did ultimate disservice, since it enlisted sympathy less for the poems judged on their own merits than for the situation of the poet, "the least favoured by circumstances, and the most destitute of friends, of any that ever existed." So promoted, Clare's fame was a nine-days' wonder. A second collection, *The Village Minstrel* (1821), sold less well; and the two ensuing volumes, *The Shepherd's Calendar* (1827) and *The Rural Muse* (1835), were stillborn, despite their higher artistry. During these years Clare was at no time so free from financial worries that he could avoid seeking agricultural employment to help support his wife and the seven children who arrived at regular

168

intervals. A variety of other factors contributed to the mental distress under which his sanity eventually gave way: increasing ill-health, nagging negotiations with publishers who were slow to print and slower to pay for his verses, despondency over moving from his beloved Helpston. In 1837 he was placed under the humane care of Dr. Matthew Allen at High Beech, Epping. From this institution he escaped in 1841, only to be committed after five months of freedom to the Northampton General Lunatic Asylum, where he passed the remainder of his life.

Clare's spirit never submitted to the body's captivity, and some of his finest lyrics came out of the bleak years of confinement for madness. "I wrote," he once said, "because it pleased me in sorrow, and when happy it makes me happier; and so I go on. . . . I pursued pleasure in many paths and never found her so happily as when I sang imaginary songs to the woodland solitudes and winds of autumn." Clare's poetry is the product of an intuitive identification with nature, yielding that "spontaneous overflow of powerful feelings" of which Wordsworth spoke. In an asylum letter of 1848, addressed to his son, he recalled: "in my boyhood Solitude was the most talkative vision I met with Birds bees trees flowers all talked to me incessantly louder than the busy hum of men. . . ." Of natural descriptions he made a vehicle for personal emotion which in later years intensified to the visionary ardor of Blake's poems or of Samuel Palmer's drawings in that artist's Shoreham period. Communion with the vital beauty encountered everywhere in his lonely walks conferred "the dower of self-creating joy" through which he was able triumphantly to surmount the bitterness of his lot:

> *I live in love, sun of undying light,*
> *And fathom my own heart for ways of good . . .*

Clare, who never learned to spell or punctuate, left little prose, most of it unpublished during his lifetime. In 1824–25 he drafted a number of letters to his publisher, James Augustus Hessey, for a projected *Natural History of Helpstone* in imitation of White's work. These "Biographys of Birds & Flowers" provide supplementary evidence of the author's extraordinary intimacy with the flora and fauna of his native region. (One botanist counted references to more than 120 plants in Clare's poetry, of which at least forty-two were for the first time identified as Northamptonshire species.) More arresting than the range and accuracy of his knowledge, however, is the prevailing tone of tender sympathy which characterizes the natural observations of this shy and gentle recluse.

From *Natural History Letters*

I ALWAYS think that this month the prophet of spring brings
many beautys to the landscape tho a carless observer woud
laugh at me for saying so who believes that it brings nothing
because he does not give himself the trouble to seek them—I
always admire the kindling freshness that the bark of the
different sorts of trees & underwood asume in the forest—
the foulroyce twigs kindle into a vivid color at their tops as
red as woodpiegons claws the ash with its grey bark & black
swelling buds the Birch with it 'paper rind' & the darker
mottled sorts of hazle & black alder with the greener hues of
sallow willows & the bramble that still wears its leaves with
the privet of a purple hue while the straggling wood briar
shines in a brighter & more beautiful green even then leaves
can boast at this season too odd forward branches in the new
laid hedges of whitethorn begin to freshen into green before
the arum dare peep out of its hood or the primrose & violet
shoot up a new leaf thro the warm moss & ivy that shelters
their spring dwellings the furze too on the common wear
a fairer green & ere & there an odd branch is coverd with
golden flowers & the ling or heath nestling among the long
grass below (coverd with the witherd flowers of last year)
is sprouting up into fresh hopes of spring the fairey rings
on the pastures are getting deeper dyes & the water weeds
with long silver green blades of grass are mantling the
stagnant ponds in their summer liverys I find more beautys in
this month then I can find room to talk about in a letter . . .

171

March 6

The little Robin has begun his summer song in good
earnest he was singing at my chamber window this morning
almost before daylight as he has done all this week & at
nightfall he comes regularly to his old plumb tree & starts
again—there is a plaintive sweetness in the song of this bird
that I am very fond of it may be calld an eternal song for it is
heard at intervals all the year round & in the Autumn when
the leaves are all fled from the trees there is a mellancholy
sweetness in it that is very touching to my feelings—the
Robin is one of the most familiar birds that a village land-
scape posseses & it is no less beloved for even children leave
its nest unmolested but the Wren & the Martin are held in the
like veneration with a many people who will not suffer their
nests to be destroyed—the Robin seems to be fond of the
company & haunts of men it builds its nest close to his cottage
in the hovel or outhouse thatch or behind the woodbine or
sweetbriar in the garden wall nor does it seem to make any
secret of its dwelling were its only enemy is the cat to whom
its confidence of saftey often falls a prey—& it seeks its food
by his door on the dunghill or on the garden beds nay it will
even settle on the gardeners spade while he is at work to
watch the worm that he throws up & unbares & in winter it
will venture into the house for food & become as tame as a
chicken—we had one that usd to come in at a broken pane in
the window three winters together I always knew it to be our
old visitor by a white scar on one of the wings it grew so tame
that it woud perch on ones finger & take the crumbs out of the
hand it was very much startld at the cat at first but after a
time it took little notice of her further than always contriving
to keep out of her way—it woud never stay in the house at
night tho it would attempt to perch on the chair spindles &

clean its bill & ruffle its feathers & put its head under its wing as if it had made up its mind to stay but somthing or other always molested it when it suddenly sought its old broken pane & departed when it was sure to be the first riser in the morning

What I observed most remarkable in its manner was that it never attempted to sing all the time it visited us what became of it at last I never knew but I suppose some cat destroyd it—it has been a common notion among heedless observers that the robin frequents nowhere but in villages but this is an erroneous one for it is found in the deepest solitudes of woods & forrests were it lives on insects & builds its nest on the roots or stools of the underwood or under a hanging bank by a dyke side which is often mistook for that of the nightingales. I have often observed its fondness for man even here for in summer I scarcely cross a wood but a Robin suddenly falls in my path to court my acquaintance & pay me a visit were it hops & flutters about as if pleasd to see me & in winter it is the woodman's companion for the whole day & the whole season who considers it as his neighbour & friend

It is not commonly known that the robin is a very quarrelsome bird it is not only at frequent warfare with its own species but attacks boldly every other small bird that comes in its way & is generally the conqueror I have seen it chase the house sparrow which tho a very pert bird never ventures to fight it hedgesparrows linnets & finches that crowd the barn doors in winter never stand against its authority but flye from its interferances & acknowledge it the cock of the walk & he always seems to consider the right of the yard is his own

The Wren is another of these domestic birds that has found favour in the affections of man the hardiest gunner will rarely attempt to shoot either of them & tho it loves to haunt the same places as the Robin it is not so tame & never ventures to seek the protection of man in the hardest winter blasts it finds its food in stackyards & builds its nest mostly in

173

the roof of hovels & under the eaves of sheds about the habitations of man tho it is often found in the cowshed in closes & sometimes aside the roots of underwood in the woods its nest is made of green moss & lind with feathers the entrance is a little hole in the side like a corkhole in a barrel it lays as many as 15 or 16 white eggs very small & faintly spotted with pink spots it is a pert bird among its fellows & always seems in a conceited sort of happiness with its tail strunted up oer its back & its wings dropping down—its song is more loud than the Robins & very pleasant tho it is utterd in broken raptures by sudden starts & sudden endings it begins to sing in March & continues till the end of Spring when it becomes moping & silent

The hedge Sparrow may be called one of these domestic birds for it is fond of frequenting gardens & homesteads near villages it is a harmless peaceable bird & not easily alarmed at the approach of man its song is low & trifling it builds its nest early in the Spring in hedges & close bushes green about gardens of moss lined with fine wool & cowhair it lays 5 eggs of a very fine blue nay it may be calld a green blue they are clear without spots it feeds on insects & small seeds & is frequently robd of its eggs by the cuckoo who leaves one of her own in its stead which the hedgesparrow hatches & brings up with an unconscious fondness & if she lays any more eggs of her own after the cuckoo has deposited hers it is said that the young cuckoo has the instinct to thrust the young sparrows out of the nest to occupy it himself wether this be true or not I cannot say for I never witnessd it tho I have found a young cuckoo in the hedgesparrows nest & in the wagtails also but in no other birds beside these two seem to be the selected foster parents of its young The hedgesparrow is very early at building its nest I found one last year in a box tree with three eggs on the 3rd of February the birds had built in the same bush 3 years together—a sharp blast happend when the young was just hatchd & perishd them & she brought off another brood in the same nest

Helpstone [n.d.]

I forgot to say in my last that the Nightingale sung as
common by day as night & as often tho its a fact that is not
generaly known your Londoners are very fond of talking
about the bird & I believe fancy every bird they hear after
sunset a Nightingale I remember while I was there last while
walking with a friend in the fields of Shacklwell we saw a
gentleman & lady listening very attentive by the side of a
shrubbery & when we came up we heard them lavishing
praises on the beautiful song of the nightingale which hap-
pend to be a thrush but it did for them & they listend &
repeated their praise with heartfelt satisfaction while the bird
seemed to know the grand distinction that its song had gaind
for it & strove exultingly to keep up the deception by attempt-
ing a varied & more louder song the dews was ready to fall
but the lady was heedless of the wet grass tho the setting sun
as a traveller glad to rest was leaning his enlarged rim on the
earth like a table of fire & lessening by degrees out of sight
leaving night & a few gilt clouds behind him such is the
ignorance of Nature in large Citys that are nothing less than
overgrown prisons that shut out the world and all its
beautys
The nightingale as I said before is a shoy bird if any one
approaches too near her secret haunts its song ceases till they
pass when it is resumd as loud as before but I must repeat
your quotation from Chaucer to illustrate this

The new abashèd nightingale
That stinteth first when she beginneth sing
When that she heareth any herde's tale
Or in the hedges any [wight] stirring
& after siker doth her voice outring

As soon as they have young their song ceases & is heard no
more till the returning may after they cease singing they

175

make a sort of gurring guttural noise as if calling the young to their food I know not what its for else but they make this noise continually & doubtless before the young leave the nest I have said all I can say about the Nightingale—In a thicket of blackthorns near our village called 'bushy close' we have great numbers of them every year but not so many as we used to have like the Martins & Swallows & other birds of passage they seem to diminish but for what cause I know not

As to the cuckoo I can give you no further tidings that what I have given in my last Artis has one in his collection of stuffed birds (but I have not sufficient scientific curiosity about me to go & take the exact description of its head rump & wings the length of its tail & the breadth from the tips of the extended wings these old bookish descriptions you may find in any natural history if they are of any gratification

for my part I love to look on nature with a poetic feeling which magnifys the pleasure I love to see the nightingale in its hazel retreat & the cuckoo hiding in its solitudes of oaken foliage & not to examine their carcasses in glass cases yet naturalists & botanists seem to have no taste for this practical feeling they merely make collections of dryd specimens class-ing them after Linnaeus into tribes & familys & there they delight to show them as a sort of ambitious fame with them 'a bird in the hand is worth two in the bush' well everyone to his hobby

I have none of this curiosity about me tho I feel as happy as they can about finding a new species of field flower or but-terflye which I have not seen before yet I have no desire further to dry the plant or torture the butterflye by sticking it on a cork board with a pin—I have no wish to do this if my feelings woud let me I only crop the blossom of the flower or take the root from its solitudes if it woud grace my garden & wish the fluttering butterflye to settle till I can come up with it to examine the powderd colours on its wings & then it may dance off again from fancyd dangers & welcome) I think your feelings are on the side of Poetry for I have no

176

specimens to send you so be as it may you must be content with my descriptions & observations I always feel delighted when an object in nature brings up in ones mind an image of poetry that describes it from some favourite author you have a better opportunity of consulting books than I have therefore I will set down a list of favourite Poems & Poets who went to nature for their images so that you may consult them & share the feelings & pleasures which I describe—your favourite Chaucer is one Passages in Spenser Cowley's grasshopper & Swallow Passages in Shakespear Milton's Allegro & Penseroso & Parts of Comus the Elizabethan Poets of glorious memory Gay's Shepherds Week Green's Spleen Thomson's Seasons Collins Ode to Evening Dyer's Grongar Hill & Fleece Shenstone's Schoolmistress Gray's Ode to Spring T. Warton's April Summer Hamlet & Ode to a friend Cowper's Task Wordsworth Logans Ode to the Cuckoo Langhorne's Fables of Flora Jago's Blackbirds Bloomfield Witchwood Forest Shooters hill &c with Hurdis's Evening Walk in the village Curate & many others that may have slipped my memory

it might seem impertinent in me to advise you what to read if you misunderstood my meaning for I dont only do it for your pleasure but I wish you to make extracts from your readings in your letters to me so that I may feel some of my old gratifications agen—a clown may say that he loves the morning but a man of taste feels it in a higher degree by bringing up in his mind that beautiful line of Thomsons 'The meek eyd morn appears mother of dews' The rustic sings beneath the evening moon but it brings no associations he knowns nothing about Miltons description of it 'Now comes still evening on & twilight grey hath in her sober livery all things clad' nor of Collins Ode to Evening

the man of taste looks on the little Celandine in Spring & mutters in his mind some favourite lines from Wordsworths address to that flower he never sees the daisy without thinking of Burns & who sees the taller buttercup carpeting the

177

closes in golden fringe without a remembrance of Chatter-
ton's beautiful mention of it if he knows it 'The kingcup
brasted with the morning dew' other flowers crowd my imag-
ination with their poetic assosiations but I have no room for
them the clown knows nothing of these pleasures he knows
they are flowers & just turns an eye on them & plods bye
therefore as I said before to look on nature with a poetic eye
magnifies the pleasure she herself being the very essence &
soul of Poesy if I had the means to consult & the health to
indulge it I should crowd these letters on Natural History
with lucious scraps of Poesy from my favourite Minstrels &
make them less barren of amusement & more profitable of
perusal In my catalogue of poets I forgot Charlotte Smith
whose poetry is full of pleasing images from nature—Does
Mr. Whites account of the Cuckoo & Nightingale agree with
mine look & tell me in your next

P.S. I can scarcely believe the account which you mention
at the end of your letter respecting the mans 'puzzling him-
self with doubts about the Nightingales singing by day &
about the expression of his notes whether they are grave or
gay'—you may well exclaim 'what solemn trifling' it betrays
such ignorance that I can scarcely believe it—if the man does
but go into any village solitude a few miles from London next
may their varied music will soon put away his doubts of its
singing by day—nay he may get rid of them now by asking
any country clown the question for its such a common fact
that all know of it—& as to the 'expression of its notes' if he
has any knowledge of nature let him ask himself whether
Nature is in the habit of making such happy seeming songs
for sorrow as that of the Nightingales—the poets indulgd in
fancys but they did not wish that those matter of fact men
the Naturalists shoud take them for facts upon their
credit—What absurditys for a world that is said to get wiser
and wiser every day—

178

Feb 7 [1825]

You ask me wether I have resumed my botanizing & naturalizing excursions & you will laugh at my comencement for I have been seriously & busily employd this last 3 weeks hunting Pooty shells & if you are not above them I must get you to assist me in the arangement or classification of them I have been making some drawings of them but they are so miserable that I must send the shells with them

There is a pleasing association attachd to these things they remind me & I think every one of happy hours who has not been a gatherer of them in his schoolboy days—how anxious I usd to creep among the black thorn thickets & down the hedge sides on my hands & knees seeking them as soon as the sun lookd warm on the hedges & banks & wakend the daisey to open its golden eye & the arum to throw up its fine green leaves I cannot forget such times as these we usd to gather them to string on thread as birds eggs are strung & sometimes to play with them at what we calld 'cock fighting' by pressing the knibbs hard against each other till one broke—I think there is one shell peculiar to our neighbourhood & almost to one spot in it it is a large one of a yellow green color with a black rim round the base there is another yellow one very common which we calld when boys 'painted Ladys' but the one I imagine as a scarce one is very different from this—they are found in low places by brook sides the snail is of a blackish yellow & appears to feed on a species of brooklime—there is another not very common I have stiled it the yellow one banded the others are common the red one banded the red self & the red many banded & small many banded with a mottld sort calld badgers by schoolboys—there is many others but they all seem variations of the same kinds the large mozzld garden snail is well known but I found many of them in a spot where it woud puzzle reason to know how they got there

179

A person had been digging a dyke in the old roman bank by the side of a fence & in some places it was 6 feet deep & in the deepest places I found the most shells most of them of the large garden kind which had been clarsified as it were in the sandy soil in which they were bedded I suppose them to have lain ever since the road was made & if that is so what a pigmy it makes of the pride of man Those centurions of their thousands & 10 thousands that commanded those soldiers to make these roads little thought that the house of a poor simple snail horn woud outlive them & their proudest temples by centurys it is almost a laughable gravity to reflect so profoundly over a snail horn but every trifle owns the triumph of a lesson to humble the pride of man—every trifle also has a lesson to bespeak the wisdom & forethought of the Deity I was struck to-day with a new Discovery I stood looking over the wall of a bridge at the brook rippling beneath me & observd a large shell & on examining it I found it a sort of fresh water Periwinkle of which there are several varietys in our brooks but none that has the peculiar construction that this one has which is a sort of Lid that it opens & shuts at pleasure that fits as close as the lid of a snuff box & keeps out the water when ever it chuses to be weary of [ ] or wants to be dry in its boat its joint as it were attached & sticks under the chin & is of no more inconvenience than a mans beard when it is open it serves the double purpose of clogs or shoes to keep the sharp gravelly bottom of the brooks from hurting its tender flesh which it might easily do if it were not thus guarded

The instinct of the snail is very remarkable & worthy notice tho such things are lookd over with a carless eye—it has such a knowledge of its own speed that it can get home to a moment to be safe from the sun as a moment too late woud be its death—as soon as the sun has lost its power to hurt in the evening it leaves its hiding place in search of food which it is generally aware were to find if it is a good way off it makes no stoppages in the road but appears to be in great haste & when it has divided its time to the utmost by travel-

Snail-shells, by William Daniell, 1809

ling to such a length as will occupy all the rest of its spare
time to return its instinct will suddenly stop & feed on what it
finds there & if it finds nothing it will go no further but return
homewards & feed on what it chances to meet with & if after
it gets home the sun shoud chance to be under a cloud it will
potter about its door way to seek food but it goes no further &
is ready to hide when the sun looks out—when they find any
food which suits them they will feed on it till it lasts & travel
to this same spot as accurately as if they knew geography or
was guided by a mariners compass—the power of instinct in
the most trifling insect is very remarkable & displays the
omnipotence of its maker in an illustrious manner nature is a
fine preacher & her sermons are always worth atten-
tion . . .

March 25th 1825

I took a walk to-day to botanize & found that the spring had
taken up her dwelling in good earnest she has covered the
woods with the white anemone which the children call Lady
smocks & the harebells are just venturing to unfold their blue
drooping bells the green is coverd with daiseys & the little
Celandine the hedge bottoms are crowded with the green
leaves of the arum were the boy is peeping for pootys with
eager anticipations & delight—the sallows are cloathed in
their golden palms were the bees are singing a busy welcome
to spring they seem uncommonly fond of these flowers &
gather round them in swarms—I have often wonderd how
these little travellers found their way home agen from the
woods & solitudes were they journey for wax & honey I have
seen them to-day at least 3 miles from any village in Langley
wood working at the palms & some of them with their little
thighs so loaded with the yellow dust as to seem almost
unable to flye it is curious to see how they collect their load
they keep wiping their legs over their faces to gather the dust

that settles there after creeping in the flowers till they have got a sufficient load & then they flye homewards to their hives—I have heard that a man curious to know how far his bees travelld in a summers day got up early one morning & stood by one of the hives to powder them as they came out with fine flour to know them agen & in the course of an hour afterwards he observd some of them at the extremity of the Lordship & having to go to the market that day he passd by a turnip field in full flower about 5 miles from home & to his supprise he found some of his own in their white powdered coats busily humming at their labour with the rest—the Ivy berrys too are quite ripe & the wood pigeons are busily fluskering among the Ivied dotterels on the skirts of the common they are very fond of them—& a little nameless bird with a black head & olive green back & wings—not known—it seems to peck the Ivy berries for its food & I have remarked that it comes as soon as they are ripe to the Ivy trees & dissapears from them when they are gone—I fancy it is one of the tribe of the Titmice & I have often found a nest clinging by the side of trees among the Ivy which I think belongs to it I know nothing further of its Life & habits—I think I had the good luck to-day to hear the bird which you spoke of last march as singing early in spring & which you so appropriatly named the mock nightingale for some of its notes are exactly similar I heard it singing in 'Open Wood' & was startled at first to think it was the nightingale & tryd to creep into the thicket to see if I coud discover what bird it was but it seemd to be very shoy & got farther from me as I approachd till I gave up the pursuit—I askd some woodmen who were planting underwood at the time wether they knew the bird & its song seemed to be very familiar to them they said it always came with the first fine days of spring & assured me it was the wood chat but they coud not agree with each others opinion for another believd it to be the large black cap or black headed Titmouse so I coud get nothing for fact but I shall keep a sharp lookout when I hear it

183

again—you have often wished for a blue Anemonie the Ane-
monie pulsatilla of botanists & I can now send you some for I
have found some in flower to-day which is very early but it is
a very early spring the heathen mythology is fond of indulg-
ing in the metamorphing of the memory of lovers & heroes
into the births of flowers & I coud almost fancy that this blue
Anemonie sprang from the blood or dust of the romans for it
haunts the roman bank in this neighbourhood & is found no
were else it grows on the roman bank agen Swordy well & did
grow in great plenty but the plough that destroyer of wild
flowers has rooted it out of its long inherited dwelling it
grows also on the roman bank agen Burghley Park in Bar-
nack Lordship it is a very fine flower & is easily cultivated by
transporting some of its own soil with it a heathy sandy soil
seems to suit it best—you enquired last summer wether we
had any plants indegenous to our neighbourhood I think we
have some but I dont know much of the new christning
system of modern botany that has such a host of alphabetical
arrangements as woud fill a book to describe the Flora of a
Village like the types of the Chinese characters that fill a
printing house to print one book with—we have a very fine
fern of the maiden hair kind that grows large with a leaf very
like the hemlock but of a much paler green & another very
small one that grows on the old stools of sallows in damp
hollows in the woods & by the sides of brooks & rivers we
have also the thorn pointed fern of Linnaeus that grows on
one spot in a dyke by Harrisons Closes near a roman station &
the harts tongue that grows on the brinks of the badger holes
in Open wood in fact we have a many ferns there is a beauti-
ful one which a friend of mine calls the 'Lady fern' growing
among the boggy spots on Whittlesea Mere & a dwarf willow
grows there about a foot high which it never exceeds it is also
a place very common for the cranberry that trails by the
brink of the mere there are several water weeds too with very
beautiful or peculiar flowers that have not yet been honored
with christnings from modern botany—we have a great va-

riety of Orchises among them the Bee orchis & Spider orchis are reckond the finest both of them may be found in an old deserted quarry calld Ashton stone pits—but perhaps they are more common on Whittering Heath were grows the 'Cross leaved heath' & a fine tall yellow flower of the Mullein species which the villagers call Goldilocks these are all the rare flowers that I am acquainted with & botanists will come miles to gather them which makes me fancy they are not common elsewhere I will send you some dryd specimens in their successions of flowering this season—have you never heard that croaking jarring noise in the woods at this early season I heard it to-day & went into the woods to examine what thing it was that caused the sound & I discoverd that it was the common green woodpecker busily employd at boring his holes which he effected by twisting his bill round in the way that a carpenter twists his wimble with this difference that when he has got it to a certain extent he turns it back & pecks awhile & then twists agen his beak seems to serve all the purposes of a nail paper gough & wimble effectually what endless new lessons may we learn from nature

[April 21, 1825]

. . . It has been often asserted that young frogs & fish will fall from the clouds in storms & it has often [been] wrongly asserted when the phenomena has sprung from natural causes—I have seen thousands of young frogs crossing a common after a shower but I found that they had left their hiding places & pursued their journeys after the shower began early in the morning early risers may see swarms of young frogs leaving their birth places & emigrating as fast as they can hop to new colonys & as soon as the sun gets strong they hide in the grass as well as they are able to wait the approach of night to be able to start again but if in the course of the day showers happen to fall they instantly seize the chance & proceed on their journey till the sun looks out &

185

puts a stop to their travelling again as to young fish I always found them in holes that were very near neighbours to brooks & had held communications (tho not then) with them in wet weather when dykes were full—it has been asserted that eels fall with rain in ponds it has been so asserted because they did not know how to account for it any other way—once when I was a young man on staying late at a feast I cross[ed] a meadow about midnight & saw to my supprise quantitys of small nimble things emigrating across it a long way from any water I thought at first they were snakes but I found on a closer observation they were young eels making for a large pond called the pool with as much knowledge as if they were acquainted with the way I thought this a wonderful discovery then but I have since observd the same thing in larger eels going from one pond to another in the day time & I caught two very large ones in the act of emigrating

Blackbirds & Thrushes particularly the former feed in hard winters upon the shell snailhorns by hunting them from the hedge bottoms & wood stulps & taking them to a stone where they brake them in a very dexterous manner—any curious observer of nature may see in hard frosts the shells of pootys thickly litterd round a stone in the lanes & if he waits a short time he will quickly see one of these birds coming with a snailhorn in his bill which he constantly taps on the stone till it is broken he then extracts the snail & like a true sportsman eagerly hastens to hunt them again in the hedges or woods where a frequent rustle of their little feet is heard among the dead leaves

A golden Plovers nest was found on Southorp heath or at least the young plovers for they make no nest—& they were taken to a clergyman at Barnack who ascertained what they were

When Woodpeckers are making or boring their holes in the spring they are so attentive over their labours that they are easily caught by boys who watch them when they are half-hid in the holes they are making & climbing softly up the

186

tree make them prisoners—a nest thus left unfinished is
never resumed by another—the male makes the holes gener-
ally & when finished sets up a continued cry to invite a
companion that seldom fails to join him in seeking materials
for lining the nest—the pied woodpecker never bores holes in
the body of the tree but in the larger grains very high up &
always on the underneath side so that they are inaccessible to
nest hunting boys—it is easy to see where the tribe are
making new nests by the litter they make at the foot of the
tree as if it were sawdust

There are two sorts of the hedge roses or hip brambles
easily distinguished one has a greyish green rough hairy leaf
this is not common it grows in a hedge on the south west
corner of Ailsworth heath

The other has a glossy green leaf without hairs & is com-
mon on every old hedge

When the young of the Nightingale leave the nest the old
ones bring them out of the woods into old hedgerows & bushy
borders about the fields—where they seem to be continually
hunting along the roots & hedge bottoms for food Their
hants here are easily known from the plaintive noise of 'toot
toot' that the old ones are constantly making at passers bye
where the path running by a hedge side make such intrusions
frequent the firetail & the Robin make a similar noise—the
Nightingale often makes another noise of 'Chur chur' which
on hearing I have seen the young one instantly hopping down
from the hedge into the bottom of the dyke & when she made
the noise of 'toot toot' they would in a moment be all as still as
if nothing was there but the old one

I always took the 'chur chur' as a food call & the tooting
noise as a token of alarm

I have often been amused with the manners & habits of
Insects but I am not acquainted with entomology to know the
names they go bye—when I was following my avocations of
husbandry last summer at weeding in a beanfield while sit-
ting at dinner I observed one of those small green nimble

187

beetles repeatingly running up to some object & then retreat-
ing again at last my curiosity urged me to examine what he
coud be at when I found that he was attacking a large moth &
when ever the moth made a trial to escape (which it coud not
do for the weeds) & struggled it retreated back & as soon as it
was still it returnd to the attack again at length the moth
became quite exausted & the beetle with the utmost dexterity
began to bite off his wings & whenever the moth made faint
struggles instantly fell to wounding him agen in the body as
if he had not sufficiently disabled him then he returned to the
wings which he soon got off & as soon as he accomplished it
he paused a while by the body as if on the watch wether his
object needed any further butchering to dispatch him & on
finding him lying quite still he then took a wide circuit all
round the body as if like a murderer he was afraid of being
seen & taken—then he nimbled off somwere as if he had
accomplished his object going about his business & I won-
derd what his object coud be in killing the moth & then
leaving him but before I had much time for reflection the
beetle again made his appearance with a companion they
went round the moth without attempting to seize it & seemd
in a consulting posture for some seconds when both of them
started agen in contrary directions & bye & bye both returned
each leading in his tracks a companion & then one of them
instantly started agen while the other three took a circuit
round the moth presently the beetle that went out returned
with two more companions & the company making 6 in all
when they came up instantly began as if the whole family was
now got together to make their dinner on the moth they first
turnd him over on his back & fed on his body 3 on each side &
when satisfied they all joined help in hand & dragd the
remainder of their prey home to a little hole between the
furrows & dissapeard—I was much astonished at the time &
made up my mind that Insects have a language to convey
their Ideas to each other & it always appears that they posses
the faculty in a greater degree than the large animals

188

From *Nature Notes*

Hawks

HAWKS are beautiful objects when on the wing I have often stood to view a hawk in the sky trembling its wings & then hanging quite still for a moment as if it was as light as a shadow & could find like the clouds a resting place upon the blue air

There are a great many different sorts of hawks about us & several to which I am a stranger too

There is a very large blue one almost as big as a goose they fly in a swopping heavy manner not much unlike the flye of a heron you may see an odd one often in the spring swimming close to the green corn & ranging over an whole field for hours together it hunts leverets & partridges & pheasants I saw one of these which a man had wounded with a gun he had stupified it only for when he got it home it was as fierce & as live as ever the wings when extended was of a great length it was of a blue-grey color hued with deeper tinges of the same its beak was dreadfully hookd & its claws long & of a bright yellow with a yellow ring round each eye which gave a fierce & very severe look at the sight of a cat it put itself in a posture for striking as if it meant to seize it as prey but at a dog it seemd rather scared & sat on its tail end in a defensive posture with its eyes extended & its talons open making at the same time an earpiercing hissing noise which dismayd the dog who woud drop his tail & sneak out as if in fear they tyd a piece of tarmarking & tetherd it in a barn were they kept it 3 or 4 days when it gnawed the string from its leg & effected its liberty by getting thro the barnholes in the wall it ate nothing all that time they offerd it carrion but it woud take no notice of it what its name is I know not they call it the blue hawk

There is a small blue hawk often mistaken for the cuckoo I know nothing of it further then seeing it often on the wing & a rare one about the size of a blackbird of a mottld color & with a white patch of feathers on the back of the head one of these sort was shot here in the summer by a field keeper I have never seen anything like it before

Last year I had two tame hawks of what species I cannot tell they were not quite so large as the sparrow hawk their wings & back feathers was of a red brown color sheathd wi black their tails was long & barrd with black & their breasts was of a lighter color & spotted their eyes was large & of a dark piercing blue their beaks was very much hookd with a sharp projecting swell in the top mandible not unlike the swell in the middle of the hookd bill usd by hedgers & called by them a tomahawk This made an incision like a knife in tearing its food the bottom mandible was curiously shortend as it were for the hook to lap over & seemd as tho nature had clippd the end off with scissors for that purpose their legs was short & yellow with a tuft of feathers over each thigh like the bantam fowl a property belonging to most of the hawk tribe They grew very tame & woud come at a call or whistle when they were hungry They made a strange noise that piercd the ear with its shrillness they was very fond of wash- ing themselves often doing it twice a day in winter after being fed they woud play in the garden running after each other & seizing bits of clods or fallen apples in their claws or catching at flies when they rested they usd always to perch on one leg with the other drawn up among their feathers they always lovd to perch on the topmost twig of the trees in the garden were they woud sit in a bold & commanding attitude one was much larger than the other & the large one was much the tamest When I went awalking in the fields it woud attempt to flye after me & as I was fearful of losing it I usd to drive it back but one day it took advantage of watching & following me & when I got into the fields I was astonishd & startld to see a hawk settle on my shoulder it was mine who had watchd me out of the town & took a short cut to flye after me I thought it woud flye away for good so I attempted to catch it but it woud not be made a prisoner & flew to the trees by the road side I gave it up for lost but as soon as I got out of sight it set up a noise & flew after me agen & when I got upon the heath were there· were no trees it woud settle upon the ground before me & if I attempted to catch it it woud run & hide in the rabbit burrows & when I left it took wing & flew after me & so it kept on to the other end of my journey when it found home as soon as I did after this I took no more heed of losing them tho they woud be missing for days together a boy caught one by suprise & hurt it so that it dyd & the tamest dyd while I was absent from home 4 days it refusd food & hunted for me every morning & came to sit in my empty chair as it woud do till I got up They thought it fretted itself to death in my absence but I think the meat I gave was too strong for it & I believd it was not well a good while before I left it I felt heartily sorry for my poor faithful affectionate hawk

On Ants

It has been a commonly believd notion among such naturalists that trusts to books & repeats the old error that ants hurd up & feed on the curnels of grain such as wheat & barley but every common observer knows this to be a falsehood I have noticd them minutely & often & never saw one with such food in its mouth they feed on flyes & caterpillars which I have often seen them tugging home with & for which they climb trees & the stems of flowers—when they first appear in the spring they may be seen carrying out ants in their mouths of a smaller size which they will continue to do a long time transporting them away from home perhaps to form new colonys—they always make a track & keep it & will go for furlongs away from their homes fetching bits of bents & others lugging away with flyes or green maggots which they pick off of flowers & leaves some when overloaded are joind by others till they get a sufficient quantity to master it home—I have often minded that two while passing each other woud pause like old friends longparted see & as if they suddenly reccolected each other they went & put their heads together as if they shook hands or saluted each other when a shower comes on an unusual bustle ensues round their nest some set out & suddenly turn round again without fetching anything home others will hasten to help those that are loaded & when the rain begins to fall the others will leave their loads & make the best of their way as fast as they can their general employment is the gathering of bents &c to cover their habitation which they generally make round an old root which they cut into holes like an honeycomb these holes lead & communicate into each other for a long way in the ground in winter they lye dormant but quickly revive if exposd to the sun there is nothing to be seen of food in their habitations then I have observd stragglers that crawl about the grass seemingly without a purpose & if they accidentally fall into the track of those at labour that quickens their pace & sudden retreat I have fancied these to be the idle & discontented sort of radicals to the government

The smaller ants calld pismires seem to be under a different sort of government at least there is not that regularity observd among them in their labours as there is among the large ones they do not keep one track as the others do but creep about the grass were they please they are uncommonly fond of bread (which the larger ants will not touch) & when the shepherd litters his crumble from his dinner bag on their hill as he often will to observe them it instantly creates a great bustle among the little colony & they hasten away with

192

it as fast as they can till every morsel is cleand up when they
pause about as if looking for more—it is commonly believd
by carless observers that every hillock on greens & commons
has been first rooted up & afterwards occupied by these little
tenants but on the contrary most of the hills they occupy are
formed by themselves which they increase every year by
bringing up a portion of mold on the surface finely powdered
on which they lay their eggs to receive the warmth of the sun
& the shepherd by observing their wisdom in this labour
judges correctly of the changes of the weather in fact he finds
it an infallible almanack when fine weather sets in their eggs
are brought nearly to the top of the new addition to their hill
& as soon as ever a change is about to take place nay at the
approach of a shower they are observd carrying them deeper
down to safer situations & if much wet is coming they en-
tirely disappear with them into the bottom of the castle were
no rain can reach them for they generally use a composition of
clay in making the hills that forces off the wet & keeps it from
penetrating into their cells if the crown of one of the hills be
taken off with a spade it will appear pierced with holes like a
honeycomb—these little things are armd with stings that
blister & torture the skin with a pain worse than the keen
nettle There is a smaller sort still of a deep black color that
like the large ones have no sting I once when sitting at my
dinner hour in the fields seeing a colony of the red pismires
near one of these black ones tryd the experiment to see wether
they woud associate with each other & as soon as I put a black
one among them they began to fight with the latter after
wounding his antagonist (seeming to be of inferior strength)
curld up & dyd at his feet I then put a red one to the colony of
the blacks which they instantly seized & tho he generaly con-
trivd to escape he appeard to be terribly wounded & no doubt
was a cripple for life—these little creatures will raise a large
tower of earth as thick as a mans arm in the form of a sugar
loaf to a foot or a foot & a half high in the grain & long grass
for in such places they cannot meet the sun on the ground so

193

they raise these towers on the top of which they lay their eggs
& as the grass or grain keeps growing they keep raising their
towers till I have met with them as tall as ones knee

Sparrows

3 SORTS The common house Sparrow The Hedge Sparrow &
Reed Sparrow often calld the fen sparrow The common spar-
row is well known but not so much in a domesticated state as
few people think it worth while bringing up a sparrow When
I was a boy I kept a tamed cock sparrow 3 years it was so
tame that it would come when calld & flew where it pleasd
when I first had the sparrow I was fearful of the cat killing it
so I usd to hold the bird in my hand toward her & when she
attempted to smell of it I beat her she at last woud take no
notice of it & I venturd to let it loose in the house they were
both very shoy at each other at first & when the sparrow
venturd to chirp the cat woud brighten up as if she intended
to seize it but she went no further than a look or smell at
length she had kittens & when they were taken away she
grew so fond of the sparrow as to attempt to caress it the
sparrow was startld at first but came to by degrees & venturd
so far at last [as] to perch upon her back puss would call for it
when out of sight like a kitten & woud lay mice before it the
same as she woud for her own young & they always livd in
harmony so much the sparrow woud often take away bits of
bread from under the cat's nose & even put itself in a posture
of resistance when offended as if it reckoned her no more than
one of its kind In winter when we coud not bear the door open
to let the sparrow come out & in I was alowd to take a pane
out of the window but in the spring of the third year my poor
tom Sparrow for that was the name he was calld by went out
& never returnd I went day after day calling out for tom &

eagerly eying every sparrow on the house but none answerd the name for he woud come down in a moment to the call & perch upon my hand to be fed I gave it out that some cat which it mistook for its old favourite betrayed its confidence & destroyed it

John Leonard Knapp

Plate VII.

A drawing of toadstools by John Leonard Knapp,
from his The Journal of a Naturalist

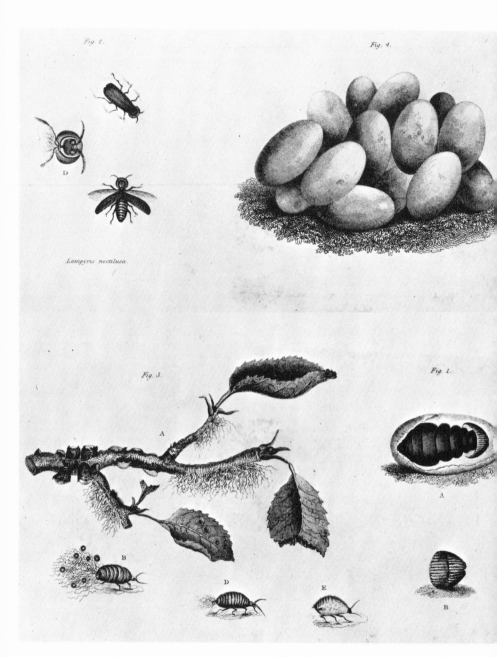

Other plates by Knapp from The Journal of a Naturalist

John Leonard Knapp

⌈1767–1845⌉

The example of Gilbert White inspired successive genera-
tions of amateur naturalists whose observations of the rural
scene constitute a neglected, but delightful category of
nineteenth-century literary activity. This body of writing had its
roots in the English system of land tenure, and, as much as the
novels of Jane Austen, was the fine flower of a social order
deriving its privileges from inherited property. The country
gentry possessed the wealth, the leisure, and the cultivation of
mind which required only the further stimulus of outdoor life to
foster an interest in scientific pursuits. John Leonard Knapp
represents this type to perfection.

Knapp was the son of the rector of Shenley in Buckingham-
shire. He served first in the navy and then in the Herefordshire
and Northamptonshire militia, achieving the rank of captain in
the latter. In 1813 he retired to Alveston near Bristol, where he
raised a large family and passed the rest of his life in unassuming
contentment. During his early years Knapp had been wont to
spend his summers in extended botanical excursions, from which
he derived the materials for his *Gramina Britannica, or Repre-
sentations of the British Grasses*, published in 1804. The work is
charmingly illustrated by the author's own delicate and minutely
accurate drawings. Two genera of grasses bearing his name bear
witness to Knapp's eminence as a botanist. Between 1820 and
1830 he contributed to *Time's Telescope* a series of articles,
entitled "The Naturalist's Diary." These descriptions of natural
phenomena encountered in daily walks about his estate in the
west of England were incorporated in *The Journal of a Natural-
ist*, which appeared anonymously in 1829 and went through
three more editions in the ensuing decade.

Knapp's model was *The Natural History of Selborne*, which,
as he wrote, "early impressed on my mind an ardent love for all

the ways and economy of nature." However, he modestly disclaimed any intent to rival White's masterpiece in unsystematically presenting his own "plain observations of nature, the produce often of intervals of leisure and shattered health, affording no history of the country; a mere outline of rural things; the journal of a traveller through the inexhaustible regions of Nature."

Despite its lack of pretension, *The Journal of a Naturalist* is rich in lore that could only have been accumulated through many years of patient and loving attention to every manifestation of animate being in one restricted locality; and Knapp imparts his findings in a manner that movingly combines poetic sensibility with natural piety. Curiosity habitually gives way to a sense of marvel at the mysterious dispensations which ensure continuity through change in the organic world. Thus, the behavior of the lowly dung-beetle provokes such characteristic reflections as the following:

Surrounded as we are by wonders of every kind, and existing only by a miraculous concurrence of events, admiration seems the natural avocation of our being; nor is it easy to pronounce, amidst such a creation, what is most wonderful. But few things appear more incomprehensible than the constant production and re-absorption of matter, impressed upon us even by these very dorrs. An animal falls to the ground and dies; myriads of creatures are now summoned by a call, by an impulse of which we have no perception, to remove it, and prepare it for a new combination; chemical agencies, fermentation, and solution, immediately commence their actions to separate the parts; and in a short time, of all this great body, nothing remains but the framework or bones, perhaps a little hair or some wool —all the rest is departed we know not whither! Worms and insects have done their parts; the earth has received a portion, and the rest, converted into gases and exhalable matters, has dispersed all over the region, which, received into vegetable circulation, is again separated and changed, becomes modified anew, and nourishes that which is to continue the future generations of life. The petal of the rose;

200

the pulp of the peach; the azure and the gold on the wing of the insect; all the various productions of the animal and vegetable world; the very salts and compounds of the soil, are but the changes some other matters have undergone, which have circulated through innumerable channels since the first production of all things, and no particle been lost . . .

From *The Journal of a Naturalist*

. . . THE ivy (*hedera helix*), the dark-looking ivy, almost covers with its thick foliage the pollards in our hedgerows; and, creeping up the sides of the old barn and chimney of the cottage, nearly hides them from our sight, affording a sheltered roosting-place to many poor birds, and is almost their only refuge in the cold season of the year. But the ivy can boast of much more extensive service to the poor wayfaring beings of creation, than the merely affording them a covering from the winds of winter. Those two extreme quarters of our year, autumn and spring, yield to most animals but a very slender and precarious supply of food; but the ivy, in those periods, saves many from want and death; and the peculiar situations, in which it prefers to flourish, are essential to the preservation of this supply, as in less sheltered ones it would be destroyed. In the month of October the ivy blooms in profusion, and, spreading over the warm side of some neglected wall, or the sunny bark of the broad ash on the bank, its flowers become a universal banquet to the insect race. The great black fly (*musca grossa*), and its numerous tribe, with multitudes of small winged creatures, resort to them; and there we see those beautiful animals, the latest birth of the year, the admiral (*vanessa atalanta*) and peacock (*vanessa Iö*) butterflies, hanging with expanded wings, like open flowers themselves, enjoying the sunny gleam, and feeding on the sweet liquor that distils from the nectary of this plant. As this honey is produced in succession by the early or later expansion of the bud, it yields a constant supply of food, till the frosts of November destroy the insects, or drive them to

202

their winter retreats. Spring arrives; and in the bitter months of March, April, and even May at times, when the wild products of the field are nearly consumed, the ivy ripens its berries, and then almost entirely constitutes the food of the missel thrush, wood-pigeon, and some other birds; and now these shy and wary birds, that commonly avoid the haunts of man, constrained by hunger, will approach our dwellings, to feed upon the ripe berries of the ivy. Now, too, the blackbird and the thrush resort to its cover, to conceal their nests. These early-building birds find little foliage at this period sufficient to hide their habitations; and did not the ivy lend its aid to preserve them, and no great number are preserved, perhaps few nests would be hidden from the young eyes that seek them. The early expansion of the catkins of the sallow (*salix caprea*), and others of the willow tribe, whence the bee extracts its first food, and the late blooming of this ivy, are indispensable provisions for the existence of many of the insect race; the "young raven does not cry in vain," nor is any thing abandoned by that Power which called it into being.

We all seem to love the ivy—

The wanton ivy, wreath'd in amorous twines,

more than any other uncultured evergreen that we possess; yet it is difficult satisfactorily to answer why we have this regard for it. As a lover of the lone, the ivy-mantled ruin, I have often questioned with myself the cause and basis of my regard for that which was but a fragment of what might have been formerly splendid, and intrinsically possessed but little to engage admiration, yet, wreathed in the verdure of the ivy, was admired; but was never satisfied, perhaps unwilling to admit the answer that my mind seemed to give. The ivy is a dependant plant, and delights in waste and ruin. We do not often tolerate its growth when the building is in repair and perfect; but if time dilapidate the edifice, the ivy takes possession of the fragment, and we call it beautiful; it adorns the castle, but is an indispensable requisite to the remains of the monastic pile. There is an abbey in the north of England, which has been venerated by all its late possessors. It is trimmed, made neat, and looks, perhaps, much as it did formerly, except being in ruins. The situation is exquisite, the remains are splendid, yet with many it fails to excite such interest as it should do. It is a bare reality. A ruin in the west of England once interested me greatly. The design of revisiting and drawing it was expressed at the time. A few days only elapsed, but the inhabitant of a neighbouring cottage had most kindly laboured hard in the interval, and pulled down "all the nasty ivy, that the gentleman might see the ruin." He did see it, but every charm had departed. These two instances, from many that might be advanced, manifest that ivy most frequently gives to these ancient edifices the idea of beauty, and contributes chiefly to influence our feelings when viewing them. The ruins of a fortress, or warlike tower, may often historically interest us, from the renown of its founder or its possessor, some scene transacted, some villain punished, hero triumphant, or cause promoted, to which we wished success: but the quiet, secluded, monastic cell, or chapel, has no tale to tell; history hardly stays to note even its founder's name, and all the rest is doubt and darkness; yet, shrouded in its ivied folds, we reverence the remains, we call it picturesque, we draw, we engrave, we lithograph the ruin. We do not regard this ivy as a relic of ancient days—as having shadowed the religious recluse, and with it often, doubtless, piety and faith, for it did not hang around the building in old time, but is comparatively a modern upstart, a sharer of monastic spoils, a usurper of that which has been abandoned by another. The tendril pendant from the orient window, lightly defined in the ray which it excludes, twining with graceful ease round some slender shaft, or woven amid the tracery of the florid arch, is elegantly ornamental, and gives embellishment to beauty; but the main body of the ivy is dark, sombre, massy; yet, strip it from the pile, and we call it sacrilege, the interest of the whole is at an end, the effect ceases,

A moment seen, then lost for ever.

Yet what did the ivy effect? what has departed with it? This evanescent charm perhaps consists in the obscurity, in the sobriety of light it occasioned, in hiding the bare reality, and giving to fancy and imagination room to expand, a plaything to amuse them.

We still retain the name of this plant as given by Pliny, though we know no reason why it was so called; but the word "helix," winding about, or twisting, is sufficiently apposite.

The foxglove (*digitalis purpurea*) is found with us in one or two places only, rather existing than flourishing, manifesting, like many other plants, a marked partiality to particular soils. It produces an abundance of seed, yet seems to wander little from the station its progenitors had fixed on, as if that alone was congenial to its habits; but with us the soil varies greatly. In the West of England, it thrives and increases with particular luxuriance; but many counties may be searched in vain for a single specimen. It seems to prefer a sandy, gravelly, or loose drained soil; not I think vegetating in strong retentive earths. We have few indigenous plants, not one, perhaps, which we have so often summoned to aid us in our distresses as the foxglove: no plant, not even the colchicum, has been more the object of our fears, our hopes, our trust, and disappointment, than this: we have been grateful for the relief it has afforded, and we have mourned the insufficiency of its powers:—

> ————*Thy last, sole aid* (*which art can give*)
> *The woe-worn parent seeks, and, hoping, clings*
> *In tearless wretchedness to thee; watches*
> *With anxious heart thy subtle progress through*
> *The day, and of thee fitful dreams through all*
> *The night—*
> ———*spare, if thou*

Canst, his hopeless grief; save worth, save beauty,
From añ early grave.

As a mere flower, the digitalis is a very handsome plant; and could we rely upon its yielding the virtues it is considered to possess, or could we regulate or control its influence, it would exist unrivalled for beauty and worth amidst our island plants. Why such a name as "foxesgloves" was bestowed upon this plant it is difficult to say, perhaps from the bare resemblance to finger-cases presented by its flowers: but I am not one of those who cavil or jeer at the common, or "vulgar names," as we are in the habit of denominating the unscientific appellations of plants; for we must remember that the culling of herbs and simples, and compounding preparations from them, to relieve the sufferings of nature, were the first rudiments of all our knowledge, the most grateful exertion of human talent, and, after food and clothing, the most necessary objects of life. In ages of simplicity, when every man was the usual dispenser of good or bad, benefit or injury, to his household or his cattle—ere the veterinary art was known, or the drugs of other regions introduced, necessity looked up to the products of our own clime, and the real or fanciful virtues of them were called to the trial, and manifests the reasonableness of bestowing upon plants and herbs such names as might immediately indicate their several uses, or fitness for application; when distinctive characters, had they been given, would have been little attended to; and hence, the numbers found favourable to the cure of particular complaints, the ailments of domestic creatures, or deemed injurious to them. Modern science may wrap up the meaning of its epithets in Greek and Latin terms; but in very many cases they are the mere translations of these despised, "old, vulgar names." What pleasure it must have afforded the poor sufferer in body or in limb,—what confidence he must have felt of relief, when he knew that the good neighbour who came to bathe his wounds, or assuage his inward torments, brought with him such things as "all-heal, break-stone, bruise-wort, gout-weed, fever-few" (*fugio*), and twenty other such comfortable mitigators of his afflictions; why their very names would almost charm away the sense of pain! The modern recipe contains no such terms of comfortable assurance: its meanings are all dark to the sufferer; its influence unknown. And then the good herbalist of old professed to have plants which were "all good:" they could assuage anger by their "loosestrife;" they had "honesty, truelove, and heartsease." The cayennes, the soys, the ketchups, and extratropical condiments of these days, were not required, when the next thicket would produce "poor man's pepper, sauce alone, and hedge-mustard;" and the woods and wilds around, when they yielded such delicate viands as "fat hen, lambs-quarters, way-bread, butter and eggs, with codlins and cream," afforded no despicable bill of fare. No one ever yet thought of accusing our old simplers of the vice of avarice, or love of lucre; yet their "thrift" is always to be seen: we have their humble "pennywort, herb twopence, moneywort, silverweed, and gold." We may smile, perhaps, at the cognomens, or the commemorations of friendships, or of worth, recorded by the old simplers, at their herbs, "Bennet, Robert, Christopher, Gerard, or Basil;" but do the names so bestowed by modern science read better, or sound better? it has "Lightfootia, Lapeyrousia, Hedwigia, Schkuhria, Scheuchzeria;" and surely we may admit, in common benevolence, such partialities as "good King Henry, sweet William, sweet Marjory, sweet Cicely, Lettuce, Mary Gold, and Rose." There are epithets, however, so very extraordinary, that we must consider them as mere perversions, or at least incapable of explanation at this period. The terms of modern science waver daily; names undergo an annual change, fade with the leaf, and give place to others; but the ancient terms, which some may ridicule, have remained for centuries, and will yet remain, till nature is swallowed up by art. No: let our ancient herbalists, "a grave and whiskered race," retain the honours due to their labours, which were most needful and important ones at those periods: by them were many of the casualties and sufferings of man and beast relieved; and, by aid of perseverance, better constitutions to act upon, and faith to operate, than we possess, they probably effected cures, which we moderns should fail to accomplish if attempted.

Upon an old bank, tangled with bushes and rubbish, we find in abundance that very early translated, and perfectly domesticated flower, the cottage snowdrop (*galanthus nivalis*): a plant that is undoubtedly a native of our island, for I have seen it in situations where nature only could introduce it, where it was never planted by the hand of man, or strayed from any neighbouring cultivation. Yet in most places where we find this flower, it is of manifest or suspicious origin; and with us it partakes of this latter character, though no remains of any ancient dwelling are observable near it. The damask rose, the daffodil, or the stock of an old bullace plum, will long remain, and point out where once a cottage existed; but all these, and most other tokens, in time waste away and decay; while the snowdrop will remain, increase, and become the only memorial of man and his labours. Many flowers present strong distinctive characters, or will, at least often do, excite in us variable feelings: the primrose, and the daisy, if not intrinsically gay, call forth cheerful and pleasing sensations; and the aspect or glance of some others will awaken different affections. The snowdrop is a melancholy flower. The season in which the "fair maids of February" come out, is the most dreary and desolate of our year: they peep through the snow that often surrounds them, shivering and cheerless: they convey no idea of reviving nature, and are scarcely the harbingers of milder days, but rather the emblem of sleety storms, and icy gales (snowdrop weather), and wrap their petals round the infant germ, fearing to admit the very air that blows; and, when found beyond the verge of cultivation, they most generally remind us of some deserted dwelling, a family gone, a hearth that smokes no more. A

208

lover of cold, it maintains the beautiful ovate form of its flower only in a low temperature; warmth expanding the petals, vitiating its grace, and destroying its character. It seems to preserve its native purity free from every contamination; it will become double, but never wanders into varieties, is never streaked or tinged with the hues of other flowers.

One of our pasture grasses is particularly affected by dry weather. Several are injured frequently by drought acting upon the stalk, not molesting the root, but withering the succulent base of the straw, which arises from the upper joint; in consequence of which, the panicle and connecting straw dry away, while the foliage and lower leaves remain uninjured. None are so obnoxious to this injury as the yellow oat-grass (*avena flavescens*), and in some seasons almost the whole of its panicles will be withered in a field of surrounding verdure. Pastures that are grazed must from circumstances be drier than those covered with herbage fit for the scythe; yet, from some unknown cause, this oat-grass seems less injured in this respect in grazing grounds, than in those where the herbage is reserved for mowing.

The plain, simple, unadorned vervain (*verbena officinalis*) is one of our most common, and decidedly waste-loving plants. Disinclined to all cultured places, it fixes its residence by way-sides, and old stone quarries, thriving under the feet of every passing creature. The celebrity that this plant obtained in very remote times, without its possessing one apparent quality, or presenting by its manner of growth, or form, any mysterious character to arrest the attention, or excite imagination, is very extraordinary, and perhaps unaccountable: most nations venerated, esteemed, and used it; the ancients had their Verbenalia, at which period the temples and frequented places were strewed and sanctified with vervain; the beasts for sacrifice, and the altars, were verbenated, the one filleted, the other strewed, with the sacred herb; no incantation or lustration was perfect without the aid of this

plant. That mistletoe should have excited attention in days of
darkness and ignorance is not a subject of surprise, from the
extraordinary and obscure manner of its growth and propa-
gation, and the season of the year in which it flourishes; for
even the great Lord Bacon ridicules the idea of its being
propagated by the operations of a bird as an "idle tradition,"
saying, that the sap which produces this plant is such as the
"tree doth excerne and cannot assimilate." These circum-
stances, and its great dissimilarity from the plant on which it
vegetates, all combine to render it a subject of superstitious
wonder: but that a lowly, ineffective herb like our vervain
should have stimulated the imaginations of the priests of
Rome, of Gaul, and of Greece, the magi of India, and the
Druids of Britain, is passing comprehension; and, as Pen-
nant observes, "so general a consent proves that the custom
arose before the different nations had lost all communication
with each other." We might with some appearance of reason,
perhaps, name the Druids of Gaul as the point, whence
certain mysteries and observances were conveyed to the
priesthood of various nations; but it would be difficult to
assign a motive for their fixing upon such plants as vervain,
and some others, to give efficacy to their ceremonies and rites.
In some of the Welsh counties vervain is known by the name
of "llyssiaur hudol," the enchanter's plant. It seems to have
had ascribed to it the power of curing the bites of all rabid
animals, arresting the progress of the venom of serpents,
reconciling antipathies, conciliating friendships, &c. Gerard,
after detailing some of its virtues from Pliny, observes, that
"many odde old wives' fables are written of vervaine tending
to witchcraft and sorcerie, which you may read elsewhere,
for I am not willing to trouble you with reporting such trifles
as honest ears abhorre to hear." To us moderns its real
virtues are unknown; regular practice does not allow that it
possesses any medicinal efficacy, and its fanciful peculiarities
are in no repute; yet it seems to hanker after its lost fame, and
lingers around the dwellings of man, for though not solely

found about our habitations, as Miller thought, yet gener-
ally, when perceived, it is near some inhabited or ruined
residence, not as a stray from cultivation, but from prefer-
ence. Our village doctresses, an almost extinct race of useful,
valuable women, the consolers, the comforters, and often
mitigators of the ailments of the poor, still make use of
vervain tea as a strengthener, and the dried powder of its
leaves as a vermifuge; but probably in another generation all
the venerated virtues of the vervain will be consigned to
oblivion. This plant seems to be the native growth of many
districts in Europe, Asia, and Africa.

The dyers' weed, yellow weed, weld, or wold (*reseda
luteola*), thrives in all our abandoned stone quarries, upon
the rejected rubbish of the lime-kilns, and waste places of the
roads, apparently a perfectly indigenous plant. Unmindful of
frost, or of drought, it preserves a degree of verdure, when
nearly all other vegetation is seared up by these extremes in
exposed situations. It was, and is yet, I believe, cultivated in
England for the use of the dyer. We import it, however, into
Bristol from France, and it sells in that city for ten shillings
per cwt. in a dry state. It gives a fine, permanent, yellow
colour to cottons, silks, and woollens, in a variety of shades,
by the aid of alum, &c. A blue tincture changes these to as
fine a green. Injury has certainly been occasioned by writers
on agricultural affairs recommending, without due inquiry,
the culture of this or that crop; and I would not incur a
censure that I blame in another; yet I cannot but suggest the
possible profit that might arise from the culture of this plant.
If foreigners derive sufficient encouragement to import it,
notwithstanding the charges of freight, port duties, and vari-
ous consequent expenses, why can it not be grown with us,
and afford superior remuneration, not having such deduc-
tions to diminish the profits? The culture of its seems very
simple, the manner of conducting the crop, and harvesting
the product, attended with little trouble or risk. Marshal
prefers a good soil; others again say, that it becomes stalky in

a rich soil. With us it grows luxuriantly, three or four feet high, on a thin, stony, undressed soil, apparently the very station it prefers; and we have about as much land of this kind, not intrinsically worth ten shillings an acre. It might be rash to predict the amount of a crop in such soils, but a ton to an acre is said to be but a small allowance; yet the produce of only this quantity, which would procure in the market a return of ten pounds, without any expenditure for manure, no more manual labour after the seed is sown, for nine months, than three thinnings, and cleanings with the hoe, and the crop harvested within the year, would be no trifling profit, and may be deserving of some consideration. The bark, the wood, the flower, the leaves of many of our native trees and plants afford a yellow dye; we have no colour so easily produced as this is; and it is equally remarkable that, amidst all the varied hues of spring, yellow is the most predominant in our wild and cultured plants. The primrose, cowslip, pilewort, globe-flower, butter-cup, cherlock, crocus, all the cabbage tribe, the dandelions, appear in this dress. The very first butterfly, that will

> ——— *aloft repair,*
> *And sport and flutter in the fields of air,*

is the sulphur butterfly (*gonepteryx rhamni*), which in the bright sunny mornings of March we so often see under the warm hedge, or by the side of some sheltered copse, undulating and vibrating like the petal of a primrose in the breeze. The blossoms of many of our plants afford for the decoration of the fair a vast variety of colours and intermediate tints, but they are all of them, or nearly so, inconstant or fugitive before the light of the sun, or mutable in the dampness of the air, except those obtained from yellow flowers: circumstances may vary the shade, but yet it is mostly permanent. Yellow is again the livery of autumn, in all the shades of ochre and of orange; the "sere and yellow leaf" becomes the general cast of the season, the sober brown comes next, and then decay.

Many impressions commonly fade away and become effaced as other objects create fresh sensations; but the love of nature, where the regard has been a settled principle, is more permanent, and influences the feelings as long as the occupations of life preserve any interest in our minds. As a child, I viewed the wild field flowers, and cropped them with delight; as a young botanist, culled with rapture the various species, returning often and again to my almost exhaustless treasure in the copse; and even now in the "sere and yellow leaf," when, in some mild vernal evening, I stroll through the grove, see the same floral splendour which year after year has been spread before me, I mark it with admiration and surprise, find it enchanting still, and fancy the present loveliness superior to all that has been before. There we see that beautiful little brilliant of the earth, like the name it bears (day's-eye), cheerful and pleasing to all. The exquisite chasteness of mien, and form of this flower, the contrast of its colours, and simplicity of attitude which it displays when springing from out its grassy tuft, can hardly be surpassed by any from another region. By its side peeps out the bright gleeful blue eyes of the little germander speedwell, in joyful gaiety—a lowly domestic plant that loves and seeks alliance with its kind, and in small family associations, by united splendour, decorates the foliage around; and there we find the stitchwort, mingling her snowy bloom, immaculately pure, with pallid green: too delicate to vegetate alone, it seeks the shelter of the hedge or copse, trembles when the breeze goes by, and seems an emblem of innocence and grace. And there the bright-flowered lotus with its pea-like bloom, in social union glows as burnished gold, animating and gilding with its lustre all the tribes that spring near it; and fifty others, too, we note, which, though common and disregarded by reason of our familiarity with them, or expelled from favour by the novelty of far-fetched fair ones, deserve more attention than we are disposed to afford them. There are few plants which we look upon with more perfect contempt than that common product of every soil, the 'dandelion.' Every child knows it, and the little village groups which perambulate the hedges for the first offspring of the year, amuse themselves by hanging circlets of its stalks linked like a chain round their necks; yet if we examine this in all the stages of its growth, we shall pronounce it a beautiful production; and its blossom, though often a solitary one, is perhaps the very first that enlivens the sunny bank of the hedge in the opening year, peeping out from withered leaves, dry stalks, and desolation, as a herald, telling us that nature is not dead, but reposing, and will awaken to life again. And some of us, perhaps, can remember the pleasure it afforded us in early days, when we first noticed its golden blossoms under the southern shelter of the cottage hedge, thinking that the 'winter was past,' and that 'the time of the singing of birds was come;' and yet, possibly, when seen, it may renew some of that childish delight, though the fervour of expectation is cooled by experience and time. The form of this flower, with its ligulate petals many times doubled, is elegant and perfect; the brightness and liveliness of the yellow, like the warm rays of an evening sun, are not exceeded in any blossom, native or foreign, that I know of: and this, having faded away, is succeeded by a head of down, which, loosened from its receptacle, and floating in the breeze, comes sailing calmly along before us, freighted with a seed at its base; but so accurately adjusted is its bouyant power to the burden it bears, that steadily passing on its way, it rests at last in some cleft or cranny in the earth, preparatory to its period of germination, appearing more like a flight of animated creatures than the seed of a plant. This is a very beautiful appointment! but so common an event as hardly to be noticed by us; yet it accomplishes effectually the designs of nature, and plants the species at distances and in places that no other

COMMON DANDELION.

(Leontodon Taraxacum.)

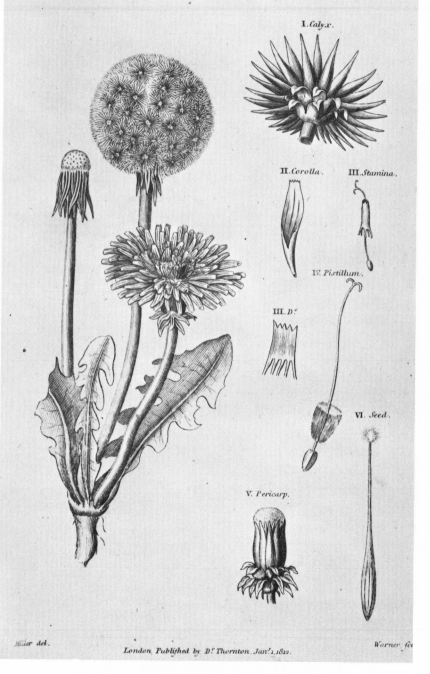

I. *Calyx.*

II. *Corolla.*   III. *Stamina.*

IV. *Pistillum.*

III. *D.º*

VI. *Seed.*

V. *Pericarp.*

Miller del.

London, Published by Dᵣ Thornton, Janᵧ 1, 1812.

Warner fc

From Robert John Thornton, The British Flora

contrivance could so easily and fitly effect. The seeds, it is true, might have fallen and germinated around the parent plant, but this was not the purport of nature; yet may seem to some a very unnecessary contrivance for the propagation of a common dandelion, whose benefits to mankind as a medicine, though retained in our pharmacopœias, and occasionally resorted to, seem of no great importance. Nor are we sensible that its virtues are essential to any portion of the creation; but this very circumstance should abate our pride, our assumed pretensions of knowledge, as we may be assured that its existence, though hidden from us, is required in the great scheme of nature, or such elaborate and sufficient contrivances for its continuation and increase would never have been called into action by nature, who is so remarkably simple in all her actions, economical in her ways, and frugal of her means.

Charles Waterton

Charles Waterton.

in his 42nd year.

*Engraved portrait of Charles Waterton, 1871,
after a painting by Charles Willson Peale*

Rook, by John Gould, from his The Birds of Great Britain, *1862–73*

Charles Waterton

[1782–1865]

Charles Waterton is remembered less for his eminence as a naturalist than for the extraordinarily eccentric conduct which marked his career from beginning to end: his escapade of scaling the façades of St. Peter's and the Castello di Sant' Angelo in Rome; his vow, taken at the death of his young wife in 1830, to sleep henceforth only on the floor and with a block of wood for pillow; his practice of draining large quantities of blood from his veins and dosing himself with calomel as a cure-all for every malady and physical accident. Waterton's biographers, fascinated by such Shandyean perversities of behavior, have ignored the fact that they were as often as not subservient to scientific pursuits. Thus, his lifelong prowess in climbing trees barefoot had been developed so that he could study the nesting-habits of birds; and his talents as a taxidermist enabled him to achieve startling realism in the mounting of species.

Waterton came of a very ancient landowning line of militantly devout Catholics, whose ancestral seat was Walton Hall in Yorkshire. He attended the Jesuit school at Stonyhurst, where a venerated teacher persuaded him to abstain from strong drink for the rest of his life and where he acquired enough Latin to supply the tag-lines which embellished his future writings. From his earliest years Waterton, like Darwin, exhibited an adventurous passion for natural history, little compatible with formal education; this proclivity the good fathers at Stonyhurst were sensible enough to harness to practical ends. "By a mutual understanding," Waterton wrote in his *Autobiography*, "I was considered ratcatcher to the establishment, and also fox-taker, foumart-killer, and crossbow-charger at the time when the young rooks were fledged."

When twenty-two Waterton embarked in 1804 for Demerara in British Guiana to take over the management of three large plantations belonging to his family. From these years in tropical South America date his first important scientific investigations. In 1812 he made during the rainy season a perilous journey through the interior to the Brazilian frontier in search of tribesmen who could instruct him in the preparation of the virulent native poison *curare*. A later collecting expedition in 1820 produced one of Waterton's most fantastic exploits: the hooking and subjugation of a savage cayman, involving the equestrian dexterity recounted in the following passage: "I sprung up and jumped on his back, turning half round as I vaulted, so that I gained my seat with my face in the right position. I immediately seized the forelegs and by main force twisted them on his back; thus they served me for a bridle." In 1825 Waterton published *Wanderings in South America*, which is not only one of the liveliest and most entertaining of travel books, but which also contains much lastingly important information, such as the author's descriptions of the then little-known characteristics of the sloth and anteater.

On eventually settling down at Walton Hall, Waterton inclosed its 259 acres of park and lake within a wall three miles long, erected to keep out foxes, badgers, poachers, and all such marauders. He thus created the first wild-life sanctuary and inaugurated the work now carried on by the Audubon Society. Not only was all gunning banned within this preserve; but to the indignation of his sporting neighbors, the owner insisted on protecting all kinds of predators, crows, hawks, owls, even weasels, the usefulness of which in exterminating vermin he rightly defended in advance of his time. His only sworn enemy was the Hanoverian rat, which he seems to have detested partly out of political prejudice, as a further obnoxious legacy of the Whig settlement! Waterton's success in encouraging owls, rooks, herons, kingfishers, and waterfowl to breed on his property saved many varieties of wild life from extinction in the region. Anecdotes relating to his experiments and observations are divertingly narrated in the three series of *Essays on Natural History*, which, together with sections of his informal *Autobiography*, appeared in 1838, 1844, and 1857.

Waterton's scientific reputation has suffered from the after-effects of the animosity which he stirred up among confreres

during his lifetime. He refused to conform to orthodox proce-
dures, as in the use of proper Latin terminology to describe
species; and he lost no opportunity to engage in controversy with
representatives of the class which he contemptuously called
closet scientists. His learned contemporaries were incensed by the
whimsical style in which he announced his findings; by suspi-
cions, usually ungrounded, of the veracity of his tall tales; and by
his penchant for practical jokes, as when he skilfully distorted a
stuffed specimen of the Red Howler monkey to resemble a primi-
tive form of human life. Nevertheless, the *Wanderings in South
America* leave no doubt either of Waterton's great intrepidity
and resourcefulness as an explorer or of the meticulous accuracy
of his observations in the field. It was, however, in the sancturary
at Walton Park that he erected over many years the true memo-
rial to his farsighted and compassionate dealings with the natural
world. Although apocryphal, the legend that a long line of birds
accompanied the funeral cortege of boats bearing his body to its
lakeside grave is a fitting tribute to the life work of the first great
pioneer in the cause of conservation.

From *Essays on Natural History*

The Barn Owl, and the Benefits It Confers on Man.

THIS pretty aërial wanderer of the night often comes into my room; and after flitting to and fro, on wing so soft and silent that he is scarcely heard, he takes his departure from the same window at which he had entered. I own I have a great liking for this bird; and I have offered it hospitality and protection on account of its persecutions, and for its many services to me,—I say services, as you will see in the sequel. I wish that any little thing I could write or say might cause it to stand better with the world at large than it has hitherto done: but I have slender hopes on this score; because old and deep-rooted prejudices are seldom overcome; and when I look back into the annals of remote antiquity, I see too clearly that defamation has done its worst to ruin the whole family, in all its branches, of this poor, harmless, useful friend of mine. Ovid, nearly two thousand years ago, was extremely severe against the owl. In his "Metamorphoses" he says,—

> *"Fœdaque fit volucris, venturi nuncia luctus,*
> *Ignavus bubo, dirum mortalibus omen."*

In his "Fasti" he openly accuses it of felony,—

> *"Nocte volant, puerosque petunt neutricis egentes."*

Lucan, too, has hit it hard,—

> *"Et lætæ jurantur aves, bubone sinistro:"*

and the Englishman who continued the "Pharsalia" says,—

222

"Tristia mille locis Stygius dedit omina bubo."

Horace tells us that the old witch Canidia used part of the plumage of the owl in her dealings with the devil,—

"Plumamque nocturnæ strigis."

Virgil, in fine, joined in the hue and cry against this injured family,—

"Solaque culminibus ferali carmine bubo
Sæpe queri, et longas in fletum ducere voces."

In our own times we find that the village maid cannot return home from seeing her dying swain without a doleful salutation from the owl,—

"Thus homeward as she hopeless went
The churchyard path along,
The blast grew cold, the dark owl scream'd
Her lover's funeral song."

Amongst the numberless verses which might be quoted against the family of the owl, I think I only know of one little ode which expresses any pity for it. Our nursery-maid used to sing it to the tune of "The Storm," "Cease, rude Boreas, blustering railer." I remember the first two stanzas of it:—

"Once I was a monarch's daughter,
And sat on a lady's knee;
But am now a nightly rover,
Banish'd to the ivy tree,

"Crying, hoo, hoo, hoo, hoo, hoo, hoo,
Hoo, hoo, hoo, my feet are cold!
Pity me, for here you see me,
Persecuted, poor and old."

I beg the reader's pardon for this exordium. I have introduced it, in order to show how little chance there has been,

223

from days long passed and gone to the present time, of studying the haunts and economy of the owl, because its unmerited bad name has created it a host of foes, and doomed it to destruction from all quarters. Some few certainly, from time to time, have been kept in cages and in aviaries. But nature rarely thrives in captivity, and very seldom appears in her true character when she is encumbered with chains, or is to be looked at by the passing crowd through bars of iron. However, the scene is now going to change; and I trust that the reader will contemplate the owl with more friendly feelings, and quite under different circumstances. Here, no rude schoolboy ever approaches its retreat; and those who once dreaded its diabolical doings are now fully satisfied that it no longer meddles with their destinies, or has anything to do with the repose of their departed friends. Indeed, human wretches, in the shape of body-snatchers, seem here in England to have usurped the office of the owl in our churchyards—"*et vendunt tumulis corpora rapia suis.*"

Up to the year 1813, the barn owl had a sad time of it at Walton Hall. Its supposed mournful notes alarmed the aged housekeeper. She knew full well what sorrow it had brought into other houses when she was a young woman; and there was enough of mischief in the midnight wintry blast, without having it increased by the dismal screams of something which people knew very little about, and which everybody said was far too busy in the churchyard at night-time. Nay, it was a well-known fact, that if any person were sick in the neighbourhood, it would be for ever looking in at the window, and holding a conversation outside with somebody, they did not know whom. The gamekeeper agreed with her in everything she said on this important subject; and he always stood better in her books, when he had managed to shoot a bird of this bad and mischievous family. However, in 1813, on my return from the wilds of Guiana, having suffered myself and learned mercy, I broke in pieces the code of penal laws which the knavery of the gamekeeper and the lamentable ignorance of the other servants had hitherto put in force, far too successfully, to thin the numbers of this poor, harmless, unsuspectinng tribe. On the ruin of the old gateway, against which, tradition says, the waves of the lake have dashed for the better part of a thousand years, I made a place with stone and mortar about four feet square, and fixed a thick oaken stick firmly into it. Huge masses of ivy now quite cover it. In about a month or so after it was finished, a pair of barn owls came and took up their abode in it. I threatened to strangle the keeper if ever, after this, he molested either the old birds or their young ones; and I assured the housekeeper that I would take upon myself the whole responsibility of all the sickness, woe, and sorrow that the new tenants might bring into the Hall. She made a low curtsy, as much as to say, "Sir, I fall into your will and pleasure." But I saw in her eye, that she had made up her mind to have to do with things of fearful and portentous shape, and to hear many a midnight wailing in the surrounding woods. I do not think that, up to the day of this old lady's death, which took place in her eighty-fourth year, she ever looked with pleasure or contentment on the barn owl, as it flew round the large sycamore trees which grew near the old ruined gateway.

When I found that this first settlement on the gateway had succeeded so well, I set about forming other establishments. This year I have had four broods, and I trust that next season I can calculate on having nine. This will be a pretty increase, and it will help to supply the place of those which, in this neighbourhood, are still unfortunately doomed to death by the hand of cruelty or superstition. We can now always have a peep at the owls, in their habitation on the old ruined gateway, whenever we choose. Confident of protection, these pretty birds betray no fear when the stranger mounts up to their place of abode. I would here venture a surmise, that the barn owl sleeps standing. Whenever we go to look at it, we invariably see it upon the perch, bolt upright; and often with its eyes closed, apparently fast asleep. Buffon and Bewick err (no doubt unintentionally) when they say that the barn owl snores during its repose. What they took for snoring was the cry of the young birds for food. I had fully satisfied myself on this score some years ago. However, in December 1823, I was much astonished to hear this same snoring kind of noise, which had been so common in the month of July. On ascending the ruin, I found a brood of young owls in the apartment.

Upon this ruin is placed a perch, about a foot from the hole at which the owls enter. Sometimes at mid-day, when the weather is gloomy, you may see an owl upon it, apparently enjoying the refreshing diurnal breeze. This year (1831) a pair of barn owls hatched their young, on the 7th of September, in a sycamore tree near the old ruined gateway.

If this useful bird caught its food by day,* instead of hunting for it by night, mankind would have ocular demonstration of its utility in thinning the country of mice; and it would be protected and encouraged everywhere. It would be with us what the ibis was with the Egyptians. When it has young, it will bring a mouse to the nest about every twelve or fifteen minutes. But in order to have a proper idea of the enormous quantity of mice which this bird destroys, we must examine the pellets which it ejects from its stomach in the place of its retreat. Every pellet contains from four to seven skeletons of mice. In sixteen months from the time that the apartment of the owl on the old gateway was cleaned out, there has been a deposit of above a bushel of pellets. The barn owl sometimes carries off rats. One evening I was sitting under a shed, and killed a very large rat as it was coming out of a hole, about ten yards from where I was watching it. I did not go to take it up, hoping to get another shot. As it lay there, a barn owl pounced upon it and flew away with it. This bird has been known to catch fish. Some years ago, on a fine

* Though the barn owl usually hunts during the night, still I have repeatedly seen it catching mice in the daytime, even when the sun shone bright.—C. W.

Barn Owl and Young at the Nest in a Dead Tree, by John Gould

evening in the month of July, long before it was dark, as I was standing on the middle of the bridge, and minuting the owl by my watch, as she brought mice into her nest, all on a sudden she dropped perpendicularly into the water. Thinking that she had fallen down in epilepsy, my first thoughts were to go and fetch the boat; but before I had well got to the end of the bridge, I saw the owl rise out of the water with a fish in her claws, and take it to the nest. This fact is mentioned by the late much revered and lamented Mr. Atkinson, of Leeds, in his *Compendium*, in a note, under the signature of W., a friend of his, to whom I had communicated it a few days after I had witnessed it.

I cannot make up my mind to pay any attention to the description of the amours of the owl by a modern writer; at least the barn owl plays off no buffooneries here, such as those which he describes. An owl is an owl all the world over, whether under the influence of Momus, Venus, or Diana.

When farmers complain that the barn owl destroys the eggs of their pigeons, they lay the saddle on the wrong horse. They ought to put it on the rat. Formerly, I could get very few young pigeons till the rats were excluded effectually from the dovecot. Since that took place, it has produced a great abundance every year, though the barn owls frequent it, and are encouraged all around it. The barn owl merely resorts to it for repose and concealment. If it were really an enemy to the dovecot, we should see the pigeons in commotion as soon as it begins its evening flight—but the pigeons heed it not; whereas, if the sparrowhawk or hobby should make its appearance, the whole community would be up at once; proof sufficient that the barn owl is not looked upon as a bad, or even a suspicious, character by the inhabitants of the dovecot.

Till lately a great and well-known distinction has always been made betwixt the screeching and the hooting of owls. The tawny owl is the only owl which hoots; and when I am in the woods after poachers, about an hour before daybreak, I hear with extreme delight its loud, clear, and sonorous notes, resounding far and near through hill and dale. Very different from these notes is the screech of the barn owl. But Sir William Jardine informs us that this owl hoots; and that he has shot it in the act of hooting. This is stiff authority; and I believe it because it comes from the pen of Sir William Jardine. Still, however, methinks that it ought to be taken in a somewhat diluted state; we know full well that most extraordinary examples of splendid talent do, from time to time, make their appearance on the world's wide stage. Thus Franklin brought down fire from the skies—*"Eripuit fulmen cœlo, sceptrumque tyrannis."* Paganini has led all London captive by a single piece of twisted catgut—*"Tu potes reges comitesque stulios ducere."* Leibnitz tells us of a dog in Germany that could pronounce distinctly thirty words. Goldsmith informs us that he once heard a raven whistle the tune of the "Shamrock," with great distinctness, truth, and humour. With these splendid examples before our eyes, may we not be inclined to suppose that the barn owl which Sir William shot, in the absolute act of hooting, may have been a gifted bird of superior parts and knowledge (*una de multis*, as Horace said of Miss Danaus), endowed, perhaps, from its early days with the faculty of hooting, or else skilled in the art by having been taught it by its neighbour, the tawny owl? I beg to remark, that though I unhesitatingly grant the faculty of hooting to this one particular individual owl, still I flatly refuse to believe that hooting is common to barn owls in general. Ovid in his sixth book, *Fastorum*, pointedly says that it screeched in his day:—

> *"Est illis strigibus nomen; sed nominis hujus*
> *Causa, quod horrenda stridere nocte solent."*

The barn owl may be heard shrieking here perpetually on the portico, and in the large sycamore trees near the house. It shrieks equally when the moon shines and when the night is rough and cloudy; and he who takes an interest in it may here see the barn owl the night through when there is a moon; and he may hear it shriek when perching on the trees, or when it is on wing. He may see it and hear it shriek, within a few yards of him, long before dark; and again, often after day-break, before it takes its final departure to its wonted resting-place. I am amply repaid for the pains I have taken to protect and encourage the barn owl; it pays me a hundred-fold by the enormous quantity of mice which it destroys throughout the year. The servants now no longer wish to persecute it. Often, on a fine summer's evening, with delight I see the villagers loitering under the sycamore trees longer than they would otherwise do, to have a peep at the barn owl as it leaves the ivy-mantled tower: fortunate for it, if in lieu of exposing itself to danger by mixing with the world at large, it only knew the advantage of passing its nights at home; for here—

> *"No birds that haunt my valley free*
> *To slaughter I condemn;*
> *Taught by the Power that pities me,*
> *I learn to pity them."*

The Rook

LAST year, I partly promised that, on some dismal winter's evening, I would sit me down and write the history of the rook. The period has now arrived. Nothing can be more gloomy and tempestuous than the present aspect of the heavens. The wind is roaring through the naked branches of the sycamores, the rain beats fiercely on the eastern windows, and the dashing of the waves against the walls of the island, warns us that one of November's dark and stormy nights is close at hand; such a night, probably, as that in which Tam O'Shanter unfortunately peeped into Kirk Alloway. Foreign-ers tell us that on these nights Englishmen are prone to use the knife, or a piece of twisted hemp, to calm their agitated spirits. For my own part, I must say that I have an insuperable repugnance to such anodynes; and were a host of blue devils conjured up by November's fogs just now to assail me, I would prefer combating the phantoms with the weapons of ornithology, rather than run any risk of disturbing the economy of my jugular vein, by a process productive of very unpleasant sensations, before it lulls one to rest.

According to my promise, I will now pen down a few remarks on the habits of the rook, which bird, in good old sensible times, was styled *frugilegus*. It is now pronounced to be *prædatorius*. Who knows but that our great ones in ornithology may ultimately determine to call it up to the house of hawks?

If this useful bird were not so closely allied to the carrion crow in colour and in shape, we should see it sent up to the tables of the rich as often as we see the pigeon. But prejudice forbids the appearance of broiled rook in the lordly mansion. If we wish to partake of it, we must repair to the cottage of the lowly swain, or, here and there, to the hall of the homely country squire, whose kitchen has never been blessed by the presence of a first-rate cook, and whose yearnings for a good and wholesome dish are not stifled by the fear of what a too highly polished world will say.

There is no wild bird in England so completely gregarious as the rook, or so regular in its daily movements. The ringdoves will assemble in countless multitudes, the finches will unite in vast assemblies, and waterfowl will flock in thousands to the protected lake during the dreary months of winter; but when the returning sun spreads joy and consolation over the face of nature, their congregated numbers are dissolved, and the individuals retire in pairs to propagate their respective species. The rook, however, remains in society the year throughout. In flocks it builds its nest, in flocks it seeks for food, and in flocks it retires to roost.

About two miles to the eastward of this place are the

231

woods of Nostell Priory, where, from time immemorial, the rooks have retired to pass the night. I suspect, by the observations which I have been able to make on the morning and evening transit of these birds, that there is not another roosting-place for, at least, thirty miles to the westward of Nostell Priory. Every morning, from within a few days of the autumnal to about a week before the vernal equinox, the rooks, in congregated thousands upon thousands, fly over this valley in a westerly direction, and return in undiminished numbers to the east, an hour or so before the night sets in. In their morning passage, some stop here; others, in other favourite places, farther and farther on—now repairing to the trees for pastime, now resorting to the fields for food, till the declining sun warns those which have gone farthest to the westward, that it is time they should return. They rise in a mass, receiving additions to their numbers from every intervening place, till they reach this neighbourhood in an amazing flock. Sometimes they pass on without stopping, and are joined by those which have spent the day here. At other times they make my park their place of rendezvous, and cover the ground in vast profusion, or perch upon the surrounding trees. After tarrying here for a certain time, every rook takes wing. They linger in the air for a while, in slow revolving circles, and then they all proceed to Nostell Priory, which is their last resting-place for the night. In their morning and evening passage, the loftiness or lowliness of their flight seems to be regulated by the state of the weather. When it blows a hard gale of wind, they descend the valley with astonishing rapidity, and just skim over the tops of the intervening hills, a few feet above the trees; but, when the sky is calm and clear, they pass through the heavens at a great height, in regular and easy flight.

Sometimes these birds perform an evolution, which is, in this part of the country, usually called the shooting of the rooks. Farmers tell you that this shooting portends a coming wind. He who pays attention to the flight of birds has, no doubt, observed this downward movement. When rooks have risen to an immense height in the air, so that, in appearance, they are scarcely larger than the lark, they suddenly descend to the ground or to the tops of trees exactly under them. To effect this, they come headlong down on pinion a little raised, but not expanded in a zig-zag direction (presenting alternately their back and breast to you), through the resisting air, which causes a noise similar to that of a rushing wind. This is a magnificent and beautiful sight to the eye of an ornithologist. It is idle to suppose for a moment that it portends wind. It is merely the ordinary descent of the birds to an inviting spot beneath them, where, in general, some of their associates are already assembled, or where there is food to be procured. When we consider the prodigious height of the rooks at the time they begin to descend, we conclude that they cannot effect their arrival at a spot perpendicular under them by any other process so short and rapid.

Rooks remain with us the year throughout. If there were a deficiency of food, this would not be the case; for when birds can no longer support themselves in the place which they have chosen for their residence, they leave it, and go in quest of nutriment elsewhere. Thus, for want of food, myriads of wild fowl leave the frozen north and repair to milder climates; and in this immediate district, when there is but a scanty sprinkling of seeds on the whitethorn bush, our flocks of fieldfares and of redwings bear no proportion to those in times of a plentiful supply of their favourite food. But the number of rooks never visibly diminishes; and, on this account, we may safely conclude that, one way or other, they always find a sufficiency of food. Now, if we bring as a charge against them, their feeding upon the industry of man, as, for example, during the time of a hard frost, or at seed-time, or at harvest, at which periods they will commit depredations, if not narrowly watched, we ought in justice to put down in their favour the rest of the year, when they feed entirely upon insects. Should we wish to know the amount of noxious insects destroyed by rooks, we have only to refer to a most valuable and interesting paper on the services of the rook, signed T. G. Clitheroe, Lancashire, which is given in the *Magazine of Natural History*, vol. vi., p. 142. I wish every farmer in England would read it, they would then be convinced how much the rook befriends them.

Some author (I think Goldsmith) informs us, that the North American colonists got the notion into their heads that the purple grakle was a great consumer of their maize; and these wise men of the west actually offered a reward of threepence for the killed dozen of the plunderers. This tempting boon soon caused the country to be thinned of grakles, and then myriads of insects appeared, to put the good people in mind of the former plagues of Egypt. They damaged the grass to such a fearful extent that, in 1749, the rash colonists were obliged to procure hay from Pennsylvania, and even from England. Buffon mentions, that grakles were brought from India to Bourbon, in order to exterminate the grasshoppers. The colonists, seeing these birds busy in the new-sown fields, fancied that they were searching for grain, and instantly gave the alarm. The poor grakles were proscribed by Government, and in two hours after the sentence was passed, not a grakle remained in the island. The grasshoppers again got the ascendancy, and then the deluded islanders began to mourn for the loss of their grakles. The governor procured four of these birds from India, about eight years after their proscription, and the State took charge of their preservation. Laws were immediately framed for their protection, and lest the people should have a hankering for grakle pie, the physicians were instructed to proclaim the flesh of the grakle very unwholesome food. Whenever I see a flock of rooks at work in a turnip-field, which, in dry weather, is often the case, I know that they have not assembled there to eat either the turnips or the tops, but that they are employed in picking out a grub which has already made a lodgment in the turnip.

Last spring I paid a visit, once a day, to a carrion crow's nest on the top of a fir tree. In the course of the morning in which she had laid her fifth egg, I took all the eggs out of the nest, and in their place I put two rooks' eggs, which were within six days of being hatched. The carrion crow attended on the stranger eggs, just as though they had been her own, and she raised the young of them with parental care. When they had become sufficiently large I took them out of the nest, and carried them home. One of them was sent up to the gamekeeper's house, with proper instructions; the other remained with me. Just at this time, an old woman had made me a present of a barn-door hen. "Take it, sir," said she, "and welcome; for if it stays here any longer, we shall be obliged to kill it. When we get up to wash in the morning, it crows like a cock. All its feathers are getting like those of a cock; it is high time that it was put out of the way, for when hens turn cocks people say that they are known to be very unlucky; and if this thing is allowed to live, we don't know what may happen. It has great spurs on its legs, and last summer it laid four eggs. If I had had my own way, it would have been killed when it first began to crow." I received the hen with abundant thanks; and, in return, I sent the old woman a full-bred Malay fowl. On examining the hen, I found her comb very large; the feathers on the neck and rump much elongated; the spurs curved, and about an inch and a quarter long; the two largest feathers in her tail arched, and four or five smaller arched ones, of a beautiful and glossy colour, hanging down on each side of the tail. In a word, this hen had so masculine an appearance, that, when strangers looked at her, they all took her to be a cock, and it was with difficulty I persuaded them that she was a hen. We allowed her the range of a sheltered grass-plot, flanked on one side by holly trees, and open to the lake on the other. Here, also, was placed, in a cage, the young rook which I had taken from the nest of the

235

carrion crow. The hen showed such an antipathy to it, that, whenever I held it to her, she would immediately fly at it. When visitors came to inspect her, I had only to take the rook out of the cage, and pit it against her, when she would stand upright, raise the long feathers on her neck, and begin to cackle, cluck, and crow. One morning the rook had managed to push aside a bar in front of its cage. A servant, in passing by, looked into it, and missed the bird. The hen had also disappeared. On search being made, they were both found floating side by side, dead, in the lake below. We conjectured that the hen had pursued the rook after its escape from the cage, and that the wind, which blew very strong that morning, had forced them both into a watery grave. I had still one rook left at the gamekeeper's. It was kept in a cage, which was placed on a little stand in his garden; and I had given orders that upon no account was it to be allowed to go at large. The feathers remained firm at the base of the bill till the 15th of August, on which day the keeper perceived that a few feathers had dropped from the lower mandible, and were lying at the bottom of the cage. In a couple of weeks more, the lower mandible had begun to put on a white scurvy appearance, while here and there a few feathers had fallen from the upper one. This is the purport of the keeper's information to me, on my return home from Bavaria. On the 31st of the same month, a terrible storm set in. By what the keeper told me, the night must have been as dark and dismal as that in which poor King Lear stood in lamentation, and exposed his hoary locks to the four rude winds of heaven. A standard white-hart cherry tree, perhaps the finest in Yorkshire, and which, for many generations, had been the pride and ornament of this place, lost two large branches during the gale; and in the morning, when the keeper rose, he found the cage shattered and upset, and driven to the farthest corner of his garden. The rook was quite dead. It had lost its life, either through the inclemency of that stormy night, or through bruises received in the fall of the cage. Thus both the rooks

236

were unlucky. The old woman, no doubt, could clearly trace their misfortunes to her crowing hen. However, the experiment with the two young rooks, though not perfect, has nevertheless been of some use. It has shown us that the carrion crow makes no distinction betwixt its own eggs and those of the rook; that it can know nothing of the actual time required to sit upon eggs in order to produce the young; that the young of the rook will thrive under the care of the carrion crow, just as well as under that of its own parents; and, finally, that the feathers fall off from the root of the rook's bill by the order of nature, as was surmised by the intelligent Bewick, and not by the process of the bird's thrusting its bill into the earth, in search of food, as is the opinion of some naturalists.

The rook advances through the heavens with a very regular and a somewhat tardy beat of wing! but it is capable of proceeding with great velocity when it chooses; witness its pursuit and attack on the sparrowhawk and kestrel. It is apt to injure, in the course of time, the elm trees on which it builds its nest, by nipping off the uppermost twigs. But this, after all, is mere conjecture. The damage may be caused by an accumulation of nests, or by the constant resort of such a number of birds to one tree. Certain, however, it is, that when rooks have taken possession of an elm tree for the purpose of incubation, the uppermost branches of that tree are often subject to premature decay.

Though the flocks of rooks appear to have no objection to keep company, from time to time, with the carrion crows, in a winter's evening, before they retire to roost, still I can never see a carrion crow build its nest in a rookery. There was always a carrion crow's nest here, in a clump of high Scotch pines, near the stables, till the rooks got possession of the trees; the carrion couple then forsook the place; the rooks were dislodged from this clump of trees, and then a pair of carrion crows (the same, for aught I know to the contrary) came and built their nest in it.

237

The rook lays from three to five eggs, varying much, like those of the carrion crow, in colour, shape, and size. After the rooks have built and even lined their nests, they leave them, on the approach of night, to repair to the general rendezvous at Nostell Priory; but as soon as they begin to lay, they then no longer quit the trees at night, until they have reared their young. When this has been effected, we see large flocks of them resorting to the different woods of the neighbourhood to pass the night. This they continue to do till a few days before the autumnal equinox, when, for reasons which baffle all conjecture, they begin to pass over this valley every morning in a westerly direction, and return in the evening to their eastern roosting-place in the woods of Nostell Priory.

Rooks are observed to keep up a very close and friendly intercourse with starlings and jackdaws; but on looking at them in the fields, the observer will perceive that, while the jackdaws mix promiscuously with the rooks, both in their flight and in searching for food, the starlings always keep in their own flock. This circumstance has long engaged my attention, but I am no further advanced in the investigation than I was on the first day on which I set out. It is one of the many secrets in the habits of birds, which will, perhaps, be for ever concealed from our view.

Charles George
William St. John

Drawing by Charles St. John

Drawings by Charles St. John

Charles George William
St. John

[1809–1856]

The British love of field sports has made extensive contributions to the literature of natural history. For the true sportsman the pursuit of game cannot be divorced from its setting; and the exercise of skill with rod and gun may well become the excuse rather than the guiding motive which leads the angler or hunter to seek ever closer intimacy with his prey. The writings of Charles St. John are a classic exemplification of how the pleasures of the chase may sharpen perception of the beauties of nature and awaken the passion for scientific knowledge.

St. John's family connection was aristocratic; he was the son of a general and the grandson of Frederick, second viscount Bolingbroke. During his boyhood years at Midhurst School he became an ardent fisherman and nurtured a motley collection of insects and pet animals. Later he served for a period as clerk in the Treasury, under which bondage, we are told, he chafed "like a caged eagle." Release came in 1833 when his cousin, Lord Bolingbroke, loaned him a shooting-box in Sutherland. Marriage in the following year brought financial independence and allowed him henceforth to reside at various localities in northern Scotland, especially Moray, where the close proximity of moors, lochs, and mountains to the seacoast offered not only plentiful game, but also unusual opportunities for observing bird life. Stricken by paralysis in 1853, St. John vainly sought to regain health in the south of England. When he died three years later, the skull of a favorite retriever was by his own wish buried at his feet.

With humorous self-deprecation St. John said of the way of life he had made for himself:

. . . I am one of the unproductive class of the genus Homo, who, having passed a few years amidst the active turmoil of cities, and in places where people do most delight to congregate, have at last settled down to live a busy kind of idle life. Communing much with the wild birds and beasts of our country, a hardy constitution and much leisure have enabled me to visit them in their own haunts, and to follow my sporting propensities without fear of the penalties which are apt to follow a careless exposure of oneself to cold and heat, at all hours of night and day. Though by habit and repute a being strongly endowed with the organ of destructiveness, I take equal delight in collecting round me all living animals, and watching their habits and instincts; my abode is, in short, a miniature menagerie. My dogs learn to respect the persons of domesticated wild animals of all kinds, and my pointers live in amity with tame partridges and pheasants; my retrievers lounge about amidst my wild-fowl, and my terriers and beagles strike up friendship with the animals of different kinds whose capture they have assisted in, and with whose relatives they are ready to wage war to the death. A common and well kept truce exists with one and all.

That St. John became a writer was largely owing to a fortunate accident. He had been in the habit of keeping desultory field notes; and some of these, including the stirring exploit of "The Muckle Hart of Benmore," were incorporated in an article which his friend Cosmo Innes, Sheriff of Moray, submitted in 1845 to the *Quarterly Review*. The enthusiastic response of its editor, J. G. Lockhart, encouraged St. John to publish *Short Sketches of the Wild Sports and Natural History of the Highlands* (1846), in the wake of which followed two equally delightful works: *A Tour in Sutherlandshire* (1849) and, posthumously, *Natural History and Sport in Moray* (1863).

Just as the writings of Wordworth's circle had drawn attention to the English Lakes fifty years before, so the charm of St. John's account of the still remote fastnesses of northern Scotland created at mid-century a vogue among sportsmen and nature lovers for exploring those regions. Furthermore, his observations

242

possess considerable scientific value, since, rejecting hearsay, he had early resolved never to write about anything which did not fall within the compass of his own experience. With the passing of time his gun was oftener employed to bring down rare specimens than to add to the day's bag; and the sportsman's keen eye took a less belligerent cast as it gained sympathetic insight into the all-pervading harmony of the natural world. The endearing qualities which make St. John's books unique in the literature of sport are illustrated in such passages as the following:

> Always graceful, a roebuck is peculiarly so when stripping some young tree of its leaves, nibbling them off one by one in the most delicate and dainty manner. I have watched a roe strip the leaves off a long bramble shoot, beginning at one end and nibbling off every leaf. My rifle was aimed at his heart and my finger was on the trigger, but I made some excuse or other for not killing him, and left him undisturbed—his beauty saved him.

Or in this description of a meeting as the author was returning empty-handed from a day of neglected opportunities hunting along the coast:

> The ferryman at the river where I pass tells me that he "is thinking I have had a long travel, but that I have not got much *ven-ni-son*." In both surmises he is not far wrong, but I have enjoyed my long and rough walk as much—ay, and much more—than I should have done the best battue in Norfolk, or the best day's grouse shooting in Perthshire.

From *Short Sketches of the Wild Sports and Natural History of the Highlands*

Chapter XIV

Anecdotes and Instinct of Dogs—Anecdotes of Retriever —Shepherds' Dogs—Sagacity—Dogs and Monkey— Bulldog—Anecodotes of Shooting a Stag—Treatment of Dogs.

So MUCH has been written, and so many anecdotes told, of the cleverness and instinct of dogs, that I am almost afraid to add anything more on the subject, lest I should be thought tedious. Nevertheless I cannot refrain from relating one or two incidents illustrating the instinct, almost amounting to reason, that some of my canine acquaintances have evinced, and which have fallen under my own notice. Different dogs are differently endowed in this respect, but much also depends on their education, manner of living, &c. The dog that lives with his master constantly, sleeping before his fire, instead of in the kennel, and hearing and seeing all that passes, learns, if at all quick-witted, to understand not only the meaning of what he sees going on, but also, frequently in the most wonderful manner, all that is talked of. I have a favourite retriever, a black water-spaniel, who for many years has lived in the house, and been constantly with me; he understands and notices everything that is said, if it at all relates to himself or to the sporting plans for the day: if at breakfast-time I say, without addressing the dog himself, "Rover must stop at home to-day, I cannot take him out," he never attempts to follow me; if, on the contrary, I say, however quietly, "I shall take Rover with me to-day," the moment that breakfast is over he is all on the *qui vive*, following me wherever I go, evidently aware that he is to be allowed to accompany me. When left at home, he sits on the step of the front door, looking out for my return, occasionally howling and barking in an ill-tempered kind of voice; his great delight is going with me when I hunt the woods for roe and deer. I had some covers about five miles from the house, where we were accustomed to look for roe: we frequently made our plans over night while the dog was in the room. One day, for some reason, I did not take him: in consequence of this, invariably when he heard us at night forming our plan to beat the woods, Rover started alone very early in the morning, and met us up there. He always went to the cottage where we assembled, and sitting on a hillock in front of it, which commanded a view of the road by which we came, waited for us; when he saw us coming, he met us with a peculiar kind of grin on his face, expressing, as well as words could, his half doubt of being well received, in consequence of his having come without permission: the moment he saw that I was not angry with him, he threw off all his affectation of shyness, and barked and jumped upon me with the most grateful delight.

As he was very clever at finding deer, I often sent him with the beaters or hounds to assist, and he always plainly asked me on starting, whether he was to go with me to the pass, or to accompany the men. In the latter case, though a very exclusive dog in his company at other times, he would go with any one of the beaters, although a stranger to him, whom I told him to accompany, and he would look to that one man for orders as long as he was with him. I never lost a wounded roe when he was out, for once on the track he would stick to it, the whole day if necessary, not fatiguing himself uselessly, but quietly and determinedly following it up. If the

245

roe fell and he found it, he would return to me, and then lead me up to the animal, whatever the distance might be. With red-deer he was also most useful. The first time that he saw me kill a deer he was very much surprised; I was walking alone with him through some woods in Ross-shire, looking for woodcocks; I had killed two or three, when I saw such recent signs of deer, that I drew the shot from one barrel, and replaced it with ball. I then continued my walk. Before I had gone far, a fine barren hind sprung out of a thicket, and as she crossed a small hollow, going directly away from me, I fired at her, breaking her backbone with the bullet; of course she dropped immediately, and Rover, who was a short distance behind me, rushed forward in the direction of the shot, expecting to have to pick up a woodcock; but on coming up to the hind, who was struggling on the ground, he ran round her with a look of astonishment, and then came back to me with an expression in his face plainly saying, "What have you done now?—you have shot a cow or something." But on my explaining to him that the hind was fair game, he ran up to her and seized her by the throat like a bulldog. Ever afterwards he was peculiarly fond of deer-hunting, and became a great adept, and of great use. When I sent him to assist two or three hounds to start a roe—as soon as the hounds were on the scent, Rover always came back to me and waited at the pass: I could enumerate endless anecdotes of his clever feats in this way.

Though a most aristocratic dog in his usual habits, when staying with me in England once, he struck up an acquaintance with a ratcatcher and his curs, and used to assist in their business when he thought that nothing else was to be done, entering into their way of going on, watching motionless at the rats' holes when the ferrets were in, and as the ratcatcher told me, he was the best dog of them all, and always to be depended on for showing if a rat was in a hole, corn-stack, or elsewhere; never giving a false alarm, or failing to give a true one. The moment, however, that he saw me, he instantly cut his humble friends, and denied all acquaintance with them in the most comical manner.

The shepherds' dogs in the mountainous districts often show the most wonderful instinct in assisting their masters, who, without their aid, would have but little command over a large flock of wild black-faced sheep. It is a most interesting sight to see a clever dog turn a large flock of these sheep in whichever direction his master wishes, taking advantage of the ground, and making a wide sweep to get round the sheep without frightening them, till he gets beyond them, and then rushing barking from flank to flank of the flock, and bringing them all up in close array to the desired spot. When, too, the shepherd wishes to catch a particular sheep out of the flock, I have seen him point it out to the dog, who would instantly distinguish it from the rest, and follow it up till he caught it. Often I have seen the sheep rush into the middle of the flock, but the dog, though he must necessarily have lost sight of it amongst the rest, would immediately single it out again, and never leave the pursuit till he had the sheep prostrate, but unhurt, under his feet. I have been with a shepherd when he has consigned a certain part of his flock to a dog to be driven home, the man accompanying me farther on to the hill. On our return we invariably found that he had either given up his charge to the shepherd's wife or some other responsible person, or had driven them, unassisted, into the fold, lying down himself at the narrow entrance to keep them from getting out till his master came home. At other times I have seen a dog keeping watch on the hill on a flock of sheep, allowing them to feed all day, but always keeping sight of them, and bringing them home at a proper hour in the evening. In fact it is difficult to say what a shepherd's dog would not do to assist his master, who would be quite helpless without him in a Highland district.

Generally speaking these Highland sheepdogs do not show much aptness in learning to do anything not connected in some way or other with sheep or cattle. They seem to have

247

been brought into the world for this express purpose, and for no other.

They watch their master's small crop of oats or potatoes with great fidelity and keenness, keeping off all intruders in the shape of sheep, cattle, or horses. A shepherd once, to prove the quickness of his dog, who was lying before the fire in the house where we were talking, said to me, in the middle of a sentence concerning something else—"I'm thinking, Sir, the cow is in the potatoes." Though he purposely laid no stress on these words, and said them in a quiet unconcerned tone of voice, the dog, who appeared to be asleep, immediately jumped up, and leaping through the open window, scrambled up the turf roof of the house, from which he could see the potato-field. He then (not seeing the cow there) ran and looked into the byre where she was, and finding that all was right, came back to the house. After a short time the shepherd said the same words again, and the dog repeated his look-out; but on the false alarm being a third time given, the dog got up, and wagging his tail, looked his master in the face with so comical an expression of interrogation, that we could not help laughing aloud at him, on which, with a slight growl, he laid himself down in his warm corner, with an offended air, and as if determined not to be made a fool of again.

Occasionally a poaching shepherd teaches his dog to be of great service in assisting him to kill game. I remember one of these men, who was in the habit of wiring hares, and though the keepers knew of his malpractices, they were for some time unable to catch him in the act, in consequence of his always placing his three dogs as videttes in different directions, to warn him of the approach of any person. A herd-boy at the farm near my house puts his dog to a curious use. A great part of his flock are sent to pasture on the carse-ground across the river, and when the boy does not want to go across to count them and see that they are all right, deterred from doing so by the water being flooded, or from any other reason, he sends his dog to swim across and collect the sheep on the opposite bank, where he can see them all distinctly. Though there are other sheep on the carse belonging to different people, the dog only brings his own flock. After they are counted and pronounced to be all right by the boy, the dog swims back again to his master.

Were I to relate the numberless anecdotes of dogs that have been told me, I could fill a volume.

I am often amused by observing the difference of temper and disposition which is shown by my own dogs—as great a difference, indeed, as would be perceived among the same number of human beings.

Having for many years been a great collector of living *pets*, there is always a vast number of these hangers-on about the house—some useful, some ornamental, and some neither the one nor the other.

Opposite one window of the room I am in at present are a monkey and five dogs basking in the sun, a bloodhound, a Skye terrier, a setter, a Russian poodle, and a young Newfoundland bitch, who is being educated as a retriever; they all live in great friendship with the monkey, who is now in the most absurd manner searching the poodle's coat for fleas, lifting up curl by curl, and examining the roots of the hair. Occasionally, if she thinks that she has pulled the hair, or lifted one of his legs rather too roughly, she looks the dog in the face with an inquiring expression to see if he is angry. The dog, however, seems rather to enjoy the operation, and showing no symptoms of displeasure, the monkey continues her search, and when she sees a flea catches it in the most active manner, looks at it for a moment, and then eats it with great relish. Having exhausted the game on the poodle, she jumps on the back of the bloodhound bitch, and having looked into her face to see how she will bear it, begins a new search, but finding nothing, goes off for a game at romps with the Newfoundland dog. While the bloodhound bitch, hearing the voice of one of the children, whom she has taken a particular fancy to, walks off to the nursery, the setter lies dozing and dreaming of grouse; while the little terrier sits with ears pricked up, listening to any distant sounds of dog or man that she may hear; occasionally she trots off on three legs to look at the back door of the house, for fear any rat-hunt or fun of that sort may take place without her being invited. Why do Highland terriers so often run on three legs? particularly when bent on any mischief? Is it to keep one in reserve in case of emergencies? I never had a Highland terrier who did not hop along constantly on three legs, keeping one of the hind legs up as if to rest it.

The Skye terrier has a great deal of quiet intelligence, learning to watch his master's looks, and understand his meaning in a wonderful manner. Without the determined blind courage of the English bull terrier, this kind of dog shows great intrepidity in attacking vermin of all kinds, though often his courage is accompanied by a kind of shyness and reserve; but when once roused by being bit or scratched in its attacks on vermin, the Skye terrier fights to the last, and shows a great deal of cunning and generalship, as well as courage. Unless well entered, when young, however, they are very apt to be noisy, and yelp and bark more than fight. The terriers which I have had of this kind show some curious habits, unlike most other dogs. I have observed that when young they frequently make a kind of seat under a bush or hedge, where they will sit for hours together, crouched like a wild animal. Unlike other dogs too, they will eat (though not driven by hunger) almost any thing that is given them, such as raw eggs, the bones and meat of wild-ducks, or wood-pigeons, and other birds, that every other kind of dog, however hungry, rejects with disgust. In fact, in many particulars, their habits resemble those of wild animals; they always are excellent swimmers, taking the water quietly and fearlessly when very young. In tracking wounded deer I have occasionally seen a Skye terrier of very great use, leading his master quietly, and with great precision, up to the place where the deer had dropped, or had concealed himself; appearing too to be acting more for the benefit of his master, and to show the game, than for his own amusement. I have no doubt that a clever Skye terrier would in many cases get the sportsman a second shot at a wounded deer with more certainty than almost any other kind of dog. Indeed, for this kind of work, a quiet though slow dog often is of more use than the best deer-hound. I at one time had an English bulldog, who accompanied me constantly in deer-stalking; he learned to crouch and creep up to the deer with me, never showing himself, and seemingly to understand perfectly what I wished him to do. When necessary I could leave him for hours together, lying alone on the hill, when he would never stir till called by me. If a deer was wounded, he would follow the track with untiring perseverance, distinguishing the scent of the wounded animal, and singling it out from the rest, never making a mistake in this respect; he would also follow the stag till he brought him to bay, when, with great address in avoiding the horns, he would rush in and seize him either by the throat or the ear, holding on till I came up, or, as he once did, strangling the animal, and then coming back to show me where he had left it.

In driving some woods one day in Ross-shire, a fine stag broke into a wide opening; two or three sportsmen were stationed at some distance above me; as the deer passed, I saw the light puff of smoke, and heard the crack of their rifles as they fired. At every shot the poor animal doubled with the most extraordinary bounds; he tried to turn back to the cover from which he had been driven, but the shouts of the beaters deterred him, and after stopping for a moment to deliberate, he came back fully determined to cross the opening, in order to gain the shelter of some large woods beyond it. He was galloping across it, when crack went another rifle, the ball striking with a splash into a small pool of water close to him, this turned him towards me, and down he came in my direction as hard as he could gallop; he appeared to be coming

251

directly at me: just as he was about a hundred yards from me, a shout from the beaters, who were coming in view, turned him again, and he passed me, going *ventre à terre*, with his head up and his horns back over his shoulders, giving me a good broadside shot; I fired, and he reeled, turning half round. Bang went my other barrel, and the stag rolled over like a rabbit, with a force and crash that seemed as if it would have broken every bone in his body. Up he got again, and went off, apparently as sound as ever, into the large wood, passing close to a sportsman who was loading; when in the wood, we saw him halt for a moment on a hillock and take a good steady look at us all, who were lost in astonishment at his escape after having been so fairly upset. He then went off at a steady swinging gallop, and we heard him long after he was out of view crushing through the dry branches of the young fir-trees. "Bring the dog," was the cry, and a very large animal, something between a mastiff and a St. Bernard, was brought; the dog went off for a little while, barking and making a great noise, but after rushing up against half a dozen trees, and tumbling over amongst the hidden stones, he came back limping and unwilling to renew the hunt. I had left my bulldog with a servant at a point of the wood some distance off, and I proposed sending for him; one of the sportsmen, who had never seen him engaged in this kind of duty, sarcastically said, "What, *that* dog who followed us to-day, as we rode up? He can be no use; he looks more fit to kill cats or pin a bull." Our host, however, who was better acquainted with his merits, thought otherwise; and when the bulldog came wagging his tail and jumping up on me, I took him to the track and sent him upon it; down went his nose and away he went as hard as he could go, and quite silently. The wood was so close and thick that we could not keep him in sight, so I proposed that we should commence our next beat, as the dog would find me wherever I was, and the strangers did not seem much to expect any success in getting the wounded stag. During the following beat we saw the dog for a moment or two pass an opening, and the next instant two deer came out from the thicket into which he had gone. "He is on the wrong scent, after all," said the shooter, who stood next to me. "Wait, and we will see," was my answer.

We had finished this beat and were consulting what to do, when the dog appeared in the middle of us, appearing very well satisfied with himself, though covered with blood, and with an ugly tear in his skin all along one side. "Ah!" said some one, "he has got beaten off by the deer." Looking at him, I saw that most of the blood was not his own, the wound not being at all deep; I also knew that once having had hold of the deer, he would not have let go as long as he had life in him. "Where is he, old boy? take us to him," said I; the dog perfectly understanding me, looked up in my face, and set off slowly with a whine of delight. He led us through a great extent of wood, stopping every now and then that we might keep up with him; at last he came to the foot of a rock where the stag was lying quite dead with his throat torn open, and marks of a goodly struggle all round the place; a fine deer he was too, and much praise did the dog get for his courage and skill: I believe I could have sold him on the spot at any price which I had chosen to ask, but the dog and I were too old friends to part, having passed many years together, both in London, where he lived with my horses and used to run with my cab, occasionally taking a passing fight with a cat; and also in the country, where he had also accompanied me in many a long and solitary ramble over mountain and valley.

In choosing a young dog for a retriever, it is a great point to fix upon one whose ancestors have been in the same line of business. Skill and inclination to become a good retriever are hereditary, and one come of good parents scarcely requires any breaking, taking to it naturally as soon as he can run about. It is almost impossible to make some dogs useful in this way, no teaching will do it unless there be a natural inclination—a first-rate retriever *nascitur non fit*. You may

253

break almost any dog to carry a rabbit or bird, but it is a different thing entirely to retrieve satisfactorily, or to be uniformly correct in distinguishing and sticking to the scent of the animal which is wounded.

In the same way pointing is hereditary in pointers and setters, and puppies of a good breed, and of a well educated ancestry, take to pointing at game as naturally as to eating their food,—and not only do they, of their own accord, point steadily, but also back each other, quarter their ground regularly, and in fact instinctively follow the example of their high bred and well brought up ancestors. For my own part, I think it quite a superfluous trouble crossing a good breed of pointers with fox-hound, or any other kind of dog, by way of adding speed and strength,—you lose more than you gain, by giving at the same time hard-headedness and obstinacy. It is much better, if you fancy your breed of pointers or setters to be growing small or degenerate, to cross them with some different family of pointers or setters of stronger or faster make, of which you will be sure to find plenty with very little trouble. It is a great point in all dogs to allow them to be as much at liberty as possible; no animal kept shut up in a kennel or place of confinement can have the same use of his senses as one who is allowed to be at large to gain opportunities of exerting his powers of observation and increase his knowledge in the ways of the world. Dogs who are allowed to be always loose are very seldom mischievous and troublesome, it is only those who are kept too long shut up and in solitude that rush into mischief the moment they are at liberty; of course it is necessary to keep dogs confined to a certain extent, but my rule is to imprison them as little as possible. Mine, therefore, seldom are troublesome, but live at peace and friendship with numerous other animals about the house and grounds, although many of those animals are their natural enemies and objects of chace: dogs, Shetland ponies, cats, tame rabbits, wild ducks, sheldrakes, pigeons, &c., all associate together and feed out of the same hand; and the only

one of my pets whose inclination to slaughter I cannot sub-
due, is a peregrine falcon, who never loses an opportunity of
killing any duck or hen that may venture within his reach.
Even the wild partridges and wood-pigeons, who frequently
feed with the poultry, are left unmolested by the dogs. The
terrier, who is constantly at warfare with cats and rabbits in a
state of nature, leaves those about the house in perfect peace;
while the wildest of all wild fowl, the common mallards and
sheldrakes, eat corn from the hand of the "hen-wife."

Though naturally all men are carnivorous, and therefore
animals of prey, and inclined by nature to hunt and destroy
other creatures, and although I share in this our natural
instinct to a great extent, I have far more pleasure in seeing
these different animals enjoying themselves about me, and in
observing their different habits, than I have in hunting down
and destroying them.

Chapter XXXI

The Badger: Antiquity of; Cleanliness; Abode of; Food;
  Family of—Trapping Badgers—Anecdotes—Escape of
  Badger—Anecdotes—Strength of—Cruelty to.

AMONGST the aboriginal inhabitants of our wilder districts,
who are likely to be soon extirpated, we may reckon that
ancient, peaceable, and respectable quadruped, the badger;
of an ancient family he certainly is—the fossil remains which
have been found, prove his race to have been co-existent with
that of the mammoths and megatheriums which once wan-
dered over our islands. Though the elk and beaver have long
since ceased to exist amongst us, our friend the brock still
continues to burrow in the solitary and unfrequented recesses
of our larger woods. Persevering and enduring in his every-
day life, he appears to have been equally so, in clinging to
existence during the numerous changes which have passed

over the face of the globe since the first introduction of his family into it. Notwithstanding the persecutions and indignities that he is unjustly doomed to suffer, I maintain that he is far more respectable in his habits than we generally consider him to be. "Dirty as a badger," "stinking as a badger," are two sayings often repeated, but quite inapplicable to him. As far as we can learn of the domestic economy of this animal when in a state of nature, he is remarkable for his cleanliness—his extensive burrows are always kept perfectly clean, and free from all offensive smell; no filth is ever found about his abode; everything likely to offend his olfactory nerves is carefully removed. I, once, in the north of Scotland, fell in with a perfect colony of badgers; they had taken up their abode in an unfrequented range of wooded rocks, and appeared to have been little interrupted in their possession of them. The footpaths to and from their numerous holes were beaten quite hard; and what is remarkable and worthy of note, they had different small pits dug at a certain distance from their abodes, which were evidently used as receptacles for all offensive filth; every other part of their colony was perfectly clean. A solitary badger's hole, which I once had dug out, during the winter season, presented a curious picture of his domestic and military arrangements—a hard and long job it was for two men to achieve, the passage here and there turned in a sharp angle round some projecting corners of rock, which he evidently made use of when attacked, as points of defence, making a stand at any of these angles, where a dog could not scratch to enlarge the aperture, and fighting from behind his stone buttress. After tracing out a long winding passage, the workmen came to two branches in the hole, each leading to good-sized chambers: in one of these was stored a considerable quantity of dried grass, rolled up into balls as large as a man's fist, and evidently intended for food; in the other chamber there was a bed of soft dry grass and leaves—the sole inhabitant was a peculiarly large old dog-badger. Besides coarse grasses, their food consists of

256

various roots; amongst others, I have frequently found about their hole the bulb of the common wild blue hyacinth. Fruit of all kinds and esculent vegetables form his repast, and I fear that he must plead guilty to devouring any small animal that may come in his way, alive or dead; though, not being adapted for the chace, or even for any very skilful strategy of war, I do not suppose that he can do much in catching an unwounded bird or beast. Eggs are his delight, and a partridge's nest with seventeen or eighteen eggs must afford him a fine meal, particularly if he can surprise and kill the hen-bird also; snails and worms which he finds above ground during his nocturnal rambles are likewise included in his bill of fare. I was one summer evening walking home from fishing in Loch Ness, and having occasion to fasten up some part of my tackle, and also expecting to meet my keeper, I sat down on the shore of the loch. I remained some time, enjoying the lovely prospect: the perfectly clear and unruffled loch lay before me, reflecting the northern shore in its quiet water. The opposite banks consisted, in some parts, of bright green sward, sloping to the water's edge, and studded with some of the most beautiful birch-trees in Scotland; several of the trees spreading out like the oak, and with their ragged and ancient-looking bark resembling the cork-tree of Spain—others drooping and weeping over the edge of the water in the most lady-like and elegant manner. Parts of the loch were edged in by old lichen-covered rocks; while farther on a magnificent scaur of red stone rose perpendicularly from the water's edge to a very great height. So clearly was every object on the opposite shore reflected in the lake below, that it was difficult, nay impossible, to distinguish where the water ended and the land commenced—the shadow from the reality. The sun was already set, but its rays still illuminated the sky. It is said that from the sublime to the ridiculous there is but one step;—and I was just then startled from my reverie by a kind of grunt close to me, and the apparition of a small waddling grey animal, who was busily employed in hunting

257

about the grass and stones at the edge of the loch; presently another, and another, appeared in a little grassy glade which ran down to the water's edge, till at last I saw seven of them busily at work within a few yards of me, all coming from one direction. It at first struck me that they were some farmer's pigs taking a distant ramble, but I shortly saw that they were badgers, come from their fast-nesses rather earlier than usual, tempted by the quiet even-ing, and by a heavy summer shower that was just over, and which had brought out an infinity of large black snails and worms, on which the badgers were feeding with good appe-tite. As I was dressed in grey and sitting on a grey rock, they did not see me, but waddled about, sometimes close to me; only now and then as they crossed my track they showed a slight uneasiness, smelling the ground, and grunting gently. Presently a very large one, which I took to be the mother of the rest, stood motionless for a moment listening with great attention, and then giving a loud grunt, which seemed perfectly understood by the others, she scuttled away, followed by the whole lot. I was soon joined by my attendant, whose approach they had heard long before my less acute ears gave me warning of his coming. In trapping other vermin in these woods, we constantly caught badgers—sometimes sev-eral were found in the traps; I always regretted this, as my keeper was most unwilling to spare their lives, and I fancy seldom did so. His arguments were tolerably cogent, I must confess. When I tried to persuade him that they were quite harmless, he answered me by asking—"Then why, Sir, have they got such teeth, if they don't live, like a dog or fox, on flesh?— and why do they get caught so often in traps baited with rabbits?" I could not but admit that they had most carnivorous-looking teeth, and well adapted to act on the offensive as well as defensive, or to crunch the bones of any young hare, rabbit, or pheasant that came in their way. When caught in traps, they never left part of their foot behind them and so escaped, as foxes and other vermin frequently do; but they display very great strength and dexterity in drawing up the peg of the trap, and this done, they will carry off the heaviest trap to an amazing distance, over rock or heather. They never attempt to enter their hole with a trap dangling to their foot, but generally lay up in some furze-bush or thicket; on these occasions we invariably found them, by tracking them with a dog who generally attended the trapper, and which dog was peculiarly skilful in tracking animals of this kind. Rover (for that was his name), a strong water-spaniel, was very fond of, and took great interest in, trapping; if he accompanied the keeper when placing his traps overnight, he would often start alone in the morning to take a survey of them, and either kill any animal he found captive, or, if he was not very confident of being the strongest, he would return impatiently for the man, and, running before him, point out plainly where every head of vermin was caught. As for getting into a trap himself, he was far too cunning, but always halting a few yards to leeward of them, and sniffing the air, would at once know if anything was caught. If a cat, marten-cat, or any smaller animal was there, he at once rushed in and killed it; but he waited for the assistance of his friend the keeper to dispatch any larger animal.

To return to the badger, and his food. One of his most favourite repasts is the contents of the nest of the wasp or wild bee, great numbers of which he must destroy. However far under ground the hive may be, and in however strong and difficult a situation, he digs them up, and, depending on his rough coat and long hair as a protection from their stings, devours comb, larvæ, honey, and insects. Many a wasps' nest I have found dug up in this way, and often far from the badger's usual abode; but the tracks of the animal always made it evident who had been the robber.

The badger is easily tamed, and will (if taken young and well used) become much attached to his master. When first caught, their efforts to escape show a degree of strength and ingenuity which is quite wonderful, digging and tearing at

259

their prison with the strength of a rhinoceros. When first imprisoned, if looked at, he immediately rolls himself up into a ball and remains quite motionless. As soon as the coast is clear again, he continues his attempts to escape; but if unsuccessful, he soon becomes contented in his confinement. I one day found a badger not much hurt in a trap. Tying a rope to his hind leg, I drove him home before me, as a man drives a pig, but with much less trouble, for he made no attempts at escape, but trotted quietly ahead, only occasionally showing a natural inclination to bolt off the main path whenever he passed any diverging road, all of which were probably familiar haunts of the unlucky beast. When at home I put him into a paved court, where I thought he could not possibly escape. The next morning, however, he was gone; having displaced a stone that I thought him quite incapable of moving, and then digging under the wall, he got away.

The badger always puts me in mind of a miniature bear, and to this family he evidently belongs. His proportions are similar to those of the bear; his manner of placing his feet on the ground is like that of a bear, and is very peculiar. Beyond the marks of his toes, which, five in number, mark the ground in nearly a straight line, are the impressions of his strong, sharp nails, apparently unconnected with, and at the distance of an inch or two from the rest of his track. These long and powerful nails are a formidable weapon, and in engagements with dogs he makes good use of them, inflicting fearful and sometimes fatal wounds. Though a quiet animal, and generally speaking not much given to wandering, I have occasionally fallen in with his unmistakeable track miles from any burrow. His habits are wholly nocturnal, and it is only in the summer evenings, when the darkness lasts but a few hours, that he is ever met with whilst it is light. During winter he not only keeps entirely within his hole, but fills up the mouth of it to exclude the cold and any troublesome visitor who might intrude on his slumbers. Frequently, however, tempted by mild weather in the winter, he comes out for

Studies of Badgers, by J. G. Millais

some good purpose of his own—either to enjoy the fresh air or to add to his larder; but never does he venture out in frost or snow. Sometimes I have known a badger leave the solitude of the woods and take to some drain in the cultivated country, where he becomes very bold and destructive to the crops, cutting down wheat and ravaging the gardens in a surprising manner. One which I know to be now living in this manner derives great part of his food during the spring from a rookery, under which he nightly hunts, feeding on the young rooks that fall from their nests or on the old ones that are shot. This badger eludes every attempt to trap him. Having more than once run narrow risks of this nature, he has become so cunning that no one can catch him. If a dozen baited traps are set, he manages to carry off the baits and spring every trap, always with total impunity to himself. At one time he was watched out to some distance from his drain, and traps were then put in all directions round it, but, by jumping over some and rolling over others, he escaped all. In fact, though a despised and maltreated animal, when he has once acquired a certain experience in worldly matters, few beasts show more address and cunning in keeping out of scrapes. Though eaten in France, Germany, and other countries, and pronounced to make excellent hams, we in Britain despise him as food, though I see no reason why he should not be quite as good as any pork.

The badger becomes immensely fat. Though not a great eater, his quiet habits and his being a great sleeper prevent his being lean.

The immense muscular power that he has in his chest and legs enables him to dig with great rapidity, while his powerful jaws (powerful, indeed, beyond any other animal of his size) enable him to tear away any obstacle in the shape of roots, &c. that he meets with. He can also stand with perfect impunity a blow on his forehead which would split the frontal bone of an ox. This is owing to its great thickness, and

262

also to the extra protection of a strong ridge or keel which runs down the middle of his head. A comparatively slight blow on the back of his head kills him. In his natural state he is more than a match for any animal that would be inclined to molest him, and can generally keep at bay any dog small enough to enter his hole. Fighting at advantage from behind some stone or root, he gives the most fearful bites and scratches, while the dog has nothing within his reach to attack save the badger's formidable array of teeth and claws.

Though nearly extinct as one of the *feræ naturæ* of England, the extensive woods and tracts of rocks in the north of Scotland will, I hope, prevent the badger's becoming, like the beaver and other animals, wholly a creature of history, and existing only in record. Much should I regret that this respectable representative of so ancient a family, the comrade of mammoths and other wonders of the antediluvian world, should become quite extirpated. Living, too, in remote and uncultivated districts, he very seldom commits any depredations deserving of death or persecution, but subsists on the wild succulent grasses and roots, and the snails and reptiles which he finds in the forest glades, or, on rare occasions, makes capture of young game or wounded rabbits or hares, but I do not believe that he does or can hunt down any game that would not otherwise fall a prey to crow or weasel, or which has the full use of its limbs. It is only wounded and injured animals that he can catch.

It is difficult to understand how any person who is not lost to every sense of humanity and shame can take delight in the cowardly and brutal amusement of badger-baiting—instead of amusement, I should have said, the disgusting exhibition of a peaceable and harmless animal worried by fierce and powerful dogs. The poor badger, too, has probably been kept for a length of time in a confined and close hutch, thereby losing half his energy and strength; while the dogs, trained

263

to the work and in full vigour of wind and limb, attack him in the most tender and vulnerable parts. Truly, I always feel a wish to make the badger and his keeper change places for a few rounds. Not that I would pay the former so bad a compliment as to suppose that he would take delight in tormenting even so great a brute as his gaoler must be.

Drawing by Charles St. John

264

Philip Henry Gosse

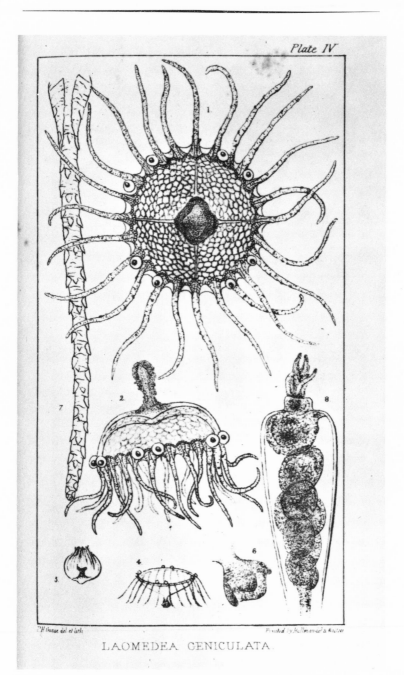

LAOMEDEA GENICULATA.

Illustration by Philip Henry Gosse from his
A Naturalist's Rambles on the Devonshire Coast

Sticklebacks and Nest, from H. Gervais and R. Boulart, Les Poissons, 1876

Philip Henry Gosse
[1810–1888]

U ntil well into the age of Darwin, theology and science con-
tinued to go comfortably hand in hand. Thus, Philip
Henry Gosse, who presided as lay minister over a small and
rigidly fundamentalist sect of Christians, was at the same time
one of the most eminent of Victorian zoologists, finding every-
where imprinted on the natural world evidences of divine handi-
work. This strange mating of passions is fully portrayed in two
works by Edmund Gosse, whose fine biography of Philip Henry,
published in 1890, was followed in 1907 by the autobio-
graphical *Father and Son*, with its moving account of the clash in
temperament between a pietistic father and a freethinking
son.

Gosse's early life was adventurous. At the age of seventeen he
left England to become clerk in a counting-house at the port of
Carbonear in Newfoundland. The isolation of this remote out-
post fostered the growth of scientific interests, and he turned to
the study of entomology, in which he was entirely self-taught.
After eight years in Newfoundland, Gosse tried his hand at
farming in the province of Quebec, and then wandered south to
Alabama, where he taught school in a primitive backwoods
community. On his return to England in 1839 he took up the
literary career in which he won recognition as the author of
learned papers as well as of popular works on science, many of
them sponsored by the Society for Promoting Christian Knowl-
edge. His first publication was *The Canadian Naturalist* (1840),
derived from the notebooks which he had kept during his three
years' residence on the Canadian border. During 1844–46 Gosse
spent eighteen months in Jamaica, where he devoted himself
principally to the ornithological investigations recorded in *The
Birds of Jamaica* (1847) and *A Naturalist's Sojurn in Jamaica*
(1851). In these volumes the author, who was the son of an

267

accomplished miniaturist, brought to perfection the accurate and beautifully colored drawings from life which illustrated all of his subsequent studies in natural history.

Overwork drove Gosse to the Devon coast in 1852 to regain his health; with this region, in which he resided for the remainder of his life, his most important and original scientific findings are associated. *Actinologia Britannica: A History of the British Sea-Anemones and Corals* (1858–60), which provided the first systematic analysis of the order Actinoidea, including thirty-four hitherto unidentified species of the lovely sea-anemone, long remained the standard work on its subject. But Gosse was not only a pioneer in the exploration of marine fauna; his lively descriptions of the curious and fascinating forms of life teeming in tidal pools converted successive generations of seaside vacationers into would-be naturalists. This vogue was encouraged by Gosse's experiments with salt-water aquaria, which he undertook to further his own researches, but which were, in his son's words, "instantly accepted by naturalists and amateurs alike, and became to the one a portable studio of biology, to the others a charming and fashionable toy."

For all the rigor of his zoological classifications, Gosse belongs in the great tradition of field naturalists descending from Gilbert White. The Preface to *A Naturalist's Sojourn in Jamaica* gives the following eloquent statement of how he viewed his calling:

> That alone is worthy to be called natural history which investigates and records the condition of living things, of things in a state of nature; if animals, of *living* animals: —which tells of their 'sayings and doings,' their varied notes and utterances, songs and cries; their actions in ease, and under the pressure of circumstances; their affections and passions towards their young, towards each other, towards other animals, towards man; their various arts and devices to protect their progeny, to procure food, to escape from their enemies, to defend themselves from attacks; their ingenious resources for concealment; their stratagems to overcome their victims; their modes of bringing forth, of feeding, and of training their offspring; the relations of their structure to their wants and habits; the countries in

268

which they dwell; their connection with the inanimate world around them, mountain or plain, forest or field, barren heath or bushy dell, open savannah or wild hidden glen, river, lake or sea:—this would be indeed *zoology*, viz. the science of *living* creatures.

The charm and vivacity of Gosse's writing is nowhere better exemplified than in the delightful series of books devoted to his collecting expeditions along the shores and in the waters of southwestern England: *A Naturalist's Rambles on the Devonshire Coast* (1853); *The Aquarium* (1854); *Tenby* (1856); and *A Year at the Shore*, "a sort of sea-shepherd's calendar," which appeared at monthly intervals throughout 1864 in the illustrated monthly, *Good Words*. In these works Charles Kingsley well remarked Gosse's "power of bringing out the human side of science, and giving to seemingly dry disquisitions and animals of the lowest type, by little touches of pathos and humour, that living and personal interest, to bestow which is generally the special function of the poet."

From *A Year at the Shore*

May

WE are far from having exhausted the treasures of the teeming sands. Another visit to their broad expanse may yield other objects of interest not inferior to those we lately discovered there. Let us, then, seek the shore, where our humble friend the shrimper, with his wading horse, under the guidance of his shrill-voiced little son, still pursues his indefatigable calling.

Again the keer-drag is drawn up the tawny beach, the bag is untied, and the sparkling, crawling, jumping heap spreads itself over the sand, beyond the limits of the insufficient cloth.

A little silvery fish wriggles from the mass, and, by a few lateral vibrations, in an instant buries himself in the soft wet sand, all but the upper surface of his head and back. Our attention is drawn towards this object; but our friend the shrimper shouts rather abruptly a note of warning. "Mind what ye be 'bout! that 'ere's pison! He's a sting-bull, he is." Thus armed, we use caution in our approaches, and look well before we touch. As we see it now, it certainly presents a noteworthy appearance. A large head, with a wide mouth opening at very upward angles; two staring eyes, set in the crown so as to look upward instead of sideways, and intently watching our intentions; a short fin on the back, of which the membrane is of the deepest velvet black, and the rays, which are stout sharp spines, are white; these rays are now stretched to the utmost, like a fan widely expanded, so as to offer the threatening points in all directions to a foe;—these are all the features we can discern, except a narrow line of olive presently lost in the sand, which marks the buried body.

In spite of the good man's earnest warnings to have nothing to do with so venomous a creature, we must contrive to take possession of it for study at home; and by the aid of our hand-net we find no difficulty in lifting it and transferring it, an unwilling guest, to a glass jar of sea-water. We now discern it more fully and distinctly; though it manifests its indignation at this tyrannical suspension of the *Habeas Corpus* Act, by flouncing around the glass, and scattering the water hither and thither. This wrath, however, gradually subsides, and our captive philosophically makes up his mind to his fate.

It is the Lesser Weever, a name corrupted from the French, who call it Vive, from the length of time which the fish will *live* out of its native element. It also bears the names of sting-fish, sting-bull, and sea-cat, among English fishermen; on the shores of the Mediterranean it bears the title of spider, and the ancient Romans called it sea-dragon. The specific names,—*vipera* and *draco*, viper and dragon—which are appropriated to this species and another which is nearly allied to it, make up an extensive list of aliases, all combining to give this pretty little fish a thoroughly bad reputation. All these titles point to a habit and a power possessed by it of inflicting severe wounds, which without doubt are of a highly inflammatory character, and are slow and difficult to cure. These are effected by the rays of the first dorsal fin, which, as we have just seen, are erected and spread in a way which indicates a perfect consciousness of their power, and by certain spines, long and acute, set on the gill-covers, one on each, pointing backward. These all are of needle-like sharpness, and are wielded most effectively. Yarrell tells us that if trod upon, or only touched, while on the watch, nearly buried in

271

the sand at the bottom of the water, it strikes with force either upwards or sideways; and Pennant says that he had seen it direct its blows with as much judgment as a fighting cock. Fishermen hold it in great dread; and the name of sting-bull is said to be due to its power of piercing even the proverbial thickness of a bull's hide.

Cuvier considers the imputation of venom to the wounds made by the Weever as a popular error. He says, "They cannot inject into the wounds they inflict with their spines any poisonous substance, properly so called; but, as these spines are very strong and sharp-pointed, and can no doubt pierce the flesh to a considerable depth, these wounds, like all others of the same description, may produce dangerous consequences if care is not taken to enlarge them, and to allow the blood to flow; this perhaps, is the most certain, as the simplest remedy, and much preferable to the boasted applications of the ancients."

This is oracular; but it does not appear that the decision of the great French anatomist was grounded on any definite experiments. Mr. Couch, on the other hand, has known three men wounded successively in the hand by the same fish (the Greater Weever), and the consequences have been felt in a few minutes as high as the shoulder. It is certain that the spinous bristles of certain caterpillars have the power of inflicting envenomed wounds, which in some cases even prove fatal, notwithstanding the minuteness of the organs, and evidence appears very strong for the injection of some highly irritant poison by means of these prickles of the Weevers.

The flesh of these fishes is esteemed for the table; but such is the general apprehension of danger attendant upon touching them, heightened also by their great tenacity of life, that the fishermen usually cut off the first dorsal and the gill-spines as soon as they capture them; while in Spain and France these precautions are enforced by legal penalties, on such fishes being exposed in the market without having been disarmed.*

According to Mr. Couch smart friction of the wounded part with olive-oil is the most effectual remedy; and this fact again suggests analogy of the evil with the effects produced by the bites of venomous snakes and the stings of insects.†

Our little fish is not uncomely in its form or the distribution of its sober colours. The upper parts are light olive, with lines of ill-defined reddish spots running lengthwise; the sides are silver-grey, tenderly washed with blue; the under parts pearly white: the cheeks and operculum are richly adorned with pearly reflections; these parts are destitute of scales, which is the chief distinction between this species and the Greater Weever, after the size; this species rarely exceeding five or six inches in length, whereas its congener attains double those dimensions, and even more.

In the tank, it is not particularly interesting; it grovels on the bottom among the pebbles, and will cover its body with the sediment so far as it is able; where it lies for hours, watching upward. Doubtless this is its habitual mode of obtaining its food; lying motionless in wait, nearly concealed, the eyes and the mouth both opening upwards, so that the former can observe, and the latter seize, any vagrant crustacean, or annelid, or young fish-fry that unsuspectingly swims within reach. Its motions when its energies are aroused are rapid, sudden, and forcible; and it probably rarely misses its victim when it makes its snap; while the multitude of minute creatures that roam continually over every part of the sea-bottom give no lack of opportunities for the exercise of its

---

* So old Drayton, in his "Polyolbion" sings, quaintly enough, and with a noble defiance of grammar: —
     "*The Weever, which, although his prickles venom be,*
     By fishers cut away, which buyers seldom see,
     Yet for the fish he bears, 'tis not accounted bad."

† Since the above was written, the question has been set at rest, by Dr. Günther's and Mr. Byerley's actual discovery of poison-glands in connexion with these spines.

instincts. He fares sumptuously, no doubt.

Here is in the drag a specimen of an interesting tribe of fishes. It is the young of the common Thornback, a little thing about five inches in width, and in its infantile grace and beauty much more attractive than the older ones we are accustomed to see on the fishmonger's table. It flaps and flutters in impatience at being dragged out of its element, and exposed to ungenial air: we will quiet its anxiety by lifting it into yonder shallow rock-pool. Now watch it. How easily and gracefully it glides around its new abode, moving along by an undulation of the edges of the broad pectoral fins, a movement which Yarrell describes as something between flying and swimming. Now it lies still on the sand-floor of the pool, motionless, save that the two oval orifices just behind the eyes are constantly opening and closing, by the drawing across each or back, of a film which exactly resembles an eyelid, and which on examination with a lens we see to be edged with a delicate fringe. The action is so closely like the winking of an eye, that an observer seeing the fish for the first time might readily suppose the orifices to be the organs of vision. They are, however, outlets of the gills, called spiracles; the ordinary gill-apertures are five on each side, placed semi-circularly on the inferior surface of the body, as you see when I turn the fish on its back,—a demonstration which it resents and resists with all its might: these upper orifices communicate with the gill-chambers by canals, and you may see the water now and then strongly driven out of them.

The eyes are these knobs just in front of the spiracles; or rather these are the orbits, the pupil looking sideways and somewhat downward. If you use the lens again, you perceive that there is a singular protection to the pupil in the form of a fan-like array of about a dozen stiff points arching over it.

The general form of the fish is beautifully symmetrical; it is nearly a rhomboid, with the two front sides slightly excavated, and the two posterior sides convex. At the point where these latter unite, there are two smaller fins (the ventrals), and the body is continued very slender to a considerable length, tapering to a point, near which two upright dorsals are placed. The pectorals, as in all this tribe, are of enormous size, forming the lateral angles of the rhomboid, and extending in front of the head to the tip of the snout.

The colours are beautiful, but not at all gaudy. A warm olive brown is the ground hue, on which numerous roundish black spots, with softly blending outlines, are set in symmetrical patterns, and there are also rows of pale spots. This combination of hues is elegant. The slender prolongation of the body is edged with a narrow stripe of pure white. The colour of the whole under surface is richly iridescent, like mother-of-pearl.

At present we see only a few of the curved spines appearing, chiefly in the vicinity of the eyes, which in the adult become so conspicuous and remarkable; being something like strong rose-spines, each set on an oval button of bone, imbedded in the skin.

Another draught presents us with the Fifteen-spined Stickleback, a little fish, remarkable for its form, but much more so for its habits. It is ordinarily about five or six inches in length, very slender and lithe, from which circumstance, combined with a protrusion of the jaws, which gives it a sinister expression, it is on some parts of the coast called the Sea-Adder. The lower jaw projects considerably beyond the upper, which indicates that the fish habitually takes its food from a point above the level of its own body. The dorsal and anal fins are high and short, so as to form, when erected, nearly equal-sided triangles; but the former is preceded by fifteen minute sharp erectile spines, each of which has its own little membrane, and all together represent the spinous portion of the dorsal fin in such fishes as have but one, as the Blennies, or the first dorsal in such as have two, as the Weevers. The caudal is narrowly lozenge-formed, as ordinarily carried, but becomes fan-like when expanded. The colours are deep sepia, or olive-brown, cast into streaks and

275

irregular clouds, on the sides, where they are interrupted by white, and by a rich golden yellow, that extends over the inferior surface: the dorsal and anal fins are white, each crossed by a broad conspicuous band of brown; the eyes have golden irides.

We frequently see this attractive little fish hovering about the long tufts of wrack and tangle that hang from perpendicular rocks, and from the quays and wharves of our harbours. It diligently hunts about for its minute crustacean prey, in picking off which it assumes all varieties of position "between the horizontal and perpendicular, with the head downward or upward," thrusting its projecting snout into the tufted weed, and snatching its morsel with a sudden jerk.

It is, however, in its domestic relations that this little fish presents itself in the most interesting aspect. It was known ages ago to Aristotle, that some fishes are in the habit of forming nests, in which they deposit their eggs, and bring up their young with a parental care not inferior to that of birds. Until lately, however, this fact was supposed to be fabulous; and fishes were believed by the greatest masters of modern zoology to be utterly destitute of the parental instinct. Recent research has in this, as in so many instances, proved the exactitude of the old Stagyrite's knowledge, and we now know that several fishes of different families nidificate. The Sticklebacks, most of which inhabit in common our marine and fresh waters, are remarkable for the manifestation of this faculty, as was first shown by Mr. Crookenden, of Lewisham, in 1834, and as has since been proved, with many interesting details, by Mr. A. Hancock and Mr. Warington. Our Sea-Adder, which is exclusively marine, was first ascertained to be a nest-builder by the late Dr. George Johnston, who mentioned the fact in the "Transactions of the Berwickshire Naturalists' Club" in 1839. But the most interesting account is that of Mr. R. Q. Couch, who noticed the facts on the coast of Cornwall, and thus records them in a paper read before the Royal Institution of that county:—

"During the summers of 1842 and 1843, while searching for the naked mollusks of the county, I occasionally discovered portions of sea-weed and the common coralline (*Corallina officinalis*) hanging from the rocks in pear-shaped masses, variously intermingled with each other. On one occasion, having observed that the mass was very curiously bound together by a slender, silken-looking thread, it was torn open, and the centre was found to be occupied by a mass of transparent, amber-coloured ova, each being about the tenth of an inch in diameter. Though examined on the spot with a lens, nothing could be discovered to indicate their character. They were, however, kept in a basin, and daily supplied with sea-water, and eventually proved to be the young of some fish. The nest varies a great deal in size, but rarely exceeds six inches in length, or four inches in breadth. It is pear-shaped, and composed of sea-weed or the common coralline as they hang suspended from the rock. They are brought together, without being detached from their places of growth, by a delicate opaque white thread. This thread is highly elastic, and very much resembles silk, both in appearance and texture: this is brought round the plants, and tightly binds them together, plant after plant, till the ova, which are deposited early, are completely hidden from view. This silk-like thread is passed in all directions through and around the mass, in a very complicated manner. At first the thread is semi-fluid, but by exposure it solidifies; and hence contracts and binds the substance forming the nest so closely together that it is able to withstand the violence of the sea, and may be thrown carelessly about without derangement. In the centre are deposited the ova, very similar to the masses of frog-spawn in ditches.

"Some of these nests are formed in pools, and are consequently always in water: others are frequently to be found between tide-marks, in situations where they hang dry for several hours in the day; but whether in the water or liable to hang dry, they are always carefully watched by the adult

277

animal. On one occasion I repeatedly visited one every day for three weeks, and invariably found it guarded. The old fish would examine it on all sides, and then retire for a short time, but soon returned to renew the examination. On several occasions I laid the eggs bare, by removing a portion of the nest; but when this was discovered, great exertions were made to re-cover them. By the mouth of the fish the edges of the opening were again drawn together, and other portions torn from their attachments and brought over the orifice, till the ova were again hid from view. And as great force was sometimes necessary to effect this, the fish would thrust its snout into the nest as far as the eyes, and then jerk backwards till the object was effected. While thus engaged it would suffer itself to be taken by the hand, but repelled any attack made on the nest, and quitted not its post so long as I remained; and to those nests that were left dry between tide-marks, the guardian fish always returned with the returning tide, nor did they quit the post to any great distance till again carried away by the receding tide."

It is worthy of note that the newly-hatched young from these nests were so unlike the full-grown Stickleback, and so like the common smooth Blenny, that Mr. Couch concluded that there had been some error in his observation, and that the nest truly belonged to the latter fish. Further research, however, proved that the Stickleback was indeed the parent; and the transition from the infantile Blenny-like outline of the face, high, bluff, and almost perpendicular, to the true Stickleback outline, long, slender, pointed, with the far-projecting lower jaw, is something remarkable.

But now the tide has reached its lowest mark; and as we wander over the wet sand at its very verge, our attention is attracted by every tiny object that breaks the uniform level, even at a considerable distance. Some of these are worm-casts thrown up by busy Annelids, working away in the sand to reach a lower and therefore a wetter level, as the upper stratum dries in the sun. But others are Crabs, of two or three species. One of them is the somewhat uncommon and very beautiful *Portumnus variegatus*, of which a great number are left by the sea, but all of them dead; some of them, however, from their freshness, only recently defunct. The shape of the carapace, or body-shell, is very elegant, and the colours, though sober—a light drab, mottled and pencilled with pale lilac—are pleasing: the hindmost pair of feet terminate in thin swimming-plates, but they are narrow, and exhibit the natatory character in only a subordinate degree.

Other Crabs are alive and active, though, to be sure, in a somewhat sluggish way. Here we catch sight of a slight movement in the wet sand, and, stooping, we perceive a pair of antennæ, much beset with short bristles, projecting from the surface. They wag to and fro, and presently up pushes a shelly head, with its pair of stalked and jointed eyes, and two tremendously long angular arms, furnished with awkward-looking nippers at their extremities. Another effort, and the whole Crab emerges from his sandy burrow, and displays his pale buff-coloured shell, wrinkled across, and armed with sharp spiny points at its front and edges. We easily take him up, for his means of escape are feeble, as he uncouthly shuffles on his short legs over the sand; and his bellicose instincts are not strongly developed, nor, if they were, have those long levers of arms any formidable powers of offence. Latreille gave to the genus the title of *Corystes;* which signifies a warrior armed for battle, from κόρυς, a helmet, but its inoffensiveness belies the appellation. Pennant had already conferred on the species the name of *Cassivelaunus*, the ancient British chief immortalized by Cæsar. If you were to ask me why this obscure crab should bear a name so renowned, I can answer only by conjecture. The carapace is marked by wrinkles, which, while in some specimens they suggest nothing, in others, especially old males, bear the strongest and most ludicrous resemblance to the face of an ancient man. I have taken specimens in which the *vraisemblance* was so

279

perfect as to strike me, and others to whom I showed it, with amazement. Now Pennant, as is well known, had strong sympathies with his British ancestry; and perhaps, by a not extravagant stretch of imagination, his playful fancy saw the features of the grand old Celtic warrior perpetuated on this Crab, which he first met with, too, be it remembered, on the Welsh coast.

Mr. Couch, in his Cornish Fauna, notices the unusual length of the antennæ. "These organs," he says, "are of some use beyond their common office of feelers; perhaps, as in some other crustaceans, they assist in the process of excavation; and, when soiled by labour, I have seen the Crab effect their cleaning by alternately bending the joints of their stalks, which stand conveniently angular for this purpose. Each of the long antennæ is thus drawn along the brush that fringes the internal face of the other, until both are cleared of every particle that adhered to them." This suggested use of the antennæ does not seem to me to be a very felicitous guess of the excellent Cornish naturalist: I should fancy them to be somewhat inefficient instruments in excavation: perhaps I can help him to a better. I have observed that, when these Crabs are kept in an aquarium, they are fond of sitting bolt upright, the antennæ placed close together, and also pointing straight upward from the head. This is, doubtless, the attitude in which the animal sits in its burrow, for the tips of the antennæ may often be seen just projecting from the sand. When the chosen seat has happened to be so close to the glass side of the tank as to bring the antennæ within the range of a pocket lens, I have minutely investigated these organs, without disturbing the old warrior in his meditation. I immediately saw, on each occasion, that a strong current of water was continuously pouring up from the points of the approximate antennæ. Tracing this to its origin, it became evident that it was produced by the rapid vibration of the foot-jaws, drawing in the surrounding water, and pouring it off upwards *between the united antennæ*, as through a long tube. Then, on examining these organs, I perceived that the form and arrangement of their bristles did indeed constitute each antenna a semi-tube, so that when the pair were brought face to face the tube was complete. It is difficult to make this arrangement intelligible by mere words; but I may say that if either of the antennæ were broken off in the middle and viewed vertically, the bristles would be seen to project from each side of the inner face, in a curved form, each making about a fourth of a circle, so that the two corresponding bristles enclose, with the body of the antenna, a semicircle. Of course, those of the opposite antenna make another semicircle, and, when placed face to face, the points of the bristles just cross each other, and a circle is enclosed. Now, the whole length of the antennæ (about an inch and a half) is closely beset with these bristles, and thus a long row of rings is formed with very narrow interspaces between them; and these rings do in effect constitute a tube quite sufficient to retain the stream of water that is poured through it.

I think then that we may, with an approach to certainty, conclude that the long antennæ are intended to keep a passage open through the sand, from the bottom of the burrow to the superincumbent water, for the purpose of pouring off the waste water, rendered effete by having bathed the gills; and it is one of those exquisite contrivances and appropriations of structure to habit which are so constantly exciting our admiration in the handiwork of the ever blessed God, which cannot be predicated by the *à priori* reasoner, however astute, but are ever rewarding the research of the patient observer.

Our walk along the sands with steady downcast poring gaze suddenly ends, and we find ourselves among low ledges of black rock (ruddy, however, in its recent fractures, for it is the old red sandstone), clad with sweltering weed, and intersected by little sparkling pools and basins, in which the tiny fishes and entangled prawns shoot hither and thither at our approach. It is the low-lying ridge in the midst of the broad

281

sandy bight that I have already spoken of. Well, *n'importe;* there is plenty of game to be obtained here, and all is fish that comes to our net. What have we here, creeping over the broad brown leathery leaf of this *Laminaria?* Is it a little scrap torn from an old newspaper? It looks like it at the first glance, only that it moves steadily onward with a smooth gliding motion, which shows that it possesses a life of its own. Examine it closely: it is exactly like a bit of white paper, about as large as a rose leaf, and cut into that shape, only with an even edge, its clear white surface marked all over with black parallel lines, some thinner, some thicker, running lengthwise, and as clear as if drawn with a pen. What answers to the base of the leaf is the head of the creature, the pointed end being the tail, where the two most strongly marked black lines meet; from the head end arise two curious ear-like leaflets, which are studded with crowded black dots, and are thrown back upon the general surface. With a lens we may discern on the surface of the body, just between these ear-like tentacles, a group of black specks. These are ascertained to be veritable eyes, notwithstanding their number, for they have a cornea, a light-refracting body surrounded with pigment, and a nerve-bulb.

As the animal glides over the surface of the smooth weed, or over the inequalities of the rough rock, we see that its thin papery margin is frequently thrown up into waves, or folds, more or less distinctly revealing the inferior surface. The movement is very even and uniform, but the mode by which it is effected has not been satisfactorily explained. It has been asserted that certain staff-like bristles which project from the skin are used as oars, but this seems doubtful. It is certain that the whole body of the animal, as of the entire class to which it belongs, is densely clothed with minute vibratory cilia; and these, while they probably serve as organs of locomotion in freely swimming, do also without doubt make the whole skin a highly delicate and sensitive organ of touch.

It is asserted of the near allies of this species, and probably

Illustration by Gosse for his A Year at the Shore
Fifteen-spined Stickleback (*above*); *Lesser Weever* (*below*)

Banded Flat-worm and Long-worm;
another illustration by Gosse for A Year at the Shore

is equally true in this case, that if an individual be cut to pieces, every portion continues to live and feel, from whatever part of the body it may be taken; and what is not a little remarkable, each piece, even if it be the end of the tail, as soon as the first moment of pain and irritation has passed, begins to move in the same direction as that in which the entire animal was advancing, as if the body were actuated throughout by the same impulse; and, moreover, every division, even if it is not more than the eighth or tenth part of the creature, will become complete and perfect in all its organs.

You would naturally expect to find the creature's mouth at the front end, where the two tentacles are placed, and the group of eyes, but you would search for it there in vain. It is, in fact, situated most strangely in the very midst of the belly; that is, at the very centre of the inferior surface. And its structure is not less peculiar than its locality. It consists of an orifice, in the midst of which lies a sort of trumpet of enormous extent when opened, but when not in active use thrown into many folds, which, when the animal wishes to seize prey, are thrust forth, and being partly opened, take the appearance of many irregular tentacles radiating in all directions, at the centre of which is the œsophagus, leading immediately into a much ramified intestine. The name which is given to this elegant and interesting creature is *Eurylepta vittata*.

But here is another member of the same class of strange creatures. On turning up a large flat stone, we expose to the light of day what might readily be mistaken for a very long thong of black leather, or rather a narrow strip of Indian-rubber, twisted and tied together, and coiled in all possible contortions. If you take hold of it, you find it not so easy to secure it as you expected, for it is excessively lubricous and soft, and withal so extensile and so tough, that you may pull one of the coils to almost any length without lifting the rest of the creature. However, you at last contrive to raise the slippery subject, and commit it safe to your tank at home, in which it will live an indefinite while; often invisible for weeks at a time, lying concealed under some of the stones, then seen perhaps in every corner of your aquarium at once, stretching from one stone to another, and coiling around every groin and projection, folded back upon itself, until in the multitude of convolutions you despair of finding head, tail, or any end at all to the uncouth vermin. You may soon discover the signs of its presence, however, in another way, for its voracity is great, and it is a ferocious foe to the tube-dwelling worms; such as the lovely *Sabellæ* and *Serpulæ*, thrusting its serpent-like head into their tubes, and dragging out the hapless tenant to be quickly swallowed.

The animal is named *Nemertes Borlasii*, or sometimes *Borlasia longissima*, in allusion to Dr. Borlase, the historian of Cornwall. It is also occasionally termed the Long-worm, *par excellence*, a name whose appropriateness will appear from the fact that it sometimes reaches a length of thirty feet, with a breadth of an eighth of an inch.

Mr. Kingsley has drawn the portrait of this ciliated worm; and if he has painted it in somewhat dark colours, and manifested more than a common measure of antipathy to it, we must confess that the physical and moral lineaments of the subject do in some degree justify the description. I will quote his vivid words.

"There are animals in which results so strange, fantastic, even seemingly horrible, are produced, that fallen man may be pardoned if he shrinks from them in disgust. That, at least, must be a consequence of our own wrong state; for everything is beautiful and perfect in its place. It may be answered, 'Yes, in its place; but its place is not yours. You had no business to look at it, and must pay the penalty for intermeddling.' I doubt that answer: for surely, if man have liberty to do anything, he has liberty to search out freely his Heavenly Father's works; and yet every one seems to have his antipathic animal, and I know one bred from his childhood to zoology by land and sea, and bold in asserting, and honest in feeling, that all without exception is beautiful, who yet cannot, after handling, and petting, and admiring all day long every uncouth and venomous beast, avoid a paroxysm of horror at the sight of the common house-spider. At all events, whether we were intruding or not, in turning this stone, we must pay a fine for having done so; for there lies an animal, as foul and monstrous to the eye as 'hydra, gorgon, or chimera dire,' and yet so wondrously fitted for its work, that we must needs endure for our own instruction to handle and look at it. Its name I know not (though it lurks here under every stone), and should be glad to know. It seems some very 'low' Ascarid or Planarian worm. You see it? That black, slimy, knotted lump among the gravel, small enough to be taken up in a dessert-spoon. Look now, as it is raised and its coils drawn out. Three feet! Six—nine at least, with a capability of seemingly endless expansion; a slimy tape of living caoutchouc, some eighth of an inch in diameter, a dark chocolate-black, with paler longitudinal lines. It is alive? It hangs helpless and motionless, a mere velvet string across the hand. Ask the neighbouring Annelids and the fry of the rock fishes, or put it into a vase at home, and see. It lies motionless, trailing itself among the gravel; you cannot tell where it begins or ends; it may be a strip of dead sea-weed, *Himanthalia lorea*, perhaps, or *Chorda filum;* or even a tarred string. So thinks the little fish who plays over and over it, till he touches at last what is too surely a head. In an instant a bell-shaped sucker mouth has fastened to its side. In another instant, from one lip, a concave double proboscis, just like a tapir's (another instance of the repetition of forms), has clasped him like a finger, and now begins the struggle; but in vain. He is being 'played,' with such a fishing-rod as the skill of a Wilson or a Stoddart never could invent; a living line, with elasticity beyond that of the most delicate fly-rod, which follows every lunge, shortening and lengthening, slipping and twining round every piece of gravel and stem of sea-weed, with a tiring drag such as no Highland wrist or step could ever bring to bear on salmon or trout. The victim is tired now; and slowly, yet dexterously, his blind assailant is feeling and shifting along his side, till he reaches one end of him; and then the black lips expand, and slowly and surely the curved finger begins packing him end foremost down into the gullet, where he sinks, inch by inch, till the swelling which marks his place is lost among the coils, and he is probably macerated into a pulp long before he has reached the opposite extremity of his cave of doom. Once safe down, the black murderer contracts again into a knotted heap, and lies like a boa with a stag inside him, motionless and blest."

Charles Kingsley

*A twelfth-century illustration of St. Guthlac Besieged by Devils
in the Guise of Animals*

Ruffs, by E. Neale, from Dresser's A History of the Birds of Europe, 1871–81

Charles Kingsley

[1819–1875]

No eminent Victorian touched the life of his age at more points than did Charles Kingsley in the course of a protean career. For more than thirty years he was Rector of Eversley in Hampshire; but the faithful discharge of his parish duties amidst circumstances of unusual domestic felicity could not begin to exhaust the energies of so virile and strenuous a temperament. An eager, though not always judicious controversialist and an eloquent preacher, he took a leading role in the Christian Socialist movement, which sought to minister to the material as well as the spiritual needs of the working classes. In particular, Kingsley campaigned militantly in behalf of measures to promote public health and sanitation. With the tempering down of his radical sympathies came ecclesiastical preferment, first as Chaplain to Queen Victoria, and then, in succession, as Canon of Chester and of Westminster. Royal patronage was also responsible for his appointment as Professor of Modern History at Cambridge University, where he was for a time tutor to the Prince of Wales. Kingsley's voluminous writings include novels of social protest (*Alton Locke, Tailor and Poet*, 1850), historical fiction (*Hypatia*, 1853 and *Hereward the Wake*, 1866), and two immortal works for younger readers (*Westward Ho!*, 1855 and *The Water Babies*, 1863).

Throughout his busy life Kingsley sought periodic relaxation in his twin passions for field sports and nature studies, which had been engendered by his clergyman father and fostered by early teachers. A lecture, delivered in 1848, concludes his plea for a museum of natural history at Reading on this characteristic note:

. . . I, for one, would be happy to add something from the flora and fauna of those moorlands, where I have so long enjoyed the wonders of nature; never, I can honestly say, alone; because when man was not with me, I had companions in every bee, and flower, and pebble; and never idle, because I could not pass a swamp, or a tuft of heather, without finding in it a fairy tale of which I could but decipher here and there a line or two, and yet found them more interesting than all the books, save one, which were ever written upon earth.

While residing at Torquay in 1854, Kingsley fell under the spell of the researches in marine zoology being conducted by Philip Henry Gosse. There resulted one of his most delightful excursions into the realm of popular science: *Glaucus; or, The Wonders of the Shore* (1855). It was this work which first brought Kingsley to the attention of the scientifically minded Prince Consort. Nearly twenty years later, when he was Canon of Chester, he found time to organize a class in botany for clerks and shopkeepers, whose enthusiastic response to his weekly lectures and field trips led to the formation of the Chester Natural History Society. A pleasantly revealing anecdote is related of the extensive American tour which Kingsley made in the year before his death. During an evening lecture in Colorado Springs an unfamiliar beetle lighted on his manuscript. The speaker took the insect in his hand for close inspection, and having identified the species to his satisfaction, released it—all without interrupting the lively flow of his discourse.

Kingsley's literary reputation rests most securely on his talent for descriptive writing. In addition to the finely evocative treatment of landscape in such novels as *Two Years Ago* and *Hereward the Wake*, his most accomplished sketches are gathered in *Prose Idylls: New and Old* (1873), which combine natural lore with the sportsman's joy in the exercise of his outdoor skills. Devonshire and the Fenlands of eastern England, the regions where Kingsley passed his adventure-loving boyhood, retained a pre-eminent place in his affections. "The Fens" was originally published in *Good Words* in 1867 at a time when the progres-

292

sive work of drainage had irremediably altered the face of that remarkable district, equally dear to the heart of the poet Clare. Kingsley's "idyll" is thus a work of imaginative reconstruction, informed equally by the author's own nostalgic recollections, by historical and antiquarian zeal for a more remote past, and by omnivorous scientific curiosity.

The Foss Dyck, Lincoln, a water-color by Peter De Wint (1784–1849)

293

From *Prose Idylls: New and Old*

The Fens

A CERTAIN sadness is pardonable to one who watches the destruction of a grand natural phenomenon, even though its destruction bring blessings to the human race. Reason and conscience tell us, that it is right and good that the Great Fen should have become, instead of a waste and howling wilderness, a garden of the Lord, where

> *All the land in flowery squares,*
> *Beneath a broad and equal-blowing wind,*
> *Smells of the coming summer.*

And yet the fancy may linger, without blame, over the shining meres, the golden reed-beds, the countless waterfowl, the strange and gaudy insects, the wild nature, the mystery, the majesty—for mystery and majesty there were—which haunted the deep fens for many a hundred years. Little thinks the Scotsman, whirled down by the Great Northern Railway from Peterborough to Huntingdon, what a grand place, even twenty years ago, was that Holme and Whittlesea, which is now but a black, unsightly, steaming flat, from which the meres and reed-beds of the old world are gone, while the corn and roots of the new world have not as yet taken their place.

But grand enough it was, that black ugly place, when backed by Caistor Hanglands and Holme Wood, and the patches of the primæval forest; while dark-green alders, and pale-green reeds, stretched for miles round the broad lagoon, where the coot clanked, and the bittern boomed, and the sedge-bird, not content with its own sweet song, mocked the notes of all the birds around; while high overhead hung, motionless, hawk beyond hawk, buzzard beyond buzzard, kite beyond kite, as far as eye could see. Far off, upon the silver mere, would rise a puff of smoke from a punt, invisible from its flatness and its white paint. Then down the wind came the boom of the great stanchion-gun; and after that sound another sound, louder as it neared; a cry as of all the bells of Cambridge, and all the hounds of Cottesmore; and overhead rushed and whirled the skein of terrified wild-fowl, screaming, piping, clacking, croaking, filling the air with the hoarse rattle of their wings, while clear above all sounded the wild whistle of the curlew, and the trumpet note of the great wild swan.

They are all gone now. No longer do the ruffs trample the sedge into a hard floor in their fighting-rings, while the sober reeves stand round, admiring the tournament of their lovers, gay with ears and tippets, no two of them alike. Gone are ruffs and reeves, spoonbills, bitterns, avosets; the very snipe, one hears, disdains to breed. Gone, too, not only from Whittlesea but from the whole world, is that most exquisite of English butterflies, *Lycæna dispar*—the great copper; and many a curious insect more. Ah, well, at least we shall have wheat and mutton instead, and no more typhus and ague; and, it is to be hoped, no more brandy-drinking and opium-eating; and children will live and not die. For it was a hard place to live in, the old Fen; a place wherein one heard of 'unexampled instances of longevity,' for the same reason that one hears of them in savage tribes—that few lived to old age at all, save those iron constitutions which nothing could break down.

And now, when the bold Fen-men, who had been fighting water by the help of wind, have given up the more capricious element for that more manageable servant fire; have replaced their wind-mills by steam-engines, which will work in all weathers; and have pumped the whole fen dry—even too dry, as the last hot summer proved; when the only bit of the primæval wilderness left, as far as I know, is 200 acres of sweet sedge and *Lastræa thelypteris* in Wicken Fen: there can be no harm in lingering awhile over the past, and telling of what the Great Fen was, and how it came to be that great flat which reaches (roughly speaking) from Cambridge to Peterborough on the south-west side, to Lynn and Tattershall on the north-east, some forty miles and more each way.

To do that rightly, and describe how the Fen came to be, one must go back, it seems to me, to an age before all history; an age which cannot be measured by years or centuries; an age shrouded in mystery, and to be spoken of only in guesses. To assert anything positively concerning that age, or ages, would be to show the rashness of ignorance. 'I think that I believe,' 'I have good reason to suspect,' 'I seem to see,' are the strongest forms of speech which ought to be used over a matter so vast and as yet so little elaborated.

'I seem to see,' then, an epoch after those strata were laid down with which geology generally deals; after the Kimmeridge clay, Oxford clay, and Gault clay, which form the impervious bedding of the fens, with their intermediate beds of coral-rag and green sand, had been deposited; after the chalk had been laid on the top of them, at the bottom of some ancient ocean; after (and what a gulf of time is implied in that last 'after'!) the boulder-clay (coeval probably with the 'till' of Scotland) had been spread out in the 'age of ice' on top of all; after the whole had been upheaved out of the sea, and stood about the same level as it stands now: but before the great valley of the Cam had been scooped out, and the strata were still continuous, some 200 feet above Cambridge and its colleges, from the top of the Gogmagogs to the top of Madingley Rise.

In those ages—while the valleys of the Cam, the Ouse, the Nene, the Welland, the Glen, and the Witham were sawing themselves out by no violent convulsions, but simply, as I believe, by the same slow action of rain and rivers by which they are sawing backward into the land even now—I 'seem to see' a time when the Straits of Dover did not exist—a time when a great part of the German Ocean was dry land. Through it, into a great estuary between North Britain and Norway, flowed together all the rivers of north-eastern Europe—Elbe, Weser, Rhine, Scheldt, Seine, Thames, and all the rivers of east England, as far north as the Humber.

And if a reason be required for so daring a theory—first started, if I recollect right, by the late lamented Edward Forbes—a sufficient one may be found in one look over a bridge, in any river of the east of England. There we see various species of Cyprinidæ, 'rough' or 'white' fish—roach, dace, chub, bream, and so forth, and with them their natural attendant and devourer, the pike.

Now these fish belong almost exclusively to the same system of rivers—those of north-east Europe. They attain their highest development in the great lakes of Sweden. Westward of the Straits of Dover they are not indigenous. They may be found in the streams of south and western England; but in every case, I believe, they have been introduced either by birds or by men. From some now submerged 'centre of creation' (to use poor Edward Forbes's formula) they must have spread into the rivers where they are now found; and spread by fresh water, and not by salt, which would destroy them in a single tide.

Again, there lingers in the Cam, and a few other rivers of north-eastern Europe, that curious fish the eel-pout or 'burbot' (*Molva lota*). Now he is utterly distinct from any other fresh-water fish of Europe. His nearest ally is the ling (*Molva vulgaris*); a deep-sea fish, even as his ancestors have been. Originally a deep-sea form, he has found his way up the rivers, even to Cambridge, and there remains. The rivers by which he came up, the land through which he passed, ages and ages since, have been all swept away; and he has never found his way back to his native salt water, but lives on in a strange land, degraded in form, dwindling in numbers, and now fast dying out. The explanation may be strange: but it is the only one which I can offer to explain the fact—which is itself much more strange—of the burbot being found in the Fen rivers.

Another proof may be found in the presence of the edible frog of the Continent at Foulmire, on the edge of the Cambridge Fens. It is a moot point still with some, whether he was not put there by man. It is a still stronger argument against his being indigenous, that he is never mentioned as an article of food by the mediæval monks, who would have known—Frenchmen, Italians, Germans, as many of them were—that he is as dainty as ever was a spring chicken. But if he be indigenous, his presence proves that once he could either hop across the Straits of Dover, or swim across the German Ocean.

But there can be no doubt of the next proof—the presence in the Fens (where he is now probably extinct) and in certain spots in East Anglia, which I shall take care not to mention, of that exquisite little bird the 'Bearded Tit' (*Calamophilus biarmicus*). Tit he is none; rather, it is said, a finch, but connected with no other English bird. His central home is in the marshes of Russia and Prussia; his food the mollusks which swarm among the reed-beds where he builds; and feeding on those from reed-bed to reed-bed, all across what was once the German Ocean, has come the beautiful little bird with long tail, orange tawny plumage, and black moustache, which might have been seen forty years ago in hundreds on every reed-pond of the Fen.

One more proof—for it is the heaping up of facts, each minute by itself, which issues often in a sound and great result. In draining Wretham Mere, in Norfolk, not so very far from the Fens, in the year 1856, there were found embedded in the peat moss (which is not the Scotch and Western *Sphagnum palustre* but an altogether different moss, *Hypnum fluitans*), remains of an ancient lake-dwelling, sup-

Burbot or Eel-pout, by A. F. Lydon, 1879

ported on piles. A dwelling like those which have lately attracted so much notice in the lakes of Switzerland: like those which the Dyaks make about the ports and rivers of Borneo; dwellings invented, it seems to me, to enable the inhabitants to escape not wild beasts only, but malaria and night frosts; and, perched above the cold and poisonous fogs, to sleep, if not high and dry, at least high and healthy.

In the bottom of this mere were found two shells of the fresh-water tortoise, *Emys lutaria*, till then unknown in England.

These little animals, who may be seen in hundreds in the meres of eastern Europe, sunning their backs on fallen logs, and diving into the water at the sound of a footstep, are eaten largely in continental capitals (as is their cousin the terrapin, *Emys picta*, in the Southern States). They may be bought at Paris, at fashionable restaurants. Thither they may have been sent from Vienna or Berlin; for in north France, Holland, and north-west Germany they are unknown. A few specimens have been found buried in peat in Sweden and Denmark; and there is a tale of a live one having been found in the extreme south part of Sweden, some twenty years ago.* Into Sweden, then, as into England, the little fresh-water tortoise had wandered, as to an extreme limit, beyond which the change of climate, and probably of food, killed him off.

But the emys which came to the Wretham bog must have had a long journey; and a journey by fresh water too. Down Elbe or Weser he must have floated, ice-packed, or swept away by flood, till somewhere off the Doggerbank, in that great network of rivers which is now open sea, he or his descendants turned up Ouse and Little Ouse, till they found a mere like their old Prussian one, and there founded a tiny colony for a few generations, till they were eaten up by the savages of the table dwelling; or died out—as many a human

* For these details I am indebted to a paper in the *Annals of Natural History*, for September 1862, by my friend, Professor Alfred Newton, of Cambridge.

family has died out—because they found the world too hard.

And lastly, my friend Mr. Brady, well known to naturalists, has found that many forms of Entomostraca are common to the estuaries of the east of England and to those of Holland.

It was thus necessary, in order to account for the presence of some of the common animals of the fen, to go back to an epoch of immense remoteness.

And how was that great lowland swept away? Who can tell? Probably by no violent convulsion. Slow upheavals, slow depressions, there may have been—indeed must have been—as the sunken fir-forests of Brancaster, and the raised beach of Hunstanton, on the extreme north-east corner of the Wash, testify to this day. But the main agent of destruction has been, doubtless, that same ever-gnawing sea-wash which devours still the soft strata of the whole east coast of England, as far as Flamborough Head; and that great scavenger, the tide-wave, which sweeps the fallen rubbish out to sea twice in every twenty-four hours. Wave and tide by sea, rain and river by land; these are God's mighty mills in which He makes the old world new. And as Longfellow says of moral things, so may we of physical:—

Though the mills of God grind slowly, yet they grind
    exceeding small.
Though He sit, and wait with patience, with exact-
    ness grinds He all.

The lighter and more soluble particles, during that slow but vast destruction which is going on still to this day, have been carried far out to sea, and deposited as ooze. The heavier and coarser have been left along the shores, as the gravels which fill the old estuaries of the east of England.

From these gravels we can judge of the larger animals which dwelt in that old world. About these lost lowlands wandered herds of the woolly mammoth, *Elephas primigen-*

ius, whose bones are common in certain Cambridge gravels, whose teeth are brought up by dredgers, far out in the German Ocean, off certain parts of the Norfolk coast. With them wandered the woolly rhinoceros (*R. tichorhinus*), the hippopotamus, the lion—not (according to some) to be distinguished from the recent lion of Africa—the hyæna, the bear, the horse, the reindeer, and the musk ox; the great Irish elk, whose vast horns are so well known in every museum of northern Europe; and that mighty ox, the *Bos primigenius*, which still lingered on the Continent in Cæsar's time, as the urus, in magnitude less only than the elephant,—and not to be confounded with the bison, a relation of, if not identical with, the buffalo of North America,—which still lingers, carefully preserved by the Czar, in the forests of Lithuania.

The remains of this gigantic ox, be it remembered, are found throughout Britain, and even into the Shetland Isles. Would that any gentleman who may see these pages would take notice of the fact, that we have not (so I am informed) in these islands a single perfect skeleton of *Bos primigenius;* while the Museum of Copenhagen, to its honour, possesses five or six from a much smaller field than is open to us; and be public-spirited enough, the next time he hears of ox-bones, whether in gravel or in peat (as he may in the draining of any northern moss), to preserve them for the museum of his neighbourhood—or send them to Cambridge.

But did all these animals exist at the same time? It is difficult to say. The study of the different gravels is most intricate—almost a special science in itself—in which but two or three men are adepts. It is hard, at first sight, to believe that the hippopotamus could have been the neighbour of the Arctic reindeer and musk ox: but that the woolly mammoth not only may have been such, but was such, there can be no doubt. His remains, imbedded in ice at the mouth of the great Siberian rivers, with the wool, skin, and flesh (in some cases) still remaining on the bones, prove him to have been fitted for a cold climate, and to have browsed upon the scanty shrubs of Northern Asia. But, indeed, there is no reason, *à priori*, why these huge mammals, now confined to hotter countries, should not have once inhabited a colder region, or at least have wandered northwards in whole herds in summer, to escape insects, and find fresh food, and above all, water. The same is the case with the lion, and other huge beasts of prey. The tiger of Hindostan ranges, at least in summer, across the snows of the Himalaya, and throughout China. Even at the river Amoor, where the winters are as severe as at St. Petersburg, the tiger is an ordinary resident at all seasons. The lion was, undoubtedly, an inhabitant of Thrace as late as the expedition of Xerxes, whose camels they attacked; and the 'Nemæan lion,' and the other lions which stand out in Grecian myth, as having been killed by Hercules and the heroes, may have been the last remaining specimens of that *Felis spelæa* (undistinguishable, according to some, from the African lion), whose bones are found in the gravels and the caverns of these isles.

And how long ago were those days of mammoths and reindeer, lions and hyænas? We must talk not of days, but of ages: we know nothing of days or years. As the late lamented Professor Sedgwick has well said:—

'We allow that the great European oscillation, which ended in the production of the drift (the boulder clay, or till), was effected during a time of vast, but unknown length. And if we limit our inquiries, and ask what was the interval of time between the newest bed of gravel near Cambridge, and the oldest bed of bog-land or silt in Cambridgeshire and Norfolk, we are utterly at a loss for a definite answer. The interval of time may have been very great. But we have no scale on which to measure it.'

Let us suppose, then, the era of 'gravels' past; the valleys which open into the fen sawn out by rivers to about their present depth. What was the special cause of the fen itself? why did not the great lowland become a fertile 'carse' of firm alluvial soil, like that of Stirling?

One reason is, that the carse of Stirling has been upheaved some twenty feet, and thereby more or less drained, since the time of the Romans. A fact patent and provable from Cramond (the old Roman port of Alaterna) up to Blair Drummond above Stirling, where whales' skeletons, and bone tools by them, have been found in loam and peat, twenty feet above high-water mark. The alluvium of the fens, on the other hand, has very probably suffered a slight depression.

But the main reason is, that the silt brought down by the fen rivers cannot, like that of the Forth and its neighbouring streams, get safe away to sea. From Flamborough Head, in Yorkshire, all down the Lincolnshire coast, the land is falling, falling for ever into the waves; and swept southward by tide and current, the debris turns into the Wash between Lincolnshire and Norfolk, there to repose, as in a quiet haven.

Hence that vast labyrinth of banks between Lynn and Wisbeach, of mud inside, brought down by the fen rivers; but outside (contrary to the usual rule) of shifting sand, which has come inward from the sea, and prevents the mud's escape—banks parted by narrow gullies, the delight of the gunner with his punt, haunted by million wild-fowl in winter, and in summer hazy steaming flats, beyond which the trees of Lincolnshire loom up, raised by refraction far above the horizon, while the masts and sails of distant vessels quiver, fantastically distorted and lengthened, sometimes even inverted, by a refraction like that which plays such tricks with ships and coasts in the Arctic seas. Along the top of the mud banks lounge the long black rows of seals, undistinguishable from their reflection in the still water below; distorted too, and magnified to the size of elephants. Long lines of sea-pies wing their way along at regular tide-hours, from or to the ocean. Now and then a skein of geese paddle hastily out of sight round a mud-cape; or a brown robber gull (generally Richardson's Skua) raises a tumult of screams, by making a raid upon a party of honest white gulls, to frighten them into vomiting up their prey for his benefit; or a single cormorant flaps along, close to the water, towards his fishing ground. Even the fish are shy of haunting a bottom which shifts with every storm; and innumerable shrimps are almost the only product of the shallow barren sea: beside, all is silence and desolation, as of a world waiting to be made.

So strong is the barrier which these sea-borne sands oppose to the river-borne ooze, that as soon as a sea-bank is built—as the projectors of the 'Victoria County' have built them—across any part of the estuary, the mud caught by it soon 'warps' the space within into firm and rich dry land. But that same barrier, ere the fen was drained, backed up for ages not only the silt, but the very water of the fens; and spread it inland into a labyrinth of shifting streams, shallow meres, and vast peat bogs, on those impervious clays which floor the fen. Each river contributed to the formation of those bogs and meres, instead of draining them away; repeating on a huge scale the process which may be seen in many a highland strath, where the ground at the edge of the stream is firm and high; the meadows near the hillfoot, a few hundred yards away, bogland lower than the bank of the stream. For each flood deposits its silt upon the immediate bank of the river, raising it year by year; till—as in the case of the 'Levée' of the Mississippi, and probably of every one of the old fen rivers—the stream runs at last between two natural dykes, at a level considerably higher than that of the now swamped and undrainable lands right and left of it.

If we add to this, a slope in the fen rivers so extraordinarily slight, that the river at Cambridge is only thirteen and a half feet above the mean sea-level, five-and-thirty miles away, and that if the great sea-sluice of Denver, the key of all the eastern fen, were washed away, the tide would back up the Cam to within ten miles of Cambridge; if we add again the rainfall upon that vast flat area, utterly unable to escape through rivers which have enough to do to drain the hills

around; it is easy to understand how peat, the certain prod-
uct of standing water, has slowly overwhelmed the rich
alluvium, fattened by the washing of those phosphatic green-
sand beds, which (discovered by the science of the lamented
Professor Henslow) are now yielding round Cambridge
supplies of manure seemingly inexhaustible. Easy it is
to understand how the all-devouring, yet all-preserving
peat-moss swallowed up gradually the stately forests of fir
and oak, ash and poplar, hazel and yew, which once grew
on that rank land; how trees, torn down by flood or
storm, floated and lodged in rafts, damming the waters back
still more; how streams, bewildered in the flats, changed
their channels, mingling silt and sand with the peat-moss;
how Nature, left to herself, ran into wild riot and chaos more
and more; till the whole fen became one 'Dismal Swamp,' in
which the 'Last of the English' (like Dred in Mrs. Stowe's
tale) took refuge from their tyrants, and lived, like him, a
free and joyous life awhile.

For there were islands, and are still, in that wide fen,
which have escaped the destroying deluge of peat-moss; out-
crops of firm land, which even in the Middle Age preserved
the Fauna and Flora of the primæval forest, haunted by the
descendants of some at least of those wild beasts which
roamed on the older continent of the 'gravel age.' The all-
preserving peat, as well as the monkish records of the early
Middle Age, enable us to repeople, tolerably well, the
primæval fen.

The gigantic ox, *Bos primigenius*, was still there, though
there is no record of him in monkish tales. But with him had
appeared (not unknown toward the end of the gravel age)
another ox, smaller and with shorter horns, *Bos longifrons;*
which is held to be the ancestor of our own domestic short-
horns, and of the wild cattle still preserved at Chillingham
and at Cadzow. The reindeer had disappeared, almost or
altogether. The red deer, of a size beside which the largest
Scotch stag is puny, and even the great Carpathian stag

306

inferior, abound; so does the roe, so does the goat, which one is accustomed to look on as a mountain animal. In the Wood-wardian Museum there is a portion of a skull of an ibex—probably *Capra sibirica*—which was found in the drift gravel at Fulbourne. Wild sheep are unknown. The horse occurs in the peat; but whether wild or tame, who can tell? Horses enough have been mired and drowned since the Romans set foot on this island, to account for the presence of horses' skulls, without the hypothesis of wild herds, such as doubtless existed in the gravel times. The wolf, of course, is common; wild cat, marten, badger, and otter all would expect; but not so the beaver, which nevertheless is abundant in the peat; and damage enough the busy fellows must have done, cutting trees, damming streams, flooding marshes, and like selfish speculators in all ages, sacrificing freely the public interest to their own. Here and there are found the skulls of bears, in one case that of a polar bear, ice-drifted; and one of a walrus, probably washed in dead after a storm.

Beautiful, after their kind, were these fen-isles, in the eyes of the monks who were the first settlers in the wilderness.

The author of the History of Ramsey grows enthusiastic, and, after the manner of all monks, somewhat bombastic also, as he describes the lonely isle which got its name from the solitary ram who had wandered thither, either in some extreme drought or over the winter ice, and never able to return, was found, fat beyond the wont of rams, feeding among the wild deer. He tells of the stately ashes—most of them cut in his time, to furnish mighty beams for the church roof; of the rich pastures painted with all gay flowers in spring; of the 'green crown' of reed and alder which girdled round the isle; of the fair wide mere with its 'sandy beach' along the forest side: 'a delight,' he says, 'to all who look thereon.'

In like humour, William of Malmesbury, writing in the first half of the twelfth century, speaks of Thorney Abbey and isle. 'It represents,' he says, 'a very Paradise, for that in pleasure and delight it resembles heaven itself. These marshes abound in trees, whose length without a knot doth emulate the stars. The plain there is as level as the sea, which with green grass allures the eye, and so smooth that there is nought to hinder him who runs through it. Neither is therein any waste place: for in some parts are apple trees, in other vines, which are either spread on the ground or raised on poles. A mutual strife is there between nature and art; so that what one produces not, the other supplies. What shall I say of those fair buildings, which 'tis so wonderful to see the ground among those fens upbear?'

But the most detailed picture of a fen-isle is that in the second part of the Book of Ely; wherein a single knight of all the French army forces his way into the isle of St. Ethel-dreda, and, hospitably entertained there by Hereward and his English, is sent back safe to William the Conqueror, to tell him of the strength of Ely isle.

He cannot praise enough—his speech may be mythical; but as written by Richard of Ely, only one generation after, it must describe faithfully what the place was like—the won-ders of the isle: its soil the richest in England, its pleasant pastures, its noble hunting-grounds, its store of sheep and cattle (though its vines, he says, as a Frenchman had good right to say, were not equally to be praised), its wide meres and bogs, about it like a wall. In it was, to quote roughly, 'abundance of tame beasts and of wild stag, roe, and goat, in grove and marsh; martens, and ermines, and fitchets, which in hard winter were caught in snares or gins. But of the kind of fish and fowl which bred therein, what can I say? In the pools around are netted eels innumerable, great water wolves, and pickerel, perch, roach, burbot, lampreys, which the French called sea-serpents; smelts, too; and the royal fish, the turbot [surely a mistake for sturgeon], are said often to be taken. But of the birds which haunt around, if you be not tired, as of the rest, we will expound. Innumerable geese, gulls, coots, divers, water-crows, herons, ducks, of which, when there is most plenty, in winter, or at moulting time, I have seen hundreds taken at a time, by nets, springes, or birdlime,' and so forth; till, as he assures William, the Frenchmen may sit on Haddenham field blockading Ely for seven years more, 'ere they will make one ploughman stop short in his furrow, one hunter cease to set his nets, or one fowler to deceive the birds with springe and snare.'

And yet there was another side to the picture. Man lived hard in those days, under dark skies, in houses—even the most luxurious of them—which we should think, from draughts and darkness, unfit for felons' cells. Hardly they lived; and easily were they pleased, and thankful to God for the least gleam of sunshine, the least patch of green, after the terrible and long winters of the Middle Age. And ugly enough those winters must have been, what with snow-storm and darkness, flood and ice, ague and rheumatism; while through the long drear winter nights the whistle of the wind and the wild cries of the water-fowl were translated into the howls of witches and demons; and (as in St. Guthlac's case) the delirious fancies of marsh fever made fiends take hideous shapes before the inner eye, and act fantastic horrors round the old fen-man's bed of sedge.

The Romans seem to have done something toward the draining and embanking of this dismal swamp. To them is attributed the car-dyke, or catch-water drain, which runs from many miles from Peterborough northward into Lincolnshire, cutting off the land waters which flow down from the wolds above. To them, too, is to be attributed the old Roman bank, or 'vallum,' along the sea-face of the marsh-lands, marked to this day by the names of Walsoken, Walton, and Walpoole. But the English invaders were incapable of following out, even of preserving, any public works. Each village was isolated by its own 'march' of forest; each yeoman all but isolated by the 'eaves-drip,' or green lane round his farm. Each 'cared for his own things, and none for those of others'; and gradually, during the early Middle Age, the

309

fen—save those old Roman villages—returned to its primæval jungle, under the neglect of a race which caricatured local self-government into public anarchy, and looked on every stranger as an alien enemy, who might be lawfully slain, if he came through the forest without calling aloud or blowing a horn. Till late years, the English feeling against the stranger lasted harsh and strong. The farmer, strong in his laws of settlement, tried at once to pass him into the next parish. The labourer, not being versed in law, hove half a brick at him, or hooted him through the town. It was in the fens, perhaps, that the necessity of combined effort for fighting the brute powers of nature first awakened public spirit, and associate labour, and the sense of a common interest between men of different countries and races.

But the progress was very slow; and the first civilisers of the fen were men who had nothing less in their minds than to conquer nature, or call together round them communities of men. Hermits, driven by that passion for isolated independence which is the mark of the Teutonic mind, fled into the wilderness, where they might, if possible, be alone with God and their own souls. Like St. Guthlac of Crowland, after wild fighting for five-and-twenty years, they longed for peace and solitude; and from their longing, carried out with that iron will which marked the mediæval man for good or for evil, sprang a civilisation of which they never dreamed.

Those who wish to understand the old fen life, should read Ingulf's *History of Crowland* (Mr. Bohn has published a good and cheap translation), and initiate themselves into a state of society, a form of thought, so utterly different from our own, that we seem to be reading of the inhabitants of another planet. Most amusing and most human is old Ingulf and his continuator, 'Peter of Blois'; and though their facts are not to be depended on as having actually happened, they are still instructive, as showing what might, or ought to have happened, in the opinion of the men of old.

Even more naïve is the Anglo-Saxon life of St. Guthlac,

310

written possibly as early as the eighth century, and literally translated by Mr. Goodwin, of Cambridge.

There we may read how the young warrior-noble, Guthlac ('The Battle-Play," the "Sport of War'), tired of slaying and sinning, bethought him to fulfil the prodigies seen at his birth; how he wandered into the fen, where one Tatwin (who after became a saint likewise) took him in his canoe to a spot so lonely as to be almost unknown, buried in reeds and alders; and among the trees, nought but an old 'law,' as the Scots still call a mound, which men of old had broken into seeking for treasure, and a little pond; and how he built himself a hermit's cell thereon, and saw visions and wrought miracles; and how men came to him, as to a fakir or shaman of the East; notably one Beccel, who acted as his servant; and how as Beccel was shaving the saint one day, there fell on him a great temptation: Why should he not cut St. Guthlac's throat, and install himself in his cell, that he might have the honour and glory of sainthood? But St. Guthlac perceived the inward temptation (which is told with the naïve honesty of those half-savage times), and rebuked the offender into confession, and all went well to the end.

There we may read, too, a detailed account of a Fauna now happily extinct in the fens: of the creatures who used to hale St. Guthlac out of his hut, drag him through the bogs, carry him aloft through frost and fire—'Develen and luther gostes'—such as tormented likewise St. Botolph (from whom Botulfston = Boston, has its name), and who were supposed to haunt the meres and fens, and to have an especial fondness for old heathen barrows with their fancied treasure hoards; how they 'filled the house with their coming, and poured in on every side, from above, and from beneath, and everywhere. They were in countenance horrible, and they had great heads, and a long neck, and a lean visage; they were filthy and squalid in their beards, and they had rough ears, and crooked nebs, and fierce eyes, and foul mouths; and their teeth were like horses' tusks; and their throats were

311

filled with flame, and they were grating in their voice; they had crooked shanks, and knees big and great behind, and twisted toes, and cried hoarsely with their voices; and they came with such immoderate noise and immense horror, that him thought all between heaven and earth resounded with their voices. . . . And they tugged and led him out of the cot, and led him to the swart fen, and threw and sunk him in the muddy waters. After that they brought him into the wild places of the wilderness, among the thick beds of brambles, that all his body was torn. . . . After that they took him and beat him with iron whips; and after that they brought him on their creaking wings between the cold regions of the air.'

But there are gentler and more human touches in that old legend. You may read in it, how all the wild birds of the fen came to St. Guthlac, and he fed them after their kind. How the ravens tormented him, stealing letters, gloves, and what not, from his visitors; and then, seized with compunction at his reproofs, brought them back, or hanged them on the reeds; and how, as Wilfrid, a holy visitant, was sitting with him, discoursing of the contemplative life, two swallows came flying in, and lifted up their song, sitting now on the saint's hand, now on his shoulder, now on his knee. And how, when Wilfrid wondered thereat, Guthlac made answer, 'Know you not that he who hath led his life according to God's will, to him the wild beasts and the wild birds draw the more near.'

After fifteen years of such a life, in fever, agues, and starvation, no wonder if St. Guthlac died. They buried him in a leaden coffin (a grand and expensive luxury in the seventh century) which had been sent to him during his life by a Saxon princess; and then, over his sacred and wonder-working corpse, as over that of a Buddhist saint, there rose a chapel, with a community of monks, companies of pilgrims who came to worship, sick who came to be healed; till, at last, founded on great piles driven into the bog, arose the lofty wooden Abbey of Crowland; in its sanctuary of the four

rivers, its dykes, parks, vineyards, orchards, rich plough-
lands, from which, in time of famine, the monks of Crowland
fed all people of the neighbouring fens; with its tower with
seven bells, which had not their like in England; its twelve
altars rich with the gifts of Danish Vikings and princes, and
even with twelve white bear-skins, the gift of Canute's self;
while all around were the cottages of the corrodiers, or folk
who, for a corrody, or life pittance from the abbey, had given
away their lands, to the wrong and detriment of their
heirs.

But within these four rivers, at least, was neither tyranny
nor slavery. Those who took refuge in St. Guthlac's peace
from cruel lords must keep his peace toward each other, and
earn their living like honest men, safe while they did so; for
between those four rivers St. Guthlac and his abbot were the
only lords, and neither summoner, nor sheriff of the king, nor
armed force of knight or earl, could enter 'the inheritance of
the Lord, the soil of St. Mary and St. Bartholomew, the most
holy sanctuary of St. Guthlac and his monks; the minister
free from worldly servitude; the special almshouse of most
illustrious kings; the sole refuge of any one in worldly tribu-
lation; the perpetual abode of the saints; the possession of
religious men, specially set apart by the common council of
the realm; by reason of the frequent miracles of the holy
confessor St. Guthlac, an ever-fruitful mother of camphire in
the vineyards of Engedi; and by reason of the privileges
granted by the kings, a city of grace and safety to all who
repent.'

Does not all this sound—as I said just now—like a voice
from another planet? It is all gone; and it was good and right
that it should go when it had done its work, and that the
civilisation of the fen should be taken up and carried out by
men like the good knight, Richard of Rulos, who, two gener-
ations after the Conquest, marrying Hereward's grand-
daughter, and becoming Lord of Deeping (the deep
meadow), thought that he could do the same work from the

hall of Bourne as the monks did from their cloisters; got permission from the Crowland monks, for twenty marks of silver, to drain as much as he could of the common marshes; and then shut out the Welland by strong dykes, built cottages, marked out gardens, and tilled fields, till 'out of slough and bogs accursed, he made a garden of pleasure.'

Yet one lasting work those monks of Crowland did, besides those firm dykes and rich corn lands of the Porsand, which endure unto this day. For within two generations of the Norman conquest, while the old wooden abbey, destroyed by fire, was being replaced by that noble pile of stone whose ruins are still standing, the French abbot of Crowland sent French monks to open a school under the new French donjon, in the little Roman town of Grante-brigge; whereby—so does all earnest work, however mistaken, grow and spread in this world, infinitely and for ever—St. Guthlac, by his canoe-voyage into Crowland Island, became the spiritual father of the University of Cambridge in the old world; and therefore of her noble daughter, the University of Cambridge, in the new world which fen-men, sailing from Boston deeps, colonised and Christianised, 800 years after St. Guthlac's death.

The drainage of the fens struggled on for these same 800 years slowly, and often disastrously. Great mistakes were made; as when a certain bishop, some 700 years ago, bethought him to make a cut from Littleport drain to Rebeck (or Priests'-houses), and found, to his horror and that of the fen-men, that he had let down upon Lynn the pent-up waters of the whole higher bogs; that rivers were running backwards, brooks swelling to estuaries, and the whole north-eastern fen ruinate, to be yet more ruinate by banks confusedly thrown up in self-defence, till some order was restored in 1332, and the fens prospered—such little of them as could be drained at all—for nigh two hundred years. Honour, meanwhile, to another prelate, good Bishop Morton, who cut the great leam from Guyhirn—the last place at which one could see a standing gallows, and two Irish reapers hanging in chains, having murdered the old witch of Guyhirn for the sake of hidden treasure, which proved to be some thirty shillings and a few silver spoons.

The belief is more general than well-founded that the drainage of the fens retrograded on account of the dissolution of the monasteries. The state of decay into which those institutions had already fallen, and which alone made their dissolution possible, must have extended itself to these fen-lands. No one can read the account of their debts, neglect, malversation of funds, in the time of Henry VIII., without seeing that the expensive works necessary to keep fen-lands dry must have suffered, as did everything else belonging to the convents.

It was not till the middle or end of Elizabeth's reign that the recovery of these 'drowned lands' was proceeded with once more; and during the first half of the seventeenth century there went on, more and more rapidly, that great series of artificial works which, though often faulty in principle, often unexpectedly disastrous in effect, have got the work done, as all work is done in this world, not as well as it should have been done, but at least done.

To comprehend those works would be impossible without maps and plans; to take a lively interest in them impossible, likewise, save to an engineer or a fen-man. Suffice it to say, that in the early part of the seventeenth century we find a great company of adventurers—more than one Cromwell among them, and Francis, the great and good Earl of Bedford, at their head—trying to start a great scheme for draining the drowned 'middle level' east of the Isle of Ely. How they sent for Vermuyden, the Dutchman, who had been draining in North Lincolnshire, about Goole and Axholme Isle; how they got into his hands, and were ruined by him; how Francis of Bedford had to sell valuable estates to pay his share; how the fen-men looked on Francis of Bedford as their champion; how Charles I. persecuted him meanly, though indeed Bedford had, in the matter of the 'Lynn Law' of 1630, given way, as desperate men are tempted to do, to something like sharp practice unworthy of him; how Charles took the work into his hands, and made a Government job of it; how Bedford died, and the fen-men looked on him as a martyr; how Oliver Cromwell arose to avenge the good earl, as his family had supported him in past times; how Oliver St. John came to the help of the fen-men, and drew up the so-called 'Pretended Ordinance' of 1649, which was a compromise between Vermuyden and the adventurers, so able and useful that Charles II.'s Government were content to call it 'pretended' and let it stand, because it was actually draining the fens; and how Sir Cornelius Vermuyden, after doing mighty works, and taking mighty moneys, died a beggar, writing petitions which never got answered; how William, Earl of Bedford, added, in 1649, to his father's 'old Bedford River' that noble parallel river, the Hundred foot, both rising high above the land between dykes and 'washes,' *i.e.* waste spaces right and left, to allow for flood water; how the Great Bedford Rivers silted up the mouth of the Ouse, and backed the floods up the Cam; how Denver sluice was built to keep them back; and so forth, – all is written, or rather only half or quarter written, in the histories of the fens.

Another matter equally, or even more important, is but half written—indeed, only hinted at—the mixed population of the fens.

The sturdy old 'Girvii,' 'Gyrwas,' men of the 'gyras' or marshes, who in Hereward's time sang their three-man glees, 'More Girviorum tripliciter canentes,' had been crossed with the blood of Scandinavian Vikings in Canute's conquest; crossed again with English refugees from all quarters during the French conquest under William. After the St. Bartholomew they received a fresh cross of Huguenot, fleeing from France—dark-haired, fiery, earnest folk, whose names and physiognomies are said still to remain about Wisbeach, Whittlesea, and Thorney. Then came Vermuyden's Dutchmen, leaving some of their blood behind them. After the battle of Dunbar another cross came among them, of Scotch prisoners, who, employed by Cromwell's Government on the dykes, settled down among the fen-men to this day. Within the memory of man, Scotchmen used to come down into the fens every year, not merely for harvest, but to visit their expatriated kinsmen.

To these successive immigrations of strong Puritan blood, more than even the influence of the Cromwells and other Puritan gentlemen, we may attribute that strong Calvinist element which has endured for now nigh three centuries in the fen; and attribute, too, that sturdy independence and self-help which drove them of old out of Boston town, to seek their fortunes first in Holland, then in Massachusetts over sea. And that sturdy independence and self-help is not gone. There still lives in them some of the spirit of their mythic giant Hickafrid (the Hickathrift of nursery rhymes), who, when the Marshland men (possibly the Romanised inhabitants of the wall villages) quarrelled with him in the field, took up the cart-axle for a club, smote them hip and thigh, and pastured his cattle, in their despite, in the green cheese-fens of the Smeeth. No one has ever seen a fen-bank break, without honouring the stern quiet temper which there is in these men, when the north-easter is howling above, the spring-tide roaring outside, the brimming tide-way lapping up to the dyke-top, or flying over in sheets of spray; when round the one fatal thread which is trickling over the dyke—or worse, through some forgotten rat's hole in its side—hundreds of men are clustered, without tumult, without complaint, marshalled under their employers, fighting the brute powers of nature, not for their employer's sake alone, but for the sake of their own year's labour and their own year's bread. The sheep have been driven off the land below; the cattle stand ranged shivering on high dykes inland; they will be saved in punts, if the worst befall. But a hundred spades, wielded by practised hands, cannot stop that

317

tiny rathole. The trickle becomes a rush—the rush a roaring waterfall. The dyke-top trembles—gives. The men make efforts, desperate, dangerous, as of sailors in a wreck, with faggots, hurdles, sedge, turf: but the bank will break; and slowly they draw off; sullen, but uncomplaining; beaten, but not conquered. A new cry rises among them. Up, to save yonder sluice; that will save yonder lode; that again yonder farm; that again some other lode, some other farm, far back inland, but guessed at instantly by men who have studied from their youth, as the necessity of their existence, the labyrinthine drainage of lands which are all below the water level, and where the inner lands, in many cases, are lower still than those outside.

So they hurry away to the nearest farms; the teams are harnessed, the waggons filled, and drawn down and emptied; the beer-cans go round cheerily, and the men work with a sort of savage joy at being able to do something, if not all, and stop the sluice on which so much depends. As for the outer land, it is gone past hope; through the breach pours a roaring salt cataract, digging out a hole on the inside of the bank, which remains as a deep sullen pond for years to come. Hundreds, thousands of pounds are lost already, past all hope. Be it so, then. At the next neap, perhaps, they will be able to mend the dyke, and pump the water out; and begin again, beaten but not conquered, the same everlasting fight with wind and wave which their forefathers have waged for now 800 years.

He who sees—as I have seen—a sight like that, will repine no more that the primæval forest is cut down, the fair mere drained. For instead of mammoth and urus, stag and goat, that fen feeds cattle many times more numerous than all the wild venison of the primæval jungle; and produces crops capable of nourishing a hundred times as many human beings; and more—it produces men a hundred times as numerous as ever it produced before; more healthy and long-lived—and if they will, more virtuous and more happy—than ever was Girvian in his log-canoe, or holy hermit in his cell. So we, who knew the deep fen, will breathe one sigh over the last scrap of wilderness, and say no more; content to know that—

> *The old order changeth, yielding place to new,*
> *And God fulfils himself in many ways,*
> *Lest one good custom should corrupt the world.*

Gerard Manley Hopkins

On the Bollen, Cheshire, drawing by Gerard Manley Hopkins

Dandelion, Hemlock and Ivy, drawing by Gerard Manley Hopkins, inscribed "The Field, Blunt House, Croydon. April–July 1862"

Gerard Manley Hopkins
⌈ 1844–1889 ⌉

Gerard Manley Hopkins is a discovery of the twentieth century. His poems, known during his lifetime to but a few intimates, including his literary executor Robert Bridges, the future poet laureate, were not published in collected form until 1918. Editions of the equally remarkable *Letters* and *Journals* have appeared only within the past generation. Hopkins may be said to have courted obscurity as consonant with the ascetic discipline imposed by the Jesuit priesthood. Converted while a scholar at Balliol College, Oxford, he was in 1866 received into the Roman Catholic Church by John Henry Newman. When two years later he took the decision to enter the Society of Jesus, he burned the poems which he had so far written, giving as his reason: "I saw they wd. interfere with my state and vocation." In 1877 Hopkins was ordained priest. His remaining years were divided between parish duties at Liverpool and Glasgow, and teaching in Jesuit schools and colleges. At the time of his early death he held the chair of classics at University College, Dublin.

In December 1875 five Franciscan nuns, refugees from religious persecution in Germany, were drowned in the Thames estuary. This tragic occurrence aroused Hopkins, then living at St. Beuno's College, North Wales, from seven years of poetic silence. Having secured the approval of his superior, he wrote his great elegy, "The Wreck of the Deutschland," with its daring innovations in language and prosody. His restless and versatile interests henceforth found expression not only in sporadic outbursts of superb poetry, but also in musical compositions and abstruse philological studies, too often left incomplete in the face of recurrent moods of despondency and self-doubt. The Ruskinian sensibility to natural beauty, which irradiates his verse and prose, had its graphic counterpart in Hopkins' very considerable talent for landscape drawing. "You know I once wanted to be a painter," he wrote to a friend; "But even if I could I wd. not I think, now, for the fact is that the higher and more attractive parts of the art put a strain upon the passions which I shd. think it unsafe to encounter."

Wanting religious inspiration, Hopkins would still have been counted among the most perceptive of nature poets. A scientist remarked "his genius for minute analysis of shapes and patterns," while a painter has called him "a *particularizer* in observation . . . one who by nature centred and converged on the local and the special." Years after the event a lay brother at Stonyhurst College, which Hopkins was attending in 1870, remembered how the poet's passionate attention to natural phenomena had excited concern. When the sun came out after a shower, he would rush to a favorite path to study the effects of light on the rain-washed quartz. "Ay, a strange yoong man," remarked the simple brother, "crouching down that gate to stare at some wet sand. A fair natural 'e seemed to us, that Mr. 'opkins."

Yet, the universe primarily revealed itself to Hopkins under its sacramental aspect, as testifying to the immanence of the Creator. In his own words, *This world then is word, expression, news of God.*" To convey the rapturous quality of his vision he developed a peculiary vocabulary, the key terms in which are *inscape* and *instress*. By inscape Hopkins meant that particular configuration or selfhood which constitutes each thing uniquely that which it is in distinction from all other things. The idiom of his poetry, as he admitted, was in large part determined by the effort to capture and fix the individuality of appearances in the outside world:

> But as air, melody, is what strikes me most of all in music, and design in painting, so design, pattern, or what I am in the habit of calling *inscape* is what I above all aim at in poetry. Now it is the virtue of design, pattern or inscape to be distinctive . . .

Instress relates to the sensations released by the perception of inscape; it is the dynamic revelation of divine purpose and meaning inhering within all creation:

All things therefore are charged with love, are charged
with God and if we know how to touch them give off
sparks and take fire, yield drops and flow, ring and tell of
him.

In addition to its intrinsic excellence as the intermittent record
of Hopkins' imaginative life in the years 1866–1875, the *Journal* possesses additional interest as a storehouse of precise observations on which he drew in subsequent poetry. Thus, for example, a notation made in 1874:

As we drove home the stars came out thick: I leant back
to look at them and my heart opening more than usual
praised our Lord to and in whom all that beauty comes
home,

was three years later transmuted into the ecstatic opening of the
sonnet, "The Starlight Night":

Look at the stars! look, look up at the skies!
O look at all the fire-folk sitting in the air!
The bright boroughs, the circle-citadels there!

Descriptions jotted down on the scene were later transferred in
refined form to the pages of the *Journal*. As a result, the initial
response to an experience passed through a process of multiple
distillation on its way to becoming a poetic image. In some cases
one can trace through a series of prose entries the operation of the
imagination as it fused disparate impressions into a single unforgettable picture. Between 1870 and 1873 Hopkins' cloud
studies included the three following passages: "herds of towering pillow clouds, one great stack in particular over Pendle was
knoppled all over in fine snowy tufts . . ."; "bright woolpacks
that pelt before a gale in a clear sky are in the tuft"; "tall tossed
clouds . . ." Although rearranged and greatly condensed, these
phrases recognizably set the scene of the sonnet, "That Nature is
a Heraclitean Fire," written in the last year of the poet's life:

"Cloud-puffball, torn tufts, tossed pillows flaunt forth . . ."

From *Journal*

MAY 3, [1866] Cold. Morning raw and wet, afternoon fine.
Walked then with Addis, crossing Bablock Hythe, round by
Skinner's Weir through many fields into the Witney road.
Sky sleepy blue without liquidity. From Cumnor Hill saw St.
Philip's and the other spires through blue haze rising pale in
a pink light. On further side of the Witney road hills, just
fleeced with grain or other green growth, by their dips and
waves foreshortened here and there and so differenced in
brightness and opacity the green on them, with delicate
effect. On left, brow of the near hill glistening with very
bright newly turned sods and a scarf of vivid green slanting
away beyond the skyline, against which the clouds shewed
the slightest tinge of rose or purple. Copses in grey-red or
gray-yellow—the tinges immediately forerunning the open-
ing of full leaf. Meadows skirting Seven-bridge road volup-
tuous green. Some oaks are out in small leaf. Ashes not out,
only tufted with their fringy blooms. Hedges springing
richly. Elms in small leaf, with more or less opacity. White
poplars most beautiful in small grey crisp spray-like leaf.
Cowslips capriciously colouring meadows in creamy drifts.
Bluebells, purple orchis. Over the green water of the river
passing the slums of the town and under its bridges swallows
shooting, blue and purple above and shewing their amber-
tinged breasts reflected in the water, their flight unsteady
with wagging wings and leaning first to one side then the
other. Peewits flying. Towards sunset the sky partly swept,
as often, with moist white cloud, tailing off across which are
morsels of grey-black woolly clouds. Sun seemed to make a

bright liquid hole in this, its texture had an upward northerly sweep or drift from the W, marked softly in grey. Dog violets. Eastward after sunset range of clouds rising in bulky heads moulded softly in tufts or bunches of snow—so it looks—and membered somewhat elaborately, rose-coloured. Notice often imperfect fairy rings. Apple and other fruit trees blossomed beautifully. . . .

May 10. Ascension Day. Fair, with more clouds than sun. Walked alone to Fyfield or rather to a step beyond the great elm (perhaps the greatest I have ever seen) and made a sketch at the turning point. The road went under elms their light green darker printed by shadows, chestnut, sweet-smelling firs etc. Rooks cawing. Beddingfield church with good and curious E. and W. windows, but sadly neglected. Fine elms there with ground-running boughs. In timbered pasture etc beside road bluebells thick, and tufts of primrose, and campion, the two latter or two former matching grace-fully but not so well the three. One effect of sky was a straight line as by a ruler parting white and soft blue, and rolling reefs shaded with pearl grey hanging from this to the earth-line.

Children with white rods beating bounds of St. Michael's parish.

June 6. Grey, with some rain. Evening fine. Aspens thick in leaf but not so the sycamores even yet, or possibly they are this summer or at this time of the summer very thin. A mass of buttercup floating down under one of the Godstow bridges. A barge, I find, not only wrinkles smooth water by a wedge outlined in parallel straight lap-waves but also, before-and without these, shallower ones running, say midway, be-tween those of the wedge and a perpendicular to the cur-rent.

July 6. Hard thunder-showers, fine between, passing clouds. Sun coming out after one of these showers in morning hotly made ground smoke, gravel as well as lawn, some time. Lawn shews half-circle curves of the scythe in parallel ranks. Beeches seen from behind the house scatter their tops in charming tufted sheep-hooks drooping towards each other and every way. Layers or shelves of the middle cedar not level but in waved lips like silver plate. Soft vermilion leather just-budded leaves on the purple beech, and the upper sprays ruddy in the sunlight: whole effect rich, the leaves too being crisply pinched like little fingered papers. Carnations if you look close have their tongue-shaped petals powdered with spankled red glister, which no doubt gives them their brilliancy: sharp chip shadows of one petal on another: the notched edge curls up and so is darked, which gives them graceful precision. Green windows of cabbages in sunshine. The roses: their richness, variety, etc will no doubt always make them necessary to the poets. Take colour: there are some pink-grey or lilac a little way off upon their dead-green bushes, there are the yellow ones with packed pieces blushing yellower at the foot, the *coupe d'Hebe* pink outside and dry bright-grained rose-pink where the leaves turn out, etc. Then for shape, some flat and straggling have fissures twisting inwards upon the centre, some are globed and with the inner petals drawn geometrically across each other like laces of boddices at the opera with chipped-back little tight rolls at the edge. . . .

July 7. Fine.—Passing cloud-shadows soaking the woods. Pleasant precision of hay-cocks and swathes with shadow on one side. Bleached look of uncut fields. Those ox-eye-like flowers in grain fields smell deliciously. Strange pretty scatter-droop of barley ears, their beards part outside like the fine crispings of smooth running water on piers etc. Holding one up to the sky so that the top hairs should be about horizontal (the rest following their radiation down to the ear itself, which would hang down) noticed the instant after removing it a tiny needle-like sort of rain in the air at right angles of course to the line of the spikes. Whiteness of the pine-buds. Lombardy poplars built high and with dice-like leaves. Soar of the poplar. Walked a new way at Finchley and saw Mr. Bickersteth on bridge over the Brent. On a windy day the leaves of trees, e.g. the plane, get and keep a certain pose of turning up from the pitch of the wind. Gable-shaped droop of firs, yews etc like that of an open hand from the wrist.

July 11. Dull and shallow sunlight. Saw an olive-coloured snake on hedge of Finchley wood and just before its slough in the road—or at all events a slough. Oats: hoary blue-green sheaths and stalks, prettily shadow-stroked spikes of pale green grain. Oaks: the organisation of this tree is difficult. Speaking generally no doubt the determining planes are concentric, a system of brief contiguous and continuous tangents, whereas those of the cedar would roughly be called horizontals and those of the beech radiating but modified by droop and by a screw-set towards jutting points. But beyond this since the normal growth of the boughs is radiating and the leaves grow some way in there is of course a system of spoke-wise clubs of green—sleeve-pieces. And since the end shoots curl and carry young and scanty leaf-stars these clubs are tapered, and I have seen also the pieces in profile with chiselled outlines, the blocks thus made detached and lessening towards the end. However the star knot is the chief thing: it is whorled, worked round, a little and this is what keeps up the illusion of the tree: the leaves are rounded inwards and figure out ball-knots. Oaks differ much, and much turns on the broadness of the leaf, the narrower giving the crisped and starry and Catherine-wheel forms, the broader the flat-pieced mailed or shard-covered ones, in

329

which it is possible to see composition in dips etc on wider bases than the single knot or cluster. But I shall study them further. . . .

July 13. Fine. All day faint long tails, getting thicker as the day went on, and at one time there were some like long ringlets, namely curls shaping out a hollow screw. Rows of cloud lay across sky at sunset, their lit parts yellow, below which was the curious opaque blue one sometimes sees with that colour.—To Midhurst, then walked to West Lavington and back, seeing the church, built 15 years ago. I should like to see it again for it looked immature and strange. The bowered lanes to Lavington skirting Cowdery Park were charming and the gloom in the thicket of the park, where yews shewed and chestnut leaves—hoary opaque green. Walked again later towards the downs, heard more wood-larks, and found a glowworm. Just beyond the town (of Midhurst) runs the canal water looking like a river and on the steeper-rising further side the park trees make a towering and noble wall which runs along to the left and turns and embays a quarter of a mile away, the whole having the blocky short cresting which freely grown park trees show. There were oaks and other trees, one beech I noticed especially scattering forwards from the press brown point-sprays, but the great feature is the Spanish chestnuts, their round knots tufted with white heaps of flour-and-honey blossom: this gives splendour and difference to such a growth of trees. I know now too what a tinkling brook is.

Aug. 22, [1867] Bright.—Walked to Finchley and turned down a lane to a field where I sketched an appletree. Their sprays against the sky are gracefully curved and the leaves looping over edge them, as it looks, with rows of scales. In something the same way I saw some tall young slender wych-elms of thin growth the leaves of which enclosed the light in successive eyebrows. From the spot where I sketched—under

330

an oak, beyond a brook, and reached by the above green lane between a park-ground and a pretty field—there was a charming view, the field, lying then on the right of the lane, being a close-shaven smoothly-rounded shield of bright green ended near the high road by a row of viol-headed or flask-shaped elms—not rounded merely but squared—of much beauty—dense leafing, rich dark colour, ribs and spandrils of timber garlanded with leaf between tree and tree. But what most struck me was a pair of ashes in going up the lane again. The further one was the finer—a globeish just-sided head with one launching-out member on the right; the nearer one was more naked and horny. By taking a few steps one could pass the further behind the nearer or make the stems close, either coincidingly, so far as disagreeing outlines will coincide, or allowing a slit on either side, or again on either side making a broader stem than either would make alone. It was this which was so beautiful—making a noble shaft and base to the double tree, which was crested by the horns of the nearer ash and shaped on the right by the bosom of the hinder one with its springing bough. The outline of the double stem was beautiful to whichever of the two sides you slid the hinder tree—in one (not, I think, in both) shaft-like and narrowing at the ground. Besides I saw how great the richness and subtlety is of the curves in the clusters, both in the forward bow mentioned before and in some most graceful hangers on the other side: it combines somewhat-slanted outward strokes with rounding, but I cannot very well characterise it now.—Elm-leaves:—they shine much in the sun—bright green when near from underneath but higher up they look olive: their shapelessness in the flat is from their being made, διὰ τὸ πεφυκέναι, to be dimpled and dog's-eared: their leaf-growth is in this point more rudimentary than that of oak, ash, beech, etc that the leaves lie in long rows and do not subdivide or have central knots but tooth or cog their woody twigs.

Ap. 6, [1868] Fine but sky overcast with transparent cloud, which was sometimes zoned and blown in wild 'locks'—altogether a moody sky. There were both solar and lunar halos, faint: it deserves notice. I do not know how long the first was but the latter may have lasted hours.—A budded lime against the field wall: turn, pose, and counterpoint in the twigs and buds—the *form* speaking.

Jan. 4, '69. We have had wind and rain, so that floods are out, but in temperature the weather mild to an unusual degree.—The other evening after a very bright day, the air rinsed quite clear, there was a slash of glowing yolk-coloured sunset.—On the 1st frost all day (which otherwise I do not remember for a long time), the air shining, but with vapour, the dead leaves frilled, the Park grass white with hoarfrost mixed with purple shadow.—Today—another clear afternoon with tender clouding after rain—one notices the crisp flat darkness of the woods against the sun and the smoky bloom they have opposite it. The trees budded and their sprays curled as if dressed for spring.

March 12, [1870] A fine sunset: the higher sky dead clear blue bridged by a broad slant causeway rising from right to left of wisped or grass cloud, the wisps lying across; the sundown yellow, moist with light but ending at the top in a foam of delicate white pearling and spotted with big tufts of cloud in colour russet between brown and purple but edged with brassy light. But what I note it all for is this: before I had always taken the sunset and the sun as quite out of gauge with each other, as indeed physically they are, for the eye after looking at the sun is blunted to everything else and if you look at the rest of the sunset you must cover the sun, but today I inscaped them together and made the sun the true eye and ace of the whole, as it is. It was all active and tossing out light and started as strongly forward from the field as a long stone or a boss in the knop of the chalice-stem: it is indeed by

332

stalling it so that it falls into scape with the sky.

The next morning a heavy fall of snow. It tufted and toed the firs and yews and went on to load them till they were taxed beyond their spring. The limes, elms, and Turkey-oaks it crisped beautifully as with young leaf. Looking at the elms from underneath you saw every wave in every twig (become by this the wire-like stem to a finger of snow) and to the hangers and flying sprays it restored, to the eye, the inscapes they had lost. They were beautifully brought out against the sky, which was on one side dead blue, on the other washed with gold.

At sunset the sun a crimson fireball, above one or two knots of rosy cloud middled with purple. After that, frost for two days.

Sept. 24—First saw the Northern Lights. My eye was caught by beams of light and dark very like the crown of horny rays the sun makes behind a cloud. At first I thought of silvery cloud until I saw that these were more luminous and did not dim the clearness of the stars in the Bear. They rose slightly radiating thrown out from the earthline. Then I saw soft pulses of light one after another rise and pass upwards arched in shape but waveringly and with the arch broken. They seemed to float, not following the warp of the sphere as falling stars look to do but free though concentrical with it. This busy working of nature wholly independent of the earth and seeming to go on in a strain of time not reckoned by our reckoning of days and years but simpler and as if correcting the preoccupation of the world by being preoccupied with and appealing to and dated to the day of judgment was like a new witness to God and filled me with delightful fear

Oct. 25—A little before 7 in the evening a wonderful Aurora, the same that was seen at Rome (shortly after its seizure by the Italian government) and taken as a sign of

God's anger. It gathered a little below the zenith, to the S.E.
I think—a knot or crown, not a true circle, of dull blood-
coloured horns and dropped long red beams down the sky on
every side, each impaling its lot of stars. An hour or so later
its colour was gone but there was still a pale crown in the
same place: the skies were then clear and ashy and fresh with
stars and there were flashes of or like sheet-lightning. The
day had been very bright and clear, distances smart, herds of
towering pillow clouds, one great stack in particular over
Pendle was knoppled all over in fine snowy tufts and pen-
cilled with bloom-shadow of the greatest delicacy. In the
sunset all was big and there was a world of swollen cloud
holding the yellow-rose light like a lamp while a few sad
milky blue slips passed below it. At night violent hailstorms
and hail again next day, and a solar halo. Worth noticing too
perhaps the water-runs were then mulled and less beautiful
than usual

Dec. 19 or thereabouts a very fine sunrise: the higher
cloud was like seams of red candle-wax

On April 29 or thereabouts *at sunset* in the same quarter of
the sky I saw, as far as I could remember it, almost the very
same scape, the same colour and so on, down to a wavy wisp
or rather seam above the rest—and this made by the sun
shining from the West instead of the East. It was not so
brilliant though

The winter was long and hard. I made many observations
on freezing. For instance the crystals in mud.—Hailstones
are shaped like the cut of diamonds called brilliants.—I
found one morning the ground in one corner of the garden
full of small pieces of potsherd from which there rose up
(and not dropped off) long icicles carried on in some way
each like a forepitch of the shape of the piece of potsherd it
grew on, like a tooth to its root for instance, and most of them
bended over and curled like so many tusks or horns or/best of

all and what they looked likest when they first caught my eye/the first soft root-spurs thrown out from a sprouting chestnut. This bending of the icicle seemed so far as I could see not merely a resultant, where the smaller spars of which it was made were still straight, but to have flushed them too.—The same day and others the garden mould very crisp and meshed over with a lace-work of needles leaving (they seemed) three-cornered openings: it looked greyish and like a coat of gum on wood. Also the smaller crumbs and clods were lifted fairly up from the ground on upright ice-pillars, whether they had dropped these from themselves or drawn them from the soil: it was like a little Stonehenge—Looking down into the thick ice of our pond I found the imprisoned air-bubbles nothing at random but starting from centres and in particular one most beautifully regular white brush of them, each spur of it a curving string of beaded and diminishing bubbles—The pond, I suppose from over pressure when it was less firm, was mapped with a puzzle of very slight clefts branched with little sprigs: the pieces were odd-shaped and sized—though a square angular scaping could be just made out in the outline but the cracks ran deep through the ice markedly in planes and always the planes of the cleft on the surface. They remained and in the end the ice broke up in just these pieces

End of March and beginning of April, [1871]—This is the time to study inscape in the spraying of trees, for the swelling buds carry them to a pitch which the eye could not else gather—for out of much much more, out of little not much, out of nothing nothing: in these sprays at all events there is a new world of inscape. The male ashes are very boldly jotted with the heads of the bloom which tuft the outer ends of the branches. The staff of each of these branches is closely knotted with the places where buds are or have been, so that it is something like a finger which has been tied up with string and keeps the marks. They are in knops of a pair, one on each side, and the knops are set alternately, at crosses with the knops above and the knops below, the bud of course is a short smoke-black pointed nail-head or beak pieced of four lids or nippers. Below it, like the hollow below the eye or the piece between the knuckle and the root of the nail, is a half-moon-shaped sill as if once chipped from the wood and this gives the twig its quaining in the outline. When the bud breaks at first it shews a heap of fruity purplish anthers looking something like unripe elder-berries but these push open into richly-branched tree-pieces coloured buff and brown, shaking out loads of pollen, and drawing the tuft as a whole into peaked quains—mainly four, I think, two bigger and two smaller

The bushes in the woods and hedgerows are spanned over and twisted upon by the woody cords of the honeysuckle: the cloves of leaf these bear are some purple, some grave green. But the young green of the briars is gay and neat and smooth as if cut in ivory.—One bay or hollow of Hodder Wood is curled all over with bright green garlic

The sycomores are quite the earliest trees out: some have been fully out some days (April 15). The behaviour of the opening clusters is very beautiful and when fully opened not the single leaves but the whole tuft is strongly templed like the belly of a drum or bell

The half-opened wood-sorrel leaves, the centre or spring of the leaflets rising foremost and the leaflets dropping back like ears leaving straight-chipped clefts between them, look like some green lettering and cut as sharp as dice

The white violets are broader and smell; the blue, scentless and finer made, have a sharper whelking and a more winged recoil in the leaves

Take a *few* primroses in a glass and the instress of—brilliancy, sort of starriness: I have not the right word—so simple a flower gives is remarkable. It is, I think, due to the strong swell given by the deeper yellow middle

'The young lambs bound As to the tabour's sound'.

They toss and toss: it is as if it were the earth that flung them, not themselves. It is the pitch of graceful agility when we think that.—April 16—Sometimes they rest a little space on the hind legs and the forefeet drop curling in on the breast, not so liquidly as we see it in the limbs of foals though

Bright afternoon; clear distances; Pendle dappled with tufted shadow; west wind; interesting clouding, flat and lying in the warp of the heaven but the pieces with rounded outline and dolphin-backs shewing in places and all was at odds and at Z's, one piece with another. Later beautifully delicate crisping. Later rippling . . .

[May 9] This day and May 11 the bluebells in the little wood between the College and the highroad and in one of the Hurst Green cloughs. In the little wood/ opposite the light/ they stood in blackish spreads or sheddings like the spots on a snake. The heads are then like thongs and solemn in grain and grape-colour. But in the clough/ through the light/ they came in falls of sky-colour washing the brows and slacks of the ground with vein-blue, thickening at the double, vertical themselves and the young grass and brake fern combed vertical, but the brake struck the upright of all this with light winged transomes. It was a lovely sight.—The bluebells in your hand baffle you with their inscape, made to every sense: if you draw your fingers through them they are lodged and struggle/ with a shock of wet heads; the long stalks rub and click and flatten to a fan on one another like your fingers themselves would when you passed the palms hard across one another, making a brittle rub and jostle like the noise of a hurdle strained by leaning against; then there is the faint honey smell and in the mouth the sweet gum when you bite them. But this is easy, it is the eye they baffle. They give one a fancy of panpipes and of some wind instrument with stops—a trombone perhaps. The overhung necks—for growing they are little more than a staff with a simple crook but in water, where they stiffen, they take stronger turns, in the head like sheephooks or, when more waved throughout, like the waves riding through a whip that is being smacked—what with these overhung necks and what with the crisped ruffled bells dropping mostly on one side and the gloss these have at their footstalks they have an air of the knights at chess. Then the knot or 'knoop' of buds some shut, some just gaping, which makes the pencil of the whole spike, should be noticed: the inscape of the flower most finely carried out in the siding of the axes, each striking a greater and greater slant, is finished in these clustered buds, which for the most part are not straightened but rise to the end like a tongue and this and their tapering and a little flattening they have make them look like the heads of snakes

[June 19] Later—The Horned Violet is a pretty thing, gracefully lashed. Even in withering the flower ran through beautiful inscapes by the screwing up of the petals into straight little barrels or tubes. It is not that inscape does not govern the behaviour of things in slack and decay as one can see even in the pining of the skin in the old and even in a skeleton but that horror prepossesses the mind, but in this case there was nothing in itself to shew even whether the flower were shutting or opening

The 'pinion' of the blossom in the comfrey is remarkable for the beauty of the coil and its regular lessening to its centre. Perhaps the duller-coloured sorts shew it best

July 8—After much rain, some thunder, and no summer as yet, the river swollen and golden and, where charged with air, like ropes and hills of melting candy, there was this day a thunderstorm on a greater scale—huge rocky clouds lit with livid light, hail and rain that flooded the garden, and thunder ringing and echoing round like brass, so that there is in a manner earwitness to the χαλκεον οὐρανόν. The lightning seemed to me white like a flash from a lookingglass but

Mr. Lentaigne in the afternoon noticed it rose-coloured and lilac. I noticed two kinds of flash but I am not sure that sometimes there were not the two together from different points of the same cloud or starting from the same point different ways—one a straight stroke, broad like a stroke with chalk and liquid, as if the blade of an oar just stripped open a ribbon scar in smooth water and it caught the light; the other narrow and wire-like, like the splitting of a rock and danced down-along in a thousand jags. I noticed this too, that there was a perceptible interval between the blaze and first inset of the flash and its score in the sky and that that seemed to be first of all laid in a bright confusion and then uttered by a tongue of brightness (what is strange) running up from the ground to the cloud, not the other way

Feb. 23, [1872]—A lunar halo: I looked at it from the upstairs library window. It was a grave grained sky, the strands rising a little from left to right. The halo was not quite round, for in the first place it was a little pulled and drawn below, by the refraction of the lower air perhaps, but what is more it fell in on the nether left hand side to rhyme the moon itself, which was not quite at full. I could not but strongly feel in my fancy the odd instress of this, the moon leaning on her side, as if fallen back, in the cheerful light floor within the ring, after with magical rightness and success tracing round her the ring the steady copy of her own outline. But this sober grey darkness and pale light was happily broken through by the orange of the pealing of Mitton bells

Another night from the gallery window I saw a brindled heaven, the moon just marked by a blue spot pushing its way through the darker cloud, underneath and on the skirts of the rack bold long flakes whitened and swaled like feathers, below / the garden with the heads of the trees and shrubs

furry grey: I read a broad careless inscape flowing through-
out

At the beginning of March they were felling some of the
ashes in our grove

March 23— . . . Saw a lad burning bundles of dry hon-
eysuckle: the flame (though it is no longer freshly in my
mind) was brown and gold, brighter and glossier than glass
or silk or water and ran reeling up to the right in one long
handkerchief and curling like a cartwhip

March 26—Snow fallen upon the leaves had in the night
coined or morselled itself into pyramids like hail. Blade
leaves of some bulbous plant, perhaps a small iris, were like
delicate little saws, so hagged with frost. It is clear that
things are spiked with the frost mainly on one side but why
this is and how far different things on the same side at the
same time I have not yet found

March 30, Holy Saturday—warm, with thunder, odd tufts
of thin-textured very plump round clouds something like the
eggs in an opened ant-hill

July 19—The ovary of the blown foxglove surrounded by
the green calyx is perhaps that conventional flower in Pointed
and other floriated work which I could not before identify. It
might also be St. John's-wort
Stepped into a barn of ours, a great shadowy barn, where
the hay had been stacked on either side, and looking at the
great rudely arched timberframes—principals(?) and tie-
beams, which make them look like bold big *A*s with the
cross-bar high up—I thought how sadly beauty of inscape
was unknown and buried away from simple people and yet
how near at hand it was if they had eyes to see it and it could
be called out everywhere again . . .

Aug. 10—I was looking at high waves. The breakers

Note. The curves of the returning wave overlap, the angular space between is smooth but covered with a network of foam . The advancing wave already broken, and now only a mass of foam, upon the point of encountering the reflux of the former. Study from the cliff above, Freshwater Gate. July 23.

Waves, drawing by Gerard Manley Hopkins, inscribed "Study from the cliff above, Freshwater Gate. July 23" always are parallel to the coast and shape themselves to it except where the curve is sharp however the wind blows. They are rolled out by the shallowing shore just as a piece of putty between the palms whatever its shape runs into a long roll. The slant ruck or crease one sees in them shows the way of the wind. The regularity of the barrels surprised and charmed the eye; the edge behind the comb or crest was as smooth and bright as glass. It may be noticed to be green behind and silver white in front: the silver marks where the air begins, the pure white is foam, the green/solid water. Then looked at to the right or left they are scrolled over like mouldboards or feathers or jibsails seen by the edge. It is pretty to see the hollow of the barrel disappearing as the white combs on each side run along the wave gaining ground till the two meet at a pitch and crush and overlap each other

About all the turns of the scaping from the break and flooding of wave to its run out again I have not yet satisfied myself. The shores are swimming and the eyes have before them a region of milky surf but it is hard for them to unpack the huddling and gnarls of the water and law out the shapes and the sequence of the running: I catch however the looped or forked wisp made by every big pebble the backwater runs over—if it were clear and smooth there would be a network from their overlapping, such as can in fact be seen on smooth sand after the tide is out—; then I saw it run browner, the foam dwindling and twitched into long chains of suds, while the strength of the back-draught shrugged the stones together and clocked them one against another

Looking from the cliff I saw well that work of dimpled foamlaps—strings of short loops or halfmoons—which I had studied at Freshwater years ago

It is pretty to see the dance and swagging of the light green tongues or ripples of waves in a place locked between rocks

Aug. 16—Big waves. There is a stack of rocks beyond the bay connected with the slope of the green banks by a neck of grass. Like an outwork or breakwater to the stack is a long block consisting of a table or platform of even height sloping forward to the sea and flanked by two squarelike taller towers or shoulders, all shining when wet like smooth coal and cut and planed like masonry. The sea was breaking on all the stack and striking out all the ledges and edges at each breaker like snow does a building. In the narrow channel between this outwork and the main stack it was all a lather of foam, in which a spongy and featherlight brown scud bred from the churning of the water roped and changed, riding this and that, but never got clear of the channel. The overflow of the last wave came in from either side tilting up the channel and met halfway, each with its own moustache. When the wave ran very high it would brim over on the sloping shelf below me and move smoothly and steadily along it like the palm of a hand along a table drawing off the dust. In the channel I saw (as everywhere in surfy water) how the laps of foam mouthed upon one another. In watching the sea one should be alive to the oneness which all its motion and tumult receives from its perpetual balance and falling this way and that to its level

Feb. 24, [1873]—In the snow flat-topped hillocks and shoulders outlined with wavy edges, ridge below ridge, very like the grain of wood in line and in projection like relief maps. These the wind makes I think and of course drifts, which are in fact snow waves. The sharp nape of a drift is sometimes broken by slant flutes or channels. I think this must be when the wind after shaping the drift first has changed and cast waves in the body of the wave itself. All the world is full of inscape and chance left free to act falls into an order as well as purpose: looking out of my window I caught it in the random clods and broken heaps of snow made by the cast of a broom. The same of the path trenched by footsteps in ankledeep snow across the fields leading to Hodder wood through which we went to see the river. The sun was bright, the broken brambles and all boughs and banks limed and cloyed with white, the brook down the clough pulling its way by drops and by bubbles in turn under a shell of ice

In March there was much snow

April 8—The ashtree growing in the corner of the garden was felled. It was lopped first: I heard the sound and looking out and seeing it maimed there came at that moment a great pang and I wished to die and not to see the inscapes of the world destroyed any more

May 30—The swifts round and scurl under the clouds in the sky: light streamers were about; the swifts seemed rather to hang and be at rest and to fling these away row by row behind them like spokes of a lighthung wheel

Nov. 8, [1874]—Walking with Wm. Splaine we saw a vast multitude of starlings making an unspeakable jangle. They would settle in a row of trees; then, one tree after another, rising at a signal they looked like a cloud of specks of black snuff or powder struck up from a brush or broom or shaken from a wig; then they would sweep round in whirlwinds—you could see the nearer and farther bow of the rings by the size and blackness; many would be in one phase at once, all narrow black flakes hurling round, then in another; then they would fall upon a field and so on. Splaine wanted a gun: then 'there it would rain meat' he said. I thought they must be full of enthusiasm and delight hearing their cries and stirring and cheering one another

Francis Kilvert

The Moccas Park Oak, by J. G. Strutt, 1830

Stonehenge, a pencil drawing by John Constable, inscribed by the artist "15 July 1820"

Francis Kilvert
⌈1840–1879⌉

First published in 1938–40, the *Diary* of the Rev. Francis Kilvert shone through the war-dimmed literary atmosphere of England like a parting gleam from those sun-drenched late Victorian summer afternoons which the author so loved. The three volumes of selections were garnered from twenty-two notebooks in which a forgotten west-of-England clergyman had recorded the quiet tenor of his days in the decade of the 1870's. Kilvert's brief life was circumscribed by the parishes in which he served: first as his father's assistant at Langley Burrell in Wiltshire, then as curate of Clyne in Radnorshire, and finally as rector successively of St. Harmon's in Radnorshire and Bredwardine in Herefordshire. He died of peritonitis within a month after his marriage in 1879. The least known to history of all the writers represented in this collection, he may yet seem the most alive because of the intimacy to which his candid and vivacious journal invites the reader.

Gently born and Oxford educated, Kilvert was by temperament and inclination perfectly suited to his calling. The portrait that emerges from his pages is of a devout, modest, and cheerful young cleric who was unfailingly attentive to the needs of his parishioners, especially the ailing and aged. By nature disarmingly susceptible, he was perpetually falling in love with one or another of the young girls whose families he visited in his daily rounds. Towards children and dumb animals he exhibited an instinctive sympathy that made him a participant in their joys and sorrows. Indeed, one of the most poignant passages in the *Diary* was occasioned by the author's surprised recognition that he possessed so great a capacity for endearing himself to others:

What is it? What is it? What do they all mean? It is a strange and terrible gift, this power of stealing hearts and exciting such love.

Kilvert was sensitive to music and painting, and he was a fluent, if unremarkable versifier. He felt a special affinity for George Herbert, William and Dorothy Wordsworth, Lamb, and Tennyson, with most of whom he shared a mildly melancholiac habit of mind, mitigated by a lively sense of the ludicrous.

Like Hardy and the Brontës, Kilvert has now given his name to a region. The Kilvert country is that lovely and secluded corner of England which lies along the Welsh border, watered by the Wye and within sight of the Black Mountains. On one level his journal depicts the leisurely and hospitable existence enjoyed by the country gentry, with their pastimes of archery and croquet, of lawn tennis (called "sphairistike!") and skating, of picnics and expeditions to gather wildflowers, all punctuated by pleasant holidays in Wales and Cornwall and the Isle of Wight. But the writer was equally at home "villaging" with the humbler rural populace, sharing their gossip, credulously perpetuating their local superstitions, taking part in the ancient folk and religious festivals which still lingered on in that countryside. Much of Kilvert's writing is time-haunted and veined with nostalgia; and he seems to have maintained his *Diary*, in part at least, out of an intuition that he was a late but not untypical lingerer amidst pastoral scenes that were vanishing. "Why do I keep this voluminous journal?" he asks at one point:

> I can hardly tell. Partly because life appears to me such a curious and wonderful thing that it almost seems a pity that even such a humble and uneventful life as mine should pass altogether away without some such record as this, and partly too because I think the record may amuse and interest some who come after me.

Yet, paradoxically, the way of life memorialized in the *Diary* survives in its timeless, rather than its fugitive aspect. Deeper than Kilvert's regret for the transience of all things human lay the joy of kinship with the unchanging rhythms of the natural world. For all his conviviality, he had the true countryman's passion for solitude. "It is a fine thing to be out on the hills alone," he writes:

> A man can hardly be a beast or a fool alone on a great mountain. There is no company like the grand solemn beautiful hills. They fascinate and grow upon us and one had a feeling and a love for them which one has for nothing else.

A tireless walker, he was abroad in all seasons; and from communion with the perennial beauty and vitality of the earth sprang that ever-renewed sense of wonder at nature's bounty which comes through so freshly in passage after passage.

From *Diary*

Wednesday, 16 March [1870]

I ate so much hare that I could hardly walk and saw stars, but at 4 went up the hill by the Bron Penllan and Little Wern y Pentre. The lane between Little Wern y Pentre and the Tall Trees infamous, so deep and soft that it is almost impossible to feel bottom. Mrs. Williams plunging down the lane through the mud and fording the pools with a sack of swedes on her back. In the meadow between the Tall Trees and Sunny Bank was singing the first lark I have noticed this year. He was coming down, his song stopped suddenly and he dropped to his nest.

Below Tybella a bird singing unseen reminded me how the words of a good man live after he is silent and out of sight 'He being dead yet speaketh'.

Also the scent of an unseen flower seemed like the sweet and holy influence of a good kind deed which cannot be concealed though the deed itself may be hidden. On to Cefn y Blaen where a 'King' once lived. Alas for the pretty merry yellow haired lassie who used to make this house so bright. Three rather nice rosy black haired grey eyed girls. The men sitting at tea but they had finished and went out as I came in. A tall spare old man with a wild eye and a night cap rose from the chimney corner, came forward and shook me by the hand respectfully, claiming acquaintance as he had seen me at Wernnewydd. Round the corner of the Vicar's Hill to Little Twyn y Grain, passing by the Great Twyns which I am happy to see is falling into ruin, the window frames

350

falling in. How well I remember and how short a time ago it seems though nearly five years. I never pass the house without thinking of that afternoon when after neglecting Margaret Thomas' dying son for a long time I went to call and was inexpressibly shocked to find that he had died only ten minutes before . . .

Faint sunshine on Bryngwyn Hill and a cold cheery gleam of water from the great peat bog below on the edge of which stands the grey cluster of buildings and the tall dark yew of Llanshifr. I went down there and waded across the yard to the house through a sea of mud and water. The kitchen was very dark, the bank rising steep in front of the window. Mrs. Morgan gave me some tea and cake. On the settle sat a man perfectly still, silent and in such a dark corner that I could not see his face. On a stool in the chimney corner sat little girl 'Ellen' holding a baby lately vaccinated, both sound asleep, and Mrs. Morgan very anxious lest the girl should 'fall the baby'. Morgan anxious to get out to his ewes and lambs and a tall girl strode into the kitchen crying in a peculiar strident voice that 'a ewe was going up Cae Drws alone' as if about to yean. Morgan went out with some hot milk and showed me the remains of the moat, where the Scotch pedlar was hidden after being murdered for the sake of his pack while lodging in the house and where his skeleton was found when the moat was cleared out. The moat that is left is a broad deep formidable ditch and rather a long pond at one end of the house and full of water. It extended once all round the house and had to be crossed by a bridge. Llanshifr a fearfully wet swampy place, almost under water and I should think very unhealthy. One of the twin yews was lately blown down and cut up into gate posts which will last twice as long as oak. The wood was so hard that Morgan said it turned many of the axes as if they were made of lead. Other axes splintered and broke upon the wood and the old yew was a crucial test of the axes. I wonder in which of these yews Gore hid the penknife before his death which made him restless as hidden iron is said to do, and caused his spirit to come back rummaging about the house and premises and frightening people out of their wits. Maria Lake used to tell me this story. It was getting dusk as I left Llanshifr and after I had plunged about for some time in the swampy Wern up to my ancles in water I lost my bearings and missed the way, so that I might have been belated but that I heard the welcome clank of plough chains as the team came down home and Joe the Llanshifr ploughman directed me up to the Holly House near which in the top of the steep bank I heard children's voices and Hannah and Aaron Gore were gathering 'chats'. They guided me to a 'glat' which I tumbled over. I met old Williams the patriarch of Crowther's Pool coming away from the Holly House, a grand old man, hale, fresh and upright, contented and dignified. I asked his age. 'Eighty seven, if I live till the 6th of old March' (that is the day after tomorrow). Struck over the top of the Vicar's Hill and as I passed Cross Fordd the frogs were croaking snoring and bubbling in the pool under the full moon.

Saturday, Easter Eve, 16 April

I awoke at 4.30 and there was a glorious sight in the sky, one of the grand spectacles of the Universe. There was not a cloud in the deep wonderful blue of the heavens. Along the Eastern horizon there was a clear deep intense glow neither scarlet nor crimson but a mixture of both. This red glow was very narrow, almost like a riband and it suddenly shaded off into the deep blue. Opposite in the west the full moon shining in all its brilliance was setting upon the hill beyond the church steeple. Thus the glow in the east bathed the church in a warm rich tinted light, while the moon from the west was casting strong shadows. The moon dropped quickly down behind the hill bright to the last, till only her rim could be seen sparkling among the tops of the orchards on the hill.

The sun rose quickly and his rays struck red upon the white walls of Pen Llan, but not so brilliantly as in the winter sunrisings. I got up soon after 5 and set to work on my Easter sermon getting two hours for writing before breakfast. At ten Mr. V. came in and we arranged that I should preach tomorrow morning and go on to Bettws and go out driving with him and his brother this afternoon.

At 11 I went to the school to see if the children were gathering flowers and found they were out in the fields and woods collecting moss, leaving the primroses to be gathered later in the day to give them a better chance of keeping fresh. Next I went to Cae Mawr. Mrs. Morrell had been very busy all the morning preparing decorations for the Font, a round dish full of flowers in water and just big enough to fit into the Font and upon this large dish a pot filled and covered with flowers all wild, primroses, violets, wood anemones, wood sorrel, periwinkles, oxlips and the first blue bells, rising in a gentle pyramid, ferns and larch sprays drooping over the brim, a wreath of simple ivy to go round the stem of the Font, and a bed of moss to encircle the foot of the Font in a narrow band pointed at the corners and angles of the stone with knots of primroses. At 2 o'clock Hetty Gore of the Holly House came down from Cefn y Blaen and upset all my arrangements for the afternoon saying that old William Pritchard there was very ill not likely to live and wishes to see me this afternoon that I might read to him and give him the Sacrament. Hetty Gore thought he might not last many days. So I was obliged to go to the Vicarage explain and give up my drive. Found the schoolmaster and a friend staying with him just going out to get moss and carrying the East window sill board from the Church to the school to prepare it for tomorrow with the text 'Christ is Risen' written in primroses upon moss. Shall I ever forget that journey up the hill to Cefn y Blaen in this burning Easter Eve, under the cloudless blue, the scorching sun and over the country covered with a hot dim haze? I climbed up the Bron panting in the sultry afternoon heat. Went up the fields from Court Evan Gwynne to Little Wern y Pentre and envied the sheep that were being washed in the brook below, between the field and the lane, by Price of Great Wern y Pentre and his excited boys. The peewits were sweeping rolling and tumbling in the hot blue air about the Tall Trees with a strange deep mysterious hustling and quavering sound from their great wings. . . .

Coming back it was cooler for the fierceness of the sun was tempered and I met a refreshing cool breeze. When I reached the village I refreshed myself at home with some beer and then went to the school where I found Mr. and Mrs. Evans at work with their friend's help on the board covered with moss and primroses, the children bringing the flowers, and the text half done. When it was done the board was taken to the church and left there all night in a cool shady place where the morning sun would not touch it, for if it were laid in its place in the East window over night the early morning sun would wither the delicate fragile beauty of the primroses. I sent Mary Jane Evans with a basket to Cae Bont Dingle for some more primroses to dress Mr. Henry Venables' grave the first thing on Easter morning and when she brought them I took them to Annie Powell and asked her to tie them up in bunches and she was delighted to do it, her father sitting by and helping her. Then I went to the wheelwright and got Henry Anthony to give me some strips of wood to make crosses, one for Mrs. Archdeacon Venables' and one for Mrs. Lester Venables' grave. I took the crosses to the school with some of Annie Powell's primrose bunches which we put into water while Mrs. Evans skilfully covered the crosses with moss and put them to float all night in a tub of water that the moss might revive and grow green, ready to be pointed early in the morning with five primrose bunches apiece.

When I started for Cefn y Blaen only two or three people were in the churchyard with flowers. Hetty Gore and Mrs. Morgan of Cold Blow etc. But now the customary beautiful Easter Eve Idyll had fairly begun and people kept arriving from all parts with flowers to dress the graves. Children were coming from the town and from neighbouring villages with baskets of flowers and knives to cut holes in the turf. The roads were lively with people coming and going and the churchyard a busy scene with women and children and a few men moving about among the tombstones and kneeling down beside the green mounds flowering the graves. An evil woman from Hay was dressing a grave. (Jane Phillips). I found a child wandering about the tombs looking for her father's grave. She had found her grandfather's and had already dressed it with flowers. The clerk was banking up and watering the green mounds not far off and I got him to come and show the child where her father's grave lay. He soon found it for he knows almost every grave in the churchyard. And then I helped the child to dress the long narrow green mound with the flowers that remained in her basket, some of which came from the Cabalva greenhouse. We found two more graves of her family close by her father's, an uncle of hers and a child, a cousin or sister. The two brothers lay side by side. My little friend had lavished so much of her flower wealth upon her grandfather's grave that there was not much left for the others and we were obliged to economize and make our scanty store go as far as possible. I showed her how to arrange the flowers in the form of a cross, and she went away satisfied and happy at the result of her work. This child is the granddaughter of poor old Parry of the Pentre. I used to see her there and she remembered me. I found Annie Dyke standing among the graves with her basket of flowers. A pretty picture she would have made as she stood there with her pure fair sweet grave face and clustering brown curls shaded by her straw hat and her flower basket hanging on her arm. It is her birthday to-day. I always tell her she and the cuckoos came together. So I went home and got a little birthday present I had been keeping for her, which I bought in the Crystal Palace in January, a small ivory brooch, with the carved figure of a stag. I took the little box which held it out into the churchyard and gave it to her as she was standing watching while the wife of one of her father's workmen, the shepherd, flowered the grave that she came to dress, for her.

More and more people kept coming into the churchyard as they finished their day's work. The sun went down in glory behind the dingle, but still the work of love went on through the twilight and into the dusk until the moon rose full and splendid. The figures continued to move about among the graves and to bend over the green mounds in the calm clear moonlight and warm air of the balmy evening. Water was in great request for the ground was very hard and dry and wanted softening before flowers could be bedded in the turf. The flowers most used were primroses, daffodils, currant, [word illegible] laurel and box. A pretty wreath of greenhouse flowers lay upon the high flat tomb of Mrs. Williams of Pipton but no one seemed to know who placed it there. I took Annie Dyke into the church to see Mrs. Morrell's work at the Font which looked beautiful and so fresh and dewy, all the flowers having their stems in water and being well sprinkled.

At 8 o'clock there was a gathering of the Choir in the Church to practise the two anthems for to-morrow, and the young people came flocking in from the graves where they had been at work or watching others working, or talking to their friends, for the Churchyard on Easter Eve is a place where a great many people meet. The clerk's wife had been cleaning the church for Easter Day and the clerk had kept the church jealously locked as there were so many strangers about in the churchyard. He now unlocked the steeple door and let us in that way. There was a large gathering of the Choir and two or three people stole in from the churchyard afterwards to hear the anthems practised. The anthems went very nicely and sounded especially well from the chancel. The moonlight came streaming in broadly through the chancel windows. When the choir had gone and the lights were out and the church quiet again, as the schoolmaster and his friend stood with me at the Church door in the moonlight we were remarking the curious fact that this year Good Friday like the Passover has fallen upon the 15th day of the month and the full moon. As I walked down the Churchyard alone the decked graves had a strange effect in the moonlight and looked as if the people had laid down to sleep for the night out of doors, ready dressed to rise early on Easter morning. I lingered in the verandah before going to bed. The air was as soft and warm as a summer night, and the broad moonlight made the quiet village almost as light as day. Everyone seemed to have gone to rest and there was not a sound except the clink and trickle of the brook.

Easter Day, 17 April

The happiest, brightest, most beautiful Easter I have ever spent. I woke early and looked out. As I had hoped the day was cloudless, a glorious morning. My first thought was 'Christ is Risen'. It is not well to lie in bed on Easter morning, indeed it is thought very unlucky. I got up between five and six and was out soon after six. There had been a frost and the air was rimy with a heavy thick white dew on hedge, bank and turf, but the morning was not cold. Last night poor Mrs. Chalmers was in trouble because she had not been able to get any flowers to dress her husband's grave and Miss Chalmers was in deep distress about it. Some boys who had promised to bring them some primroses had disappointed them. So I thought I would go and gather some primroses this morning and flower the grave for them. I strolled down the lane till I came in sight of the full mill pond shining between the willow trunks like a lake of indefinite size. Here and there the banks and road sides were spangled with primroses and they shone like stars among the little brakes and bramble thickets overhanging the brook. A sheep and lamb having broken bounds were wandering about the lane by themselves and kept on fording and refording the brook where it crosses the road to get out of my way. The mill was silent except for the plash of the water from 'the dark round of the dripping wheel'. The mill pond was full, but I forgot to look at the sun in it to see if he was dancing as he is said to do on Easter morning. There was a heavy white dew with a touch of hoar frost on the meadows, and as I leaned over the wicket gate by the mill pond looking to see if there were any primroses in the banks but not liking to venture into the dripping grass suddenly I heard the cuckoo for the first time this year. He was near Peter's Pool and he called three times quickly one after another. It is very well to hear the cuckoo for the first time on Easter Sunday morning. I loitered up the lane again gathering primroses where I could from among the thorn and bramble thickets and along the brook banks, not without a good many scratches. Some few grew by the mill pond edge and there was one plant growing on the trunk of a willow some way from the ground. The children have almost swept the lane clear of primroses for the same purpose for which I wanted them. However I got a good handful with plenty of green leaves and brought them home.

The village lay quiet and peaceful in the morning sunshine, but by the time I came back from primrosing there was some little stir and people were beginning to open their doors and look out into the fresh fragrant splendid morning. Hannah Whitney's door was open. I tied my primroses up in five bunches, borrowed an old knife etc. and a can of water from Mary and went to Mrs. Powell's for the primroses Annie had tied for me last night, but no one in the house was up and the door was locked. Anthony and Richard Brooks were standing in the road by the churchyard wall and I asked them if they could show me Mr. Chalmers' grave. Richard Brooks came along with me and showed me where he believed it to be, and it proved to be the right grave. So I made a simple cross upon it with my five primrose bunches. There were a good many people about in the churchyard by this time finishing flowering the graves that could not be done overnight, watering the flowers and looking at last night's work. Jane Davies and a girl seeing me at work came and dressed the rest of the four Chalmers graves. By this time Mrs. Powell was just opening her door so I went to the house with Charlie Powell and got the primroses which had been in water all night and were exquisitely fresh and fragrant. With these five bunches I made a primrose cross on the turf at the foot of the white marble cross which marks Mr. Henry Venables' grave. Then I went to the school.

It was now 8 o'clock and Mrs. Evans was down and just ready to set about finishing the moss crosses. She and Mary Jane went out to gather fresh primroses in the Castle Clump as last night's were rather withered. The moss had greatly improved and freshened into green during the night's soaking and when the crosses were pointed each with five small bunches of primroses they looked very nice and pretty because so very simple. Directly they were finished I carried them to the churchyard and placed them standing, leaning against the stone tombs of the two Mr. Venables. People came up to look at the crosses and they were much admired. Then I ran home to dress and snatched a mouthful of breakfast.

There was a very large congregation at morning church the largest I have seen for some time, attracted by Easter and the splendour of the day, for they have here an immense reverence for Easter Sunday. The anthem went very well and Mr. Baskerville complimented Mr. Evans after church about it, saying that it was sung in good tune and time and had been a great treat. Mr. V. read prayers and I preached from 1 John III.2,3 about the Risen Body and Life. There were more communicants than usual: 29. This is the fifth time I have received the Sacrament within four days. After morning service I took Mr. V. round the churchyard and showed him the crosses on his mother's, wife's, and brother's graves. He was quite taken by surprise and very much gratified. I am glad to see that our primrose crosses seem to be having some effect for I think I notice this Easter some attempt to copy them and an advance towards the form of the cross in some of the decorations of the graves. I wish we could get the people to adopt some little design in the disposition of the flowers upon the graves instead of sticking sprigs into the turf aimlessly anywhere, anyhow and with no meaning at all. But one does not like to interfere too much with their artless, natural way of showing their respect and love for the dead. I am thankful to find this beautiful custom on the increase, and observed more and more every year. Some years ago it was on the decline and nearly discontinued. On Easter Day all the young people come out in something new and bright like butterflies. It is almost part of their religion to wear something new on this day. It was an old saying that if you don't wear something new on Easter Day, the crows will spoil everything you have on. Mrs. Chalmers tells me that if it is fine on Easter Day it is counted in Yorkshire a sign of a good harvest. If it rains before morning church is over it is a sign of a bad harvest.

Between the services a great many people were in the churchyard looking at the graves. I went to Bettws Chapel in the afternoon. It was burning hot and as I climbed the hill the perspiration rolled off my forehead from under my hat and fell in drops on the dusty road. Lucretia Wall was in chapel looking pale and pretty after her illness. I went into the farmhouse after Chapel and when I came away Lucretia and Eliza both looking very pretty were leading little Eleanor about the farmyard between them, a charming home picture. Coming down the hill it was delightful, cool and pleasant. The sweet suspicion of spring strengthens, deepens, and grows more sweet every day. Mrs. Pring gave us lamb and asparagus at dinner.

Tuesday, 14 March [1871]

The afternoon had been stormy but it cleared towards sunset.

Gradually the heavy rain clouds rolled across the valley to the foot of the opposite mountains and began climbing up their sides wreathing in rolling masses of vapour. One solitary cloud still hung over the brilliant sunlit town, and that whole cloud was a rainbow. Gradually it lost its bright prismatic hues and moved away up the Cusop Dingle in the shape of a pillar and of the colour of golden dark smoke. The Black Mountains were invisible, being wrapped in clouds, and I saw one very white brilliant dazzling cloud where the mountains ought to have been. This cloud grew more white and dazzling every moment, till a clearer burst of sunlight scattered the mists and revealed the truth. This brilliant white cloud that I had been looking and wondering at was the mountain in snow. The last cloud and mist rolled away over the mountain tops and the mountains stood up in the clear blue heaven, a long rampart line of dazzling glittering snow so as no fuller on earth can white them. I stood rooted to the ground, struck with amazement and overwhelmed at the extraordinary splendour of this marvellous spectacle. I never saw anything to equal it I think, even among the high Alps. One's first involuntary thought in the presence of these magnificent sights is to lift up the heart to God and humbly thank Him for having made the earth so beautiful. An intense glare of primrose light streamed from the west deepening into rose and crimson. There was not a flake of snow anywhere but on the mountains and they stood up, the great white range rising high into the blue sky, while all the rest of the world at their feet lay ruddy rosy brown. The sudden contrast was tremendous, electrifying. I could have cried with the excitement of the overwhelming spectacle. I wanted

361

someone to admire the sight with me. A man came whistling along the road riding upon a cart horse. I would have stopped him and drawn his attention to the mountains but I thought he would probably consider me mad. He did not seem to be the least struck by or to be taking the smallest notice of the great sight. But it seemed to me as if one might never see such a sight again. The great white range which had at first gleamed with an intense brilliant yellow light gradually deepened with the sky to the indescribable red tinge that snowfields assume in sunset light, and then the grey cold tint crept up the great slopes quenching the rosy warmth which lingered still a few minutes on the summits. Soon all was cold and grey and all that was left of the brilliant gleaming range was the dim ghostly phantom of the mountain rampart scarce distinguishable from the greying sky.

Friday, 11 August

A woodpigeon has built her nest in a fir on the lawn, and it is beautiful to hear her soft continual cooing among the branches. After going to the post I strolled down the meadows past Westhay and Lombard's farm to the upper bridge on the Blackwater. The limpid water ran as clear as air in the sunshine over the yellow pebbles and the still smooth pools, brimmed cool dark and glassy in the shade.

The lovely lanes beyond were checquered with sunlight and green shade. As I sat upon a fallen tree by the lane side, a gleam of white shirt sleeves came up the lane between the trees and through the alternate bars of light and shade, and two lusty young men went up to the hay fields of Stoneborough, one with fair hair carrying a scythe over his shoulder. Then came the quick tramp of hoofs and a labourer rode up the steep lane on a dark brown cob. The lane led on to a breezy common, glowing purple with heather. The pimpernel blazed in the grass with wide open scarlet eyes, and the woods were lighted in their dark green depths by the scarlet

362

bunches of the rowan berries. The scent of the hay came mixed with the aromatic odour of the fir trees drawn out by the sun. The wood path was carpeted soft with millions of fir needles and the voices of the gamekeeper's children at play and the barking of a dog came merrily up through the plantations.

In a field among the woods the flax sheaves stood in shocks like wheat, the fine-hung bells on their wiry hair stalks rustling and quaking in the breeze like wag wantons. A mare and foal stood in the shade among the flax sheaves.

In the afternoon I went to pay a farewell visit to the lime avenue. It looked more like a vast church than ever and the strong low sunlight which came up the green aisle seemed to be pouring through a great distant window. The sunlight streamed between the dark tree trunks, a soft cool breeze rustled the limes overhead and the checquering shadow of the leaves danced and flickered on the rich floor sunny and golden green.

Saturday, 27 January [1872]

Banging of guns, rabbit shooting at Wye Cliff.

Then the Radnorshire postman coming from Llowes blew his horn.

I set out for Pwlldwrgi to get some wild snowdrops along the river side by the Otter's Pool for Mrs. Venables. Opposite Clyro Court I met the brothers Venables returning from a walk. Mr. George Venables came yesterday. He said they had been walking on the high common above Brynyrhydd and he never saw the Fan of Brecon look so beautiful, the outline of the mountain quite clear, but the interstices filled with a tender mist.

I went down to the river side by the Llowes path stile and by the old hollow blasted oak, the uncanny oak, the haunted oak which bears such bad repute, and then climbed along the slippery foreshore and mud banks steeply sloping of the sinking river. After scrambling through some bushes and crossing a rushing runnel brawling from its spring on the high bank above I clambered up into the old green road. And there by the old green road side and on the bank of a little rushing brook the wild snowdrops, the 'Fair Maids of February', grew in myriads, with closed eyes and hanging heads. How white and pure and stainless they looked in the deepening twilight. They grew among the thorns and ragged bushes, peeping through the dead leaves and dry tussocks of bleached and withered grass, here and there bowing over and round a soak and contrasting their pure white blossoms with the moist black earth.

Overhead on the high bank above the nine tall poplar spires shot into the sky, but the evening was so still that not a twig trembled or waved and the poplars towered as motionless as church steeples.

Below the grey river hurried past with a tumultuous rushing current washing heavily and lapping against its mud shores, and higher up the stream the water swirled fiercely round the sharp corner and boiled in the deep Pwlldwrgi, the Pool of the water dog or water beast, the Otter's Pool. The road was very still. No one seemed to be passing, and the birds sang late and joyfully in the calm mild evening as if they thought it must be spring. A white mist gathered in the valley and hung low along the winding course of the river. Mingled with the rushing of the brooks the distant voices and laughter of children at play came floating at intervals across the river and near at hand a pheasant screeched now and then and clapped his wings or changed his roost from tree to tree like a man turning in his bed before he falls asleep.

And down under the poplars out of sight in their lowly hidden place, courting no one's notice, the lovely snowdrops hung their pure white heads and closed their eyes in sleep as the night fell.

So simple, so humble, yet so brave. It comes before the crocus dares. I love the snowdrop, the first of all the flowers, the harbinger of Spring. God's New Year's gift to the earth, the Fair Maid of February, the daughter of the earth and the snow.

And so pure, so spotlessly, stainlessly pure. Who is it that calls the snowdrop the 'pure pale penitent'?

But to me it always seems to be 'the penitent absolved'. Oh that all our sins might thus be washed away and we be presented spotless through the Saviour's atoning blood.

Saturday, 18 May

Hay Fair still going on. To get out of the sight and sound of it I went up the unfrequented path from Penllan to the Wern below Gwernfydden to look for bog beans to give to Mrs. Venables on Whitsun Day. The marshy ground was thick with the trefoil bean leaves, but not a blossom had yet opened. I found a gate beside a sheltered hedge, in a sunny nook convenient for reading, and returning to the village I climbed Penllan again with that charming book *Lettice Lisle** and established myself in my sunny corner on the gate sheltered from the East wind by the high green hedge and secure from intrusion on a path that led to nowhere and therefore sacred from the folks returning from the fair. It was a quiet peaceful beautiful place. There was no sound to be heard but the singing of the birds, and nothing to be seen but the blue mountains rising over the sunny golden green oaks of Penllan Wood and the blue sky above all. No living thing seemed to be moving except a rising lark and a small blue butterfly which fluttered along the sunny side of the hedge. Presently as I sat perfectly still upon the gate reading I heard a sharp little rustling in the hedge close by me as if some small fourfooted animal were bustling busily about. In a minute or two afterwards came out of the bank on to the

* By Frances Parthenope, Lady Verney, a sister of Florence Nightingale.

open path before the gate a beautiful little creature coloured a deep rich chestnut red except its throat and belly which were pure white. It carried in its mouth a mouse or a young rat. Apparently it did not see me. At all events he took no notice and was not the least startled. He passed under the gate carrying the mouse and went into the hedge on the opposite side of the path. But he did not seem to know what to do with the mouse and soon came out again, still carrying it in his mouth. I made a slight noise on purpose and the weasel dropped his prey on the path and retreated into the hedge. I got down off the gate, picked up the mouse and placed it a few feet further off in front of the gate and then resumed my seat to watch the result. The weasel was not at all abashed. He came to the mouth of the hole in the hedge, rested his little forepaws upon a bit of stick, stood up, and looked round him with his quick brilliant watchful eyes to see what had become of his mouse. Then the beautiful slender creature came out upon the path and began darting about like lightning trying to discover his prey by scent. I never saw any living thing move with such extraordinary swiftness.

The mouse was only 3 or 4 feet from him, but the weasel could not see it, and as I had lifted the mouse from the ground he could not follow it along the earth by scent. So he was completely at fault. He must have been extraordinarily blind or shortsighted. After darting about on the path close by the gate for a few minutes the weasel gave up the search and went back into the original hedge to hunt another mouse and I heard him rustling and bustling about in the bank for some time after.

Saturday, 26th July [1873]

Up at 6.30 and out at 7 o'clock in a lovely bright breezy morning, the dew shining after rain.

I stole out at the back door to avoid disturbing anyone and

I believe Rawlings the gardener thought I was gone mad or going to commit suicide for he ran anxiously out of his shoe house and looked after me to see which way I was going. The meadows were clean swept and washed and the lattermath from which the hay had been cleared gleamed brilliant green after the rain. I followed the lanes past West Hay, and presently came to the dry bed of a brook crossing the road. Before I could pass over it however I heard a sudden sound of water and saw a stream beginning to trickle and wind amongst the stones. The stream broadened and deepened till with a swift rush of brown turbid water the brook bed was filled and the stream poured under a little foot bridge and roared down, a small cataract, into the meadows beyond. I thought at first it was a little flood caused by the day and night's rain and just came down the valley, but a merry-faced peasant, who was on his way to a rustic festival of sheep dipping, said that the sudden stream I had seen was the water fresh loosed from the mill pound of Zealey's Mill at Phelley Holme.

The man said there were a good many trout in the brooks from ½ lb. to 2 lbs. and told me they should probably end their sheep dipping with a trout netting frolic in the evening after the work was done.

At the bottom of the hill in the sunny hollow where we crossed a little stream of limpid water clear as crystal, dazzling and gleaming over its yellow pebbles, we met a woman who in answer to my companion's enquiries directed him to the sheepwashing. And presently we came to the gate of the meadow where the rural festival was being held. A group of men whose clothes were splashed and dyed by the red wash were plunging sheep and lambs one by one into a long deep trough. The sheep went in white and came out red, protected by their dipping against the attentions of the fly, and walked away across the meadow to join the flock, shaking the red wash in showers from their close-shorn fleeces.

The lane grew more and still more lovely. The morning sunlight slanted richly across the road between the trees, or struck here and there through a break in the foliage and tipped a frond of fern with brilliant green light. Broad alternate bars of sunshine and shadow lay across the lane, the sunlight shone on the polished grey silvery stems of a row of beeches, and a tender morning mist hung dreamily over the wooded hollow of the dingle below the road.

The lane opened up into a high open common across which the morning breeze from the sea stirred freshly with a cool light after the warm shelter of the hollow lanes. Beyond the common a gate let into a shady road cool and damp, dark and quiet as a cloister. It was completely overhung by trees, and the air was filled with the fragrant aromatic scent of the fir trees and the soft carpet of fir needles with which the ground was thickly strewn. The fields of ripening wheat began to glow golden along the slopes of the blue hills and the ferns, fresh washed by the rain of the night, beamed clear and brilliant green where the sun slanted silently through the windows of the wood.

Sunday, 2 August [1874]

Between ten and eleven o'clock to-night I walked alone up and down the drive under the clear starry sky, waiting for the moon to rise behind an oak in the eastern sky and to throw the shadows of the silver weeping birches across the lawn. The night was cool and fresh and a slight mist began to rise and whiten over the meadows. Then the eastern sky brightened and behind the oak the moon rose over Bencroft ridge like a great fire. As she cleared the tops of the trees a soft golden beam stole across the turf from between the two birches, discovering and tipping here and there a bunch of white flowers in the beds and soon the shadows of the tree stems lay across the drive and the foliage of the birches was mapped upon the lawn.

Monday, 31 August

When I went out with Jock this morning to walk across the common before breakfast there as usual were the three white tiddling lambs lying round the white gate. Immediately the three bold white lambs began to play with the black dog, to hunt him about and butt him sportively, while the dog with his ears laid back pretended to be afraid of the lambs, ran away from them, bounded back, faced them and occasionally took one of them by the ear.

For the first time in my life I crossed the ancient stile between the Barrow Farm and Cottages and wandered among the quiet lonely meadows between Langley Burrell and Hardenhuish, chancing at length upon the old footpath and line of stiles now almost disused between the two villages.

I love to wander on these soft gentle mournful autumn days, alone among the quiet peaceful solitary meadows, tracing out the ancient footpaths and mossy overgrown stiles between farm and hamlet, village and town, musing of the many feet that have trodden these ancient and now well nigh deserted and almost forgotten ways and walking in the footsteps of the generations that have gone before and passed away.

In the course of my wanderings among these quiet unknown meadows I came suddenly upon a view of the White Horse and the Monument on Cherhill Down that I remember seeing as a child nearly thirty years ago. The sight brought back a flood of recollections. I remember that as a child I could see the White Horse and the monument without difficulty with the naked eye. . . .

Monday, 14 September

As I sit writing in my bedroom and looking from the window at the glorious morning spread upon the mountains

369

the Wye valley is filled full of mist from side to side. Out of the great white fog sea rises an island ridge of trees above Wye Cliff and one great solitary fir stands up alone like an isolated rock and stems the tide of the rolling mist. The sun has risen cloudless and the fog sea gleams brilliant and dazzling, and shining like silver. Now the sea of mist has swallowed up the island ridge of trees and the great solitary fir. Everything is swamped and gone down in the bright rolling flood which tosses and heaves and seems to dash itself in spray against the mountain sides.

Villaging in the morning. Saw Mrs. Chaloner, Mrs. Price of the Swan and Flora Benson my old pupil.

At noon I started with Morrell and the Vicar and Curate (Prickard and Trumper) to walk to Aberedw across the hills. It was one of the loveliest days I ever saw and the mountains were in all their beauty of light and tender blue. We sat to take our luncheon upon the turf of the Beacons beside a tinkling rivulet over against Llanbedr Church. A sweet fresh wind was moving upon the hills and brilliant gleams of green and purple cloud shadows were flying upon the great landscape. In the narrow green sunny lanes the nuts still hung from the hazel tree and a small farmer driving a herd of fat red oxen put us into the right way with the beautiful courtesy of Radnorshire. Below us Bychllyn Pool lay in its hollow like a silver shield and the heather was blooming purple upon the hills. Over the rolling moor rose the pointed cone of Penpicca Hill and we came down into the grand amphitheatre which embosoms the twin valleys and the meeting of the sweet waters of the Edw and the Wye. . . .

Thursday, 24 September

I went out upon the Common before breakfast. The morning was singularly lovely even for a fine autumn morning. A tender delicate blue mist spread its veil over the trees and distant hills, and the lilacs and the thick grass were drenched with a silvery white web of dew. Through the mist the quiet green sunshine came softly stealing over the fresh morning meadows. The air moved sweet and warm over the common. Two wood pigeons were pouring out their hearts and their tale of love from elm to elm. The bright coloured herd of cows and the silver-fleeced sheep fed quietly at distant parts of the great level pasture. There came a sharp swift hurtling of wings overhead and a large hawk rushed through the air going south. The Chippenham Church clock struck eight with a sweet musical sound and two sweet bells immediately began chiming for matins. Two boys came from the village laughing merrily.

And in the midst of all this beauty and freshness a black shadow stole over the scene, a hearse with plumes and a mourning coach rumbled along the road from Chippenham and across the bright Common. So 'sin entered into the world and death by sin'.

This afternoon I walked over to Kington St. Michael by Langley Burrell Church and Morrell Lane and the old Mausoleum and Langley Ridge and the Plough Inn. It was a day of exceeding and almost unmatched beauty, one of those perfectly lovely afternoons that we seldom get but in September or October. A warm delicious calm and sweet peace brooded breathless over the mellow sunny autumn afternoon and the happy stillness was broken only by the voices of children blackberry gathering in an adjoining meadow and the sweet solitary singing of a robin.

As I drew near Kington the sun was veiled by a great cloud, dark in the middle and white-edged, from behind which darted on different sides broad streaming rays, some dark blue, some light blue and some shining and brilliant white. Near the entrance to the village I fell in with a team of red oxen, harnessed, coming home from plough with chains rattling and the old ploughman riding the fore ox, reminding me vividly of the time when I used to ride the oxen home

371

from plough at Lanhill.

Since I was last at Kington the roof of the Chancel has been raised and a new decorated East window has replaced the early English one.

As I went down into the fair green dingle of Kenhills and crossed the little brook to the gate of the cottage and garden I thought how many things had befallen me and how much I was altered for better or worse since I last trod that path and that little plank bridge over the brook on my way from visiting poor dying Julia Lessiter. In spite of the warm afternoon sunshine the solitary cottages, low-lying on the brook, looked cold and damp, but the apples hung bright on the trees in the cottage gardens and a Virginia creeper burned like fire in crimson upon the wall, crimson among the green.

When I returned home at night the good Vicar accompanied me as far as the Plough Inn. The moon was at the full. The night was sweet and quiet. Overhead was the vast fleecy sky in which the moon was riding silently and the stillness was broken only by the occasional pattering of an acorn or a chestnut through the leaves to the ground.

Wednesday, 7 October

For some time I have been trying to find the right word for the shimmering glancing twinkling movement of the poplar leaves in the sun and wind. This afternoon I saw the word written on the poplar leaves. It was 'dazzle'. The dazzle of the poplars.

Tuesday, 3 November

This morning between breakfast and luncheon I walked up to Bowood to see the beeches by way of the Cradle Bridge, Tytherton Stanley and Studley Hill. I went into Bowood

Park by the Studley Gate and turned sharp to the left down a drive that brought me soon into the very heart and splendour of the beeches. As the sun shone through the roof of beech boughs overhead the very air seemed gold and scarlet and green and crimson in the deep places of the wood and the red leaves shone brilliant standing out against the splendid blue of the sky. A crowd of wood pigeons rose from the green and misty azure hollows of the plantation and flapped swiftly down the glades, the blue light glancing off their clapping wings. I went by the house down to the lakeside and crossed the water by the hatches above the cascade. From the other side of the water the lake shone as blue as the sky and beyond it rose from the water's edge the grand bank of sloping woods glowing with colours, scarlet, gold, orange and crimson and dark green. Two men were fishing on the further shore of an arm of the lake and across the water came the hoarse belling of a buck while a coot fluttered skimming along the surface of the lake with a loud cry and rippling splash.

> 'The wild buck bells from ferny brake,
> The coot dives merry on the lake,
> The saddest heart might pleasure take
> To see all Nature gay.'

To eye and ear it was a beautiful picture, the strange hoarse belling of the buck, the fluttering of the coot as she skimmed the water with her melancholy note, the cry of the swans across the lake, the clicking of the reels as the fishermen wound up or let out their lines, the soft murmur of the woods, the quiet rustle of the red and golden drifts of beech leaves, the rush of the waterfall, the light tread of the dappled herd of deer dark and dim glancing across the green glades from shadow into sunlight and rustling under the beeches, and the merry voices of the Marquis's children at play.

Why do I keep this voluminous journal? I can hardly tell. Partly because life appears to me such a curious and wonderful thing that it almost seems a pity that even such a humble

373

and uneventful life as mine should pass altogether away without some such record as this, and partly too because I think the record may amuse and interest some who come after me. . . .

Friday, May Eve [1875]

The young rooks cried from their nests lightly veiled in the fresh tender green of the elms around the Manor Farm, the distant Church bell went on ringing for Vespers. Across the meadow came the quick roll of a drum, as a great woodpecker tapped upon a tree, and the calling of the cuckoo chimed sweetly with the rushing of the river weir at Kellaway's Mill.

Thursday, Midsummer Day

And a lovely day it has been, soft warm and sunny. I took the young cuckoo out of his nest, put him in the great wicker cage, and hung the cage up in the hawthorn hedge close to the old nest that the hedge sparrows might feed their charge. It reminded me of William Barnes the Dorsetshire Poet's humorous lines, 'And the goocoo will soon be committed to cage, for a trespass in somebody's tree'.

Gathering strawberries. Edward Awdry came over and stayed to supper. As the day wore the weather became more and more beautiful till at last the evening grew the loveliest I think I ever saw. The rich golden light flooded the lawn and clean freshly cleared meadows, slanting through the western trees which fringe the Common's edge. Even the roan cows, and the Alderney especially, glowed with a golden tinge in the glorious evening sunlight. From the wide common over the thick waving fragrant grass came the sweet country music of the white-sleeved mowers whetting their scythes and the voices of their children at play among the fresh-cut

*Male Cuckoo and, in the Background, Young Bird
being fed by Pied Wagtail, by John Gould*

flowery swaths. The sun went down red under a delicate fringe of gold laced cloud, the beautiful Midsummer evening passed through twilight and gloaming into the exquisite warm soft Midsummer night, with its long light in the north slowly, softly lingering as Jupiter came out glorious in the south and flashed glittering through the tresses of the silver birches softly waving, and the high poplars rustled whispering and the Church clock at Draycot struck ten and I longed to sleep out of doors and dream my 'Midsummer night's dream'.

Friday, 27 August

To-day I paid my first visit to Stonehenge.

We had breakfast before Church and immediately after service Morris and I started to walk to Stonehenge, eleven miles. As we walked through the meadows towards Salisbury with the great spire ever before us pointing heavenward, Morris told me some of the adventures of Edward Hill and Lord March when they were in America shooting grizzly bears.

Passing through the beautiful Cathedral Close and the city of Salisbury we took the Devizes road and after we had walked along that road for some six miles we saw in the dim distance the mysterious Stones standing upon the Plain. We pushed on to the clump of trees which shelters the Druid's Head Inn from the S.W. winds and had a merry luncheon in a long dark parlour adorned with a large signboard style of art painting of a Druid's Head. Then we struck across the Plain towards the Stones.

The sun was hot, but a sweet soft air moved over the Plain 'wafting' the scent of the purple heather tufts and the beds of thyme and making the delicate blue harebells tremble on their fragile stems. A beautiful little wheatear flitted before us from one stone heap to another along the side of the wheel track as we struck across the firm elastic turf. Around us the

Plain heaved mournfully with great and solemn barrows, the 'grassy barrows of the happier dead'. It seemed to be holy ground and the very Acre of God. Beyond Ambresbury the Plain swelled into bolder hills, and dark clumps of trees here and there marked the crests and high places of the downs, while the white and dusty road glared away northwards in full sweep for Devizes across the great undulations of the rolling Plain.

Soon after we left the Druid's Head and struck across the turf eastward we came in sight of the grey cluster of gigantic Stones. They stood in the midst of a green plain, and the first impression they left on my mind was that of a group of people standing about and talking together. It seemed to me as if they were ancient giants who suddenly became silent and stiffened into stone directly anyone approached, but who might at any moment become alive again, and at certain seasons, as at midnight and on Old Christmas and Midsummers Eve, might form a true 'Chorea Gigantum' and circle on the Plain in a solemn and stately dance.

It is a solemn awful place. As I entered the charmed circle of the sombre Stones I instinctively uncovered my head. It was like entering a great Cathedral Church. A great silent service was going on and the Stones inaudibly whispered to each other the grand secret. The Sun was present at the service in his Temple and the place was filled with his glory. During the service we sat under the shadow of the great leaning stone upon the vast monolith which has fallen upon and crushed and which now nearly covers the Hearth or Altar Stone. Many Stones still stood upright, one leaned forward towards the East, as if bowing to the rising sun, while some had fallen flat on their faces as if prostrate with adoration before the Lamp of Heaven, or as if like Dagon they had fallen across the threshold of the Temple before the advent of a purer faith, and in reluctant acknowledgment and worship of One Greater than They.

It must be a solemn thing to pass a night among the silent

shadows of the awful Stones, to see the Sun leave his Temple in the evening with a farewell smile, and to watch for him again until at morning he enters once more by the great Eastern gate and takes his seat upon the altar stone.

As we went down the southern slope of the green plain we left the Stones standing on the hill against the sky, seeming by turns to be the Enchanted Giants, the Silent Preachers, the Sleepless Watchers, the great Cathedral on the Plain.

Passing over another ridge crested with a haystack we came down into the valley of the Avon and walked under the shade of beautiful cross avenues, dark and cool after the glare and heat of the plain, till we came to the farmhouse of Normanton, where we stopped to ask for the way to cross the river at Normanton Hatches, the only bridge hereabouts, and for a drink of water. A pretty servant maid came to the door with the information we wanted and a jug of cold sparkling water, but with a kindly and anxious inquiry if we would not like something better.

Crossing the river at Normanton Hatches we walked along the hillside through meadows and barley fields till we came to the hospitable Manor House of Great Durnford, the seat of Mr. John Pinckney, where we found Mr. and Mrs. Pinckney, Mr. Charles Everett and Major Fisher, the Champion archer of England, at luncheon. After luncheon the archers went out to shoot at a beautiful archery ground by the riverside. The ladies sat watching under the trees while the arrows flashed past with a whistling rush, and the glorious afternoon sunlight shone mellow upon the beeches, and the still soft air of the river valley was filled with the cooing of woodpigeons and the strange mournful crying of the moorhens and dabchicks, and three beautiful cows came down the glade from sunlight to shadow to their milking place, and the river flashed darkly past the boathouse and under the leaning trees, and a man rowed up the stream with his milkcans in a boat from the meadows where he had milked a distant herd of cows.

Major Fisher was not shooting like the Champion Archer of England and kept on dropping his arrows into the green. He was angry with the woodpigeons, because they divert his falcons from their game when he is hawking. 'A hunted pigeon', said the Major, 'is the fastest bird out. He will go considerably more than a mile a minute and away goes the falcon after him for miles.' He said also 'A falcon is a true gentleman (falcon gentle). He never eats a bird alive, but always breaks its neck first. The short-winged hawks eat their prey alive.' Major Fisher now keeps nothing but peregrines. He says the Gyr-falcons are becoming very scarce. He asked Morris and myself to come to his hawking lodge at Chitterne, near Heytesbury, and see him hawk for rooks.

Leaving Durnford Manor House we passed down the village between the pretty cottage gardens and the rows of elm trunks which Lord Malmesbury has lately felled, so as to devastate the pretty village. Then taking a path to the left we ascended the downs and looked down upon the well-watered valley and the shining reaches and streams of the Avon among the woods and water-meads, and Woodford Church across the river, and the fine old farm house of Hele where King Charles II slept after the Battle of Worcester. Striking across the country we came at twilight to the edge of the downs and saw Old Sarum looming before us. Up and down we climbed, the hardest steepest way through moat and over mound, till we came at dusk into the strange sad mysterious deserted city, silent but for the voices of some children at play amongst the bushes within the desolate mounds and broken walls.

Saturday, 22 April [1876]

A lovely summer morning which I spent in sauntering round the lawn at Monnington Rectory watching the waving of the birch tresses, listening to the sighing of the firs in the great solemn avenue, that vast Cathedral, and reading Rob-

379

ert Browning's 'In a Gondola' and thinking of dear Ettie. To-
day there was a luncheon party consisting of Andrew and
Mary Pope from Blakemere, Mr. and Mrs. Phillott from
Staunton-on-Wye, Houseman, and Mr. Robinson from Nor-
ton Canon. After they had left William and I walked up to
the top of Moccas Park, whence we had a glorious view of the
Golden Valley shining in the evening sunlight with the white
houses of Dorstone scattered about the green hillsides 'like a
handful of pearls in a cup of emerald' and the noble spire of
Peterchurch rising from out of the heart of the beautiful rich
valley which was closed below by the Sugar Loaf and the
Skyrrid blue above Abergavenny.

We came tumbling and plunging down the steep hillside
of Moccas Park, slipping, tearing and sliding through oak
and birch and fallow wood of which there seemed to be
underfoot an accumulation of several feet, the gathering ruin
and decay probably of centuries.

As we came down the lower slopes of the wooded hillside
into the glades of the park the herds of deer were moving
under the brown oaks and the billiant green hawthorns, and
we came upon the tallest largest stateliest ash I ever saw and
what seemed at first in the dusk to be a great ruined grey
tower, but which proved to be the vast ruin of the king oak of
Moccas Park, hollow and broken but still alive and vigorous
in parts and actually pushing out new shoots and branches.
That tree may be 2000 years old. It measured roughly 33 feet
round by arm stretching.

I fear those grey old men of Moccas, those grey, gnarled,
low-browed, knock-kneed, bowed, bent, huge, strange, long-
armed, deformed, hunchbacked, misshapen oak men that
stand waiting and watching century after century, biding
God's time with both feet in the grave and yet tiring down
and seeing out generation after generation, with such tales to
tell, as when they whisper them to each other in the mid-
summer nights, make the silver birches weep and the poplars
and aspens shiver and the long ears of the hares and rabbits

stand on end. No human hand set those oaks. They are 'the trees which the Lord hath planted'. They look as if they had been at the beginning and making of the world, and they will probably see its end.

Tuesday, 25 April

This morning William drove to Hereford with Mr. Phillott of Staunton-on-Wye to the Bishop's visitation. At ten o'clock I started in an April shower to walk to Peterchurch. I went through Moccas Park and up a deep wild picturesque lane beyond the Bredwardine Lodge. The noble spire of the fine Norman Church rises grandly in the midst of the valley, the white houses of the village are gathered round it and hard by are one or two poplars rising with golden green spires against the blue sides of the distant hills. The Church is approached over a broad rude stone pitched causeway, quaint and ancient, which borders and then bridges the broad fair steam of the Dore which flows close beneath the churchyard and the great steeple of St. Peter's Church. The Church has been well restored but I was disappointed to find the old picture of the Peterchurch Fish gone from the interior wall.

I went home another way, over the hill to Blakemere. A wild storm of hail swept down the valley but I took shelter under a hawthorn bush and the sun still went on shining. When the wild storm and white squall were over I went on up the steep lane between the dripping glancing glittering hedges, till across a dingle which separated it from the lane I saw an old man at work in a cottage garden. We exchanged greetings and gave the time of day across the dingle, and I asked him about the picture of the Peterchurch Fish. 'The Church', said the old man, 'was restored three years. I cannot justly say whether the picture of the Fish is on the wall now or not. I have only been to Church once since the Church was restored. There was a collection at the Church and I went. I don't go to Church a lot. I don't remember seeing the Fish on the wall then. The picture of the Fish was on the wall furthest from the door as you do go in. They do say the Fish was first seen at Dorston and speared there, but he got away and they hunted him down to Peterchurch and killed him close by the Church. He was as big as a salmon and had a gold chain round his neck. They do say you can see the blood now upon the stones at Dorston where the Fish was speared first.'

The lane and dingle led me up to a farmhouse on the hill from which I could see the cone of the Sugar Loaf Mountain at Abergavenny rising above the hills which shut in the Golden Valley. Passing over a fine open bit of high common land studded with rounded bosses and clumps of gorse I entered a young plantation which clothes the northern slope of the hills and came slipping, sliding, scrambling down the precipitous path of deep red mud, greasy with the rain. By dint of catching at trees and bushes and swinging myself down I arrived at length without a fall in the rich warm meadows of Blakemere. There in a field adorned with a noble pear tree of majestic height and growth in full blossom I found cowslips and the first bluebells and the young ferns uncurling their crozier heads. And the sun shone and the cuckoo called and the pear tree waved her blossoms and all the sweet flower scents went up in fragrant incense and praise to God, and I gathered cowslips and bluebells and was as happy as a child.

I came home about 3.30 very hungry and thirsty and Thersie gave me a good luncheon of cold beef. What a luxury it is to be hungry and thirsty and to be able to satisfy your hunger and thirst. Many a man would give £1,000 to be able to enjoy his food as I have done to-day. In the evening I accompanied Thersie on a round of visits to her parishioners in Monnington Common. I had never been there before. In a little cottage among meadows and apple trees we found a nice old woman, Hannah Preece, at home. Outside the door on the cottage wall hung the old dry withered birch and wittan twigs soon to be replaced on May Eve by new boughs 'to keep the old witch out' and counteract her spells during the coming year.

Saturday, 9 March [1878]

I went out for a little while on the terrace this morning and walked up and down on the sunny side of the house. After how many illnesses such as this have I taken my first convalescent walk on the sunny terrace and always at this time of year when the honeysuckle leaves were shooting green and the apricot blossoms were dawning and the daffodils in blow. But some day will come the last illness from which there will be no convalescence and after which there will be no going out to enjoy the sweet sights and sounds of the earthly spring, the singing of the birds, the opening of the fruit blossoms, the budding dawn of green leaves, and the blowing of the March daffodils. May I then be prepared to enter into the everlasting Spring and to walk among the birds and flowers of Paradise.

Richard Jefferies

Water Cress Gatherers, by J. M. W. Turner, 1819, from Liber Studiorum

Magpie.   Raven.   Jackdaw.

Magpie, Raven, Jackdaw, by Archibald Thorburn

Richard Jefferies
[1848–1887]

Richard Jefferies' writings signalize the passing of an era. He is a curiously alien figure in late Victorian England: a countryman without the physical hardihood to earn his living from the soil; a lover of books lacking the education to discipline his imagination. He became a free-lance journalist living amidst populous scenes, who described remembered pleasures for an audience of sentimental magazine readers which was content to learn about wild life at second hand. As with D. H. Lawrence, Jefferies' reputation has been fostered by a rhapsodic cult, whose members have exalted his vitalist philosophy at the expense of the factual intimacy with nature from which it was derived.

Jefferies was born on Coate Farm near Swindon in North Wiltshire. He received little formal schooling; but his father, an acutely perceptive observer of natural phenomena though an unsuccessful farmer, sharpened his senses, while a city-bred aunt encouraged his voracious reading habits. After a happy and carefree boyhood passed in the open, he went to work at the age of seventeen as a reporter for the *North Wilts Herald*, in the columns of which appeared his earliest studies of the region around Swindon. Continuing failure as a writer of fiction turned him for support to the popular periodicals of the day, which welcomed his essays depicting the charms of a vanishing rusticity. After marrying, Jefferies moved in 1877 to Surbiton on the suburban fringe of London, never to return to his birthplace.

Fresh from the land and still in good health, Jefferies published within three years the four works which securely place him among the supreme historians of the English countryside: *The Gamekeeper at Home: or, Sketches of Natural History and Rural Life* (1878); *Wild Life in a Southern County* (1879); *The Amateur Poacher* (1879); and *Round about a Great Estate* (1880). The contents of these volumes, all inspired by Wiltshire memories, were gathered from pieces which had first appeared in the *Pall Mall Gazette*. In 1881 the onset of the painful illness from which he never recovered drove Jefferies to Sussex; and henceforth the quality of his writing changes in ways best illustrated by his extraordinary autobiography, *The Story of My Heart* (1883). As though the shadow of his own impending death had its counterpart in a despairing recognition that the ancestral vitality of agricultural England was doomed, Jefferies inclined increasingly to the feverish celebration of a kind of natural mysticism. Although he scrutinized the world about him as closely and knowingly as ever and with heightened sensitivity to its loveliness, his style became more highly wrought and self-conscious, marred by mannerisms and an insistent didacticism that too often detract from the heartfelt immediacy of the experiences which the author is seeking to communicate.

No part of England is more tenaciously rooted in the past than Wiltshire. Coate is within walking distance of Wayland Smith's cave and the White Horse and Savernake Forest. The region is traversed by the Roman road and rimmed to the south, east, and west by the Downs. Sarsen-stones, tumuli, and ancient fortifications are landmarks of the country that the youthful Jefferies haunted until, like Matthew Arnold's Scholar-gipsy, he came to be regarded as its familiar spirit. "See'd ye owt on the Downs?" a yeoman was asked. "Nobbut Dick Jefferies moonin' about," came the answer. "I was sensitive to all things," Jefferies wrote,

> to the earth under, and the star-hallow round about; to the least blade of grass, to the largest oak. They seemed like exterior nerves and veins for the conveyance of feeling to me. Sometimes a very ecstasy of exquisite enjoyment of the entire visible universe filled me.

The volumes of early recollections radiate out from the home points of Coate Water and Burderop Woods to embrace not only the topography and natural history of the author's shire, but also the immemorial folkways of its inhabitants. The landscape is peopled with unforgettable figures: Keeper Haylock; Molly the bustling milkmaid; the poacher Oby; Dickon, the sporting son of the landlady of Sarsen public-house. Edward Thomas noted in

The Gamekeeper at Home the "rich, quiet ease" with which
Jefferies so magically calls back the lost world of his youth,
rendering its joys in all their spontaneity and freshness and
simplicity:

> Things occur in his pages as they do on walks, haphazard,
> and often unconnected. Descriptions, portraits, narratives,
> arguments, odds and ends of superstitions, customs, curi-
> osities, come together in Nature's own abundance. The
> writing is effortless, and in places slipshod; it hardly mat-
> ters: the breath of elaboration might have made it less rus-
> tic. As it stands it is perhaps the first thoroughly rustic
> book in English, by a countryman and about the country,
> with no alien savours whatever.

From *The Gamekeeper at Home: or, Sketches of Natural History and Rural Life*

CHAPTER VI

BIRDS AND BEASTS OF PREY

THERE are other enemies of game life besides human poachers whose numbers must be kept within bounds to ensure successful sport. The thirst of the weasel for blood is insatiable, and it is curious to watch the persistency with which he will hunt down the particular rabbit he has singled out for destruction. Through the winding subterranean galleries of the 'buries' with their cross-passages, 'blind' holes and 'pop' holes (*i.e.* those which end in undisturbed soil, and those which are simply bored from one side of the bank to the other, being only used for temporary concealment), never once in the dark close caverns losing sight or scent of his victim, he pursues it with a species of eager patience. It is generally a long chase. The rabbit makes a dash ahead and a double or two, and then halts, usually at the mouth of a hole: perhaps to breathe. By-and-by the weasel, baffled for a few minutes, comes up behind. Instantly the rabbit slips over the bank outside and down the ditch for a dozen yards, and there enters the 'bury' again. The weasel follows, gliding up the bank with a motion not unlike that of the snake; for his body and neck are long and slender and his legs short. Apparently he is not in haste, but rather lingers over the scent. This is repeated five or six times, till the whole length of the hedge-row has been traversed—sometimes up and down again. The chase may be easily observed by anyone who will keep a little in the background. Although the bank be tenanted by fifty other rabbits, past whose hiding-place the weasel must go, yet they scarcely take any notice. One or two whom he has approached too closely bolt out and in again; but as a mass the furry population remain quiet, as if perfectly aware that they are not yet marked out for slaughter.

At last, having exhausted the resources of the bank the rabbit rushes across the field to a hedgerow, perhaps a hundred yards away. Here the wretched creature seems to find a difficulty in obtaining admittance. Hardly has he disap-peared in a hole before he comes out again, as if the inhabit-ants of the place refused to give him shelter. For many animals have a strong tribal feeling, and their sympathy, like that of man in a savage state, is confined within their special settlement.

With birds it is the same: rooks, for instance, will not allow a strange pair to build in their trees, but drive them off with relentless beak, tearing down the half-formed nest, and taking the materials to their own use. The sentiment, 'If Jacob take a wife of the daughters of Heth, what good shall my life do me?' appears to animate the breasts of gregarious creatures of this kind. Rooks intermarry generation after generation; and if a black lover brings home a foreign bride they are forced to build in a tree at some distance. Near large rookeries several such outlying colonies may be seen.

The rabbit, failing to find a cover, hides in the grass and dry rushes; but across the meadow, stealing along the fur-row, comes the weasel; and, shift his place how he may, in the end, worn out and weary, bunny succumbs, and the sharp teeth meet in the neck behind the ear, severing the vein. Often in the end the rabbit runs to earth in a hole which is a *cul-de-sac*, with his back towards the pursuer. The weasel,

391

unable to get at the poll, which is his desire, will mangle the hinder parts in a terrible manner—as will the civilised ferret under similar conditions. Now and then the rabbit, scratching and struggling, fills the hole in the rear with earth, and so at the last moment chokes off his assailant and finds safety almost in the death-agony. In the woods, once the rabbit is away from the 'buries', the chase really does resemble a hunt; from furze-bush to bracken, from fern to rough grass, round and round, backwards, doubling, to and fro, and all in vain.

At such times, eager for blood, the weasel will run right across your path, almost close enough to be kicked. Pursue him in turn, and if there be no hedge or hole near, if you have him in the open, he will dart hither and thither right between your legs, uttering a sharp short note of anger and alarm, something composed of a tiny bark and a scream. He is easily killed with a stick when you catch him in the open, for he is by no means swift; but if a hedge be near it is impossible to secure him.

Weasels frequently hunt in couples, and sometimes more than two will work together. I once saw five, and have heard of eight. The five I saw were working a sandy bank drilled with holes, from which the rabbits in wild alarm were darting in all directions. The weasels raced from hole to hole and along the sides of the bank exactly like a pack of hounds, and seemed intensely excited. Their manner of hunting resembles the motions of ants; these insects run a little way very swiftly, then stop, turn to the right or left, make a short detour, and afterwards on again in a straight line. So the pack of weasels darted forward, stopped, went from side to side, and then on a yard or two, and repeated the process. To see their reddish heads thrust for a moment from the holes, then withdrawn to reappear at another, would have been amusing had it not been for the reflection that their frisky tricks would assuredly end in death. They ran their quarry out of the bank and into a wood, where I lost sight of them.

The Stoat (*Autumn, Winter, and Irish Stoat*), *by G. E. Lodge*

The pack of eight was seen by a labourer returning down a woodland lane from work one afternoon. He told me he got into the ditch, half from curiosity to watch them, and half from fear—laughable as that may seem—for he had heard the old people tell stories of men in the days when the corn was kept for years in barns, and so bred hundreds of rats, being attacked by those vicious brutes. He said they made a noise, crying to each other, short sharp snappy sounds; but the pack of five I myself saw hunted in silence.

Stoats, though not so numerous as weasels, probably do quite as much injury, being larger, swifter, stronger, and very bold, sometimes entering sheds close to dwelling-houses. The labouring people—at least, the elder folk—declare that they have been known to suck the blood of infants left asleep in the cradle upon the floor, biting the child behind the ear. They hunt in couples also—seldom in larger numbers. I have seen three at work together, and with a single shot killed two out of the trio. In elegance of shape they surpass the weasel, and the colour is brighter. Their range of destruction seems only limited by their strength: they attack anything they can manage.

The keeper looks upon weasel and stoat as bitter foes, to be ruthlessly exterminated with shot and gin. He lays to their charge deadly crimes of murder, the death of rabbits, hares, birds, the theft and destruction of his young broods, even occasional abstraction of a chicken close to his very door, despite the dogs chained there. They are not easily shot, being quick to take shelter at the sight of a dog, and when hard hit with the pellets frequently escaping, though perhaps to die. Both weasel and stoat, and especially the latter, will snap viciously at the dog that overtakes them, even when sore wounded, always aiming to fix their teeth in his nose, and fighting savagely to the last gasp. The keeper slays a wonderful number in the course of a year, yet they seem as plentiful as ever. He traps perhaps more than he shoots.

It is not always safe to touch a stoat caught in a trap; he

lies apparently dead, but lift him up, and instantly his teeth are in your hand, and it is said such wounds sometimes fester for months. Stoats are tough as leather: though severely nipped by the iron fangs of the gin, struck on the head with the butt of the gun, and seemingly quite lifeless, yet, if thrown on the grass and left, you will often find on returning to the place in a few hours' time that the animal is gone. Warned by experiences of this kind, the keeper never picks up a stoat till 'settled' with a stick or shot, and never leaves him till he is nailed to the shed. Stoats sometimes emit a disgusting odour when caught in a trap. The keeper has no mercy for such vermin, though he thinks some of his feathered enemies are even more destructive.

Twice a year the hawks and other birds of prey find a great feast spread before them; first, in the spring and early summer, when the hedges and fields are full of young creatures scarcely able to use their wings, and again in the severe weather of winter when cold and hunger have enfeebled them.

It is difficult to understand upon what principle the hawk selects his prey. He will pass by with apparent disdain birds that are within easy reach. Sometimes a whole cloud of birds will surround and chase him out of a field; and he pursues the even tenour of his way unmoved, though sparrow and finch almost brush against his talons. Perhaps he has the palate of an epicure, and likes to vary the dish of flesh torn alive from the breast of partridge, chicken, or mouse. He does not eat all he kills; he will sometimes carry a bird a considerable distance and then drop the poor thing. Only recently I saw a hawk, pursued by twenty or thirty finches and other birds across a ploughed field, suddenly drop a bird from his claws as he passed over a hedge. The bird fell almost perpendicularly, with a slight fluttering of the wings, just sufficient to preserve it from turning head-over-heels, and on reaching the hedge could not hold to the first branches, but brought up on one near the ground. It was a sparrow, and was not apparently hurt—simply breathless from fright.

All kinds of birds are sometimes seen with the tail feathers gone: have they barely escaped in this condition from the clutches of the hawk? Blackbirds, thrushes, and pigeons are frequently struck: the hawk seems to lay them on the back, for if he is disturbed that is the position his victim usually remains in. Though hawks do not devour every morsel, yet as a rule nothing is found but the feathers—usually scattered in a circle. Even the bones disappear: probably ground vermin make away with the fragments.

The hawk is not always successful in disabling his prey. I have seen a partridge dashed to the ground, get up again, and escape. The bird was flying close to the ground when struck; the hawk alighted on the grass a few yards further in a confused way as if overbalanced, and before he could reach the partridge the latter was up and found shelter in a thick hedge.

The power to hover or remain suspended in one place in the air does not, as some have supposed, depend upon the assistance of the wind, against which the hawk inclines the plane of his wings like an artificial kite. He can accomplish the feat when the air is quite still and no wind stirring. Nor is he the only bird capable of doing this, although the others possess the power in a much less degree. The common lark sometimes hovers for a few moments low down over the young green corn, as if considering upon what spot to alight. The flycatcher contrives to suspend itself momentarily, but it is by a rapid motion of the wings, and is done when the first snap at the insect has failed. It is the rook that hovers by the assistance of the wind as he rises with his broad, flat wings over a hedge and meets its full force, which counterpoises his onward impetus and sustains him stationary, sometimes compelling him to return with the current.

Hawks have a habit of perching on the tops of bare poles or dead trees, and are there frequently caught in the gin the keeper sets for them. The cuckoo, which so curiously resembles the hawk, has the same habit, and will perch on a solitary post in the middle of a field, or on those upright stones sometimes placed for the cattle to rub themselves against. Though 'wild as a hawk' is a proverbial phrase, yet hawks are bold enough to enter gardens, and even take their prey from the ivy which grows over the gable of the house. The destruction they work among the young partridges in early summer is very great. The keeper is always shooting them, yet they come just the same, or nearly; for, if he exterminates them one season, others arrive from a distance. He is particularly careful to look out for their nests, so as to kill both the old birds and to prevent their breeding. There is little difficulty in finding the nest (which is built in a high tree) when the young get to any size; their cry is unmistakable and audible at some distance.

Against sparrow-hawk and kestrel, and the rarer kinds that occasionally come down from the mountains of the north or the west—the magazines of these birds—the keeper wages ceaseless war.

So too with jay and magpie; he shoots them down whenever they cross his path, unless, as is sometimes the case, specially ordered to save the latter. For the magpie of recent years has become much less common. Though still often seen in some districts, there are other localities where this odd bird is nearly extinct. It does not seem to breed now, and you may ask to be shown a nest in vain. A magpie's nest in an orchard that I knew of was thought so great a curiosity that every now and then people came to see it from a distance. In other places the bird may be frequently met with, almost always with his partner; and so jays usually go in couples, even in winter.

The jay is a handsome bird, whose chatter enlivens the plantations, and whose bright plumage contrasts pleasantly with the dull green of the firs. A pair will work a hedge in a sportsmanlike manner, one on one side, the second on the other; while the tiny wren, which creeps through the bushes as a mouse through the grass, cowers in terror, or slips into a knot-hole till the danger is past. When the husbandman has sown his field with the drill, hardly has he left the gateway before a legion of small birds pours out from the hedgerows and seeks for the stray seeds. Then you may see the jay hop out among them with an air of utter innocence, settling on the larger lumps of clay for convenience of view, swelling out his breast in pride of beauty, jerking his tail up and down, as if to say, Admire me. With a sidelong hop and two flaps of the wing, he half springs, half glides to another coign of vantage. The small birds, sparrows, chaffinches, greenfinches—instantly scatter swiftly right and left, not rising, but with a hasty run for a yard or so. They know well his murderous intent, and yet are so busy they only put themselves just out of reach, aware that, unlike the hawk, he cannot strike at a distance. This game will continue for a long time; the jay all the while affecting an utter indifference, yet ever on the alert till he spies his chance. It is the young or weakly partridges and pheasants that fall to the jay and magpie.

The keeper also destroys owls—on suspicion. Now and then someone argues with the keeper, assuring him that they do not touch game, but this he regards as pure sentimentalism. 'Look at his beak,' is his steady reply. 'Tell me that that there bill weren't made to tear a bird's breast to bits? Just see here—all crooked and pointed: why, an owl have got a hooked bill like an eagle. It stands to reason as he must be in mischief.' So the poor owls are shot and trapped, and nailed to the side of the shed.

But upon the crow the full vials of the keeper's wrath are poured, and not without reason. The crow among birds is like the local professional among human poachers: he haunts the place and clears everything—it would be hard to say what comes amiss to him. He is the impersonation of murder. His long, stout, pointed beak is a weapon of deadly power, wielded with surprising force by the sinewy neck. From a tiny callow fledgling, fallen out of the thrush's nest, to the partridge or a toothsome young rabbit, it is all one to him. Even the swift leveret is said sometimes to fall a prey, being so buffeted by the sooty wings of the assassin and so blinded by the sharp beak striking at his eyes as to be presently overcome. For the crow has a terrible penchant for the morsel afforded by another's eyes: I have seen the skull of a miserable thrush, from which a crow rose and slowly sailed away, literally split as if by a chisel—doubtless by the blow that destroyed its sight. Birds that are at all diseased or weakly, as whole broods sometimes are in wet unkindly seasons, rabbits touched by the dread parasite that causes the fatal 'rot', the young pheasant straying from the coop, even the chicken at the lone farmstead, where the bailiff only lives and is in the fields all day—these are the victims of the crow.

Crows work almost always in pairs—it is remarkable that hawks, jays, magpies, crows, nearly all birds of prey, seem to remain in pairs the entire year—and when they have once tasted a member of a brood, be it pheasant, partridge, or chicken, they stay till they have cleared off the lot. Slow of flight and somewhat lazy of habit, they will perch for hours on a low tree, croaking and pruning their feathers; they peer into every nook and corner of the woodlands, not like the swift hawk, who circles over and is gone and in a few minutes is a mile away. So that neither the mouse in the furrow nor the timid partridge cowering in the hedge can escape their leering eyes.

Therefore the keeper smites them hip and thigh whenever he finds them; and if he comes across the nest, placed on the broad top of a pollard-tree—not in the branches, but on the trunk—sends his shot through it to smash the eggs. For if the young birds come to maturity they will remain in that immediate locality for months, working every hedge and copse and ditch with cruel pertinacity. In consequence of this unceasing destruction the crow has become much rarer of late, and its nest is hardly to be found in many woods. They breed in the scattered trees of the meadows and fields, espe-

399

cially where no regular game preservation is attempted, and where no keeper goes his rounds. Even to this day a lingering superstition associates this bird with coming evil; and I have heard the women working in the fields remark that such and such a farmer then lying ill would not recover, for a crow had been seen to fly over his house but just above the roof-tree. . . .

From *Wild Life in a Southern County*

CHAPTER X

The wood-pile—Lizards—Sheds and rickyard—The witches' brier—
Insects—Plants, flowers, and fruit.

THE farmhouse at Wick has the gardens and orchard already mentioned upon one side, and on the other are the carthouses, sheds, and rickyard. Between these latter and the dwelling runs a broad roadway for the wagons to enter and leave the fields, and on its border stands a great wood-pile. The fagots cut in the winter from the hedges are here stacked up as high as the roof of a cottage, and near by lies a heap of ponderous logs waiting to be split for firewood. From exposure to the weather the bark of the fagot sticks has turned black, and is rapidly decaying, and under it innumerable insects have made their homes.

For these, probably, the wrens visit the wood-pile continually: if in passing any one strikes the fagots with a stick, a wren will generally fly out on the opposite side. They creep like mice in between the fagots—there are numerous interstices—and thus sometimes pass right through a corner of the stack. Sometimes a pole which has been lying by for a length of time is found to be curiously chased, as it were, all over the surface under the loose bark by creeping things. They eat channels, interweaving and winding in and out, in an intricate pattern, occasionally a little resembling the Moorish style of ornamentation seen on the walls of the Alhambra. I have found poles so curiously carved like this that the idea naturally occurred of using them for cabinet-work. They might at least have supplied a hint for a design. Besides the wrens, many other birds visit the wood-pile: sparrows are perpetually coming, and on the retired side towards the meadow the robins build their nests. On the ridge, where some of the sticks project, the swallows often perch and twitter—generally a pair seem to come together.

It takes skill as well as mere strength even to do so simple a thing as to split the rough logs lying here on the ground. They are not like those Abraham Lincoln began life working at—even-grained wood, quickly divided—but tough and full of knots strangely twisted; so that it needs judgment to put the wedges in the right place.

Near the wood-pile are a well and a stone trough for thirsty horses to drink from, and as the water, carelessly pumped in by the carters' lads, frequently overflows, the ground just there is usually moist. If one of the loose oak logs that lie here with the grass growing up round it is rolled over, occasionally a lizard may be found under it. This lizard is slender, and not more than three or four inches in length, general colour a yellowish green. Where one is found a second is commonly close by. They are elegantly shaped, and quick in their motions, speedily making off. They may now and then be discovered under large stones, if there is a crevice, in the meadows. They do not in the least resemble the ordinary "land-lizard," which is a much coarser-looking and larger creature, and is not an inhabitant of this locality. At all events it is rare enough to have escaped me here, though I have often observed it in districts where the soil is light and sandy and where there is a good deal of heath-land. The land-lizards will stroll indoors if the door be left open. These lesser but more elegant lizards appear to prefer a damp spot—cool and moist, but not positively wet.

A large shed built against the side of the adjacent stable is used as a carpenter's workshop—much carpenter's work is

402

done on a farm—and here is a bench with a vice and variety of tools. When sawing, the wood operated on often "ties" the saw, as it is called—that is, pinches it—which makes it hard to work; a thin wedge of wood is then inserted to open a way, and the blade of the saw rubbed with a little grease, which the metal, heated by the friction, melts into oil. This eases the work; a little grease, too, will make a gimlet bore quicker. Country carpenters keep this grease in a horn—a cow's horn stopped at the larger end with a piece of wood and at the other by its own natural growth. Now the mice (which are everywhere on farm premises) are so outrageously fond of grease that they will spend any length of time gnaw-gnaw-gnawing till they do get at it. Right through the solid stopper of wood they eat their way, and even through the horn; so that the carpenter is puzzled to know how to preserve it out of their reach. It is of no use putting it on a shelf, because they either rush up the wall or drop from above. At last, however, he has hit upon a dodge.

He has suspended the horn high above the ground by a loop of copper wire, which projects six or eight inches from the wall, like a lamp on a bracket. The mice may get on the bench, and may run up the wall, but when they get to the wire they cannot walk out on it—like tight-rope walking—the more especially as the wire, being thin and flexible, bends and sways if they attempt it. This answers the purpose as a rule; but even here the carpenter declares that once now and then his horn is pilfered, and can only account for it by supposing that a bolder mouse than common makes a desperate leap for it, and succeeds in landing on the flat surface of the wooden stopper.

The shed has one small window only, which has no glass, but is secured by an iron bar (he needs no larger window, for all carpenters work with the door open); and through this window a robin has entered and built a nest in a quiet corner behind some timber. Though a man is at work here so often, hammering and sawing, the birds come fearlessly to their young, and pick up the crumbs he leaves from his luncheon.

Between the timber framework of the shed and the brickwork of the adjacent stable chinks have opened, and in these and in the chinks between the wooden lintel of the stable door and the bricks above it the bats frequently hide, passing the day there. Others hide in the tiles of the roof where their nests are made. The labouring lads often amuse themselves searching for these creatures, whose one object in daylight seems to be to cling to something: they will hang to the coat with the claws at the extremity of their membranous wings, and if left alone will creep out of sight into the pocket. There are two well-marked species of bats here—one small and the other much larger.

The lesser bat flies nearer to the ground, and almost always follows the contour of some object or building. They hawk to and fro for hours in the evening under the eaves of the farmhouse, and frequently enter the great garrets and the still larger cheese-room (where the cheese is stored to mature)—sometimes through the windows, and sometimes seeming to creep through holes made by sparrows or starlings in the roof. Moths are probably the attraction; of these there are generally plenty in and about old houses. Occasionally a bat will come into the sitting-room, should the doors be left open on a warm summer evening. This the old folk think an evil omen, and still worse if in its alarm at the attempts made to drive it away it should chance to knock against the candle and overturn or put it out. They think, too, that a bat seen in daytime is a bad sign. Once now and then one gets disturbed by some means in the tiles, and flutters in a helpless manner to the nearest shelter; for in daylight they seem quite at a loss, though flying so swiftly at night.

The greater bat hawks at a considerable elevation above houses and trees, and wheels and turns with singular abruptness, so that some think it a test of a good shot to bring them down. The reason, however, why many find it difficult to hit a bat is because they are unaccustomed to shoot at night, and not because of its manner of flight, for it often goes quite straight. It is also believed to be a test of good hearing to be able to hear the low shrill squeak of the bat, uttered as it flies; the same is said of the shrew mouse, whose cry is yet more faint and acute. The swift, too, has a peculiar kind of screech, but easily heard.

Beyond the stables are the cattle-sheds and cow-yards. These sheds are open on the side towards the yard, supported there by a row of wooden pillars stepped on stones to keep them from rotting. On the large cross-beams within the swallows make their nests. When the eggs are hard set the bird will sit so close that with care and a gentle manner of approach you may sometimes even stroke her back lightly with your finger without making her rise. They become so accustomed to men constantly in and out the sheds as to feel little alarm. Some build their nests higher up under the roof-tree.

To the adjoining rickyard redstarts come every summer, building their nests there; "horse-matchers" or stonechats also in summer often visit the rickyard, though they do not build in it. Some elm trees shade the ricks, and once now and then a wood pigeon settles in them for a little while. The coo of the dove may be heard frequently, but she does not build very near the house.

On this farm the rookery is at some distance in the meadows, and the rooks rarely come nearer than the field just outside the post and rails that enclose the rickyard, though they pass over constantly, flying low down without fear, unless some one chances just then to come out carrying a gun. Then they seem seized with an uncontrollable panic, and stop short in their career by a violent effort of the wings, to wheel off immediately at a tangent. Perhaps no other bird shows such evident signs of recognizing a gun. Chaffinches, it must not be forgotten, frequent the rickyard in numbers.

Finally come the rats. Though trapped, shot, and ferreted

without mercy, the rats insist on a share of the good things going. They especially haunt the pigsties, and when the pigs are served with their food feed with them at the same trough. Those old rats that come to the farmstead are cunning, fierce brutes, not to be destroyed without much difficulty. They will not step on a trap, though never so cleverly laid; they will face a ferret, unless he happens to be particularly large and determined, and bite viciously at dogs. But with all their cunning there is one simple trick which they are not up to: this is to post yourself high up above the ground, when they will not suspect your presence; a ladder is placed against a tree within easy shot of the pigsty, and the gunner, having previously arranged that everything shall be kept quiet, takes his stand on it, and from thence kills a couple perhaps at once.

On looking back, it appears that the farmhouse, garden, orchard, and rickyard at Wick are constantly visited by about thirty-five wild creatures, and, in addition, five others come now and then, making a total of forty. Of these forty twenty-six are birds, two bats, eight quadrupeds, and four reptiles. This does not include some few additional birds that only come at long intervals, nor those that simply fly over-head or are heard singing at a distance.

The great meadow hedge—the highway of the birds— where it approaches the ha-ha wall of the orchard, is lovely in June with the wild roses blooming on the briers which there grow in profusion. Some of these briers stretch forth into the meadow, and then, bent down by their own weight, form an arch crowned with flowers. There is an old super-stition about these arches of brier hung out along the hedge-row: magical cures of whooping-cough and some other dis-eases of childhood can, it is believed, be effected by passing the child at sunrise under the brier facing the rising sun.

This had to be performed by the "wise woman." There was one in every hamlet but a few years ago, and indeed here and there an aged woman retains something like a reputation for witchcraft still. The "wise woman" conducted the child entrusted to her care at the dawn to the hedge, where she knew there was a brier growing in such a position that a person could creep under it facing the east, and there, as the sun rose, passed the child through.

Dragonflies, by William Daniell, 1809

In the hollow just beneath the ha-ha wall, where it is moist, grow tall rushes; and here the great dragonfly darts to and fro so swiftly as to leave the impression of a line of green drawn suddenly through the air. Though travelling at such speed, he has the power of stopping abruptly, and instantly

407

afterwards returns upon his path. These handsome insects are often placed on mirrors as an ornament in farmhouses. The labourers will have it that they sting like the hornet; but this they say also of many other harmless creatures, seeming to have a general distrust of the insect kind. They will tell you alarming stories of terrible sufferings—arms swollen to double the natural size, necks inflamed, and so forth—caused by the bites of unknown flies. Not being able to discover what fly it is that inflicts these poisonous wounds, and having spent so many hours in the fields without experiencing such effects, I rather doubt these statements, though put forth in perfect good faith; indeed, I have often seen the arms and chests of the men in harvest time with huge bumps rising on them which they declared were thus caused. The common harvest bug, which gets under the skin, certainly does not cause such great swellings as I have seen; nor the stoat-fly, which latter is the most bloodthirsty wretch imaginable.

With a low hissing buzz, a long, narrow, and brownish-gray insect settles on your hand as you walk among the hay, and presently you feel a tingling sensation, and may watch (if you have the patience to endure the irritation) its body gradually dilate and grow darker in colour as it absorbs the blood. When once thoroughly engaged, nothing will frighten this fly away: you may crush him, but he will not move from fear; he will remain till, replete with blood, he falls off helpless into the grass.

The horses in the wagons have at this season to be watched by a boy armed with a spray of ash, with which he flicks off the stoats that would otherwise drive the animals frantic. A green spray is a great protection against flies; if you carry a bough in your hand as you walk among the meadows, they will not annoy you half so much. Such a bough is very necessary when lying *perdu* in a dry ditch in summer to shoot a young rabbit, and when it is essential to keep quiet and still. Without it it is difficult to avoid lifting the hand to knock the flies away—which motion is sure to alarm the rabbit that may at that very moment be peeping out preparatory to issuing from his hole. It is impossible not to pity the horses in the hayfields on a sultry day; despite all the care taken, their nostrils are literally black with crowds of flies, which constantly endeavour to crawl over the eyeball. Sunshine itself does not appear so potent in bringing forth insects as the close electrical kind of heat that precedes a thunderstorm. This is so well known that when the flies are more than usually busy the farmer makes haste to get in his hay, and lets down the canvas over his rick. The cows give warning at the same time by scampering about in the wildest and most ludicrous manner—their tails held up in the air—tormented by insects.

The ha-ha wall, built of loose stones, is the home of thousands upon thousands of ants, whose nests are everywhere here, the ground being undisturbed by passing footsteps. They ascend trees to a great height, and may be seen going up the trunk sometimes in a continuous stream, one behind the other in Indian file.

In one spot on the hedge of the ha-ha is a row of bee-hives; the garden wall and a shrubbery shelter them here from the north and east, and the drop of the ha-ha gives them a clear exit and entrance. This is thought a great advantage—not to have any hedge or bush in front of the hives—because the bees, heavily laden with honey or pollen, encounter no obstruction in coming home. They are believed to work more energetically when this is the case, and they certainly do seem to exhibit signs of annoyance, as if out of temper, if they get entangled in a bush. Indeed, if you chance to be pursued by an angry cloud of bees whose ire you have aroused, the only safe place is a hedge or bush, into which make haste to thrust yourself, when the boughs and leaves will baffle them. If the hive be moved to a different place, the bees that chance at the time to be out in the fields collecting honey, upon their return, finding their home gone, are evidently at a loss. They fly round, hovering about over the spot for a long time before

409

they discover the fresh position of the hive.

The great hornet, with its tinge of reddish orange, comes through the garden sometimes with a heavy buzz, distinguishable in a moment from the sound of any other insect. All country folk believe the hornet's sting to be the most poisonous and painful of any, and will relate instances of persons losing the use of their arms for a few days in consequence of the violent inflammation. Sometimes the hornet selects for its nest an aperture in an old shed near the farmhouse. I have seen their nests quite close to houses; but unless wantonly disturbed, there is not the slightest danger from them, or indeed from any other insects of this class. I think the common hive-bees are the worst tempered of any—they resent the slightest interference with their motions. The hornet often chooses an old hollow withy pollard for the site of its nest.

In the orchard there is at least one nest of the humble-bee, made at a great depth in a deserted mouse's hole. These bees have eaten away and removed the grass just round the entrance, so as to get a clear road in and out. They are as industrious as the hive bee; but as there are not nearly so many working together in one colony, they do not store up anything approaching to the same quantity of honey. There is a superstition that if a humble-bee buzzes in at the window of the sitting-room it is a sure sign of a coming visitor.

Be careful how you pick up a ripe apple, all glowing orange, from the grass in the orchard; roll it over with your foot first, or you may chance to find that you have got a handful of wasps. They eat away the interior of the fruit, leaving little but the rind; and this very hollowness causes the rind to assume richer tints and a more tempting appearance. Specked apples on the tree, whether pecked by a blackbird, eaten by wasps or ants, always ripen fastest, and if you do not mind cutting out that portion, are the best. Such a fallen apple, when hollowed out within, is a veritable torpedo if incautiously handled.

410

Wasps are incurable drunkards. If they find something sweet and tempting they stick to it, and swill till they fall senseless to the ground. They are then most dangerous, because unseen and unheard; and one may put one's hand on them in ignorance of their whereabouts. Noticing once that a particular pear tree appeared to attract wasps, though there was little or no fruit on it, I watched their motions, and found they settled at the mouth of certain circular apertures that had been made in the trunk. There the sap was slowly exuding, and to this sap the wasps came, and sipped it till they could sip no more. The tree being old and of small value, it was determined to see what caused these circular holes. They were cut out with a gouge, when the whole interior of the trunk was found bored with winding tunnels, through which a pistol bullet might have been passed. This had been done by an enormous grub, as long and large as one's finger.

Old-world plants and flowers linger still like heirlooms in the farmhouse garden, though their pleasant odour is ofttimes choked by the gaseous fumes from the furnaces of the steam-ploughing engines as they pass along the road to their labour. Then a dark vapour rises above the tops of the green elms, and the old walls tremble and the earth itself quakes beneath the pressure of the iron giant, while the atmosphere is tainted with the smell of cotton waste and oil. How little these accord with the quiet, sunny slumber of the homestead! But the breeze comes, and ere the rattle of the wheels and cogs has died away the fragrance of the flowers and green things has reasserted itself. Such a sunny slumber, and such a fragrance of flowers, both wild and cultivated, have dwelt round and over the place these two hundred years, and mayhap before that. It is perhaps a fancy only, yet I think that where men and nature have dwelt side by side time out of mind there is a sense of a presence, a genius of the spot, a haunting sweetness and loveliness not elsewhere to be found. The most lavish expenditure, even when guided by true taste, cannot produce this feeling about a modern dwelling.

411

At Wick, by the side of the garden path, grows a perfect little hedge of lavender; every drawer in the house, when opened, emits an odour of its dried flowers. Here, too, are sweet marjoram, rosemary, and rue; so also bay and thyme, and some pot-herbs whose use is forgotten, besides southern-wood and wormwood. They do not make medical potions at home here now, but the lily leaves are used to allay inflammation of the skin. The house-leek had a reputation with the cottage herbalists; it is still talked of, but I think very rarely used.

Among the flowers here are beautiful dark-petalled wallflowers, sweet-williams, sweet-brier, and pansies. In spring the yellow crocus lifts its head from among the grass of the green in front of the house (as the snowdrops did also), and here and there a daffodil. These, I think, never look so lovely as when rising from the greensward; the daffodils grow, too, in the orchard. Woodbine is everywhere—climbing over the garden seat under the sycamore tree, whose leaves are spotted sometimes with tiny reddish dots, the honeydew.

Just outside the rickyard, where the grass of the meadow has not been mown but fed by cattle, grow the tall buttercups, rising to the knee. The children use the long hollow stems as tubes wherewith to suck up the warm new milk through its crown of thick froth from the oaken milking-pail. There is a fable that the buttercups make the butter yellow when they come. But the cows never eat them, being so bitter; they eat all round close up to the very stems, but leave them standing scrupulously. The children, too, make similar pipes of straw to suck up the new cider fresh from the cider-mill, as it stands in the tubs directly after the grinding. Under the shady trees of the orchard the hare's parsley flourishes, and immediately without the orchard edge, on the "shore" of the ditch, grow thick bunches of the beautiful blue crane's-bill, or wild geranium, which ought to be a garden flower and not left to the chance mercy of the scythe. There, too, the herb Robert hides, and its foliage, turning colour, lies like crimson lace on the bank.

Even the tall thistles of the ditch have their beauty—the flower has a delicate tint, varying with the species from mauve to purple; the humble-bee visits every thistle bloom in his path, and there must therefore be sweetness in it. Then in the autumn issues forth the floating thistle down, streaming through the air and rolling like an aerial ball over the tips of the bennets. Thistle down is sometimes gathered to fill pillow-cases, and a pillow so filled is exquisitely soft. There is not a nook or corner of the old place where something interesting may not be found. Even the slates on a modern addition to the homestead are each bordered with yellow lichen—perhaps because they adjoin thatch, for slates do not seem generally to encourage the growth of lichen. It appears to prefer tiles, which therefore sooner assume an antique tint.

To the geraniums in the bow-window the hummingbird moth comes now and then, hovering over the scarlet petals. Out of the high elms drops a huge gray moth, so exactly the colour of gray lichen that it might be passed for it—pursued, of course, as it clumsily falls, by two or more birds eager for the spoil. It is feast-time with them when the cockchafers come: they leave nothing but wing-cases scattered on the garden paths, like the shields of slain men-at-arms.

In the bright sunshine, when there is not a cloud in the sky, slender beetles come forth from the cracks of the earth and run swiftly across the paths, glittering green and gold, iridescent colours glistening on their backs. These are locally called sun-beetles, because they appear when the sun is brightest. Be careful not to step on or kill one; for if you do it will certainly rain, according to the old superstition. The blackbird, when he picks up one of the larger beetles, holds it with its back towards him in his bill, so that the legs claw helplessly at the air, and thus carries it to a spot where he can pick it to pieces at his leisure.

413

The ha-ha wall of the orchard is the favourite haunt of butterflies; they seem to love its sunny aspect, and often cling to the loose stone like ornaments attached by some cunning artist. Sulphur butterflies hover here early in the spring, and later on white and brown and tiny blue butterflies pass this way, calling *en route*. Sometimes a great noble of the butterfly world comes in all the glory of his wide velvety wings, and deigns to pause awhile that his beauty may be seen.

Somewhere within doors, in the huge beams or woodwork, the death-tick is sure to be heard in the silence of the night: even now the old folk listen with a lingering dread. Give the woodwork a smart tap, and the insect stops a few moments; but it rapidly gets accustomed to such taps, and after a few ceases to take notice of them. This manner of building houses with great beams visibly supporting the ceiling, passing across the room underneath it, had one advantage. On a rainy day the children could go into the garrets or the cheese-loft and there form a swing, attaching the ropes to the hooks in the beam across the ceiling.

The brewhouse, humble though its object may be, is not without its claim to admiration. It is open from the floor to the rafters of the roof; and that roof in its pitch, the craft of the woodwork, the dull polish of the old oak, has an interest far surpassing the dead, staring level of flat lath and plaster. Noble workmanship in wood may be found, too, in some of the ancient barns; sometimes the beams are of black oak, in others of chestnut.

In these modern days men have lost the pleasures of the orchard; yet an old-fashioned orchard is the most delicious of places wherein to idle away the afternoon of a hazy autumn day, when the sun seems to shine with a soft, slumberous warmth without glare, as if the rays came through an aërial spider's web spun across the sky, letting all the beauty but not the heat slip through its invisible meshes. There is a shadowy coolness in the recesses under the trees. On the damson trunks are yellowish crystalline knobs of gum which has exuded from the bark. Now and then a leaf rustles to the ground, and at longer intervals an apple falls with a decided thump. It is silent, save for the gentle twittering of the swallows on the topmost branches—they are talking of their coming journey—and perhaps occasionally the distant echo of a shot where the lead has gone whistling among a covey. It is a place to dream in, bringing with you a chair to sit on—for it will be freer from insects than the garden seat—and a book. Put away all thought of time—often in striving to get the most value from our time it slips from us as the reality did from the dog that greedily grasped at the shadow—simply dream of what you will, with apples and plums, nuts and filberts within reach.

Dusky Blenheim oranges, with a gleam of gold under the rind; a warmer tint of yellow on the pippins. Here streaks of red, here a tawny hue. Yonder a load of great russets; near by heavy pears bending the strong branches; round black damsons; luscious egg-plums hanging their yellow ovals overhead; bullace, not yet ripe, but presently sweetly piquant. On the walnut trees bunches of round green balls—note those that show a dark spot or streak, and gently tap them with the tip of the tall slender pole placed there for the purpose. Down they come glancing from bough to bough, and striking the hard turf the thick green rind splits asunder, and the walnut itself rebounds upwards. Those who buy walnuts have no idea of the fine taste of the fruit thus gathered direct from the tree, when the kernel, though so curiously convoluted, slips its pale yellow skin easily and is so wondrously white. Surely it is an error to banish the orchard and the fruit-garden from the pleasure-grounds of modern houses, strictly relegating them to the rear, as if something to be ashamed of.

415

From *The Amateur Poacher*

CHAPTER SEVEN

THE MOUCHER'S CALENDAR

THERE were several other curious characters whom we frequently saw at work. The mouchers were about all the year round, and seemed to live in, or by the hedges, as much as the mice. These men probably see more than the most careful observer, without giving it a thought.

In January the ice that freezes in the ditches appears of a dark colour, because it lies without intervening water on the dead brown leaves. Their tint shows through the translucent crystal, but near the edge of the ice three white lines or bands run round. If by any chance the ice gets broken or upturned, these white bands are seen to be caused by flanges projecting from the under surface, almost like stands. They are sometimes connected in such a way that the parallel flanges appear like the letter 'h' with the two down-strokes much prolonged. In the morning the chalky rubble brought from the pits upon the Downs and used for mending gateways leading into the fields glistens brightly. Upon the surface of each piece of rubble there adheres a thin coating of ice: if this be lightly struck it falls off, and with it a flake of the chalk. As it melts, too, the chalk splits and crumbles; and thus in an ordinary gateway the same process may be seen that disintegrates the most majestic cliff.

The stubbles—those that still remain—are full of linnets,

416

upon which the mouching fowler preys in the late autumn. And when at the end of January the occasional sunbeams give some faint hope of spring, he wanders through the lanes carrying a decoy bird in a darkened cage, and a few boughs of privet studded with black berries and bound round with rushes for the convenience of handling.

The female yellow-hammers, whose hues are not so brilliant as those of the male birds, seem as winter approaches to flock together, and roam the hedges and stubble fields in bevies. Where loads of corn have passed through gates the bushes often catch some straws, and the tops of the gateposts, being decayed and ragged, hold others. These are neglected while the seeds among the stubble, the charlock, and the autumn dandelion are plentiful and while the ears left by the gleaners may still be found. But in the shadowless winter days, hard and cold, each scattered straw is sought for.

A few days before the new year [1879] opened I saw a yellow-hammer attacking, in a very ingenious manner, a straw that hung pendent, the ear downwards, from the post of a windy gateway. She fluttered up from the ground, clung to the ear, and outspread her wings, keeping them rigid. The draught acted on the wings just as the breeze does on a paper kite, and there the bird remained supported without an effort while the ear was picked. Now and then the balance was lost, but she was soon up again, and again used the wind to maintain her position. The brilliant cockbirds return in the early spring, or at least appear to do so, for the habits of birds are sometimes quite local.

It is probable that in severe and continued frost many hedgehogs die. On January 19 [1879], in the midst of the sharp weather, a hedgehog came to the door opening on the garden at night, and was taken in. Though carefully tended, the poor creature died next day: it was so weak it could scarcely roll itself into a ball. As the vital heat declined the fleas deserted their host and issued from among the spines. In February, unless it be a mild season, the mounds are still

417

bare; and then under the bushes the ground may be some-
times seen strewn with bulbous roots, apparently of the blue-
bell, lying thickly together and entirely exposed.

The moucher now carries a bill-hook, and as he shambles
along the road keeps a sharp look-out for briars. When he
sees one the roots of which are not difficult to get at, and
whose tall upright stem is green—if dark it is too old—he
hacks it off with as much of the root as possible. The lesser
branches are cut, and, the stem generally trimmed; it is then
sold to the gardeners as the stock on which to graft standard
roses. In a few hours as he travels he will get together quite a
bundle of such briars. He also collects moss, which is sold for
the purpose of placing in flowerpots to hide the earth. The
moss preferred is that growing on and round stoles.

The melting of the snow and the rains in February cause
the ditches to overflow and form shallow pools in the level
meadows. Into these sometimes the rooks wade as far as the
length of their legs allows them, till the discoloured yellow
water almost touches the lower part of the breast. The
moucher searches for small shell snails, of which quantities
are sold as food for cage birds, and cuts small 'turfs' a few
inches square from the green by the roadside. These are in
great request for larks, especially at this time of the year,
when they begin to sing with all their might.

Large flocks of woodpigeons are now in every field where
the tender swede and turnip tops are sprouting green and
succulent. These 'tops' are the moucher's first great crop of
the year. The time that they appear varies with the weather:
in a mild winter some may be found early in January; if the
frost has been severe there may be none till March. These the
moucher gathers by stealth; he speedily fills a sack, and goes
off with it to the nearest town. Turnip-tops are much more in
demand now than formerly, and the stealing of them a more
serious matter. This trade lasts some time, till the tops be-
come too large and garden greens take their place.

In going to and fro the fields the moucher searches the

418

banks and digs out primrose 'mars', and ferns with the root attached, which he hawks from door to door in the town. He also gathers quantities of spring flowers, as violets. This spring [1879], owing to the severity of the season, there were practically none to gather, and when the weather moderated the garden flowers preceded those of the hedge. Till the 10th of March not a spot of colour was to be seen. About that time bright yellow flowers appeared suddenly on the clayey banks and waste places, and among the hard clay lumps of fields ploughed but not sown.

The brilliant yellow formed a striking contrast to the dull brown of the clods, there being no green leaf to moderate the extremes of tint. These were the blossoms of the coltsfoot, that sends up a stalk surrounded with faintly rosy scales. Several such stalks often spring from a single clod: lift the heavy clod, and you have half a dozen flowers, a whole bunch, without a single leaf. Usually the young grasses and the seed-leaves of plants have risen up and supply a general green; but this year the coltsfoot bloomed unsupported, studding the dark ground with gold.

Now the frogs are busy, and the land lizards come forth. Even these the moucher sometimes captures; for there is nothing so strange but that someone selects it for a pet. The mad March hares scamper about in broad daylight over the corn, whose pale green blades rise in straight lines a few inches above the soil. They are chasing their skittish loves, instead of soberly dreaming the day away in a bunch of grass. The ploughman walks in the furrow his share has made, and presently stops to measure the 'lands' with the spud. His horses halt dead in the tenth of a second at the sound of his voice, glad to rest for a minute from their toil. Work there is in plenty now, for stonepicking, hoeing, and other matters must be attended to; but the moucher lounges in the road decoying chaffinches, or perhaps earns a shilling by driving some dealer's cattle home from fair and market.

By April his second great crop is ready—the watercress;

419

the precise time of course varies very much, and at first the quantities are small. The hedges are now fast putting on the robe of green that gradually hides the wreck of last year's growth. The withered head of the teazle, black from the rain, falls and disappears. Great burdock stems lie prostrate. Thick and hard as they are while the sap is still in them, in winter the wet ground rots the lower part till the blast overthrows the stalk. The hollow 'gicks' too, that lately stood almost to the shoulder, is down, or slanting, temporarily supported by some branch. Just between the root and the stalk it has decayed till nothing but a narrow strip connects the dry upper part with the earth. The moucher sells the nests and eggs of small birds to townsfolk who cannot themselves wander among the fields, but who love to see something that reminds them of the green meadows.

As the season advances and the summer comes he gathers vast quantities of dandelion leaves, parsley, sowthistle, clover, and so forth, as food for the tame rabbits kept in towns. If his haunt be not far from a river, he spends hours collecting bait—worm and grub and fly—for the boatmen, who sell them again to the anglers.

Again there is work in the meadows—the haymaking is about, and the farmers are anxious for men. But the moucher passes by and looks for quaking grass, bunches of which have a ready sale. Fledgeling goldfinches and linnets, young rabbits, young squirrels, even the nest of the harvest-trow mouse, and occasionally a snake, bring him in a little money. He picks the forget-me-nots from the streams and the 'bluebottle' from the corn: bunches of the latter are sometimes sold in London at a price that seems extravagant to those who have seen whole fields tinted with its beautiful azure. Byand-by the golden wheat calls for an army of workers; but the moucher passes on and gathers groundsel.

Then come the mushrooms: he knows the best places, and soon fills a basket full of 'buttons,' picking them very early in the morning. These are then put in 'punnets' by the greengrocers and retailed at a high price. Later the blackberries ripen and form his third great crop; the quantity he brings in to the towns is astonishing, and still there is always a customer. The blackberry harvest lasts for several weeks, as the berries do not all ripen at once, but successively, and is supplemented by elderberries and sloes. The moucher sometimes sleeps on the heaps of disused tan in a tanyard: tanyards are generally on the banks of small rivers. The tan is said to possess the property of preserving those who sleep on it from chills and cold, though they may lie quite exposed to the weather.

There is generally at least one such a man as this about the outskirts of market towns, and he is an 'original' best defined by negatives. He is not a tramp, for he never enters the casual wards and never begs—that is, of strangers; though there are certain farmhouses where he calls once now and then and gets a slice of bread and cheese and a pint of ale. He brings to the farmhouse a duck's egg that has been dropped in the brook by some negligent bird, or carries intelligence of the nest made by some roaming goose in a distant withy-bed. Or once, perhaps, he found a sheep on its back in a narrow furrow, unable to get up and likely to die if not assisted, and by helping the animal to gain its legs earned a title to the owner's gratitude.

He is not a thief; apples and plums and so on are quite safe, though the turnip-tops are not: there is a subtle casuistry involved here—the distinction between the quasi-wild and the garden product. He is not a poacher in the sense of entering coverts, or even snaring a rabbit. If the pheasants are so numerous and so tame that passing carters have to whip them out of the way of the horses it is hardly wonderful if one should disappear now and then. Nor is he like the Running Jack that used to accompany the more famous packs of foxhounds, opening gates, holding horses, and a hundred other little services, and who kept up with the hunt by sheer fleetness of foot.

Yet he is fleet of foot in his way, though never seen to run; he *pads* along on naked feet like an animal, never straightening the leg, but always keeping the knee a little bent. With a basket of watercress slung at his back by a piece of tar-cord, he travels rapidly in this way; his feet go 'pad, pad' on the thich white dust, and he easily overtakes a good walker and keeps up the pace for miles without exertion. The watercress is a great staple, because it lasts for so many months. Seeing the nimble way in which he gathers it, thrusting aside the brook-lime, breaking off the coarser sprays, snipping away pieces of root, sorting and washing, and thinking of the amount of work to be got through before a shilling is earned, one would imagine that the slow, idling life of the labourer, with his regular wages, would be far more enticing.

Near the stream the ground is perhaps peaty; little black pools appear between tufts of grass, some of them streaked with a reddish or yellowish slime that glistens on the surface of the dark water; and as you step there is a hissing sound as the spongy earth yields, and a tiny spout is forced forth several yards distant. Some of the drier part of the soil the moucher takes to sell for use in gardens and flowerpots as peat.

The years roll on, and he grows old. But no feebleness of body or mind can induce him to enter the workhouse: he cannot quit his old haunts. Let it rain or sleet, or let the furious gale drive broken boughs across the road, he still sleeps in some shed or under a straw-rick. In sheer pity he is committed every now and then to prison for vagabondage—not for punishment, but in order to save him from himself. It is in vain: the moment he is out he returns to his habits. All he wants is a little beer—he is not a drunkard—and a little tobacco, and the hedges. Some chilly evening, as the shadows thicken, he shambles out of the town, and seeks the limekiln in the ploughed field, where, the substratum being limestone, the farmer burns it. Near the top of the kiln the ground is warm; there he reclines and sleeps.

422

The night goes on. Out from the broken blocks of stone now and again there rises a lambent flame, to shine like a meteor for a moment and then disappear. The rain falls. The moucher moves uneasily in his sleep; instinctively he rolls or crawls towards the warmth, and presently lies extended on the top of the kiln. The wings of the water-fowl hurtle in the air as they go over; by-and-by the heron utters his loud call.

Very early in the morning the quarryman comes to tend his fire, and starts to see on the now redhot and glowing stones, sunk below the rim, the presentment of a skeleton formed of the purest white ashes—a ghastly spectacle in the grey of the dawn, as the mist rises and the peewit plaintively whistles over the marshy meadow.

E. D. H. JOHNSON

E. D. H. Johnson was born in Ohio in 1911, and was educated at St. Paul's School and at Princeton, Oxford, and Yale universities. He is the Holmes Professor of Belles-Lettres of Princeton University, where he has taught since 1939. He has written on all aspects of the Victorian Age, his major field of scholarly interest. He regularly contributes to the scholarly periodicals and has published two books, *The Alien Vision of Victorian Poetry*, a book of literary criticism, and *The World of the Victorians*, a critical anthology of prose and poetry. Mr. Johnson is an ornithologist, especially devoted to studying the habits of shore birds. Whenever possible, he has lived in the open, close to nature, and since 1949 he has spent his summers with his family in a house overlooking the Bay of Fundy in Nova Scotia. He is also an authority on the early English school of landscape painters and has a collection of their watercolors.